The "sacred sands" are the Indiana Dunes, the natural landscape of shifting sand hills, tamarack swamp, oak forest, gull, tern, spring lupine, and prickly pear cactus on the southern coast of Lake Michigan. For almost a century the people of Chicago came here to celebrate this primitive and sacred center, which seemed to redeem the urban machine through evocation of the unity and interdependency of living things.

Through the research of Henry Cowles, Victor Shelford, W. C. Allee, and other scientists at the University of Chicago, the Dunes became the "birthplace of ecology" in America and the classic site for the study of ecological succession. The history of the Dunes has been a continuing struggle for survival between private industry's trespass and usurpation and the advocates of the public welfare, one of the longest and most bitterly contested environmental conflicts in American history. It involved at one time or another in defense of the Dunes: Carl Sandburg, Jane Addams, Jens Jensen, Stephen Mather, Harriet Monroe, Donald Culross Peattie, Edwin Way Teale, Senator Paul Douglas, and thousands of ordinary people. It was a social democratic movement, influenced by Midwest Progressivism, and infused with a profoundly religious symbolism of ritual, communion, and sacrifice. It led to the establishment of the Indiana Dunes State Park and Indiana Dunes National Lakeshore. Nor is the story over. Plans for the Bailly Nuclear Plant Number 1 on the Dunes' perimeter were only recently dropped after a rigorous campaign against it.

J. Ronald Engel's eloquent narrative captures the power and spirit of this inspiring contemporary myth of the unifying vision of community. 32 photographs. 3 maps.

SACRED SANDS

The Voices of the Dunes

The Sand Dunes of Indiana
Courtesy of the Chicago Historical Society

SACRED SANDS

The Struggle for Community
in the Indiana Dunes

J. Ronald Engel

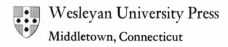

Wesleyan University Press
Middletown, Connecticut

Copyright © 1983 by J. Ronald Engel
First Edition
Published by Wesleyan University Press, 110 Mt. Vernon Street,
Middletown, Connecticut 06457
Distributed by Harper & Row, Publishers, Keystone Industrial Park,
Scranton, Pennsylvania 18512

I am grateful to Helga Sandburg for permission to print excerpts from her poems,
"The Visitor," and "Great Lake of My Childhood"; to the Sandburg Family Trust
under Agreement dated April 29, 1963, Frank M. Parker and Maurice C. Greenbaum,
Trustees, for permission to print Carl Sandburg's poem, "Dunes," and excerpts from
his poetry and writings; to David Sander for permission to print lines from his song,
"Beulah Land"; to Great Lakes Review to print an excerpt from Gary Nabhan's
poem, "Diana-Gone-Driftwood Dune Woman"; to Charles G. Bell for permission
to quote from his poem, "These Winter Dunes"; to Jeannette Vaughn Mosier for
permission to quote from her poems "Keep Your Song" and "Duneland Magic"; to
Frederick Webster Kirtland for permission to quote from "The Dunes at Gary."

Manufactured in the United States of America

For John and Beatrice Engel

Dedication Address

We have foregathered here today to dedicate a small portion of a natural landscape to posterity, that it may remain unharmed by the hand of man for all time in order that they, the children of this generation and their children's children may enjoy its beauties and from this clear air and these sparkling waters, these groves, these sands with their varied fauna and flora, receive inspiration and renew their health and youth.

This is not a little thing or a performance of only modest worth but one of the most splendid deeds that we of this generation could consummate. This landscape, although mobile and more changeable perhaps than most, has been long in the making. All the forces of nature since the beginning of time have had a part in bringing about the perfection of contour and form and color and harmony which we see before us and around us. The cosmic powers have been at work here; the great internal forces of the earth; mighty glaciers; restless waters; the wonder-working winds and the beneficent rains have done their part; while the commanding sun, center and centralized power of our portion of the universe, dominated all.

Man, the destroyer, lays a blighting hand on most of nature's works, so it is fitting that man should set apart portions of the natural landscape to remain unharmed and untouched forever, and it should be our purpose to see to it that this and other landscapes set apart from time to time remain unharmed and undefiled in fact as well as in ideal, that devastating politics be not allowed to despoil what has been set apart, that any changes or alterations which may be made in this and other landscapes be made by the friends and lovers of landscape and not by those who fail to understand.

And now I dedicate this dune landscape in the name of the great forces and materials of nature—in the name of life itself—the resultant of those materials and forces, I dedicate this park.

In the name of the elemental stuffs of which the material portion of this landscape is composed:

In the name of silicon, the great earth builder.

In the name of iron, maker of civilization.

In the names of calcium and magnesium, rock builders.

In the names of carbon and nitrogen, bases of organic life.

In the names of hydrogen and oxygen, makers of the ocean and the life-giving air.

In the name of free oxygen, the great vitalizer and the very breath of life itself.

In the name of all the elements that go to make up this planet where we dwell.

And in the name of the great forces, I dedicate:

The earth forces, gravitation, magnetism, electricity.

The forces of water, the tides, the waves and the life-giving rain.

The forces of air—the winds that never cease to blow.

And lastly, in the name of fire which, controlled, is the greatest friend of man and uncontrolled his most relentless enemy; greatest of forces; worshipped since the most ancient times; focusing point of mankind. The family gathers about the fireplace; the Indian lights his tepee fire, and where the pioneer far from civilization makes his tiny blaze, that spot is home. We are all, all fire worshippers. And overhead flames the great orb of day which controls our planet and our destiny with his mighty furnaces. When he rises golden morning awakens the earth; when he sets the sable dome of night and the quiet stars stand guard above our sleeping hours. When he moves forward spring comes to the land, and when he departs we are icebound in the throes of winter.

And in the name of the departed red man, I dedicate this park; and of the departed wild beasts of the forests; and in the name of the birds which make their homes here and of those birds of passage, pausing here in their long migrations for rest and succor.

I dedicate this park to the unborn generations of man that they may see this landscape as we have seen it, in full faith that they will have eyes to see nature, understanding to comprehend nature, and a love that will perpetuate the beauties of nature.

And I charge you, and all friends of landscape everywhere, to maintain this dune landscape untouched and undefiled that the unborn races of man may come here from whatever harassments there may be in future civilizations to tread these singing sands, to breathe this clear air, to bathe in these sparkling waters, to feel the beauties of these wide-flung colors and harmonies and so to be inspired and reanimated with greater capacity for living.

W. D. RICHARDSON,
*Address at the Council Fire
of the Friends of Our Native
Landscape, meeting at Lake
Front Park, Gary, Indiana,
Columbus Day, 1919*

Contents

Illustrations

Preface

The first insight I had into the struggle to save the Indiana Dunes came one day in the fall of 1965 when I impulsively interrupted a trip across northern Indiana and stopped at Valparaiso to attend hearings on the Indiana Dunes National Lakeshore. Until that time I had only known the Dunes through the stories that appeared from time to time in Chicago papers reporting the latest crisis in Senator Paul Douglas's crusade.

The auditorium at Valparaiso University was overflowing as one speaker after another came forward to present testimony. Toward the middle of the afternoon, a short, white-haired woman, who must have been in her late seventies, made her way down the long aisle. The audience became noticeably quieter. Taking her place in front of the committee, she drew herself up and proceeded to make a passionate plea for the preservation of the Dunes, concluding that to destroy them was to defy the values of the God-given beauty spot of the Middle West. There was loud applause. In the question period that followed, however, a hostile congressman began a personal attack. Again there was applause—this time from the opposition. Again she drew herself up and with firmness told the committee that although she did indeed reside in a town with a private beach, she and the other members of the Save the Dunes Council favored including that beach in the Lakeshore, and furthermore, she would be pleased to see the government take her home as well!

Some years later, when the council invited me to conduct a public memorial service for Dorothy Buell, it was that afternoon which I remembered.

In 1970 my wife and I moved to the Indiana Dunes. After six years of involvement in the civil rights struggle in Chicago, we were seeking a time of renewal and a place where our children might find a fresh start in contact with the land. For two all too brief years, the Dunes were our haven.

In the late afternoons, after returning from Chicago on one of the rickety old orange trains of the Chicago, South Shore and South Bend Railroad—the nation's last electric interurban—I would take our dog for long walks along the beach and into the shifting sand hills that surrounded our home. Across the lake, I could see towers of flickering lights—Chicago—from that distance a dream city, a mirage on the horizon. Always, as we retired for the night, there was the sound of waves on the beach, sometimes soft and rhythmic, sometimes hard and driving, echoing up the sides of the dune where our house was perched. And always in the morning, any season of the year, there were the cries of blue jays and cardinals in the pines at the hilltop. On summer evenings, especially, a beautiful gentleness descended on the dunes. On such occasions just to sit and listen to the sounds of the woods and the sounds of children playing was enough.

It has often occurred to me how strange it was that I could find contentment in an area so tame and so close to the metropolis. I, who had not attended my college graduation because I was so eager to reach the Sierras and embark upon a career in the National Park Service, who had considered myself the luckiest of men to serve as a seasonal ranger in the wilderness of Isle Royale during the summers of graduate school! One reason I found renewal there, I know, was that through the Dunes I relived my youth. Each year of my childhood in Baltimore was climaxed by a short vacation to the dunes and beaches of the middle Atlantic coast. But the most important reason was the Dunes themselves. I had the uncanny feeling of belonging to the land—a sense I have never had so distinctly before or since.

In the early 1970s, I chaired for a short time a committee of the Save the Dunes Council that sought to expand the Lakeshore. In company of Herb Read, Bill Hankla, Harold Olin, and Paul Strand, I tramped the Dunes from Gary to Michigan City surveying the areas that might be added to the park. I became acquainted with the immense variety of terrain and habitat and captured some sense of the grandeur of the landscape as it once was.

I soon discovered that the spirit of Dorothy Buell was very much alive. Through the round of committee and board meetings, in the midst of potluck dinners, around campfires and on hikes, I was in-

troduced to a rare community of dedicated men and women. I also
discovered that the struggle to save the Dunes had a long history,
and that those currently involved were but the latest generation
of a movement that began among Chicago Progressives at the turn
of the century. The spirit of Dorothy Buell had its antecedents
as well.

One hot and humid day in Washington, D.C., in the middle of
June 1971, Congressman J. Edward Roush of Fort Wayne, Indiana, invited his colleagues to come to his office and examine the
bill he planned to introduce to expand the Lakeshore. The night
before I had left a large map of the Indiana Dunes with one of his
assistants, who in turn had given her child the task of crayoning in
green the areas proposed for acquisition. In the morning when I
arrived at the Roush office, I was just in time to see a congressman
who strongly supported the industrialization of the area stomp out
of the room red with fury. A quick look at the map told why. Mis-
understanding her directions, the aspiring young artist had colored
the Bethlehem Steel plant green!

Later that day I told this story to Paul Douglas. The retired
Dunes veteran, battling now the onslaughts of age, sat upright, an
impressive lion-like figure, in the living room of his Washington
home. The late afternoon sun lighted his white hair and delineated
the craggy features of his face. He listened unsmiling, then gruffly
said that we were in for a long fight and that he would back us in
every way he could. Only much later did I realize why the story
of the green crayon could never be funny to Paul Douglas.

The inspiration for this book lies in such memories.

It must be said straight away that those who enacted the drama
of the Dunes had their failings as well as their virtues. If I pay scant
heed to the failings, and perhaps overstress the virtues, it is for a
reason. My purpose is to trace the emergence of a vision and to
show its impact on the course of events of a century. Those who
people these pages aimed higher than they reached; they at times
thought and acted in contradictory ways; they frequently did not
recognize their complicity in what they condemned, and often suc-
cumbed to temptations of self-righteousness. In other words the
Dunes vision was borne by an imperfect humanity. But they saw,
felt, and thought with passion; they sacrificed for their ideals, and,

most important, their ideals were worthy of their commitments. For this reason the story that follows is told through the eyes of those who loved and fought for the Dunes. The tools of critical scholarship I use are for the purpose of illuminating the depths and significance of their perceptions—not to correct or challenge them.

Of course, there are intellectual reasons for this book as well as personal ones.

The United States needs an humanitarian and environmental ethic—that is to say, an ethic that links the imperative of social justice with the imperative of environmental preservation. I join those who are convinced that no lasting change of this magnitude will occur in American society apart from a change in its culture, most specifically, its religiously based ethical traditions. Cultural change is not sufficient for social change, but it is a necessary ingredient. The two most powerful religious traditions in American society are the biblical tradition of the churches and synagogues, and the civil religion of democracy. The civil tradition is found in voluntary associations concerned for the general welfare, the legal and political heritage of the Republic, and much of American art and literature. The two traditions stand in a dialectical relationship to one another, and at their best, reinforce one another. If there is to be an environmental social ethic—an ethic of ecojustice—in the United States in the late twentieth century, both must be transformed.

It is the heritage of civil religion and public ethics that is the primary concern here.

The thesis of this book is that the campaign to save the Indiana Dunes emerged as part of an insurgent movement in the Midwest to reform the democratic faith of the nation. Based largely in Chicago, and rooted in the ethos and politics of Progressivism, this movement sought to sever the identification of democracy with competitive individualism. It conceived the meaning of democracy to be equal freedom in community, or the "cooperative commonwealth." For some members of the movement, the authentic vision of community inherent within the democratic experience was larger than human community alone. They yoked the revolutionary ideals of freedom, equality, and fraternity to the ecological principles of unity and interdependence among all forms of being.

It was this comprehensive vision of community that was associated with the Dunes landscape in the early part of the century and that motivated the campaign to preserve it. As a consequence, the eighty-year struggle to save the Dunes constitutes a prophetic chapter in the history of American public life.

The inquiry that began a decade ago, and that led, by various stages, to this book, early became interdisciplinary in character. American environmental, intellectual, and social history, local and regional studies of the Midwest, cultural geography, and the ecological sciences—all were contextual to the subject. Yet the story opened up special avenues for exploration.

The struggle to save the Dunes, "the birthplace of ecology," was not a struggle for monumental scenery, or for land of little economic value. In these respects it was an exception to the history of the national parks as described by Alfred Runte in *National Parks: The American Experience*. It involved many of the persons and themes treated by Donald Worster in *Nature's Economy: The Roots of Ecology*, Bernard Duffey in *The Chicago Renaissance in American Letters*, and Allen Davis in *Spearheads for Reform: The Social Settlements and the Progressive Movement, 1890–1914*. Yet, by virtue of the fact that in the Dunes experience these persons and themes interacted in a regional subculture intensely devoted to a specific place, unsuspected relations appeared between early twentieth-century science, literature, and reform. On a broader canvas, the Dunes movement helped create new symbols for the tradition of democratic social change described by Russell Nye in *Midwestern Progressive Politics*, while it also served as a novel political response to the cultural dilemma imaged by Leo Marx in *The Machine in the Garden: Technology and the Pastoral Ideal in America*.

The groundwork for this study was laid by contributors to the discipline of religious studies who have identified an authentic religious dimension in American public life. These include Sidney Mead in *The Lively Experiment*, Robert Bellah in *The Broken Covenant: American Civil Religion in Time of Trial*, and Catherine Albanese in *Sons of the Fathers: The Civil Religion of the American Revolution*. There are several contributions this study hopes to make to the project they began. One is to provide an account of the people's involvement in a universalistic version of the democratic faith that linked environmental and social justice concerns. Another is to suggest the symbolic importance of national and state parks and other special landscapes for environmental ethics and public policy. An implication of the study is that the mythos of the civil religion, no less than that of any other kind of religion, is sustained, criticized, and reformed by living traditions composed of sacred places, associations, rituals, art, science, literature, and philosophy, and that the future of the society is dependent upon the quality of such traditions in American culture.

This inquiry was born in many classrooms and conferences, and has led into many libraries and homes. I can make only the barest beginnings of an acknowledgment of my indebtedness to the persons who have contributed in one fashion or another to this book.

In the background of my work, there will always stand the figures of James Luther Adams, John F. Hayward, and Sidney E. Mead, my former teachers and senior colleagues at Meadville Theological School of Lombard College. Their influence is apparent in these pages. Nor would the project have taken the form it did apart from my mentors at the University of Chicago Divinity School. I am especially indebted to Gibson Winter. His early recognition of the radical religious implications of the environmental crisis, and his writing in the areas of art, philosophy, and technology as they bear upon the American future, were important in the development of my thought. Alvin Pitcher's concern for the religious substance of political community, Mircea Eliade's phenomenology of religion, and Martin Marty's quest for a defensible public theology, have left a strong imprint as well. I continue to be indebted to the Social Ethics Seminar, formed by previous students in the Ethics and Society Field, and led initially by Alan Anderson, which has formed, in recent years, the primary intellectual context for my work in religious social ethics.

Colleagues and students at Meadville/Lombard were understanding and resourceful during the long period of my absorption in this project. Two successive deans of the school, John Godbey and Gene Reeves, facilitated time for writing. Research assistants Linda Hart and Mary Scriver rendered valuable aid, as did Meadville's business manager, Randall Vaughn. Kiyo Hashimoto was a fountain of good cheer. The personal support of Peter Fleck and Neil Shadle kept me at work through difficult times.

The members of the Save the Dunes Council, especially Edward Osann, Jr., Herbert and Charlotte Read, and Sylvia Troy, were generous with their time, knowledge, and encouragement.

The following persons were generous in granting interviews and in helping in a variety of ways with my research: James Teeri, Associate Professor of Biology, and Paul Voth, Professor Emeritus of Biology, the University of Chicago; Douglas Anderson and Kenneth Gray, previous administrative assistants to Senator Douglas; Emily Taft Douglas; William Hendrickson, former Chief Scientist, and James R. Whitehouse, Superintendent, Indiana Dunes National Lakeshore; Robert Linn, former Chief Scientist, National Park Service; Louis Hasenstraub, Assistant Director of Administration, Indiana State Parks; William Beecher, Director of the Chicago Academy of Sciences; Hilda Armin, Helen Bieker, Garnet Biesel, Robert Borchers, Lee Botts, Ragna Eskil, Hazel Hannell, John Hawkinson, Eugene Knotts, Hazel Olmsted, Emma Pitcher, Gladys Rizer, David Sander, Floyd Swink, and Leon Urbain.

Richard Brauer, Malcolm Collier, Sarah Cooke, Robert Jackson, Edward Kormandy, and Christian Moe, scholars whose research interests overlap mine, offered valuable information and suggestions.

The illustrations would not have been possible without the help of Carl Armstrong of the Indiana State Museum, Indianapolis, John Forwalter, and Helga Sandburg, and the photography of Bruce Bachman at the Richard Love Galleries in Chicago, James Fischer, Nancy Hays, and John Nelson.

Research librarians of special resourcefulness were Phil Barker and Rosemary Canright at Westchester Library, Chesterton, Indiana; Carol Doty of the Morton Arboretum; Louis Hieb of the University of Arizona, Tucson; Archie Motley at the Chicago Historical Society; the late Walter Necker at Regenstein Library, University of Chicago; and Peg Schoon at Calumet Purdue. In addition to these collections, the following libraries and archives were consulted: Art Institute of Chicago, Chicago Public Library, Field Museum, Gary Public Library, Indiana Dunes National Lakeshore, Indiana State Library and Indiana Commission on Public Records,

Indianapolis, John Crerar Library, Library of Congress, Newberry Library, Prairie Club, Chicago, Richardson Sanctuary, Dune Acres, Indiana, Save the Dunes Council, Beverly Shores, Indiana, and the University of Illinois at Circle Campus.

Many authors have sung the praises of my editor, Jeannette Hopkins. I will add one more voice: she believed in the work and was at the same time its best critic.

Finally, my family has sustained the writing of this book in more ways than can be named. My father-in-law, Walter Gibb, edited the dissertation; Mark and Kirsten Engel gave me, ungrudgingly, the time to write it, and constant cheers from the sidelines; and Joan Engel, as in all things, made the living and the writing of it a matter of joy and mutual fulfillment.

J. RONALD ENGEL
Chicago,
June 1982

SACRED
SANDS

Prologue

tanding in Jackson Park on Chicago's lakefront on a clear
afternoon, one may still look across the southern tip of
Lake Michigan and see, low on the horizon, the green-
capped headlands of the Indiana Dunes. For centuries they
greeted Native Americans who traveled south by canoe to hunt
and trap in the fertile crescent of marshland at the head of the lake,
and when, in the seventeenth century, the *voyageurs* penetrated
the Great Lakes, the Dunes rose before them to mark the entrance
to the vast interior of the new continent. Although flanked and
divided by factories and towers billowing clouds of smoke, and
only a remnant of their former glory, the Dunes still rise to meet
the eye—white and radiant in the sun.

The famed Indiana Dune Country, known colloquially simply
as "the Dunes," runs intermittently for fourteen miles along the
Lake Michigan coast between the cities of Gary and Michigan
City, Indiana. Cut in half by a 2½-billion-dollar deep-water port
and steel complex, including the largest blast furnaces in North
America, and interspersed with highways, railroad lines, shopping
centers, and housing developments, it is a remnant of native landscape in the heart of the industrial Midwest. Most of what remains
is divided between the 2,200 acres of the Indiana Dunes State Park,
and the scattered jigsaw-puzzle pieces of open space that comprise
an additional 11,000 acres authorized for the Indiana Dunes National
Lakeshore.

As small and fragmentary as the Dunes landscape is, it nonetheless offers a refuge for the ten million citizens of the largest metropolitan area between the two coasts. The Dunes parks lie within an
hour's drive of Chicago's Loop, yet there one may still run barefoot through waving marram grass, explore the flora of an ancient
tamarack swamp, watch the slow beats of a great blue heron wing-
ing over a secluded pond. On a hot summer weekend, the beaches,
trails, bike paths, and campsites are filled to overflowing. In 1980

1½ million visits were made to the State Park, and 1¼ million visits to the National Lakeshore. The latter, still in the process of development, is one of America's first national recreational areas in an urban setting. Both are truly people's parks.

Given the region's history, it is a wonder that any of the Dunes remain. If the allegedly normal course of development had occurred without intervention, the Dune Country would now be completely settled and industrialized, and the megalopolis of the Midwest would extend unbroken across Indiana to the Michigan line.

After the Civil War, the great urban and industrial explosion of Chicago began to spread south and east around the rim of Lake Michigan into the Calumet region—Indiana's "last frontier." Step by step, the native landscape of dunes, fen, marsh, and prairie, considered a desert wasteland by most observers, was obliterated. In 1889 Standard Oil Company started to build its great refinery at Whiting, Indiana; in 1901 Inland Steel began to construct what was soon to become the nation's largest steel plant at East Chicago, Indiana. And in 1906 United States Steel purchased 9,000 acres of low dunes and sloughs running for seven miles along Lake Michigan and laid the foundations for the city of Gary. It was not many years before one of the largest industrial centers of the world lay at the southern end of Lake Michigan.

But something did intervene.

At the turn of the century, a small band of Chicago reformers, artists, and scientists, joined by a few sympathetic Hoosiers, began the struggle to save the Dunes. Among their number, they counted settlement house workers Jane Addams and Graham Taylor; landscape architect Jens Jensen and national park system founder Stephen Mather; poets Harriet Monroe and Carl Sandburg; artists Frank V. Dudley and Earl H. Reed, Sr.; geologist Thomas Chamberlin and ecologist Henry Cowles. These were creative spirits of the Chicago renaissance of the Progressive era. In succeeding years they added new lights to their ranks—nature writers Donald Culross Peattie and Edwin Way Teale, "Father of Indiana State Parks" Richard Lieber, and Illinois senator Paul H. Douglas. Together with the public-spirited businessmen, labor organizers, politicians, civic leaders, and plain citizens who joined them, they created a movement that lasted through World War I, the roaring twenties, the Great Depression, and World War II, and culminated in the 1950s and '60s with what one urban geographer has called "perhaps the most savage conservation-industry confrontation in history."[1]

Those in the vanguard of the Dunes struggle never numbered more than several hundred. But what they lacked in numbers, they made up in commitment and the hours, weeks, and years devoted to the cause. In some cases several generations within a single family were involved in one phase or another of the eighty-year struggle to preserve the Dunes. Testimony in the 1960s before congressional committees alone runs to several thousand pages, and by 1982 the number of bills submitted to the U.S. Congress proposing preservation of the Dunes was nearly one hundred.

The campaign that led to the establishment of the Indiana Dunes State Park in 1923 was long and difficult. But when, in 1949, the push for the final industrialization of the Dune Country came, the Dunes movement was pitted against a coalition of political and economic interests of a sort not encountered before in the American environmental experience. The alignment seeking development of the remaining Dunes included not only the interests of utilities, railroads, banks, land-holding combines, and the Bethlehem and National Steel corporations, but also virtually the entire Indiana congressional delegation and state administration. With the leadership of Paul Douglas, however, the Dunes advocates marshaled support from newspapers throughout the country, from labor unions and national environmental associations, and carried the battle through both houses of Congress until it reached President Kennedy and President Johnson. Nor did the struggle end with the establishment of the Indiana Dunes National Lakeshore in 1966—the first unit added to the national park system against the opposition of the congressional district in which it was located. The movement was spurred to repeated action during the late 1960s and '70s by new threats to the Dunes, including a nuclear power plant approved by the U.S. Atomic Energy Commission for construction immediately adjacent to the Lakeshore's boundary.

The Dunes struggle did not simply happen. Many other areas of outstanding natural significance and beauty were lost to the exploding Chicago metropolis in the last century without a murmur of protest. By no stretch of the academic imagination can the struggle be reduced to the workings of any economic, political, or geographical law. It cannot be adequately explained as a conflict between two competing political jurisdictions, or as a reaching out for cost-free benefits by either a recreation-hungry urban population or a privileged class. Eventually, thousands of citizens from Indiana as well as Illinois joined the campaign to save the Dunes. Popular sentiment in the Chicago metropolitan region in favor of their preservation was evidenced by the quarter million signatures affixed to petitions in 1958; still there was no mass uprising or mass movement of Chicagoans to save the Dunes. The career of Paul Douglas neither rose nor fell with the Dunes question, and, in fact, he found little support on the matter in the Chicago press and business community. If among those who fought for the Dunes a few stood to benefit economically from their preservation, the extent of their sacrifices demonstrated that threats to personal amenities or life-styles could not alone count as motivation for the struggle. Most homeowners near the areas in contention were either neutral or sought their industrialization.

There must then be other explanations for the struggle for the Dunes, for the fight of a small band of devoted citizens against public apathy and powerful opposition over nearly a century to save a few miles of the native landscape.

Paul Douglas, near the end of his long and distinguished senatorial career, said, "If we get this bill through, I will feel that my life has not been in vain. Until I was thirty, I wanted to save the world. Between the ages of thirty and sixty I wanted to save the country. But since I was sixty, I've wanted to save the Dunes."[2] In the closing years of the struggle for the Indiana Dunes National Lakeshore, Thomas Dustin, executive director of the Indiana Izaak Walton League, also made it clear that in his view more was involved than ordinarily met the eye. In an essay entitled "The Indiana Dunes: A Symbol," he wrote that the "driving forces behind the pitched battles to preserve what is left of the Indiana Dunes" were far more than "swings and slides, and more than so much acreage on which to play or swim." Rather, he wrote, it was a "battle for the heritage of life . . . a pride and an acknowledgement of man's relationship to his earth."[3]

In 1966, Dorothy Buell, founder and first president of the Save the Dunes Council, told the *Chicago Tribune* that there were two biblical texts for her campaign: "Where there is no vision the people perish," and "By their deeds, ye shall know them."[4]

The purpose of the book that follows is to retrieve the history of human aspiration and sacrifice associated with this unique landscape. Now that a representative portion of the landscape is preserved, it is important that the story be told. As Dorothy Buell once commented, "It is a saga worthy of respect."[5]

ONE

The Great Dunes Pageant

To Nanabozho, the High Manitou,
Here on the place his fires made bare, the place
Where his great lodge was standing in the time
Before he first created men, I call,
And breathe my prayers upon the wind to him.
Great Nanabozho, send my soul thy dreams,
For I am thine—thine prophet—and my feet
Tread here thy sands, mine eyes turn to thy sun,
My hands
Scatter the sacred seed of thy desire;
Take me and fill me with thine ancient lore.
Here stood thy lodge when pale Tawiskaron,
Thy brother, stole the sun which thou hadst made,
And bridged thy waters with his flint-ribbed ice;
Here in the chase around the world's blue rim
Thou didst o'ertake him. Here the battle raged,
Jostling the stars apart, that fight of gods,
When thou didst break Tawiskaron asunder,
And from this place, when that dark battle ceased,
Thou didst forbid the prairie grass
Ever to heal the scars of thy dead fires.
Thy sacred ground is this, and wandering feet
Alone shall tread it through the lonely years.
Here shall the prophet's vision flame, the song
Of free and lofty trails, and purple smokes
Of dreaming fires ascend. The Dreamers come;
Show them through me the years of this thy home
Great Manitou; the tribes who trod this trail,
The trickling stream of life along thy waste,
The marching pageant of thy sacred sands.

THOMAS WOOD STEVENS,

the first speech of the Prophet
from *The Historical Pageant
of the Dunes*, 1917

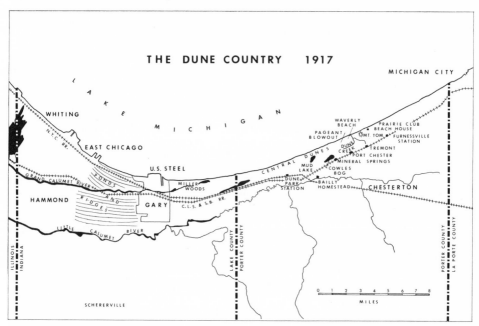

The Dune Country, 1917
Drawing by Joan G. Engel

Shortly before 3 P.M. on Memorial Day, 1917, the American flag was raised on the top of Mount Tom, the highest sand mountain in the Indiana Dunes. Thus began the great "Historical Pageant and Masque of the Sand Dunes of Indiana," an event heralded at the time as the largest outdoor drama in American history.[1]

MEMORIAL DAY, 1917

Spring comes late and uncertainly to the Dune Country. On the morning of May 30, the skies were slate gray. By noon distant lightning accompanied scattered rain showers, and by afternoon a thunderstorm threatened. As Ben Hecht reported the next day in the *Chicago Daily News*, "So far as the ghosts of LaSalle and Marquette were concerned, it couldn't have been a better day for a historical pageant. The Indiana dunes lay in an inscrutable wilderness under a gloomy sky."[2]

But the mood of the hundreds of persons trudging through a half-mile of sand to reach the amphitheater permitted little compromise with the weather. Expectant, determined, they perceived themselves making history. All day "in little black streams, they trickled across the broad face of the dunes . . . from shop girls with their luncheons in fruit boxes, to the professional critter armed with wood axes and bowie knives and knapsacks, blanket robes and sleeping cots."[3] By mid-afternoon several thousand persons had made the pilgrimage to the great bowl, or "blowout," surrounded on three sides by long, steep sand hills at the head of Lake Michigan.

For most, the day's trip had begun early, embarking in Chicago's Loop on one of the fourteen-car special trains of the Illinois Central, and debarking two hours later at Port Chester Station—fifty-one miles southeast of Chicago—in the the heart of the Dunes. Others made the trip by car, carriage, or wagon. Driving from scattered points throughout southern Wisconsin, Illinois, Indiana, and lower Michigan, they ventured at the end onto the rutted, winding dirt roads leading into the dunes north of Chesterton. There they found parking grounds for five thousand vehicles and the mayor of Gary, with the entire police force, at the scene directing traffic.

The day was the culmination of months of preparation. In February the Dunes Pageant Association was incorporated with James L. Houston, Jr., editor with the *Chicago American*, president. Among the twenty-four incorporators and thirty-one trustees were Jane Addams of Hull House; Graham Taylor of Chicago Commons; Dwight H. Perkins, architect; Bess Sheehan, Gary civic leader; Lorado Taft, sculptor; and, from the University of Chicago, Henry C. Cowles, botanist, and Rollin D. Salisbury, geographer.[4] Thomas Wood Stevens, former native of Chicago and president of the American Pageant Association, was chosen to write and produce the pageant, and Donald Robertson, founder of the Drama Players of the Chicago Theatre Society, to be pageant master and play the role of the narrator, the "Prophet." An announcement circulated in March declared that the pageant and masque to be presented May 30 and June 3, 1917, was an "artistic demonstration" to call attention to the proposed acquisition of the Dune Country as a national or state park.[5] Within weeks, fifty civic associations and numerous prominent Chicago business leaders responded to the call for cooperation and more than $10,000 was raised.

In spite of the war and a series of misunderstandings leading to strained relations between Stevens and the pageant trustees, momentum for the project grew through the spring of 1917.[6] Houston and his staff toured the region making speeches, recruiting actors, dancers, choruses, and orchestras, and parceling out responsibility for each of the six major episodes to various universities, high schools, clubs, and towns. By the end of May, the total number of participants neared one thousand. For a week before May 30, workers readied the site and actors held rehearsals on the dunes, making the country for a mile around the pageant grounds look like a tented city. Scores of volunteer receptionists, chaperons, guides, ticket and program sellers, nurses, and publicity agents waited for the crowds on Wednesday morning.

It was a dramatic experience to come over the rim of Pageant Blowout on the trail from Port Chester and suddenly to see the lake in the distance, waves rolling in cross-cutting winds, dark clouds stretching out to the horizon, and the gathering of many hundreds of persons covering the great valley in the sand hills. As Margery Currey wrote for the *Chicago Tribune:* "The whole day on the dunes was itself, in fact, the great pageant. . . . Roaming about everywhere were groups of eighteenth-century Spanish soldiers, Frenchmen, and Britishers, Miami, Mohegan, and Pottawattomie Indians, and nymphs of the dunes with silver gray draperies floating off behind them. Beautiful little processionals of gayly costumed figures silhouetted along a distant ridge against a slate-colored sky made pictures that will never leave the memory."[7]

While uniformed Camp Fire girls circulated through the throng soliciting $1 for life memberships in the National Dunes Park Association, the crowds gathered about campfires or swarmed into the little shacks, or "inns," along the beach for fish dinners and sandwiches and coffee. Some, the real "Dune Bugs," who could be distinguished from the rest of the company by the stout boots they wore and the oilskins, knapsacks, and staffs that they carried, accompanied the guides on trips to Mount Tom or Tamarack Swamp in the hinterland. Others never made it farther than the round white "Reception Tent" where Chicago philanthropist Eames McVeagh and Ethel McDurfee, secretary of the pageant association, served hot tea for visiting society folk and special guests such as Earl H. Reed, Sr., whose exhibits of etchings had done much in recent years to attract Chicagoans to the Dunes.

Shortly before 3 P.M., the skies partially cleared, and for a moment the sun colored the sands with deep yellow and brown tints. A hush fell as spectators hurried in from outlying points and actors took their assigned places. As bugles blew, a troop of Boy Scouts perched in the high branches of the dead trees on the south side of the blowout wig-wagged red semaphore flags to signal those on Mount Tom that the flag was to be raised and the drama begun. The musicians had hardly played the first notes of the "International Fantasia" by Rollinson when rain began to fall again. The spectators who had no umbrellas dug holes in the sand while the word went out: "Better wet heads than wet feet!"[8]

The stage for the pageant was the floor of the blowout, several hundred feet across. At the north or lake end, a high stand was erected for the narrator, Donald Robertson. Transplanted saplings and shrubbery demarcated the focus of action. Spectators sitting high on the slopes of the blowout had a panoramic view of the lake, beach, and stage before them, while one-half mile to the east, they could see the three peaks of Mounts Tom, Holden, and Green, named by early settlers "The Three Sisters." Several factors had led Houston and his friends to choose this blowout for the pageant. It was one of the largest and most familiar along the shoreline (known locally as the "Big Blowout," and to Chicagoans as "Jens Jensen Blowout"), directly accessible by train, and adjacent to the summer colony of Waverly Beach. It was also close to some of the places of the Dunes that were richest in history. The blowout itself was reputed to be the site of an age-old Great Council Ground, used by generations of Indians. A quarter mile east was Dune Creek, the presumed scene of a Revolutionary War skirmish. The real "stage" for the pageant was more than the floor of the blowout; it was the whole vicinity, including its historical associations.

Donald Robertson mounted the platform and the pageant began. A column of actors depicting Indians marched single file toward the stage, while others paddled canoes along the lakeshore in front of the blowout. Robertson, garbed as the Indian Prophet, in a solemn and rolling voice beseeched Nanabozho, the High Manitou, to hear his prayers and fill his soul with divine dreams and ancient lore. By all reports, at this moment, the words hardly uttered, a re-markable event occurred. George Brennan, a Chicago educator and historian, later described it: "As if in answer to the Prophet's appeal . . . while still in his pose of supplication, the heavens opened with a fierce electric display all over the lake and the Dunes, followed by continuous, deafening crashes of thunder, reverberating through the hills and valleys, which continued for some time. It was thrilling; yea, awe-inspiring!" [9]

With torrents of rain blotting out all sight and sound, the audience huddled closer in their little dugouts, while the actors ran to the dressing tents for cover. After several unsuccessful attempts to continue, the directors gave up, and Robertson shouted above the wind that weather permitting, the pageant would be given next Sunday, and that the day's tickets would be honored.

June 3 was a perfect day for the estimated crowd of twenty-five to forty thousand that darkened the sides of Pageant Blowout for the delayed performance.[10] Thousands of cars and carriages jammed the roads leading to Port Chester—many never reaching the parking grounds. The sunlight made vivid and real what the thunder and rain had blanketed in mystery at the first performance. The lake, sky, and hills were brilliant with their caps of wind-beaten trees; the spring lupine, hairy puccoon, and butterfly weed were in bloom by the trailside.

The flag was raised on Mount Tom punctually at 2:30 and for half an hour the audience joined in the singing of patriotic airs. At 3:00 the pageant began. The voices of the actors were distinctly heard up to the rim of the amphitheater as six episodes representing the history of the Dune Country processed across the landscape. Each episode was built around a particular incident which reputedly occurred in the Dunes, while it simultaneously represented a larger period and movement in the story of midwestern exploration and settlement and in the history of the nation as a whole. The title the Dunes Pageant Association chose for Steven's work. "The Dunes Under Four Flags," indicated the epic sweep of history: the times of the French missionaries and colonists, shown through incidents in the lives of Père Marquette and Sieur de LaSalle; the struggle on the frontier between British soldiers and American revolutionaries, dramatized in patriot Tom Brady's capture at Dune Creek after a raid on the British Fort St. Joseph; the daring Spanish campaign north into Michigan in 1781, portrayed by a march across the Dunes; the westward movement of American traders and army troops, dramatized by incidents surrounding John Kinzie's trading post in Chicago, and the Fort Dearborn massacre; and finally, the establishment of permanent settlements in the Northwest Territory, with their shared ambition to become the "metropolis of the West," dramatized in the life of Joseph Bailly, first white settler in the Dunes, and by the visit of Daniel Webster to the little town of City West at the mouth of Dune Creek in 1834. Present in all of the scenes were the figures of the Native Americans, telling the story of the tragic loss of the land by its original inhabitants.

As the sun's shadows lengthened across the floor of the sand bowl, the series of interpretative dances that formed the masque began. In the first scene, three groups of dancers, the first in pale gray floating draperies symbolizing the Winds, the second in blue-green symbolizing the Waves, and the third in hooded pajamas of beige symbolizing the Sands, entered the stage. To the music of Rachmaninoff's "Prelude in G Minor," they interpreted how the winds and waves, by "playing upon the yellow sands," build the dunes. Then "borne on the swift current of the wind," a second troupe appeared and with bows and tips, and short, quick runs, imitated a bevy of sandpipers lighting upon the new-formed shore.[11]

In the third dance, a congregation of wood nymphs dedicated the Dunes as their sanctuary. But one of them, a "Sorrowing Tree-Heart," senses impending destruction of the dunes, and pleads for their preservation: "Grant us these haunts of beauty, Heart of Pan, Heart of Man." As if in answer to her pleas, the concluding "Dance of the Indians" showed Indian warriors and their women rejoicing in the discovery of the Dune Country. Following the "Dagger Dance" from *Natoma* by Victor Herbert, they adopt it as their homeland, performing the ritual of the Calumet by which the land is consecrated to "Peace, Love and the Fireside."[12]

The great "Historical Pageant and Masque in the Sand Dunes of Indiana" reached its finale with a grand martial review of the six hundred actors and dancers across the floor of the blowout. George Brennan recalled: "It was a glorious sight when all of the people . . . rallied to the colors, behind

THE CALUMET
   FRENCH FLAG
      BRITISH FLAG
         SPANISH FLAG
            AMERICAN FLAG

and the Prophet, at the head of the Grand Parade, bearing the AMERICAN FLAG, led this vast assemblage of 25,000 people in singing *The Star-Spangled Banner!*"[13]

The newspapers reported the next day that as the moon rose over Mount Tom that night, hundreds of campfires dotted the dunes.

"THE PAGEANT OF BIG PURPOSE IN THE SAND DUNES"

The Dunes Pageant of 1917 must occupy a central place in any effort to understand the larger meaning of the eighty-year movement to preserve the Indiana Dunes. For those who participated, the pageant was a definitive expression of the purposes to which they were devoted. Its impact was felt for years. Frank V. Dudley was so stirred by the pageant that he resolved to devote his life to painting the Dunes.[14] Afterward, he memorialized the event in two paintings, *The Pageant* and *Port Chester Trail to Pageant Blowout*, one of which hung in the Art Institute of Chicago the following year.[15] Six years later, the memory of the pageant was vivid in the minds of those who led the successful campaign for the Indiana Dunes State Park. Mabel McIlvaine summed up in retrospect: "By this pageant the people of Indiana were able to declare this portion of lake shore and forest a State Park."[16] And forty years later, the pageant still had power to inspire fresh poetry among those working with Senator Paul H. Douglas to establish the Indiana Dunes National Lakeshore.[17]

The political context for the Dunes Pageant was a rapid succession of events which occurred prior to 1917. About 1912, a concerted campaign was spearheaded by the Prairie Club of Chicago to establish a "Sand Dunes National Park." One of the persons involved in the campaign was Stephen T. Mather, an influential Chicago civic leader and Bull Moose Republican, who had accumulated a fortune in the borax business. Mather was a member of the conservation committees of the Prairie Club and the Chicago Geographic Society, and was intimately acquainted, through a variety of connections, with most of the early leaders of the Dunes movement.

In 1914 Mather made a tour of the national parks of the West. Dissatisfied with their condition, he wrote in protest to his old college friend from the University of California, Secretary of the Interior Franklin K. Lane. Lane told Mather to come to Washington and "run them yourself." In 1915, with an appointment as assistant to the secretary, Mather set to work to put order into the administration of the national parks. Soon Mather and his own bright young assistant, Horace Albright, had joined J. Horace

McFarland, the American Civic Association, and other so-called "esthetic conservationists" in promoting the establishment of a separate bureau for the national parks within the Department of the Interior. In 1916, Mather's former confederate in Chicago civic reform, William Kent, now an independent California congressman, introduced legislation to form a National Park Service, and after extensive lobbying it was passed by Congress in the course of the summer. On August 25, President Woodrow Wilson signed into law the National Park Service Act, and Mather was quickly appointed the first director of the Service.[18]

Within two weeks of the passage of the act, Mather had arranged with newly appointed junior Senator Thomas Taggart of Indiana to introduce a resolution, which the Senate passed on September 7, authorizing a study of "the advisability of the securing by purchase or otherwise, all that portion of the counties of Lake, LaPorte, and Porter in the State of Indiana bordering on Lake Michigan and commonly known as the 'sand dunes.' . . ."[19] In late October Mather returned to Chicago to tour the Dunes and hold public hearings on the Taggart resolution. The hearings were held in the courtroom of Mather's friend, Judge C. C. Kohlsaat, on October 31. Earl Reed's etchings lined the walls and at the front of the room, to symbolize the Dune Country, there was an exhibit of prickly pear cactus. Over four hundred persons attended the hearings, with representatives of over twenty civic organizations testifying in favor of a Dunes park.

On December 20, Mather submitted his report to the Secretary of the Interior. In spite of the fact that the federal government had never purchased land for a national park, Mather recommended that it buy a good portion of the Dune Country—an area approximately twenty-five miles long by one mile deep between Gary and Michigan City, Indiana. He estimated that between nine and thirteen thousand acres of dunes and wetlands could be purchased at a cost ranging between $1.8 million and $2.6 million. A few months later, in early 1917, Lane endorsed Mather's recommendation and submitted it to Congress. In order to help the cause Mather proceeded to have the hearings published and circulated largely at his own expense.

Encouraged by these events, the organizations working for the preservation of the Dunes, led by the newly formed National Dunes Park Association, sought to give the idea as much publicity as possible. As an exercise in political "propaganda," the Dunes Pageant was an ambitious enterprise. There was widespread advance publicity, especially among the sponsoring women's clubs. Theodore Roosevelt, Governor Frank O. Lowden of Illinois, and Governor James P. Goodrich of Indiana sent messages of support. Afterward, members of Congress received copies of the "Dunes Pageant and History Book" and a mass petition signed by those who attended. Newsreels of the event were shown throughout the country, and stories carried in newspapers as far afield as New York and Philadelphia.

However, the park effort itself was aborted by events well before the pageant was presented. On April 6, 1917, the United States declared war against Germany. The new slogan became "First Save the Country, then Save the Dunes."[20] Moreover, early in 1917, Mather had a nervous breakdown and left Washington, no one had come forward to take recently defeated Senator Taggart's place as a congressional sponsor. Nonetheless, as a publicity spectacle under conditions of wartime, the Dunes Pageant must be judged a considerable success. *The New York Evening Post* drily commented, "A Pageant in war time which has nothing to do with war is not an every day occurrence."[21]

But there were other purposes at work as well.

Writing in the *Chicago Tribune* in late February, Margery Currey noted that "the point most stressed in planning the pageant is the importance it will have for the *community, using the word in a large sense*."[22] At least some of her meaning was captured by Caroline McIlvaine, librarian of the Chicago Historical Society, and a leading figure in the pageant's inception. "This patriotic pageant," she wrote in retrospect, "not only profited the project of 'saving the Dunes,' but has done something toward re-cementing the sympathies of people of all degrees and nationalities in this region."[23] One reason why "The Pageant of Big Purpose in the Sand Dunes," as one journal described it, was important to the community was because it functioned as an agency for the creation of community.[24] This was an end worth accomplishing, especially in wartime.

By creating a community united by mutual sympathy, the pageant created a political constituency for the preservation of the Dunes. But more important, it helped reconnect those present with the ongoing communion of human beings across the generations, which it was the purpose of the park to serve. The park was for the sake of the community—past, present, and future. To "Save the Dunes," as Thomas W. Allinson, one of the officers of the Dunes Pageant Association, said in a speech at Gary in April, was "not the fad of a few people but the necessity of us all," and therefore it is "not only a necessity but our duty to conserve this land of our forefathers."[25] This is why, when A. F. Knotts, president of the National Dunes Park Association, contemplated the future success of the park movement, he could think of no better form of celebration than another pageant. In his letter of congratulation to the Dunes Pageant Association on June 4, he concluded: "When the national park is secured, we will have a national pageant which will be attended by hundreds of thousands instead of thousands."[26]

There was an even more fundamental purpose at work beneath this one, a first principle upon which everything else ultimately depended. This purpose was referred to in various ways. Some alluded to a love of the land. Reported the *Gary Tribune:* "As a dramatic spectacle, the pageant was a huge success, and as for its *actual purpose* . . . it was more than successful, for thousands fell in love with the vast stretches of wild country."[27] Stoughton Cooley, writer for the *Chicago Herald,* spoke in terms of a prophetic demand: "O ye men and women of Chicago, conquering and unconquered; ye good-hearted, careless, blundering profligate citizens. . . . Pause a moment in your mad career. Lift up your eyes and behold a beauty not made by the hand of man."[28] Others talked about an ideal. In the *Prairie Club Bulletin,* Mary Kelly Graves introduced her article on "The Dunes Pageant" with the statement: "There are many ways in which man battles for his idealism. For some things he must draw the sword; for others he must insistently project his ideal until it animates and drives the multitude to realize his vision with him."[29]

This testimony indicates that the primary purpose of the Dunes Pageant was to persuade the thousands of spectators who attended to see a new vision of the Dune Country. Through the symbolism of drama, dancing, music, and poetry, its sponsors sought to convince those who, as Margery Currey noted, once knew "the Dunes only by hearsay or by assumption as tracts of colorless, sandy, uninteresting waste," that here was a place of beauty, rich in history, and pregnant with import for human values.[30]

The celebration of a vision, and the conversion of masses of one's fellow citizens to see that vision—this was no doubt the underlying motivation of the scores of volunteers who devoted money, time, and talent to the pageant's production. To show the "value and beauty of the Dunes" to the residents of Indiana and Illinois,[31] and perhaps to the rest of the nation as well, simply for its own sake, was reason enough to hold it, and the only plausible explanation why so much energy was devoted to the pageant when, by spring of 1917, there was no serious chance for passage of park legislation.

From this end, everything else flowed. Through it, those in attendance became joined to one another in one great community, and by its means, they had "burned into [their] consciousness the belief that the Dunes . . . should be perserved as a great park for the people."[32]

This was, in essence, a religious purpose. The attempt to convert other persons to a new vision of the world, so that their attitude toward others is transformed because of it, and they are motivated to form a more perfect community on its behalf, is the kind of activity characteristic of all missionary religious movements. John Dewey, who influenced many of the early leaders of the Dunes movement, defined the "religious" quality of human experience as "any activity pursued in behalf of an ideal end against obstacles and in spite of threats of personal loss because of a conviction of its general and enduring value."[33] The identification of the purpose of the pageant as religious in nature suggests that it functioned, at least implicitly, as a great collective religious ritual for those who attended. The movement that created the pageant, although many of its members might not have recognized it as such, was at root a religious movement.

PILGRIMAGE INTO SACRED SPACE AND TIME

Perhaps the single most expressive description of the Dunes Pageant was Caroline McIlvaine's: "On May 30 and again on June 3, many thousand citizens of Michigan, Indiana, and Illinois left their homes very early in the morning to join in a pilgrimage along the shore of Lake Michigan to a desert spot at its southmost curve. . . . In a vast amphitheatre carved by the winds at the summit of a sand dune the pilgrims sat down, broke bread, and confirmed one another in the verdict that this natural park preserved by the grace of God ought to be reserved forever as a national park."[34]

There are reverberations of the aboriginal tribes making their yearly pilgrimages to the ancestral shrine in the mountains, of the Israelites setting off into the desert in quest of the Promised Land, of the Moslems winding their way to Mecca. Some described the throng assembled as a "great congregation," joined in "one rare bond of fellowship," witnessing a "prophesy" and undergoing an "awakening."[35]

The historical basis for the actions of those who gathered in the Dunes in 1917 is to be found in their own unique experience of the Dune Country, in their Christian inheritance from a century of frontier settlement in the Midwest, and in a retrieval of the ritualistic means by which all human beings try to give cohesion and identity to their common life.

For several decades individuals and small groups had been coming from Chicago for free rambles in the Indiana Dunes. As the city grew, making strolls along the beaches and low dunes that once encircled Chicago less possible, the still relatively wild Dune Country became the object of that "natural desire," as attorney John O. Bowers, Sr., a participant in the early Dunes movement called it, "of those living in congested and highly artificial surroundings for contact with the primitive, the primeval."[36] When the poet Edgar Lee Masters wrote an article for the *Chicago Herald* to publicize the Dunes Pageant, it was about a composite of such walks, for him a "regular Sunday plan." Masters's walk took him by the edge of a tamarack swamp, through the oak forests of the stationary dunes, past the shifting dunes with their "undulating wastes of sand spiked by the dead bodies of trees," and along the shore, where he built a fire at the foot of a great sand hill.[37]

For many, these trips assumed the character of a pilgrimage to a sacred place. Landscape architect Jens Jensen, the most eloquent of those who first spoke out on behalf of the preservation of the Dunes, voiced a shared sentiment at the public hearings in 1916: "We need the dunes; we can never do without them. . . . How can we ever be without such a wonderful vision, a vision that we carry with us until we make our next pilgrimage?"[38]

On Memorial Day, 1908, began a more formal and ritualistic form of pilgrimage to the Dunes. On that day a committee of the Chicago Playground Association sponsored its first public "Saturday Afternoon Walking Trip" near Miller, on the eastern outskirts of Gary, Indiana. Amalia Hofer and Graham Taylor of Chicago Commons settlement house were among those who organized the trip with Jensen. Hofer later recalled it as the "first of the many great pilgrimages to the dune country" led by the association of walking enthusiasts that in 1911 became the Prairie Club. More than two hundred hikers—"women in long, full skirts with long, full 'automobile veils,' men in old clothes, only now and then one bold enough to appear in knickers"—left Chicago by train in the morning and spent the day wandering "more or less lost among the bewildering little sand hills." After a good deal of fun, including the collapse of a footbridge and the consequent dunking of Tom Allinson and John Bley in the Grand Calumet River, the two parties led by Hofer and Jensen converged upon the "beach rendezvous," to find a "campfire, with the coffee steaming in the new tin wash boiler, and the glorious stretch of rolling blue just beyond."[39]

Amalia Hofer also recalled a song from those early hikes in the Dunes:

Here's the spot we've camped on
    Many times before;
The ashes of our fires,
    Are strewn along the shore,
Let's turn the charred old back-log,
    Remembering other days,
And kindle for old time's sake

Another rousing blaze.
 Come and pile the driftwood!
  Heap it wide and high!
 Today we make burnt offering
  To the ghosts of days gone by![40]

Some of the ghosts the burning logs in the Dunes called back to life in 1917 were midwesterners who for generations had made pilgrimages to isolated places in the wilderness and gathered about campfires to sing and to become united into one community. These were the "camp-meetings" of the frontier, where the enactment of the biblical story of salvation moved thousands to conversion to a new vision of life. The camp-meeting created a new form of religious ritual for a free people yearning for a living God who would confirm their pioneer experiences of equality and neighborliness. Looking out on the evening of June 3 at the blazing campfires and tents on the Dunes landscape, and remembering the journeys that had led there, and the hours of singing and camaraderie, one might well have seen the great revival gatherings of earlier years. The content of the ritual drama celebrated in 1917 was different, but the function was similar.[41]

In 1913, five years after the "Saturday Afternoon Walking Trips" began, the pilgrimages to the Dunes were augmented by the addition of formal ceremony. The Prairie Club built a Beach House near Mount Tom, and on Columbus Day, the club invited the public to hike into the dunes and participate in the dedication service. After Thomas Allinson, head resident of Henry Booth Settlement House, spoke on "Prayer and Prairie," and Jensen dedicated the building, a masque written by another settlement worker, Mrs. Jacob Abt, entitled "The Spirit of the Dunes," was performed in a blowout nearby. Abt's allegory, cast in well-turned Elizabethan verse, portrayed through the character of Duna the mythic spirit of the Dunes. Lost, wandering alone across the landscape in search of her "loved home," the maiden Duna enters the Dune Country. Here she is courted by the four winds. The West Wind is a symbol of the seductive music of the Dunes; the East Wind a symbol of the shifting hills of golden sand; the South Wind a symbol of the flowers of spring and the languid summer breezes, the North Wind a symbol of the dappled autumn colors and winter's snowy blasts. In the variegated landscape which they create together, Duna discovers her true kingdom.[42]

Two years later, on Memorial Day, 1915, a similar program was presented to an audience of more than twelve hundred. Exercises at the Beach House included a speech by Allinson, songs by the Prairie Club Chorus, and a patriotic oration. The group hiked to the blowout a half-mile east for another masque by Abt, "The Awakening." The title was taken from the double action of the play: the awakening of a young man to the beauties of the Dunes by seeing there the awakening of summer by Sylvan and Helios. As a result of his conversion, the young man becomes an enthusiastic member of the walking club, and a faithful pilgrim to the Dunes. This production vastly impressed those who saw it, judging from the comment of the *Chesterton Tribune* the following day: "On top of a dune, with its cap blown out is a natural amphitheatre, seemingly made for staging the fantastic. . . . From the beginning of time until that day, never was such a scene enacted there."[43]

On Memorial Day, 1916, fifteen hundred persons attended a spring festival of folk dancing under the direction of the Mary Wood Hinman School, with the participation of children from Maxwell Street Settlement in Chicago, where Abt and her husband were head residents. The festival was preceded by anniversary exercises at which Earl Reed spoke on "The Dunes." It was on this occasion, according to George Brennan, that the idea for a Dunes Historical Pageant in 1917 first occurred. As Emma Doeserich in her history of the Prairie Club explains, it was the long history of successes with open air festivals, masques, and patriotic services that led to the decision by the club to organize a separate corporation called "The Dunes Pageant Association."[44]

A striking feature about these celebrations, culminating in the pageant and masque in 1917, was the archetypal character of the ritual pilgrimage to the open air amphitheater in the Dunes. The shape of the blowout resembled the natural amphitheaters of the ancient and primitive worlds. The Athenians, for example, had made regular pilgrimages to a similar bowl-like amphitheater outside the walls of their city. The Greek theater symbolized the city's graveyard, where in dramatic ritual the spirits of the past were recalled and their stories retold, both informing the present and perpetuating the society's identity. Similarly for the Hopi, when the members of the tribe seated themselves in the sacred amphitheater, they symbolically occupied the lower half-circle of the cosmos, the underworld of the dead. The amphitheater was the burial site of the ancestors, and there, through the action of religious ritual, the living could make contact with the meaning and power of the collective past.[45]

Such structural congruence suggests a further interpretation of the experience of those who made the pilgrimage to the Dunes in 1917 and watched the figures of the past reappear on the floor of the blowout before them. It is plausible to see in this twentieth-century, supposedly "secular," phenomenon, aspects of the kind of experience that characterizes all religious ceremonies which dramatically reenact the creation myth and sacred history of a people.[46]

If Thomas Wood Stevens's words are taken at their face value, his text for the pageant speaks for itself in this regard. From the opening speech, in which the Prophet tells a myth of how the world was created by the Manitou of the Dunes, Nanabozho, to the concluding benediction, when he departs,

> Leaving thy house forever to thy sons,
> My brother-spirits, dreamers, wanderers,
> Who dance upon the dunes beneath thy stars
> And lift their hearts to thy mysterious night
> And light new fires upon thine ancient hearth.[47]

the blank verse of the narrative projects the prose dialogue of the play's historical episodes into sacred time. The dream-like world created by the pageant, the world where, as Ben Hecht observed, "LaSalle again surveyed the yellow wastes, Marquette again stalked along the water's edge,"[48] was a reactualization of the time when the great founding events of the universe and the society occurred, a time which continues to exist alongside and in interpenetration with the profane ordinary time of day-to-day events. It appears that Stevens experimented for a decade with dramatic techniques to create precisely such a psychological effect.

The pageant made visible, present, and real the unification of human experience that those who were working for a Dunes park found resident in the landscape. George Brennan's description of what he believed those who witnessed the pageant *truly saw* is characteristic of a passage into liminal time and space:

This question has often been asked, "Was this great pageant worth while?" Yes, it was. For here were *crystallized the different phases of Dune character*—its beauty and its desolation—its restful peace, and the terrific evidence of its storms—its primitive wildness and the ever-changing newness of its neighboring cities—the birchbark canoe and the palatial steamer that plows the azure waters of the mighty inland ocean that washes its sandy shores—the poor Indian with his untutored mind and savage nature, and the cultured American enjoying this historic portrayal of the life of the Dunes.

All of these sights have brought to the onlooker the *true life history of the Dunes,* and have portrayed them so vividly that *they stand out as real things.*[49]

It is no wonder that the spectators were awed by the thunder and lightning following Donald Robertson's appeal to Nanabozho on the afternoon of May 30, or that one of the last Native Americans living in northern Indiana should faint with emotion. Lola Was-sur-man, a Kickapoo Indian, told a reporter that her companion had collapsed when she saw the scene depicting the forced departure of her ancestors to the Potawatomi reservation in Kansas. The presence of living Indians at the pageant, some from as far away as South Dakota, also added to the impression that it was the reenactment of authentic events.[50]

According to the creation myth of the pageant, Nanabozho had his home in the Dunes before he created human beings; it was the site of his hearth and lodge. His sacred fires created the Dunes. By making the pilgrimage to the Dunes and gathering again in fellowship, as the Prairie Club and many others had been doing for a decade and more, and as the Indian tribes, the pioneers, and the settlers of the past once did, and relighting the council fires as they had done, and as the deity of the world, Nanabozho, himself did in that primordial time when the world of the Dunes was created—by ritual reenactment—the pageant engaged these twentieth-century "moderns" in the means all peoples employ to recover their sacred history.

It was, in Brennan's words, "the true life history of the Dunes."

This history was presented as the key to the meaning of both the surrounding natural environment and the society's identity. For many in the audience of thousands sitting in silence around the sides of the great sand bowl, it must have seemed as though their own collective "inner history" was revealed to them. This region, so recently settled, doubling in population every decade, had an archaic past. Out here in the Dunes, away from the distractions of the city, this sacred past could once again live and give purpose to the present. The decision to hold the pageant was much more than the decision to stage a publicity spectacle for political effect.

"Dunes park" had two interconnected meanings, the first, political—as a public park, the Dunes could be preserved in common ownership by the people—the second, religious and symbolic. Dunes park, in the second sense, referred to the perception of the Dunes as a sacred place. According to the pageant's myth of origins, it was in the Dunes that the creative Power of the universe was first made manifest and the "world" created, and where the promise of universal community remained embodied. The Prophet declared in his concluding speech:

> Thy medicine and magic of the soul,
> Of wrongs forgotten, peace and brotherhood
> Small bloom forever 'mid thy sacred hills.[51]

LANDSCAPE AND IMAGINATION

With her ability to see to the center of things, Margery Currey wrote the following on "The Pageant of the Dunes":

> Inevitably, as man lives close to the earth and its beauty and mystery take shape for him in concrete images and ideas, the events and figures of any region come to have a significance that finally blends them together into some sort of connected story. And this makes a mythology of that region, with its basis found partly in the mystic wonder that comes to man in vast solitary spaces where there are only the sea and sky and earth, somewhat in the tiny insect and bird and animal life of the place, slightly in the historical events and the human figures who have appeared in the region, and mostly in the imagination of man, to whom the solitude is vastly expressive and the life forms intimately lovable.[52]

Well before the park campaign took such an encouraging turn in the summer of 1916, the Dunes movement had received its genesis in the imaginations of those who found the solitude of the Dune Country "vastly expressive," its life forms "intimately lovable," and who created the "mythology of that region." Among these were the members of the Prairie Club. But an even wider community of experience created the Dunes mythology, a community represented among the pageant's sponsors by such figures as the poet Harriet Monroe and the sculptor Lorado Taft. These individuals shared the aspiration in the early years of the twentieth century of creating a mythology for Chicago, embodying unique qualities of its landscape and the special promise of democracy of its people. Through such an epic myth, they hoped to influence the future of the city and its surrounding region. One of their number, Sherwood Anderson, gave their expectations voice when he wrote in *Mid-American Chants:* "Conceive if you will the mightiness of that dream that these fields and places, out here west of Pittsburg, may become sacred places. . . ."[53]

Many of the members of what has come to be called the "Chicago renaissance" focused their energies exclusively on the city itself, but those who contributed to the work of the collective imagination that produced the Dunes Pageant of 1917 included the native landscape in their vision. They saw within the new city's existential reality a latent promise that it might someday fulfill its original boast and be a "city in the garden." They believed the people lacked the capacity to see, as the Chicago architect and visionary Louis Sullivan so clearly saw, that the city and the lake and the dunes and the prairie were tied together in a single destiny. Sullivan asked: "Do you think the picture of the City one thing, the picture of the fair broad water and land another thing? The drama of the City one thing, the drama of the open another?"[54] It was this group's self-appointed task to spur their fellow citizens to answer this challenge. Of the varied means they chose—poetry, novels, painting, sculpture, architecture—none more clearly showed the communal dimension of their art, or the ecological character of their vision, than festal drama.[55]

Perhaps no one in the Dunes movement was in a better position to articulate the meaning of the pageant than Lorado Taft. In 1917

Taft stood at the center of Chicago's art establishment. On the evening of April 6, 1917, the Dunes Pageant Association invited the public to Fullerton Hall at the Art Institute for a general orientation session on the upcoming event. Taft, Stevens, and Alice Gray, a University of Chicago Phi Beta Kappa who was living alone in the Dunes, spoke to the gathering.

Taft sought to place the Dunes issue within an historical perspective. Beginning with a contrast between the hill towns of Italy, each a unique "personality," developed through centuries of isolation, and the oppressive and monotonous homogeneity of industrial America, where one cannot tell the difference between the general physiognomy of Detroit, Chicago, or San Francisco, he proceeded to comment on the prevailing effort to obliterate variety and distinctiveness of place. Then, turning to Chicago, he said: "Now, there are two great beauties of this region, two things which are distinctive. One is the lake and the other is its product, the Dunes." Yet Chicagoans had shut themselves off from the lake, and were sandmining the Dunes, destroying a heritage from the past comparable to the Colosseum of Rome or the cathedral at Rheims, each of these, like the Dunes, the "fruit of hundreds of thousands of lives," and the substance of the personality of the place. He declared that "if beauty stands for anything, it is because it binds generations of men together," and the Dunes had the power to do this for Chicago.[56]

Taft's remarks at the Art Institute stemmed from a lifelong devotion to making community of locale "interesting to itself." He regarded the cathedrals of Europe as the ideal community enterprise of their time, and yearned to find a way to engage his own city in similar undertakings. Like his friends Sullivan, Jensen, Monroe, and Stevens, he had faith that the ordinary people of his own time, properly stimulated and schooled in the great humanistic tradition of the West, could create great art, and a distinctive "Art Spirit of the Midwest" would ultimately triumph.[57] A decade before the pageant, in response to a query about a proposed "Chicago Day" festival, Taft had lamented: "We have no wandering minstrels to sing the glories of a legendary past and the heroic deeds of our ancestors." But there are other ways of "evoking memories and garlanding our historic spots with association," and the best of these is pageantry wherein "the great events of the past may be pictured and the dreams of the future foreshadowed."[58] Some of the scenes Taft suggested for the festival were later enacted in the Dunes Pageant of 1917.

The outdoor pageant and masque were ideally suited as dramatic forms to express the distinctive myth of a place, and to involve the community in which that myth lived, or ought to live, in its production. The story of a place links landscape and society together, and in outdoor drama, scene, actors, and audience are all part of the dramatic action. American and European history of the preceding several centuries provided few if any models for such drama. For this reason, the midwesterners reappropriated dramatic models from the Italian Renaissance and Elizabethan England, where the masque had received its fullest development before the Puritan Revolution, and from American tribal ceremony, and creatively blended them together to pioneer a new dramatic form appropriate to their urban setting and love of nature.[59]

In the first two decades of the twentieth century, a phenomenal interest in outdoor drama swept across America as an expression of the quest for community. Artists and dramatists, like Taft and Stevens, and settlement house workers, like Jane Addams and Graham Taylor, found outdoor festivals, pageants, and masques an effective way to counteract the fragmentation and alienation of their neighborhoods. By employing what they considered the most democratic of arts, theater, and the most democratic of the theatrical arts, outdoor theater, involving dance, music, drama, and landscape, the world the artists and reformers sought to call into being appeared in front of the audience in the hundreds of community participants cooperating together in the production of a collective work of art.[60]

The Dunes movement drew upon the ideas and experiences of this larger enthusiasm for historical pageantry and turned them to its own purposes. In 1913, for example, Stephen Mather brought William C. Langdon, president of the newly formed American Pageant Association, to Chicago to talk on "Historical Pageants in America" at the City Club. In his speech Langdon defined "pageant" as *"a drama—if it is not a drama it is not a pageant—in which the place is the hero and the development of the community is the plot*." He noted that until very recently the drama of the West, like its historic religion, was exclusively focused on the individual man or woman as the hero, with the person's life as the plot. Community drama, which may be correlated with the new community emphasis in religion, on the other hand recognizes that the community itself has a "personality" and a "life and dramatic development."[61] Langdon concluded that authentic community drama must be outdoor drama; otherwise the hero—the *public life*—is barred from the stage.

Those in Chicago like Mather and Taft, who were concerned to create a genuine public life that would express the "life and dramatic development" of the "personality" of *this place*, were sympathetic to such a radical perspective. It gave them a theoretical framework, warranted by a national movement, within which to pursue and interpret to others their native vision. They were especially helped by those intellectual leaders of the movement, such as Thomas Wood Stevens's colleague in the American Pageant Association, Thomas Dickinson, who believed that the use of nature as a "dramatic medium" in community drama meant "working with powers beyond [oneself] that will bring forth beauties better than [one's] thought." The theoreticians for the national movement often admitted openly what many Chicago Progressives believed. The reason for all the excitement was that the new drama expressed a new humanistic faith, in Dickinson's terms, a new "social metaphysical."[62]

In 1917 Stevens had close ties to the pageant movement in Chicago and throughout the nation. Recently assigned the task of founding the first university department of drama in the United States at Carnegie Institute in Pittsburgh, Stevens had been a lover of the Dunes for more than twenty years. He was poet, printer, playwright, author of short stories, painter of murals, teacher, and, in 1910, with Earl H. Reed, Sr., one of the founders of the Chicago Society of Etchers. But his principal interest was pageantry and by 1917 he had written a substantial number of such plays, including several produced by the Chicago Stage Guild and the Art Institute, and a series devoted, in various midwestern localities, to the history of the Old Northwest.[63]

Stevens's principal collaborator in Chicago was Kenneth Sawyer

Goodman. In 1913, at the behest of Jens Jensen, Goodman wrote "A Masque," later called *The Beauty of the Wild;* far less ambitious in scope than the Dunes Pageant, but more easily performed, it was written in classic masque form with sufficient generality to evoke the "genius loci" of a variety of landscape settings. The simple allegory it dramatized by means of five symbolic figures was another statement of the ecological vision of the Dunes movement. The masque began with an oboe solo from the "New World Symphony." An Indian appears on a ridge silhouetted against the sky; driven from his beloved land by the Pioneer, he says goodbye to his companion, the spirit of the place, personified by the Faun. The Pioneer is then replaced by the Builder. In conclusion, the Friend appears and pledges protection of the Faun's home. The Faun lights a fire and says:

> I pledge thee it shall leap with flame of spring,
> High as my hopes, strong as my love of freedom.
> These woods are mine and thine. Thy children's children
> Shall find me always here to welcome them.
> I pledge to thee and them my lasting calm,
> A refuge from the fret of roaring streets,
> Silence and Beauty, Peace and leafy shade,
> Unfevered days to make them whole again,
> All this, and nightly blessing of clean stars.[64]

The Goodman masque was performed for the first time on June 14, 1913, at the first annual meeting of the Friends of Our Native Landscape, near Oregon, Illinois, as part of the movement to establish White Pines State Park. Vachel Lindsay came up from Springfield for the occasion to recite his poem, "Hawk of the Rocks," and Henry Cowles brought his botany class from the University of Chicago. The masque quickly became popular among landscape preservationists in the four-state region surrounding Chicago and its performance a yearly ritual. It was given by the Friends for twenty-seven consecutive years. Many of the persons active in the Dunes movement, including Jensen, Frank V. Dudley and his wife, Maida Lewis, both of whom participated for twenty years, and botanist Herman Silas Pepoon, were active in the production of the masque. On at least one of these occasions, June 4,

1926, in the Dunes at Sawyer, Michigan, Stevens, having returned
to Chicago to become head of the Kenneth Sawyer Goodman
Theater of the Art Institute, supervised the presentation. Its last
recorded performance was at Tremont in the Indiana Dunes in
1945.

Ragna B. Eskil, who directed the masque for nineteen years, wrote
in remembrance: "This hold on people was the thing that we who
had to do with it year after year marveled at most. For, in a way, the
masque was very simple. . . . Yet its emotional power was so great
that, throughout the whole performance, no one ever stirred. . . .
The masque had that quality of binding a multitude as one. . . .
Tears ran down their cheeks at the Fawn's speech, and when the
songs were ended, they got up slowly and walked away as if they
had been in church." [65]

The Dunes Pageant and the Goodman masque were linked with
the other outdoor dramas and festivals in the Midwest and the
Dunes, not only by the circumstances of authorship and performance, but also by the aim of holding up for the citizens of the
Chicago region a mythic vision of their distinctive landscape and
history, the dream of a regional community, part urban, part rural,
part wild, characterized by reciprocity between society and nature.

THE DRAMA OF DEMOCRACY

American civil religion, like all religious traditions, is a particular
complex of symbols, beliefs, rituals, and stories. It may be defined
as the "religious symbol system which relates the citizen's role and
American society's place in space, time, and history to the conditions of ultimate existence and meaning." [66] By this definition, the
scriptures of the Jewish people are an epic account of the civil religion of Israel. Ever since the Puritan settlement, America, too, has
had a sense of epic religious significance, whether conceived as
God's New Israel or in Lincoln's fine phrase, "God's almost chosen
people." American civil religion is more implicit and loosely organized than the religion of the ancient Hebrews, but it has a ceremonial calendar, sacred texts such as the Declaration of Independence,
shrines such as the Gettysburg Battlefield, a national covenant concentrated in the symbol "democracy," and theological referents

such as the deist God of natural law. In the United States civil religious piety often is expressed through voluntary associations concerned for community welfare, political parties, and movements for social change.

Until recently, Memorial Day was an important holiday in the ceremonial calendar of American civil religion, along with Columbus Day, Thanksgiving, Washington's and Lincoln's birthdays, Fourth of July, and Labor Day. Memorial Day functioned for a century as a great ceremony of ritual renewal. The themes of sacrifice of the soldier dead for the living, the obligation of the living to sacrifice their own lives for future generations, and the affirmation of a sacred covenant binding the generations with one another and with their God expressed the belief that the American nation is perpetually reborn by those who give the "last full measure of devotion." [67]

In Chicago, before the First World War, Memorial Day (or Decoration Day) was regularly observed as the day on which to honor the memory of the soldiers who gave their lives in the Civil War, and an occasion also to pay respect to the memory of all the dead. The Dunes Pageant Association must have been especially aware, on the year that the nation entered the Great War, of the challenge to their art that this particular occasion presented. In anticipation of the event, Caroline McIlvaine told the *Chicago Daily Journal* that there would be "martial color and martial music . . . in fact, the pageant is really a patriotic rally with a picture of the valorous deeds of the past to inspire the present." [68]

As McIlvaine was the first to acknowledge, the pageant drama the pilgrims to the Dunes witnessed on May 30 was no ordinary Memorial Day celebration. It did share many of the themes of the national "cult of the dead," and it was in some sense a "patriotic rally." But Stevens and his colleagues endowed these conventional symbols with new meaning. The mythic framework in which they set their portrayal of the American past served to judge and redefine the received understandings of the civil religion and to pose a large question mark before the nation's future.

Apart from a recital of Daniel Webster's 1834 speech at City West and the finale, in which the United States flag led the procession, and the audience sang the "Star Spangled Banner," there was no other suggestion of glorification of the nation. The focus, from the opening notes of the overture's "International Fantasia," was rather on all humanity. The United States is only one of *four* Western nations that process across the landscape and whose peoples are somehow contained in the singular history of this sacred place. In different ways, by the death of a great leader, by defeat in battle, by the loss of possessions, by dashed hopes, each nation—France, Britain, Spain, the United States—shares in the common experience of mortality. The United States flag leads the procession because it is the most recent of nations to possess the land and hence, for the time being, to carry the universal ideals and hopes of humanity.[69]

The occasion suggested, and the pageant association was prepared to adopt, a radical change of perspective from a focus on the nation's passage through time and across the landscape to a focus on this place and those societies that have been its transient inhabitants. It was a shift from the customary Western homocentric viewpoint, in which the landscape is a mere condition for human action, to a geocentric viewpoint, in which the landscape, in its total evolutionary and historical development, is the primary subject of action.

The shift marked both a recovery and a revision of the original myth of America as the primordial time and place, a New World. Mary Kelly Graves tried to explain the "ideal" of the Dunes Pageant to the readers of the *Prairie Club Bulletin:*

> It is an inspiring thought that the various nations which, one after the other, have trickled across the Dune country, are now represented in such great numbers all through this district, and that the land which served as the successive battle-ground of so many nationalities is now to be fought for in bloodless battle, that it may become forever a playground for these peoples, representatives of every country in the world.[70]

The New World was a battleground as well as a paradise, and whatever retrieval of the millennial vision of America as a playground was possible in 1917 had to come to terms with that reality.

In the Dunes Pageant two meanings of the "Indian" communicate forcefully a tragic view of American history. Stevens and his fellow sponsors had a strong feeling for the Native American, both as a particular people who underwent a great tragedy, and as a mythic race. The portrayal of the Indian as the first ancestor of the Dunes embodies both these meanings, especially clear in the figure of the Prophet. Historically, the role Donald Robertson assumed was based on the life of a midwestern Shawnee chief. The Prophet and his brother, the famous warrior Tecumseh, were leaders of a League of Northwest tribes which defended Native American rights to the land against encroachment in the early nineteenth century. The Prophet and Tecumseh were both tragic figures; the cause for which they fought was doomed. As a mythic figure, however, the Prophet speaks for Everyman. Through his eyes the audience sees that the particular experience of the Indian in the Dunes is prototypical of the tragedy of all peoples, and his hopes are the same that bind all peoples together.[71]

No innocent dream of a New World Eden, nor jingoist nationalism, was presented to the citizens of Chicago on Memorial Day, 1917. The nation was redefined to include, as its first citizens, those it had destroyed before its founding. The Indian functioned as a Christ-figure: his original sacrifice permitted the pioneers to inherit this place; his passion is repeated in every generation; and his dream of "Peace, Love and the Fireside" ultimately will redeem humanity's tragic history.

The symbol of the Indian redefined even more radically the transcendent community whose origin and destiny is celebrated in the Dunes Pageant. Because the historical Indian is the archetypal person and the historical Indian lived, it was presumed, in a relationship of profound reciprocity with the rest of nature, the community whose history is at stake from the beginning of the pageant includes nature within it. The view that the Dunes enter into internal relationships with human existence, was, of course, the overwhelming burden of the whole pageant. But the primary model was provided by the Indian, the first to love the Dunes, the preservation of which was necessary for his way of life.

In the concluding masque, the Western pastoral tradition was merged with the Native American heritage to communicate a feeling for the mutuality of humanity and nature. In the program accompanying each of the dances is a short selection from the poetry of the pastoral literary tradition: from classics such as *The Tempest* by Shakespeare ("Come out unto these yellow sands/And there take hands/*** kiss'd/By the wild wave's mist."),[72] and from American contemporaries Harriet Monroe, Mabel McIlvaine, and Mary Austin. The masque, which symbolized the meaning of the pageant as a whole, portrayed the evolution of the Dune Country as a microcosm of the evolution of the earth, beginning with the formation of the dunes from wind, waves, and sand, and continuing through the appearance of various forms of life. The arrival of the Indians for the ritual of the Calumet comes as a response to the last of these dances, the pleas of the Wood People for the preservation of the Dunes. The natural landscape is taken up into an eschatological vision of the peaceable Kingdom. This was the scene painted by Frank Dudley in his picture *The Pageant*—the circle of Indians in the Council of the Calumet ringed by the audience on the sides of the blowout.

The pageant expressed a geocentric perspective most fundamentally through its symbolism of the divine. This symbolism was indirectly derived from the Native American myth of "Manabozho" (or "Nanabozho") and its close association in folklore with the legends of Hiawatha.[73] Stevens bent selected themes from the popular story to the purposes of this occasion, and made Nanabozho the Manitou, or deity of the Dunes. In so doing, he also, within the context of the pageant, made him the god of the American people who now inherited this place. The invocation of a native nature god, or some invented symbol for "spirit of place," was in keeping with all the previous pageants that were concerned for the preservation of the landscape and sought to express a mythology for the Chicago region: Mrs. Abt's "Duna," Earl R. North's "Spirit of the Dunes," Goodman's "Faun." Nothing could have constituted a more radical redefinition of the civil religion. For, in addition to the remote deistic God enshrined in the Declaration of Independence and the biblical God to whom Lincoln prayed, there was now also enshrined a symbol of divinity closer to the Roman *genius loci*, the "Pan" of Greek mythology, or the Earth Mother goddesses of the ancient Near East. The new symbol of divinity pointed to a mystical sense of *belonging to this place*, what Mircea Eliade has called "a cosmically structured feeling that goes far beyond family or ancestral solidarity."[74]

Yet, the new content the pageant sponsors were in effect proposing for their society's civil religion was no new version of primitivism. They were close to Walt Whitman in their unwillingness to give up either side of the civilization versus nature dialectic in American culture. Their profession of the creed of "man in the open air" entailed a robust affirmation of the unique powers of human creativity, as well as a hymn of praise for the native landscape. In the pageant, the dream of a "metropolis of the West"—shared by all the hamlets that sprang up in the early nineteenth century along the sandy wastes of southern Lake Michigan—was not rejected. Brennan, in his description of the vision the pageant crystallized before him, set the "poor Indian with his untutored mind and savage nature" in juxtaposition to the "cultured American." The mythic figure of the Indian and his native deity were used by Stevens and others less to romanticize primitive American life than to express the ideal of a society integrated within itself and with its natural environment.[75]

The dramatic plot of the pageant told the story of the tragic struggle throughout human history to realize such an inclusive community. The object of the struggle was possession of the sources of life: the sun, the land, the powers of production. Its redemptive meaning was in the small, but significant, actions of ordinary people who used the means of existence for the common good. The paradigm for these saving actions was the creation myth of the Dunes recited by the Prophet at the beginning of the pageant—the myth of the conflict between Nanabozho, the Manitou of life and summer, and Tawiskaron, the Manitou of winter and death, at the dawn of creation. Tawiskaron stole the sun, but Nanabozho, in a "chase around the world's blue rim," overtakes him, and in the battle that ensues, "jostling the stars apart," the sun is retrieved for the good of all. The story is repeated in each of the six episodes from the lives of the ancestors: the subterfuges of LaSalle but the gospel of Christian love preached by Marquette; the betrayal of Indian leaders as they bargain their people's hunting grounds away, but the courage of Pontiac to resist; the foolish cowardice of Tom Brady, leader of the American revolutionary forces, but the courageous trust of all persons by Joseph Bailly and his Indian wife; the ambition of the businessmen of City West to use federal funds for harbor improvements for their own advantage, but the final conclusion by one of them that the Dunes should remain free. Just as the myth of origins ended in Nanabozho's victory over Tawiskaron and the coming of summer, the concluding story told by the masque finds its climax in the universal Kingdom brought in by those who act to include the rest of nature in the great council of life.

From the perspective of eternity, the ultimate perspective of the story, the passage of humanity across the landscape was perceived as meaningless apart from this great struggle for community—the struggle between those who sought to cooperate and use the wealth of the world for the good of all beings, and those who sought to use it selfishly for their own aggrandizement. The Memorial Day drama of redemptive sacrifice binding the generations together was conceived as a drama of the long, slow, painful quest for democracy among the world's common people.

Thomas Wood Stevens believed in the possibility of civic ritual's reconstituting the body politic. In one of his earlier pageants he wrote: "Every act was born of a vision. . . . All the reformations of the world begin and end in visions which do not die."[76] The message of the pageant for Independence Day he and Goodman produced in 1911 in Jackson Park, Chicago, was how the arrival of the enacted word, the signing of the Declaration of Independence, inspired collective action—the decision of Washington's troops to persevere in the battle at New York. In 1914 Stevens and Percy Mackaye collaborated in "The Pageant and Masque of St. Louis," which similarly inspired the populace—this time the audience—to action. When Stevens got up to make his speech at the Art Institute of Chicago on April 6, following Lorado Taft, he showed films of the St. Louis pageant. "That city was obsessed by the spirit, 'Well, this ain't much of a town anyway.' At first 99 percent of the people scoffed at the pageant. After they saw it they awoke and adopted a new city charter."[77] Take Chicagoans out to the sand dunes for the pageant, Stevens concluded, and see what kind of a park they will create!

In the Dunes's ritual drama the past was imaginatively recreated in order to refound the present on a basis adequate to a more universal ideal of the future. By redefining the civil religion's myth of origins, a new beginning could be made. History was the medium for the pageant association's present concerns. And just as the original revolutionaries of 1776 were inspired to cast off what they perceived in the light of their newly revealed sacred history as their oppressor, the Chicago Progressives conceived themselves as empowered by their vision of the authentic heritage of America to cast off the oppressors of their own age.

The difference between the new version of the civil religion, what Mary Kelly Graves referred to as the "finest type of patriotism," and the old version was promptly noticed by those opposed to a park in the Dunes. A. J. Bowser, former state senator, and fiery editor of the *Chesterton Tribune* in Porter County, Indiana, wrote in an editorial that those who sponsored the pageant "might be better employed in helping save the country. Saving the Dunes to shut out industry from the lake front . . . may be a patriotic duty, but we fail to see it."[78] It was precisely the industrialization of the region at the cost of the environment, and the control of that industrialization by corporations rather than the people, that constituted the oppressor Dunes patriots sought to battle. And it was on the Dunes that a significant battle for the democratic faith was to be fought.

When Honore J. Jaxon rose to speak at the Mather hearings on behalf of the Chicago Federation of Labor and the Public Ownership League, which he claimed represented the 300,000 organized working men of the city, he announced a theme that was to have enduring reverberations throughout the history of the Dunes movement. "For thirty years we have been cut off from the lake front by railroad corporations, private hotels, private interests, and our voice has been suppressed and our protest has not been heard."[79] In the same vein, William L. Chenery observed in the *Chicago Herald:* "The sand dunes of northern Indiana in their charming way offer to Chicago and to the nation the same sort of test with which the absolute czar challenged Russia. So far as the Dunes are concerned we are as far removed from self-government as were the Russians before the famous Sunday of March 11."[80]

The "Inaugural Pageant in the Dunes," as Caroline McIlvaine named it, sought to call a new people into being. However, like the signing of the Declaration, and the presentation of the pageant in St. Louis, it publicly symbolized what had in large measure already happened, stage by stage, over the previous years. Just as the shot fired at Concord signaled the eruption of a new society that already existed, so the unfurling of the American flag by the National Dunes Park Association on the top of Mount Tom in the summer of 1916, with the declaration that the "Dunes belong to the people," symbolized the presence of a revolutionary band of citizens already determined to reclaim ownership of their land.[81] The Dunes Pageant legitimized this new voluntary society.

Two years later, Thomas Wood Stevens wrote another civic ritual for the soldier dead, but this time he recast his vision of the community for which they had sacrificed their lives in terms of the sacred covenant of a League of Nations, and the

> Rain in the spring, and sunlight after rain,
> And the rich bourgeoning of the earth . . .[82]

Only a few years later, the Dunes Pageant was to seem an event in a distant past. Within the decade, paved modern roads were to take visitors to Pageant Blowout, and the Dunes were to lose much of their remoteness and other-worldly appeal.

Yet the effects were to be felt for many years—indeed, down to the closing decades of the twentieth century, not only in the long, continuing struggle to save the Dunes, but in all the phases of cultural and political aspiration the pageant represented. The insurgent movement to preserve the Indiana Dunes cannot be understood apart from the reformed myth of American origins and destiny that gave it purpose, and the script for its actions as well.

The Sand Dunes of Indiana
Courtesy of the Chicago Historical Society

City and Dunescape—one interdependent whole
Photo by Joan Nelson

Waiting out the rain, Memorial Day, 1917
Negative by Arthur E. Anderson. Print by James C. Fisher

"See the Dunes First," guided hikes to the Dunes hinterland
Negative by Arthur E. Anderson. Print by James C. Fisher

Arriving at Pageant Blowout, June 3, 1917
Negative by Arthur E. Anderson. Print by James C. Fisher

"Historical Pageant of the Sand Dunes of Indiana," June 3, 1917
Negative by Arthur E. Anderson. Print by James C. Fisher

Pilgrimage to the Dunes, "Saturday Afternoon Walking Trips,"
Memorial Day, 1909
Courtesy of the Prairie Club

Prairie Club Beach House
Negative by Arthur E. Anderson. Print by James C. Fisher

Frank V. Dudley and his wife, Maida Lewis, in the Kenneth Goodman masque, *The Beauty of the Wild*
Courtesy of the Prairie Club

Dance from *The Awakening*, Memorial Day, 1915
Courtesy of the Gary Public Library

Jens Jensen at the Prairie Club Memorial Fountain, Indiana Dunes State Park, 1932

Negative by Arthur E. Anderson. Print by James C. Fisher

The Sandburg family at their home near Harbert, Michigan. Left to right: Carl, Helga, dog "Biff," Janet, Lillian Steichen Sandburg
Courtesy of Helga Sandburg

Earl H. Reed, *The Voices of the Dunes*, etching
Courtesy of the Art Institute of Chicago

Earl H. Reed, *The Moon in the Marsh*, etching
Courtesy of the Art Institute of Chicago

Frank V. Dudley, *View from Mt. Tom*, oil
Courtesy of the Indiana State Museum, Indiana Department of Natural Resources

Frank V. Dudley, *Sun and Shadows Meet*, oil
Courtesy of the Indiana State Museum, Indiana Department of Natural Resources

Emil Armin, *Crescendo*, oil
Courtesy of Hilda Armin

Frances Strain, *On the Beach*, oil
Courtesy of Garnet Biesel

V. M. S. Hannell,
Pine in the Dunes,
oil
Property of the author

BIRTHPLACE OF ECOLOGY

Moving mountains of sand, near Dune Park Station, Indiana, about 1900
Courtesy of the Department of Botany, University of Chicago

Henry C. Cowles (right)
and J. P. Lotsy in the
Dunes, 1922
Courtesy of the Department
of Botany, University of
Chicago

Henry C. Cowles and students on a field trip, 1910. Slide entitled: "Old Swamp soil
exposed by erosion of superjacent dune, Michigan City, Indiana."
Courtesy of the Department of Botany, University of Chicago

Sand-mining near Dune Park Station, Indiana, 1906
Courtesy of the Department of Botany, University of Chicago

POST–WORLD WAR II DUNES STRUGGLE

Dorothy R. Buell, founder of the Save the Dunes Council, 1952
Courtesy of the Save the Dunes Council

Senator Paul Douglas and Secretary of the Interior Stewart Udall in
midst of the Dunes battle, 1961

Photo by *Hammond Times*. Courtesy of Chicago Historical Society

Pilgrimage to the Central Dunes, July 23, 1961, with Howling Hill in the
distance. Left to right: Stewart Udall, Alan Bible, Paul Douglas, and
Conrad Wirth

Photo by John Nelson

Central Dunes, 1961
Photo by Herbert Read

Central Dunes, 1971. Burns Waterway Harbor and Bethlehem Steel
(taken from same site as above)
Photo by Herbert Read

The Save the Dunes Council, July 23, 1961
Courtesy of the Save the Dunes Council

Paul H. Douglas at the Indiana Dunes
Photo by John Nelson

Left to right:
Herb Read,
co-chair, Bailly
Alliance; Fred
Hershberger,
president,
U.S.W.A. Local
12775
(NIPSCO);
James Balanoff,
director,
U.S.W.A. Dis-
trict 31; Dave
Wilborn, presi-
dent, U.S.W.A.
Local 6787
(Bethlehem
Steel). Bailly
Nuclear Alliance
protests
NIPSCO
Nuclear Plant,
April 1981
Photo by Don
Blume. Courtesy of
Gary Post-Tribune

John Hawkinson at
"Picnic on Hawk's
Island," Memorial
Day, 1969
Photo by Nancy Hays

TWO

Dune Country Patriots

The lovely, wild, weird Dune country, with its
wooded hills, moving dunes, blow-outs, winding trails,
tree-laced creeks, lowland marshes, and the Great
Lake washing its shores, is known and loved by a few
hundred fortunate ones who have breathed with joy
its breezes laden with spices of the forest, caught
Mother Nature at work making and unmaking hills
and valleys, watched the violet carpet change to lupine
blue, to rose, to red and gold, then brown and white;
heard the songs of early spring, and caught the flashing
of cardinal wings against the snow.

from *"An Exhibit of the Dune Country,"*
Chicago Public Library, 1917

(*attributed to* JOHN GOULD FLETCHER)

Probably, in the "old days" when we waded at the
edge of the lake, under Doctor Elliot Downing's
direction, scooping up nets full of tiny creatures for
examination, we were too soggy to have any empathy
with a dune. Our viewpoint at that period might have
been the viewpoint of a crayfish or a clam. Later, on

the many trips when with eager ears cocked forward, we followed in the quick footsteps of Doctor Cowles, we were still much too young and vigorous, and too enchanted with the new field of Ecology, to care about sun or wind, or sand between our teeth. Our viewpoint was that of pioneer plants, such as marram grass and wormwood and tough cottonwoods. And, some years later, when we meandered in the incandescent wake of Jens Jensen, Danish landscape man, and of Harriet Monroe of *Poetry Magazine*, our heads were too high in the clouds for us to be conscious of the assault of quartz grains. Our viewpoint then was akin to that of gulls and wheeling terns. And on a recent December field trip through the dunes under the leadership of E. L. Palmer of Cornell and Edwin Way Teale, naturalist and author, our minds were too busy for our bodies to notice much. Our viewpoint here might be likened to that of inquisitive and acquisitive crows.

MAY THEILGAARD WATTS,

from *Reading the Landscape*, 1957

D une Country patriots"—so they were called by the *Chi-cago Herald* in 1917.[1] The first of their number, Jens Jensen, who began as early as 1900 to travel throughout the Chicago region proclaiming the glories of the Dunes, earned the title "Apostle of the Dunes." Thomas W. Allinson, who followed, was called the "Apostle of Conservation." Bess Vrooman Sheehan was "The Dunes Lady," Charles H. Robinson the "Dean of the Dunes," and Frank V. Dudley the "Seer of the Dunes." The poet Edwin Markham named Earl H. Reed, Sr., "The Laureate of the Dunes." Less pretentiously, they referred to themselves as "Dunites," "Beach Nuts," "Dunatics," and "Dune Bugs."

APOSTLES OF THE DUNES, PROPHETS OF DEMOCRACY

The early leaders of the Dunes movement made the pilgrimage, saw the vision, and returned to tell the story and work for its ful-fillment in the society at large. No doubt for many, "apostle" was an accurate designation; in the Western religious tradition, an apostle witnesses a revelation and is called to preach it to the world. Jensen, who understood this vocation, wrote of the Dunes that they were "the shrine at which the poet and artist worship. . . . Here the soul is touched with divine fire; and from here their mes-sages to their people are filled with sincerity and purity."[2]

Some among the Dunes leadership, however, would be better described as prophets. They also made the pilgrimage and saw the vision; but when they came to tell the story, they spoke directly on behalf of the democratic God who made it all possible. Like the Prophet in the Dunes Pageant of 1917, they spoke with authority as persons directly inspired. It was their special task to make the connections between the revelation of the Dunes and the manifes-tations of the God of democracy in other times and places. Carl Sandburg, the "Bard of Democracy," was one of these, as was Stephen Mather, the "Father of the National Parks," Richard Lieber of Indiana, the "State Park Philosopher," and Donald Cul-

ross Peattie, the "Poet of Nature." But the division between apostles and prophets is less a division between persons than between
functions, and often the two functions were performed by the
same individual. Jensen, for example, was also regarded as "Dean
of American Landscape Architects."

The Dunes movement included a much larger constellation of
persons than those who took specific leadership responsibility. Not
all of those who over the years sought the preservation of the
Dunes participated in the distinctive spirit of the movement. Sometimes, motives quite at variance with those of a universal democratic faith led individuals to join the preservation effort. On the
other hand, some, like Jane Addams, only peripherally related to
the preservation drive itself, must count as significant contributors.
They shared a devotion to the welfare of the total community,
identified that ideal with the Dunes landscape and the idea of
democracy within world history, and were acknowledged as spiritual leaders of the cause.

By 1920 it was clear who the first leaders of the Dunes movement were. They had produced pageants and festivals culminating
in the Dunes Pageant of 1917; they had founded several associations
concerned for the preservation of the Dunes, borne eloquent public witness at the hearings conducted by Stephen Mather, written
numerous articles, poems, and books, and exhibited etchings, paintings, and photographs. Some had their names officially written in
the Dunes landscape as well.

When first published by Rand McNally in 1920, Peter S. Goodman's "Map of Indiana Dunes: The Wonder Region of the Middle
West" caused quite a stir and not a little dissension within the
ranks of the movement's leadership. On a handsome blue, tan,
white, and black sheet, measuring 30″ × 30″, Goodman presented
to the public a detailed topographical map of the heart of the
Dunes, a fifteen-mile section running from Dune Park Station on
the Illinois Central Railroad on the west, to Michigan City, Indiana, on the east. Clearly shown were each of the dunes, swamps,
marshes, rivers and lakes of the Dune Country, the location of all
the houses and shacks, and every well-beaten foot trail, wagon
trail, road, and railroad line. Included too were eight photographs
of popular Dunes scenes: among them, the summit of Mount Tom,

the blowout near the Beach House, Dune Creek, and the Prairie Club colony. Goodman claimed that the map was the fruit of twenty-two years of tramping the dunes, and that he had hiked more than eight hundred miles in the last year and a half alone for its preparation.[3]

The topography of the map did not cause the distress. The "Temple of Fame," as Gary newspaperman Tom Cannon called it, which Goodman deliberately erected on top of its contours, did.[4] The temple was a pantheon for some of the better-known Dunes apostles: dunes were named in honor of Jensen and Allinson, as well as of every past president of the Prairie Club; there was a dune called "Diana Dune," in deference to the name folklore had bestowed upon Alice Gray; there was a "Pageant Dune" and a "Dudley Blowout"; other landmarks were named for well-known figures like the botanists Pepoon and Cowles, and the bird photographer, W. D. Richardson.

Goodman's new mythical geography of the Dunes particularly came as a shock to A. F. Knotts, president of the National Dunes Park Association. While his disapproval reflected in part the gap between the Dunes leadership centered in Gary, and the leadership of the Chicago-based Prairie Club, to which Goodman belonged and which he obviously favored in the names he chose to honor, a more basic issue was at stake. Knotts, like George Brennan, was a devoted historian of the Dunes, and he felt that the map, with "names so new the varnish smells,"[5] was an insult to the ancestors of the place. The *Chicago Tribune*, in its report of the map controversy, noted with some insight that "when A. F. Knotts betakes himself into that sandy region athwart Gary called the Dunes there rises before him a vision. The sands become dotted with the wigwams of the aborigines. . . . He meditates as he walks and by his side there stalk the ghosts of great sachems and medicine men." For Knotts the map was a "sacrilege against the aborigines"[6] and other immortals such as Marquette, Joliet, and Bailly. Indeed, Knotts charged, Goodman seems to think that the Prairie Club antedates the discovery of America!

In retrospect, the map shows the extent to which the Dunes movement by 1920 had identified itself with the Dunes landscape and assumed the role of a living tradition. The Chicago members of the movement perceived their leaders not as the usurpers but as the rightful successors of the original inhabitants. They were the ones who by their love of the Dunes and their struggle for democracy in the present kept alive the sacred inheritance. The conflict between Knotts and Goodman was not substantial, but the conflict between the conservative and the liberal in every tradition. Nor was it to be the last of the controversies over who has the right to name the Dunes landscape and thereby establish its meaning for the present.

Among the Dune Country patriots of the Progressive era, roughly the period 1890–1930, the Dunes movement and its informing vision took shape. During these years the personal, associational, and geographic relationships that nurtured the movement for the rest of the century were initially formed, and equally important, the Dunes tradition—the body of art and literature which expressed the movement's vision—was first created. The achievements of those who followed confirmed and augmented what was already set in motion by the apostles and prophets of these early years.

Two principal factors were responsible for the creativity of the 1890–1930 period. The first of these was the Dune Country itself. The experience of the Dunes in the early years was of a qualitatively different order from the experience of the Dunes later. In the early period they were by no means virgin country, but they were wild, and they were remote—"like a bit of a different world . . . a country of fantastic hills, with gullies and little meadows and bogs and little lakes and streamlets and forests of strange trees and flower beds of strange blooms."[7] In 1917 "no one standing on the crest of one of these mountainous billows of sand and looking over the dramatic landscape before him would dream he was standing within a few miles of Chicago and the pastoral mildness of our middle western plains."[8] In later years the same impression recurred, although with less empirical basis and less conviction.

The second principal factor was the vitality of the "religion of democracy" that permeated the early Dunes leadership. This late nineteenth- and early twentieth-century version of the civil religion was an heroic, if diffuse and sometimes contradictory, effort to refound American society on the basis of a third great national covenant.[9]

The foundational covenant of the United States was embodied in the Declaration of Independence and the Constitution. Although each of the three historic principles of the Enlightenment democratic faith—freedom, equality, and fraternity—were present in the Revolutionary covenant, it may be considered primarily a covenant of *freedom* under law, of self-government. The second great covenant was the result of the Civil War; embodied in the Fourteenth Amendment, it was a covenant of *equality* of rights for all citizens regardless of race. The third American covenant proclaimed by the prophets of the religion of democracy was a covenant of *fraternity*, of social democracy. Lincoln anticipated the third covenant in his Inaugurals and in the Gettysburg Address. Jens Jensen defined it thus: "A democracy is the highest social order man has planned, but such an order can only survive when each individual accepts his responsibility in a brotherhood bound together in service. This is the meaning of government 'of the people, by the people, and for the people.'"[10]

The aim of the new covenant was to create a more deliberate and cooperative economic and social order without sacrificing the pluralism and individual initiative of the American heritage. The shared assumption was that it was time for American society to achieve collective self-consciousness with regard to its ultimate purposes. In the face of the immense concentrations of private and corporate wealth in the new industrial order it was necessary that the society invent new institutions to assure the conditions required for liberty and equality for all the people.

Midwestern Unitarian minister Charles Ferguson captured significant themes of the new social spirit in his 1900 book *The Religion of Democracy*. The world is our home, because the natural environment is the body of God, the Incarnation is now, the "timeless Man of Nazareth" is the man of the modern spirit and his revolution of universal fraternity is the revolution of the age. The day of the self-made man is over. Now every last man and woman may go out into the open air and participate as co-creators with their fellow citizens and with God in building the city of life. "We announce the dissolution of the old regime of privilege, exclusion and monopoly, and we proclaim a new constitution according to the essential law." [11] As Ferguson's use of Christian symbols suggests, proponents of the religion of democracy appropriated biblical as well as Enlightenment motifs, especially those concerned with justice and community. This was in keeping with the view of some that the American experiment in democracy was the third testament of the Judeo-Christian tradition.

Walt Whitman, singing the praises of our common humanity *en masse*, was one of the early prophets of the religion of democracy, and William James, Josiah Royce, and John Dewey were in varying ways its theologians. Converts to the new social faith were especially prevalent among left-wing Protestants, liberal Jews, religious humanists and secularists. Political tracts of the movement, including Henry George's *Progress and Poverty*, Henry Demarest Lloyd's *Wealth Against Commonwealth*, and Herbert Croly's *The Promise of American Life*, shared the view that every person has an equal right to the fruits of the earth, and to the benefits of socially created resources and institutions. All conceived the third American covenant as a commitment by the people to take responsibility for the welfare of the oppressed. Many also included within the new covenant a new sense of responsibility for the land which is why the religion of democracy may be considered one of the spiritual centers of the Progressive conservation movement. [12]

Three other factors were responsible for the creativity of the early Dunes movement. These were the dominant cultural interests that coalesced in the movement's leadership: reform, art, and science. Each uniquely embodied the underlying principles and spirit of the religion of democracy.

Thomas Allinson, looking back at the early Dunes campaigns from sometime in the 1930s, wrote that the vitality of those years was due to the fact that the Dunes movement brought together persons prominent in art, science, and public service; "a remarkable group of persons," he commented on another occasion, "from many walks of life drawn together by the love of nature." [13] Caroline McIlvaine agreed: "As clever a group of artists, litterateurs, and sociologists as could be assembled anywhere in America!" [14] In his 1916 report to Secretary Lane, Stephen Mather chose to underscore the pluralistic character of the Dunes leadership, and to point to what he considered its most salutary result, an objective and holistic viewpoint. "Among the speakers who urged that the sand dunes be preserved as a national reservation," he wrote, "were many men and women prominent in educational, art, literary, scientific, and business circles of several states. The hearing, therefore, did not proceed as a gathering of local citizens expressing convictions based on purely local considerations, but gave me an opportunity to gain the benefit of the thought and serious study of broadgauge minds which were not influenced by selfish motives."[15]

Each of the three major cultural pursuits had a particular life of its own in Chicago, and a particular institutional locus with which it was identified. The concern for public service and reform was most pervasive. The Dune Country patriots participated in various phases of this movement, but its most specific locus was the settlement houses. The locus for art and literature, more scattered, centered around the artists' colonies and the Art Institute. The locus for science and scholarship was chiefly the University of Chicago. Each exemplified in a different way the shared quest for a new revelation of the God of democracy—a revelation that would point the way to how, in the twentieth century, the widest and deepest fraternity might undergird the ongoing struggle for freedom and equality in America.

MIDWESTERN REFORM

A common impulse toward democratic social change was channeled in several different directions in the Progressive era. Midwestern Progressivism took a distinctive direction at once peculiarly American and international. The outlook of the Dune Country patriots on the meaning of a democratic society and its relations to the natural environment was conditioned by this special midwestern political culture.[16]

To the radical adherents of the religion of democracy who gathered in Chicago at the turn of the century, the common good meant quite concretely the life of the community itself. Gathered mostly from the farms and small towns of the Midwest hinterland, the Chicago Progressives participated in the myth of the Midwest as the redemptive heartland of the nation that had remained true to the founding Jeffersonian ideals. At its best, their experience of democracy was the experience of equals who, through the mutual give and take of a variety of points of view, and through the pooling of a variety of skills and talents, built a better way of life to be shared by all. But good or bad, their experience was of specific interdependent communities and this was necessarily the framework in which they cast their dreams of freedom, equality, and justice.

The communities with which they were acquainted were not settled communities. The Midwest was the land of the immigrant, and its towns new communities in process of rapid growth. There was a voluntary, experimental character about life in the Midwest throughout the nineteenth century. Chicago author Milo Quaife noted: "All around the shores of Lake Michigan, on every inlet and creek, and for scores of miles inland, town sites were platted with enthusiastic zeal. . . ."[17] Chicago was the apogee of such zeal. As Opie Read declared in his 1893 novel *The Colossus:* "Chicago has begun to set the pace of a nervous nation's progress . . . a regathering of the forces that peopled America and then made her great among nations."[18] Most of this activity was pursued with the hope of quick prosperity, but in addition to the economic motive, there was an idealistic strain. The number of Utopian experiments bears witness to this.[19] So does Mark Twain's *Huckleberry Finn*, which celebrated the dream of pastoral fraternity rediscovered in the midst of the flow of life down the great river at the heart of the continent.[20]

One important source of the viewpoint of the Chicago Progressives was Populism. Populism in the 1880s and '90s was a party (founded July 4, 1892), a political culture, and a network of alliances. Its animating spirit was a belief in the capacity of human beings to creatively channel their competitive instincts into cooperative action, a belief that people might come together and solve their problems through various kinds of specific cooperative policies and institutions. Positively, Populism meant new self-respect for the poor and an insistence upon the rights and dignity of women. It meant working people taking their collective welfare into their own hands. This required not only individual initiative, but the cultivation of the arts of political discourse and organization. Negatively, Populism meant the rejection both of the large corporate trusts and monopolies that burgeoned in the late nineteenth century, and of the collectivist forms of socialism advocated by Marxism. The promise of the "Cooperative Commonwealth," which Populism passed on to its successors, was a third way—economically, a mixed economy with a bias toward producer cooperatives, and politically, a participatory democracy with a citizenry enlightened by intensive education and practical experience. Although necessarily transformed in the process, the ethos of Populism was carried forward into midwestern Progressivism where, reinforced by the social awakening of the middle class, its influence can be traced not only in the Progressive party of 1914, but in Progressive Republicanism, the Social Democratic party, and the liberal wing of the Democratic party.[21]

As one booster put it in the 1840s, the Midwest "is not the Garden of America, but of the world!"[22] The Jeffersonian hope for America as the land where face-to-face democracy could flourish was also the Enlightenment ideal of global citizenship. The Chicago Progressives were the heirs of a doctrine of democracy as thoroughly universalistic as it was regionally particularistic. And what city of the country gave greater promise of the realization of a genuine cosmopolitanism at the turn of the century than Chicago, as diverse as all the races, religions, occupations, and classes that immigrated to America could make it? But even Chicago was not world enough to satisfy the global yearnings of the Chicago reformers, artists, and scientists from whose ranks the Dune Country patriots were self-selected. The Chicago Progressives were proud of their Chicago citizenship, by which they meant not merely the city of Chicago, but the Chicago region, for them the center of the Midwest. They were equally as proud of their national and cosmopolitan citizenship; their hope for a renaissance of democratic community in Chicago was also the hope for a renaissance of democratic community in the nation and the world.

The stirrings of the religion of democracy were international: the themes of Ruskin, Morris, Tolstoy, and Turgenev were considered universal. Many of the Chicago reformers were eager to

make contact with those abroad who shared their ideals. They became singularly devoted to travel and by this means some of their
most creative ideas were brought to Chicago. Jane Addams returned from Ulm inspired to build a Cathedral of Humanity.
Thomas Stevens returned from a visit in 1906 to Louis Parker's
Pageant of Sherbourne, England, ready to write pageants of American history. Cowles and his colleagues at the University of Chicago
engaged in frequent personal exchanges with European scientists.
Harriet Monroe, perhaps the most indefatigable cosmopolitan of
them all, died at the age of seventy-six climbing a mountain in
Peru. There was nothing parochial about Chicago Progressivism.
At the same time, it was intensely devoted to local and regional
affairs.

All of the Dunes apostles and prophets participated in the ethos,
and many in the specific political programs, of midwestern social
democracy. Some, such as Frank Tuthill, president of the Prairie
Club in 1917, and owner of the Tuthill Springs Works in Hammond, Indiana, played only minor political roles in the movement.
Yet, as a public-spirited businessman, Tuthill could wax as eloquent as any over the "planks of our immortal platform . . . the
symphony of a re-united Democracy."[23] Others, like Jensen, who
waged a continuous war against graft in the parks of Chicago, a
war that cost him his job as superintendent of Humboldt Park in
1900, played more substantial political roles at the local and state
levels; Bess Sheehan was president of the Indiana Federation of
Clubs in the 1920s; A. F. Knotts, founder of a Populist newspaper
at Hammond in 1891, was attorney with Clarence Darrow for the
striking Pullman workers in 1894. A few, such as Carl Sandburg,
Stephen Mather, and Paul Douglas became national figures.

Chicago writers encouraged the impetus to reform by celebrating the real and ideal lives of Progressive leaders. One 1917
novel, Isaac Friedman's *The Radical*, wrote the script for Paul
Douglas's career. It chose as its hero a politician with high motives
who forged his way from the Chicago City Council to the United
States Senate to advocate the "Cooperative Commonwealth." His
hope was to hold the remaining public land for the people in per-
petuity so that they might have a safeguard against the inordinate

growth of business power and an economic base on which to build the society of the future.

Midwestern reformers of special importance to the Dunes movement were John Peter Altgeld, governor of Illinois, 1893–1896; Eugene Debs, labor organizer and Socialist candidate for president who polled nearly one million votes in 1920; and Robert M. La Follette, Sr., governor of Wisconsin, 1900–1905, and subsequently United States senator, and presidential candidate of the Progressive Independent party in 1924.

Altgeld was one of the first of the midwestern urban radicals. During his brief tenure as governor he enacted sweeping Populist and socialist inspired reforms, including child labor laws, corporation laws, civil service, tax laws, educational and penal reforms. But his most enduring contribution was his example of personal integrity and thorough dedication to social justice. Although he knew it spelled political suicide, he pardoned the Haymarket rioters, and supported the Pullman strike. He was joined in his reform campaign by Jane Addams, Henry Demarest Lloyd, and Clarence Darrow.

Eugene Debs was a native of Indiana and founder of the Social Democratic party in 1897. Although few members of the Dunes movement followed him into the Socialist party, he exerted considerable personal influence. Many sympathized with his pacifist position during the World War. Tom Knotts, labor organizer for the Pullman strike and brother of A. F. Knotts, served time in jail with Debs in 1894 and later named his son after him. Debs was a close friend of Carl Sandburg and greatly admired by Paul Douglas.

What Altgeld started in Illinois, La Follette continued with more enduring political results in Wisconsin. He built from scratch a farm-labor alliance that set the pattern for Progressive reform throughout the Midwest. La Follette learned much of his progressivism from John Bascom, who came to the University of Wisconsin as president in 1874 determined to make the school a civic as well as intellectual force in the state. One of La Follette's most influential programs, as governor, was the "Wisconsin Idea," the development of the state university as a partner in the work of public service. Under several outstanding successors to Bascom, including Thomas C. Chamberlin and his student, Charles R. Van Hise, the University of Wisconsin became a pioneer in the education of the people for democratic citizenship. Thomas Chamberlin later, as head of the Department of Geology at the University of Chicago, attracted Henry Cowles to Chicago and became a champion of the Dunes. Van Hise's 1910 volume *The Conservation of Natural Resources in the United States*, the bible of midwestern conservationism, inspired Richard Lieber's campaign for state parks in Indiana. Under the influence of Van Hise, too, outdoor drama received strong impetus at the University of Wisconsin and Thomas Wood Stevens went to Madison to work with Thomas Dickinson and Percy MacKaye.

The impact of early midwestern Progressivism upon the Dunes movement was symbolized by the six photographs Paul Douglas hung on the walls of his Senate office when he went to Washington in 1948. They were pictures of Lincoln, Jane Addams, John Peter Altgeld, Clarence Darrow, Robert La Follette, and George Norris. As he wrote later: "All six were from the soil of the Middle West and all carried with them more than a touch of greatness. I hoped that if I looked at them long enough, like the man in Hawthorne's story of the Great Stone Face, I might catch a little of their qualities."[24]

SETTLEMENT HOUSES

At the turn of the century, the special tendencies of midwestern Progressivism were focused as through a great magnifying glass on the dozens of settlement houses that ringed Chicago's Loop. Here the commitment to the democratic ideal of the community as a self-creating and self-governing whole came alive in practice. And here, in what were called at the time "Ethical Bohemias" or "cultural melting pots," the leaders of Chicago reform, art, and science met and discussed the leading ideas and movements of the day.

If, as Plato said, the end of every story is inherent in its beginning, the Dunes movement may be justly considered a creature of the settlement houses. In 1893 the residents of Hull House established the first public playground in Chicago. In 1906 Chicago

settlement workers helped found the National Playground Association, and in 1908 the Chicago branch appointed Dwight Perkins
to head a committee to survey the possibility of sponsoring regular
walks for the particular benefit of the social workers and the neighborhood residents associated with the settlement houses. This was
the beginning of the "Saturday Afternoon Walking Trips" and
the ritual hikes to the Dunes. In the 1910s Henry Booth House
sponsored annual summer camps in the Dunes, and some of the
first recorded meetings in the campaign for a Dunes park were
held at that settlement.[25]

The settlement house influence is readily apparent in the leader-
ship of the Dunes movement through the 1970s. In the early period,
in addition to the residents of Hull House, there were Mr. and
Mrs. Thomas Allinson, head residents of Henry Booth Settlement
House, and Mr. and Mrs. Jacob Abt, head residents of nearby
Maxwell Street Settlement. Chicago Commons contributed Gra-
ham Taylor and Amalia Hofer. Stephen Mather was affiliated with
Hull House and was the philanthropic founder in 1912 of the
House of Social Service in the Chicago Stockyards District. In
Gary, Bess Sheehan's "outspoken local interest" was Campbell
Friendship House.[26] Later, Sheehan's successor in the role of "Lady
of the Dunes," Dorothy Buell, was associated with Gary Neighborhood House. Sylvia Troy, who in turn succeeded Dorothy Buell as
president of the Save the Dunes Council in 1968, received a major
portion of her inspiration for a life dedicated to civic reform and
volunteer community service, and for her own profession of medical
social work, from the classes she attended as a child in a settlement
house in the East Bronx, New York.

The personal leadership exerted by the settlement workers in the
Dunes movement was significant; even more so was the vision they
carried with them to the Dunes from their work in the inner city.
This vision was closely associated in the 1890s and early 1900s
with such versions of the religion of democracy as the social idealism of Felix Adler's ethical culture movement, and the Christian
socialism advocated by Protestant proponents of the Social Gospel.

The founder of the first settlement house in America was Stanton Coit, who later became an Ethical Culture leader in London
and one of the most forthright of the preachers of the religion of

democracy at the turn of the century. Like Louis Sullivan, George Bellows, and John Dewey, all of whom influenced the Dunes apostles without ever becoming personally involved in the Dunes movement itself, Coit must be considered one of the fathers of the Dunes vision through his influence upon the settlement house movement. In 1886, after visiting Toynbee Hall in London, Coit moved to the Lower East Side of New York where he founded Neighborhood Guild. The name referred to his idea of civic reform: a system of working class community organizations which would utilize natural leadership in the city's neighborhoods to promote "all the reforms, domestic, provident or recreative which the social ideal demands."[27] When Jane Addams and Ellen Gates Starr moved into the old mansion on South Halsted Street three years later, it was with the same purpose in mind of facilitating a renaissance of organic democracy in the city.

The settlement house movement in Chicago was closely associated in its early years with the intellectual milieu of the Chicago Ethical Humanist Society. William M. Salter, first leader of the society, helped Addams and Starr in their plans for Hull House, and in 1898, with Thomas Allinson, he led the society in the founding of Henry Booth House on Chicago's near South Side. Addams frequently appeared as a "lecturer" at the Chicago Ethical Humanist Society along with such well-known midwestern religious humanists and reformers as Jenkin Lloyd Jones of All Souls Unitarian Church, Horace Kallen, protégé of William James, and George Burnham Foster of the University of Chicago. Horace Bridges, who succeeded Salter, spoke on such subjects as "The Democratic Conception of God" and "Organic Democracy versus Aristocracy." In 1915 he delivered an address on "The Poems of Harriet Monroe." Stanton Coit visited the Society in 1914, the same year that saw the publication of his book *The Soul of America*, and called for the formation of a "Church of the Republic," an independent American national church that would celebrate the religion of democracy in the United States.[28]

Allinson's vision of Henry Booth House typified an idea common to all the settlement workers, that they were in some fundamental sense returning to the geographical center and communal roots of the new urban society and beginning again. In one of his annual reports, Allinson described the Henry Booth House as situated close to the site of the sand mountain where Father Marquette lived through the first winter passed by a white man on the shore of southern Lake Michigan. Now it was the neighborhood center of the junk, iron, and metal trades, and over all was an ever-present smoke pall. However, as one of the four most congested wards of the city, it was a good place to pursue the purpose of "The House by the Side of the Road"—"helping neighbors help themselves." In 1907, when Allinson was writing, "neighbors" was defined by the line from John Latouche's "Ballad for Americans," the official song of Booth House: "I'm just an Irish-Negro-Jewish-Italian-French and English-Spanish-Russian-Chinese-Polish-Scotch-Hungarian-Litvak-Swedish-Finnish-Canadian-Greek and Turk, Czech and double-check American!" [29]

The underlying motive of the settlement workers, bluntly stated, was no less than the individual and social salvation of the human community. For them, democracy meant that the original gospel of Christian love had been saved from its erroneous association with the exclusivist doctrines of a specifically religious consciousness and was to be fulfilled through the inclusive fraternity of the social organism itself.

In the transition the "Good News" of personal redemption through Christ's sacrifice was transformed into what Graham Taylor called the "religion of Good Neighborship." The settlement idea, as one of the residents of Henry Booth House wrote in 1917, is "not service, but a feeling of social democracy or brotherhood or just plain friendship." [30] Wrote a resident of Graham Taylor's Chicago Commons: "A mission, in the ordinary sense of that word, comes from *outside* to a neighborhood or community which it regards as 'degraded'. . . . The settlement bases its existence, its hope, its endeavor on the firm foundation of Democracy—on the thesis that the people must and can and will *save themselves*." [31] Christian agape became Christian humanitarianism, which in turn was interpreted in terms of the eighteenth-century Enlightenment notion of a common humanity. "There is something primordial about (our) motives," said Jane Addams in her famous lecture,

"The Subjective Necessity for Social Settlements," "but I am perhaps not over-bold in designating them as a great desire to share
the race life. . . . There must be the overmastering belief that all
that is noblest in life is common to men as men."[32]

The settlement workers denied that they were altruistic. The
grand social principle they repeatedly evoked was reciprocity. In
addition to "democracy," the word that best expressed its embodiment in the life of the community was "common." Graham Taylor's 1896 explanation of how he chose the name for his settlement
house is a classic statement of the shared vision of the Chicago
reformers that the sacred is found in reciprocal relationships natural and common to all:

> When in search for the Settlement's name, we groped for weeks after
> some title which had at its root, if not in its form, that good old English
> word *common*. For the idea of the sharing of what each has equally
> with all, and all with each, of what belongs to no one and no class, but
> to every one of the whole body, is the idea underlying not only this
> word and its equivalents in many tongues, but the very conception of
> that community and communion in which society and religion consist,
> and which constitute the essence of the settlement motive and move-
> ment.[33]

Taylor, a Congregational minister, traced the ancestry of what
he considered the root metaphor of society and religion not to an
ecclesiastical source, but to the struggle for democracy in English
political history. He added another meaning to the symbol *common*, which also derived from English political history and which
pointed directly to how the vision of community in the inner city
was to be transferred to the vision of a Dunes park:

> As the freemen of the race organized in their early shires, municipali-
> ties and guilds, and later on combined to form one body representing
> the whole people, so the represented people, without any primary dis-
> tinction of class, came to be known as "the Commons." To this ideal of
> social democracy, the name adds the suggestion of those few patches
> of mother earth still unclaimed as private property, which at least
> afford standing room equally for all, irrespective of pecuniary circum-
> stances or social status.[34]

Artists and writers began to take a serious interest in the Dune Country in the 1890s. For the next several decades, a burst of creative activity focused upon the Dunes, associated with the Chicago renaissance in American arts and letters.[35] After World War I, this activity slackened somewhat but continued, although at a reduced pace, through World War II; even today it is quite alive. Thus there has been an unbroken line of persons who for nearly a century, finding the Dunes landscape imaginatively appealing, have sought to communicate that appeal in words, pictures, and plastic forms.

Jens Jensen began hiking through the Dune Country in 1889—five years after he and his fiancée arrived in the United States from Denmark, three years after he got his first job with the Chicago West Park Commission, one year after he planted his first garden of native wildflowers, "The American Garden," in Union Park. Jensen responded enthusiastically to the prairie and duneland surrounding Chicago. It not only reminded him of the seacoast of his native Jutland, but symbolized the freedom of movement and equality of opportunity he identified with mid-America. Jensen quickly established a career in Chicago as the leader of the "Prairie School" of landscape architecture. In 1906 he was rehired by a reform administration as superintendent of the West Side Parks. He subsequently constructed a huge conservatory in Garfield Park for which he prepared illustrations of the geologic evolution of the Midwest. The genetic approach was carried into his design of public parks and private estates. Holding that the conditions and forces natural to any environment are the logically normal ones for living in that place, Jensen shared with his friends and colleagues, Prairie School architects Louis Sullivan and Frank Lloyd Wright, the view that midwestern art should be organized around broad, simple patterns with complex details, and utilize common, native materials in an unpretentious manner. Landscape architect Wilhelm Miller credited Jensen with creating a new Middle West landscape style based on conserving original plant communities and repeating a motif of horizontal lines symbolic of the prairie.[36]

Earl Howell Reed, Sr., was also one of the early artists to discover the Dunes. The first sketching trip his son remembered accompanying him on was in 1891 to the dunes near St. Joseph, Michigan. Son of a scholarly minister and a mother who wrote books on Hindu and Buddhist literature, and brother of Myrtle Reed, a novelist whose best-known tale is *Lavender and Old Lace*, Reed was first a newspaper reporter on the *Chicago Times* and then for some years a broker on the Chicago Board of Trade. One day in 1906 or 1907, Reed took a solitary hike across the Indiana Dunes. In the midst of his rambles, as he later told the story, he received the flashing inspiration that he ought to work full time sketching and describing the beautiful world that lay around him. True to his illumination, Reed renounced the world of commerce and devoted the rest of his life to portraying the Dunes in etchings and story.[37]

Sometime before 1902, Thomas Wood Stevens had written his first literary impression of the Dunes, a poem appropriately entitled "The Spirit of the Dunes." And by 1909, "before the dunes had become a fad, when there were only two other shacks on the whole beach," as his friend and collaborator Marion Patten later remembered it, he was living there in a "darling little Japanese shack."[38]

With the popularization of the Dunes by Reed and Jensen, the "Saturday Afternoon Walking Trips," and perhaps most important of all, the completion of the Chicago, Lake Shore and South Bend Electric Railroad (later called the Chicago, South Shore, and South Bend, or colloquially the South Shore) between Chicago and Michigan City in 1908, interest in the Dunes among artists and writers increased rapidly. By 1912 Frank V. Dudley was making trips to the Dunes with the Prairie Club and beginning to paint the first of his hundreds of Dunes pictures. Ten years later, with the proceeds from the prestigious Mr. and Mrs. Frank G. Logan medal for his painting *Duneland* and its subsequent purchase by the Art Institute of Chicago, Dudley built a cabin and studio in the Dunes which he occupied for most of each year until his death in 1957.[39]

Carl Sandburg had been acquainted with the Dunes since 1906; after his return to Chicago from a job as private secretary to the Social Democratic mayor of Milwaukee and his marriage to Lillian Steichen, he walked there often. In 1914 Edgar Lee Masters wrote excitedly, "Next Monday I am going for a tramp to the sand dunes with a Swede bard."[40] This was Sandburg. Also in 1914 Harriet Monroe began publishing "Chicago Poems" in *Poetry;* in 1916 the book edition included Sandburg's poem "Dunes." In the late 1920s, Sandburg rebuilt a summer home in the dunes north of Michigan City, Indiana, and lived there year-round with his family until the end of World War II. Helga Sandburg drew upon her memories of those years for her novel *The Owl's Roost,* published in 1962.[41]

In the 1912–1919 period an efflorescence of Dunes art was spurred by the national park campaign. The period began with the exhibition of several Dunes etchings by Reed at the Paris Salon, and the publication of his first book, *The Voices of the Dunes,* a handsome volume of his etchings, each faced with a poem by a Chicago writer. By 1918 he had exhibited several times in Chicago, as well as in other cities of the United States; a permanent collection of his work was displayed in the "Reed Room" at the Art Institute of Chicago; and he had published two more books, *The Dune Country* and *Sketches in Duneland.*[42]

In 1916 the well-known landscape painter Charles Francis Browne toured the Dunes with Stephen Mather, joining Lorado Taft in putting the imprimatur of the Chicago art establishment upon the park project. In 1917, in preparation for the Dunes Pageant, the Chicago Public Library sponsored "An Exhibit of the Dune Country," etchings and photographs by members of the Prairie Club, among them L. H. Drury, Arthur E. Anderson, and Charles G. Dudley. An accompanying bulletin board featured poems of the Dunes. In the following year the first of Frank Dudley's exhibits appeared at the Art Institute, and in 1919 the Friends of Our Native Landscape ingeniously established the Dunes as one of the great regional landscapes of America in an exhibition at the Art Institute entitled "Pictures of Our Country." Artists representative of each of thirteen classic American landscapes were included; representing the Dunes were Dudley, Reed, Charles W. Dahlgreen, Ralph Fletcher Seymour, and Bertha E. Jacques.[43]

In the midst of this heady esthetic interest in the Dunes, two of the foremost American nature writers of the twentieth century were coming to maturity. On Chicago's far South Side, where city and dunes met, Robert and Elia Peattie's precocious son, Donald Culross Peattie, was spending his adolescence writing poetry and exploring the nearby lakeshore and prairie. Edwin Way Teale was spending his summers at his grandparents' farm, "Lone Oak," on the edge of the dunes near Furnessville. In 1930 Peattie published *Flora of the Dunes*, and in 1935 *An Almanac for Moderns* established his literary reputation. Teale waited until 1942 to write *Dune Boy*, which became an overnight success.[44]

In 1913 Floyd Dell and Margery Currey moved into studios on Fifty-seventh Street in Chicago's South Side neighborhood of Hyde Park. They quickly became vital figures in the art colony that had existed there since the 1893 World's Fair. By day Currey wrote for the *Chicago Tribune* and by night played hostess to a talented community of artists and writers, including at various times Ben Hecht, Theodore Dreiser, Sherwood Anderson, and Vachel Lindsay. With the South Shore railroad only steps away, providing direct access to the Dune Country for weekend outings, the Fifty-seventh Street colony became a center for the creation of Dunes art in the following two decades.

Sometime before 1920, the New England marine landscape painter Charles Biesel arrived in Chicago and took up residence in Hyde Park. Soon he rented studio space in one of the buildings on Fifty-seventh Street, joined the Prairie Club, purchased a cottage near Tremont, and began painting the Dunes. After the War he was joined by his son, Fred Biesel. Charles, Fred, his wife, Frances Strain, and their friends Emil Armin, V. M. S. Hannell, Gustaf Dalstrom, and Francis Foy were members of a close-knit group which in 1929 called itself "The Chicago Ten." Most of the younger members of this group attended classes together at the Art Institute of Chicago, where they were influenced by George Bellows and Randall Davy, and later all exhibited with the famous No-Jury Society. During this period they developed an increasing interest in painting the Dunes, and by the mid-1930s, the Biesels, Vin Hannell and his artist wife, Hazel, and the Armins had purchased or built cottages there. Other artists and writers migrated to the Dunes from the South Side of Chicago, among them the writers John and Marion Drury, the painter Ethel Crouch Browne, and the painter, writer, and wood etcher David Sander. The Dunes art created by this second generation of Chicago artists is characterized by its variety of subject matter and use of medium, its subjective vitality and its intimate feeling for both urban and natural landscapes.[45]

There were and are many other artists and writers of the Dunes. A by no means exhaustive list would include the novelists Marjorie Hill Allee, Julia Cooley Altrocchi, Meyer Levin, Elma K. Lobaugh, Arnold Mulder, and Thomas Rogers; children's book authors Seymour Fleishman and Julian May; poets Charles G. Bell, Galway Kinnell, and Jeannette Vaughn Konley; nature writers Samuel A. Harper and E. Stillman Bailey; artists J. Howard Euston, James Gilbert, John Hawkinson, John Cowan Templeton, and Dudley Crafts Watson; and photographers Jun Fujita and George Svihla.[46]

Hundreds of amateur artists and writers contributed to the Dunes tradition. David Sander wrote a reminiscence of the late 1920s: "All my life I have watched people come to the dunes. As a child I came on the train with my father and fifty other men and their wives who journeyed here from as far away as Milwaukee to paint and sketch in the natural wonderland. Just to see them debark from the orange electric traincar was a marvelous sight, handing down their easels and sketch boxes and camp stools and knapsacks and canteens. And they stood, all fifty or sixty of them, as the train pulled away, strapping on their puttees, and arranging their loads equally between both hands and their backs. Too young to paint, I would climb from dune to dune as the artists set up their paintboxes on patent tripods. It was I who ran to the lake to get them water for their watercolors and who watched with delight as I would tumble down into a sandy blowout to see six men at their easels painting away in the bright yellow sunlight."[47]

But none of these additional persons, almost all Chicagoans, change the basic contours of the history: Dunes art and literature found its first and lasting inspiration in the 1890–1930 period. Thus, while it may be said that the communal substance of the Dunes vision was most tangible in the early settlement houses, the symbols, images, and stories that expressed the vision were the creation of the greats and near-greats among the writers and artists of the Chicago renaissance.

Many of the artists and writers shared the life of the settlements as residents, students, and teachers, or as friends and spouses of the settlement workers. Hull House, especially, encouraged creative activity in the arts, and many Dunites, such as Harriet Monroe, Jens Jensen, Carl Sandburg, Donald Robertson, Kenneth Goodman, the Hannells, and Emil Armin were affiliated with it. So important were the settlement workers as heroic figures in the drama of social redemption that authors like Elia Peattie took them as subjects for their novels. It is evident that in their own associations—the Cliff Dwellers, the Fifty-seventh Street art colony, the No-Jury Society, and the art colonies in the Dunes—the artists and writers pursued a quest for a rebirth of community similar to that which motivated the settlement workers. A spirit of collegiality existed in these associations that was the counterpart to the more civic-oriented fellowship of the settlements.[48]

The identification ran even deeper than this. Like the settlement workers, the members of the Chicago renaissance were seeking a new relationship between art and democracy.

Beginning in the 1880s, Chicago was the center for a movement of artists, who, according to bookman and "Dune Bug" Ralph Fletcher Seymour, "recognized the brand of living in their neighborhood as peculiarly American, and undertook to translate their understanding of its beauty and meaning into art forms."[49] In 1903 William Dean Howells made a similar appraisal of Chicago writers. "The republic of letters," he observed, "is everywhere sufficiently republican; but in the metropolis of the Middle-west, it is so without thinking; it is so almost without feeling; and the atmospheric democracy, the ambient equality, is something that seems like the prime effect in literature of what America has been doing and saying in life ever since she first formulated herself in the Declaration."[50]

The Chicago artists and writers carried forward the Transcendentalist quest for an art and literature of democracy. But they did so under the conditions of a growing urban, industrial and corporation-dominated society, in Hamlin Garland's words, "the portentous presence" of the metropolis, not the conditions of rural New England in the 1830s.

The result was an increasing alienation during the period 1890–1930 of Chicago artists and writers from the dominant public and commercial institutions of the region. As Bernard Duffey summarizes: "The first stage of Chicago's renaissance joined hands with the second to define a literary culture deliberately hostile to and liberated from the dominant forces of a modern business America."[51] Along with this alienation went a quest for symbols and images adequate to express what they perceived as the alternative—the genuinely democratic currents of life moving within the experience of the people. Some of the Chicago artists and writers identified their vision of authentic selfhood-in-community with the relatively virgin landscape of the Indiana Dunes.

Chicago artists and writers shared with the settlement house workers the transition from conceiving of art as a force for moral uplift to seeing it as a medium of expression intrinsic to all human activity and experience. In the former view, prevalent among Chicago's cultural elite at the turn of the century, art need not challenge the economic and social relationships of the society, for it is concerned with the spiritual in a non-wordly sense and is confined to leisure-time pursuits. In the latter view, art is the authentic means of communication and production in which all classes and all phases of social life ought to participate, and which requires the development of cooperative social institutions to fulfill its function.[52]

Some of the Chicago artists and writers, like Sandburg, were exponents for the latter view from the time they first raised their voices in the city. "Art gives people the best equivalents of religion and is the real spiritual foundation of democracy," he wrote. "Any person devoting his time to making people aware of their own music and poetry is contributing to the dignity of man."[53] Others, such as Jensen and Sullivan, who for a time shared the support of the financial leaders of the city, came to see the neo-classic revival that dominated the 1893 World's Fair and inspired the Burnham Plan as a betrayal of their life and work. To them, such forms marked the emergence of a new feudal mentality bent on imposing an autocratic rule on the city and its native landscape. Harriet Monroe spoke for them all when in the 1920s she affirmed that contrary to the Puritan fathers who "considered proficiency in the arts unworthy of free and enlightened citizens," it is when the artistic dimension inherent in all human vocations is cultivated that a free and enlightened citizenry becomes possible. To succeed in grounding art in democracy and at the same time democracy in art would mean a "reversal of systems of education and schools of thought beside which the Russian revolution is a molehill to a mountain."[54]

The creative response of the makers of the Chicago Renaissance was to celebrate the original experience of the artist, and the universal experience of the people. By these means they hoped to undermine what they regarded as an oppressive economic and social superstructure. Through a disciplined stripping away of the unnecessary and transient accretions of capitalist civilization within themselves, by true *self*-education, they hoped to make contact with the recurrent feelings and ideals that joined human beings throughout history. Rebirth of self was yoked to rebirth of society. Their goal, therefore, was much the same as that of the settlement house workers who also sought the birth of social democracy through personal identification with the life of the masses. But the artists' and writers' route, like Walt Whitman's "open road," an image important to them, led primarily through the acceptance of self, what they saw as a rediscovery of the soul. The path of artistic commitment corresponded to the reformer's path of political revolt, but each involved its own special form of suffering and self-discipline.[55]

The impulse of the Chicago renaissance toward personal and social liberation led to an absorption with the naive. The simple person, the person without pretension, the person close to nature or to the root processes of industrial production, was the authentic individual who retained the sincerity and sympathy necessary for cooperative modes of life. The image of the "folk" was found in many places, but as the pageant of 1917 dramatized, it was associated most closely with the image of the Native American. Taft constructed a statue of Blackhawk on the banks of the Mississippi for which Stevens wrote the service of dedication. Reed recorded extant tales of the Dune Country Potawatomi and invented new ones of his own. Dudley and his Indian wife Maida Lewis dressed themselves in native costumes for public programs. Members of the Prairie Club carved totems and placed them in front of their tents in the Dunes. Ralph Fletcher Seymour and his fellow Cliff Dwellers danced in the Dunes "to the pounding of Kurt

Stein's Indian drum."[56] Almost everyone painted or wrote about the Indians of the Southwest. None of this was historical curiosity; rather, it was a quest for the unification of experience through vicarious identification with the original American race.

The impulse to liberation through originality of experience was evident in the *styles* of the Dunes artists and writers: in the ordinary language of Sandburg's free blank verse, in the confessional eloquence of Jensen's speeches, in the prototypical perspectives of Dudley's paintings, in the intimate detail of Hazel Hannell's dunes flowers, in the forceful simplification of Armin's paintings. These required immense sophistication and devotion to a total way of life separate from the commercialism of modern society.

The Chicago artists and writers were seeking the experience of an original revelation. Wrote Sherwood Anderson: "All this desire of revelation I found among the new acquaintances in the little converted storeroom at 57th and Stony Island." As Francis Strain's painting *The Crowd*—in which a nude woman stands unperturbed in the midst of a mob of frantic overdressed men and women—so strikingly expresses, it was the quest for a new revelation of self and brotherhood and sisterhood that the artists and writers took with them into the city. And as Sherwood Anderson's image of the baptismal rite of passage many experienced during weekend excursions out of the city indicates, this quest went with them into the Dunes as well:

> The weekends at some little town on the lake shore, six or eight of us men and women sleeping perhaps, or at least trying to sleep, under one blanket by a low fire built on the shore of the lake, even perhaps going off in the darkness to some secluded spot to bathe, all of us in the nude, it all quite innocent enough, but such a wonderful feeling in us of leading a new, free, bold life, defying what seemed to us the terribly stodgy life out of which we had all come.[57]

HARPER'S UNIVERSITY

The new University of Chicago opened its doors in 1892 on the South Side of Chicago, within the corporate limits of suburban Hyde Park, at a time when night sounds could still be heard from the nearby marshes, and dunes could still be seen stretching south along the lakeshore. William Rainey Harper, the university's first president, had come to the school determined to make it the top-ranking institution of higher learning in the Middle West, if not the country. Almost single-handedly he planned the university, and did so in accord with his own profound commitment to the religion of democracy.[58]

In 1899 Harper delivered an address, "The University and Democracy," a systematic statement of his philosophy of higher education. He posed the question: "Has democracy a religion?" and answered: "Yes; a religion with its god, its altar, and its temple, with its code of ethics and its creed. Its god is mankind, humanity; its altar, home; its temple, country. The one doctrine of democracy's creed is the brotherhood, and consequently the equality of man; its system of ethics is contained in a single word, righteousness." Harper, who was an Old Testament scholar, went on to argue that the religion of democracy was a definite religion, yet one which was also eclectic and worldwide, for it included not only much of Judaism and Christianity, but also many of the best features of other religions and systems of philosophy. The foundations of the democratic faith, in Harper's view, were naturalistic, for "democracy"—as the highest ideal of human achievement, and an actual system of social and personal life—is the product of a long period of historical evolution, grounded in the "operation of laws of life which antedate the existence of man himself."[59]

For Harper, the religion of democracy set the terms for the proper understanding of the origin and purpose of the modern university. The genesis of the university was the "democratic idea," which appeared in the guilds or "spontaneous confederations" of the twelfth century. There cooperative self-government, freedom from ecclesiastical control, and the right of free utterance first took root. The university is therefore "of the people, and for the people, whether considered individually or collectively." The contemporary task of the university was given to it by the overriding contemporary need of democracy: understanding and unification of its highest and truest principles. Harper's charge to the university of the twentieth century, which he then proceeded to explicate in some detail, was that it be no less than prophet, priest, and philosopher, indeed messiah, of a democratic society, "an agency which, in union with all others, will usher in the dawn of the day when the universal brotherhood of man will be understood and accepted by all men." [60]

Harper brought to the university in succeeding years scholars who he thought would subscribe to this mission—among them, Thomas Chamberlin in geology, John M. Coulter in botany, and John Dewey in psychology, philosophy, and education. One of the persons to whom Harper made overtures of a teaching position, but who regretfully declined, was a young man by the name of Richard Lieber. With such persons Harper set about answering what he considered the first great question before the university: "how to become one in spirit, though not necessarily in opinions." [61] The result is well known. As William James exclaimed in 1903, "The result is wonderful—a *real school*, and *real Thought*. Important thought, too! Did you ever hear of such a city or such a University? Here [at Harvard] we have thought, but no school. At Yale a school but no thought. Chicago has both." [62] The point was that at Chicago a genuine community of inquiry emerged. And in keeping with its emphasis on the pragmatic interplay of theory and action, the University of Chicago Settlement soon took its place not far from Hull House, President Harper served on the Chicago Board of Education, Dewey founded his Laboratory School, and the faculty as a whole quickly became involved in a wide range of organizations and activities devoted to the betterment of the city.

Thomas C. Chamberlin and John Merle Coulter, two of the best known men of science in the United States at the turn of the century, contributed immeasurably to the beginnings of the science of ecology at the University of Chicago, and to the scientific and symbolic importance attributed to the Indiana Dunes. Both agreed with Harper that democratic religion and social morality had their roots in the operation of natural laws open to empirical investigation and in the universal experience of humankind.

In 1892, the year he left the presidency of the University of Wisconsin to take up work as head of the Department of Geology at Chicago, Chamberlin summarized his thought on the relation of religion to the commonwealth. Public religion and ethics, he argued, were grounded in the fields of knowledge pursued by the university and in commonly shared beliefs not subject to dispute between sects and parties. Their ultimate basis was the "inherent religiousness of life" that pervades all aspects of human endeavor and the "ever-present revelation" of the Supreme Power found in the actual operations of the physical universe. Chamberlin thought in terms of a "secular theology" that might someday formulate the mandates of general revelation so that the members of society could understand the substance of civic duty. Chamberlin's premise was that "modern investigation is forcing synthetic minds irresistibly to the conviction that all things known are tied together by indissoluble bonds and constitute one great unity which is permeated and presided over by the organizing agency of the universe." Because of this general ecological viewpoint he could simultaneously turn to the physical sciences for moral instruction and affirm the "American spirit [which] welcomes all sincere endeavors to promote a better life, feeling that, whatever the errors involved may be, they will ultimately be eliminated as the result of co-working and comparison." [63]

Coulter was no less hopeful about the prospects for reconciling religion and science and placing them in service of the public good. Especially was he concerned to show that the scientific picture of progressive evolution was compatible with the "essentials" of religion found in universal human experience. Coulter was a dedicated Presbyterian layman. He was also a liberal. On several occasions there were attempts to arrange a debate between him and fundamentalist William Jennings Bryan. Near the end of his life, Coulter and his son, Merle C. Coulter, published *Where Evolution and Religion Meet*, a summary of the scientific humanitarian faith they shared. Organic evolution they defined as "that type of change in which a living organism (plant, animal, man) becomes 'better adapted to the environment,' develops and perfects the equipment with which the requirements of life are met." So understood, the principle of evolution is evident in all aspects of human experience as well as in the whole history of living organisms on earth. It finds its highest expression in those adaptations by which human beings seek to perfect their characters. In this case, the "environment" is composed mainly of other human beings, and the "requirements of life are for a more sympathetic and effective co-operation."[64] The function of religion, the Coulters concluded, is to guide the evolution of human history in such fashion that its social progress through perfection of character will be comparable to the progressive evolution of plant and animal life to more harmonious levels of adaptation with the physical environment.

The World's Columbian Exposition, held in Chicago in 1893 on the Midway adjacent to the new university, symbolized at its inception (if not in its implementation) the progressive humanitarian and naturalistic philosophy espoused by Harper, Chamberlin and Coulter. Scientists, scholars, and artists from throughout the world gathered to exchange ideas in a series of congresses, one of which was a World Parliament of Religions. Harriet Monroe, whose "Ode to Brotherhood" opened the exposition, wrote later of the architect John Wellborn Root's original vision of the fair: "He wished to express our militant democracy as he felt it, pausing after victory for a song of triumph before taking up its onward march."[65] For Louis Sullivan, the fair that *ought to have been* arose as a "gorgeous Garden City . . . within the parkland by the blue waters, oriented toward the rising sun, a token of a covenant of things to be, a symbol of the city's basic significance as offspring of the prairie, the lake and the portage."[66]

Into this visionary and challenging intellectual milieu young Henry Cowles moved in 1895. A graduate of Oberlin College in 1893, Cowles came to Chicago with a fellowship to study geology with Chamberlin and his associate, Rollin D. Salisbury. But he also attended Coulter's botany lectures, where he was introduced to the science of ecology. Coulter encouraged Cowles to combine his study of dynamic physiography with plant ecology and to pursue his doctoral research in the nearby Indiana Dunes. Cowles accepted the suggestion, beginning at the same time his life-work and his lifelong association with the Dunes.[67]

Cowles remained for his entire professional life at the University of Chicago. From 1897, when he gave his first six lectures on plant ecology, to 1931, the year of his effective retirement, more than two hundred Ph.D's were graduated by the botany department. Many of these went on to become recognized leaders in American ecology. This does not count the large number of undergraduate and graduate students who matriculated in Cowles's classes but did not earn the Ph.D.

The "Cowles School of Ecology" dominated the Department of Botany at the University of Chicago down to the time of its merger with zoology in 1968. Most important personally to Cowles among his early students was George D. Fuller, who completed his dissertation in plant ecology and morphology in 1912 on the basis of research in the Dunes. Cowles and Fuller, who were close in age, quickly became friends. After Fuller joined the faculty, they taught classes together, led field trips, and shared in the activities of Friends of Our Native Landscape. In 1933, just as Cowles was retiring and Fuller was assuming the leadership of the department, Charles E. Olmsted was invited to the university as the Coulter Fellow. He brought with him an interest in dunes ecology from previous research in the sand barrens of Connecticut, and soon established himself as the successor to the Cowles tradition at Chicago. Like Cowles and Fuller before him, Olmsted spoke out vigorously in favor of a national park in the Dunes.

But Cowles's influence did not stop at the doors of the botany department; it extended outward to other departments of the university and other scholars and institutions in the Midwest.

As Paul Voth, who served in the botany department from 1932 to 1968, later recalled, from approximately 1895 to 1930 there was a "highly sympathetic core group" of faculty and graduate students in the natural sciences at the university who were constantly crossing disciplinary lines, visiting one anothers' classes, and exchanging ideas and experiences. Among the factors that brought these men and women together, in addition to the university's pervasive spirit of collegiality, was their shared excitement over the young science of ecology and the research and teaching many of them were doing in the Chicago environs. Indicative of these relationships was the scene Stevens included in his original manuscript for the Dunes Pageant of 1917. "Three fantastic figures representing Professors"—the Scholar, the Botanist, and the Geologist—were to appear on the dunes and be chased away by a swarm of dancing mosquitoes![68]

So strong was the relationship between the early University of

Chicago natural sciences faculty and the Dunes that in 1903, after consultation with Cowles, Jensen, and others, Harper submitted a proposal to the board of trustees for the purchase of a "Biological Field and Farm" to be located in Porter County, Indiana. The proposed tract, which would "comprise the widest possible associated variety of botanical specimens and animal life within reach of the University," was to encompass 1,150 acres of duneland. This was the first recorded plan for the preservation of a portion of the Indiana Dunes.[69]

In addition to Chamberlin, Coulter, Cowles, Fuller, and Salisbury, who was co-author in 1899 with William C. Alden of *The Geography of Chicago and Its Environs*, the leadership of the "highly sympathetic core group" included: ornithologist Reuben M. Strong, who first visited the Dunes with Cowles in 1897 and who through his lifelong leadership of the Chicago Conservation Council was active in the Dunes struggle into the 1960s; Frank M. Woodruff, who began his ornithological researches in the Dunes as a graduate student in 1897, and later became director of the Chicago Academy of Sciences; Victor E. Shelford, who on the basis of his research in the Dunes helped found the science of animal ecology in the United States, and in 1913 published the first work in America on the classification of animals by environments, *Animal Communities in Temperate America, as Illustrated in the Chicago Region: A Study in Animal Ecology*; Charles C. Adams, who claimed that he offered the first course in general animal ecology in the United States at Chicago in 1902; Robert S. Platt, member of the geography department, who in 1917 participated in the first topographic mapping of the Dunes and who was active in the Save the Dunes campaign of the 1950s; and Warder Clyde Allee, who earned his Ph.D. in animal ecology in 1912 on the basis of a dissertation that included field research in the Dunes, and who was chiefly responsible for the establishment of a parallel ecological tradition at Chicago, which culminated in the publication of the epochal *Principles of Animal Ecology* in 1949.[70]

The impact of this group on the Dunes movement was immense. In spite of differences among its members, it provided through the new science of ecology, or the "study of communities," as it was also called, the naturalistic foundations for the vision of social de-

mocracy the reformers and artists brought to the Dunes landscape—a vision that most of the ecologists shared. The group also
provided a stream of recruits to the Dunes cause. Many were those
who, like May Theilgaard Watts, experienced the Dunes for the
first time and were enculturated into the privileged society of
those who loved them by a field trip sponsored by the University
of Chicago. Some teachers, like Cowles, took their classes to the
Dunes pageants and festivals, confronting them directly with the
mythology the landscape imaginatively provoked, a mythology
which they, indirectly, helped to create.[71] Through the Chicago
Academy of Sciences and similar institutions, the University of
Chicago scientists made contact with a large number of amateur
and semiprofessional naturalists in the Chicago region interested in
the topography, flowers, trees, birds and animals of the Dunes.

At the head of the university during these early years marched
the figure of Harper, whose sense of mission for the school set the
tone for the work of its departments. In the background stood the
figure of John Dewey, who, of all members of the faculty, most
fully embodied, in his person as in his philosophy, the meaning of
the Chicago School. Dewey's indirect influence upon the Dunes
movement was considerable.

In the 1880s, while an instructor at the University of Michigan,
Dewey began to work out a theology for the religion of democracy, a life's work, which culminated fifty years later with the
publication of his contextualist metaphysics, *Experience and Nature;* his esthetics, *Art as Experience;* and his philosophy of religion, *A Common Faith.* Dewey early identified the democratic
principle with the "radical, living, unity of God."[72] In his neo-
Hegelian view, the democratic movement of the modern age was a
religious movement with a supremely religious function to perform: to overcome the Western dualism of spirit and nature by
"making the spiritual the unity and law of the natural, and the
natural simply the embodied or expressed spiritual."[73] In 1888
Dewey wrote: "The next religious prophet who will have a permanent and real influence on men's lives will be the man who suc-
ceeds in pointing out the religious meaning of democracy, the
ultimate religious value to be found in the normal flow of life

itself."[74] It is apparent that Dewey considered himself to be that prophet.

Like Harper, Dewey conceived of the religion of democracy as the successor to the Hebrew and Christian traditions. But whereas Jesus revealed that the individual can through practical action participate in the divine nature, the democratic movement revealed the social and holistic character of the action that incarnates the divine nature. Dewey believed that, "Democracy thus appears as the means by which the revelation of truth is carried on. It is in democracy, the community of ideas and interest through community of action, that the incarnation of God in man (man, that is to say, as organ of universal truth) becomes a living, present thing, having its ordinary and natural sense. This truth is brought down to life; its segregation removed; it is made a common truth enacted in all departments of action, not in one isolated sphere called religious."

In Christianity, the Incarnation meant that "God is essentially and only the self-revealing, and the revelation is complete only as men come to realize Him." In democracy, the Incarnation means that "there is but one fact—the more complete movement of man to his unity with his fellows through realizing the truth of life."[75]

After he came to Chicago in 1894, Dewey stopped using theological terms, but he never tired of contrasting his vision of the common world (in which all forms of existence share) with dualism, whether the dualism between person and person or between humanity and nature, and whether the dualism appeared in the guise of spirit versus matter, values versus facts, subject versus object, or ideal versus real. Dewey struggled for the rest of his life to give intellectual precision and scope to the notion that in democratic social action the *continuity* of experience and nature is most fully realized.

The crucial terms in Dewey's philosophy were experience and art. For Dewey, the structure of experience is intrinsically transactional or social. It involves an unceasing functional interchange between organism and environment. In this broad sense, experience is a universal trait of all living things. However, the most complex and intense forms of experience are found in works of art; the universal human capacity for art is therefore rooted in biological and social evolution. The distinction that falls to humanity is the peculiar ability, by means of the imagination and symbolization of the work of art, to augment and liberate those tendencies toward unification found in nature's transactions, and consequently to contribute to the unification of human existence within itself and with nature. The successful work of art contains technology and directs it to the enhancement of transactional experience. The supreme work of art is the collective enterprise that aims to clarify and fulfill the unity in variety of the common world. This is democracy.[76]

From the time he first visited Hull House, shortly after it was founded, and began his lifelong friendship with Jane Addams, until the time he left Chicago in 1904, Dewey propounded the belief that democracy represents more than a form of government, that it is indeed, a *new way of life*, a new form of moral and spiritual association, and that its time had come. During this period he emerged as the philosopher of what Lewis Feuer has called the "Back to the People Movement" in American thought. He gave it not only intellectual respectability but an ideology.[77]

Dewey's influence at Chicago was felt throughout the university among those who shared his concern for a new social paradigm in the human and natural sciences—Edward Scribner Ames in psychology of religion, Albion W. Small and Robert E. Park in sociology, George Herbert Mead and James Hayden Tufts in philosophy, Thorstein Veblen and Clarence Ayres in economics. His influence was felt especially in the field of education, and it was by this means that he interacted most directly with leaders of the Dunes movement. The most important vehicle for the dissemination of Dewey's ideas was the University Laboratory school. Scholars from throughout the university came to teach and observe there, among them, Chamberlin, Salisbury, Coulter, and Cowles. Julia Cooley, Emily Taft, and Donald Peattie were graduated from there and Dune Bugs Bertha Parker and Richard Bijogen taught there. Nearby, in the School of Education, two dedicated Dunites served on the faculty: Zonia Baber, who taught geography, and Elliot R. Downing, whose *Naturalist in the Great Lakes Region* is a popular classic of the Dunes tradition. Of all the public school systems in the Chicago region influenced by Dewey's philosophy of the school as a social settlement, or model democratic community, none was more completely molded by his ideas than the Gary school system, and it was in this system that Bess Sheehan and Dorothy Buell, who were to be leaders in the struggle to save the Dunes, taught.[78]

In the same year, 1898, that Cowles was completing his dissertation on plant succession in the Dunes, Dewey delivered a public address, "Evolution and Ethics," at the University of Chicago. In it he formulated his own emerging environmental social ethic. With Harper, Chamberlin and Coulter, he believed that the surest foundation of the spiritual life lay in recognition that the "laws and conditions of righteousness are implicated in the working processes of the universe." The pursuit of social righteousness is essentially ecological. "Man is an organ of the cosmic process in effecting its own progress," he argued, and his progress consists in "making over a part of the environment by relating it more intimately to the environment as a whole; not, once more, in man setting himself against that environment." Dewey then went on to prophesy that *"The unwritten chapter in natural selection is that of the evolution of environments."*[79] Whether Dewey knew about Cowles's researches in the Dunes, or ever visited the Dunes, cannot be ascertained. But many of Dewey's colleagues at the university believed that few landscapes in America had greater potential for disclosing what was empirically involved in the "evolution of environments," or what, imaginatively speaking, man as "an organ of the cosmic process in effecting its own progress" might mean, than the Indiana Dunes.

THE DUNES MOVEMENT

The interchange between the reformers, artists, and scientists in the early period created the Dunes movement: a loose nexus of personal, associational, and geographical relationships, sustained by a living tradition and the shared experience of the Dunes landscape.

One example of the remarkable series of relationships that have characterized the movement over the generations is the Read family. Chicago novelist Opie Read was a good friend of Carl Sandburg, Lorado Taft, and other notables of the Chicago renaissance. His son, Philo B. Read, an artist, was a friend of Jensen and an ardent Dunatic. Philo participated in the Dunes Pageant of 1917 and worked assiduously for the Indiana Dunes State Park in the 1920s. Thirty years later he was a leader of the Save the Dunes Council. Philo's son Herbert P. Read, an architect, took up the fight for the Indiana Dunes National Lakeshore in the 1950s and continues to this day to be one of the Dunes' most outspoken advocates. Charlotte Johnson Read, his wife, became executive director of the Save the Dunes Council in 1976.

As remarkable as such personal relationships may be, the enduring influence of the first Dune Country patriots is even more striking in the history of the voluntary associations concerned for the preservation of the Dunes. In this respect, the impact of the three friends, Allinson, Jensen, and Cowles, representing respectively the interests of reform, art, and science, is particularly noteworthy. Also unusual is the high degree of overlapping membership of the associations. In the period prior to World War I, many of the same people met several times a month but wore the badge of a different group each time.

Allinson, Jensen, and Cowles were leaders in the founding of the Prairie Club in 1911. Jensen had the honor of suggesting the name, and he and Allinson both served as presidents. All three served with Mather on the club's conservation committee. Called by Samuel Harper the "High Priest in Nature's Sanctuary," the Prairie Club was for several decades the midwestern counterpart to the Appalachian Trail Club in the East and the Sierra Club in the West.

Allinson, Jensen, and Cowles, separately or together, were also active in the founding and/or leadership of at least five other organizations concerned for the Dunes. Foremost of these was the Friends of Our Native Landscape. Jensen founded the Friends in 1913 as an organization dedicated to the conservation of the "spiritual power in the American landscape."[80] It quickly grew to include chapters in Illinois, Wisconsin, and Michigan. The membership embraced the elite among the first Dunes apostles and prophets: among them, Addams, Allinson, Cowles, Dudley, Euston, Fuller, Mather, the McIlvaines, Monroe, Pepoon, Perkins, Reed, Richardson, Salisbury, Schantz, Strong, Urbain, and Woodruff. After his break with the Social Democrats in 1917, the Friends was one of the few organizations with which Carl Sandburg remained affiliated.

In the same year, the Wild Flower Preservation Society was organized by Cowles with the help of Zonia Baber, Reuben Strong, and Leon Urbain.[81] A year later, in 1914, the Prairie Club called together representatives of a variety of service organizations in Chicago to found the Conservation Council. With Cowles and Allinson present, the council took as its first project the investigation of the value of Dunes land and the securing of a map of the region desired for preservation.[82] Probably the first association to take an interest in the Dunes was the Chicago Geographic Society, founded in 1898 by Zonia Baber. Salisbury was the first president, and in 1912, when Cowles was president, Jensen and Mather were on the conservation committee. During the early years the organization met twice a month. The first three annual meetings were addressed in turn by Salisbury, Cowles, and Chamberlin.[83]

These associations were active in the drive to preserve the Dunes from the time of their founding through the 1960s. In addition to the Dunes project, they were instrumental in the establishment of the Illinois state park system and the Cook County Forest Preserves which ring Chicago.

When in 1916 the National Dunes Park Association was organized at a mass rally of several thousand persons at Waverly Beach, its first board of directors included, again, Allinson, Jensen, and Cowles, and a delegation from Indiana, among them three Gary pioneers—A. F. Knotts, his niece's husband John O. Bowers, Sr., and Bess Sheehan. Bowers was an attorney, teacher, and one-time candidate for Congress on the Progressive party ticket. Later, he became a strong advocate of the World Court and League of Nations. After the war the National Dunes Park Association remained active as the nucleus for the drive for a state park. But the dream of the association, "A National Park for the Middle West, and all the Middle West for a National Park," never died.

The geographical center for the Dunes movement has been the

neighborhood of Hyde Park, the home of the University of Chicago. Running between Fifty-third Street and the Midway Plaisance at Sixtieth Street on Chicago's South Side, Hyde Park was ideally situated for Dune Bugs because of ready access by railroad lines to the Dune Country. For more than a century, Hyde Park has symbolized Progressive reform in Chicago, and no other community has contributed more leaders to the Dunes movement, or more of its own spirit to the Dunes vision. Mather lived in Hyde Park, so did Reed, Stevens, and most members of the University of Chicago faculty. The Fifty-seventh Street art colony was near the center of the neighborhood; Dudley had his art store on Sixty-third Street. Taft built his Midway Studios on Sixty-first Street. Paul Douglas, who married Lorado Taft's daughter, Emily, while an economist on the University of Chicago faculty, got his start in Independent politics there. The influence of Hyde Park upon the Dunes movement is illustrated by the map that Earl Landgrebe, congressman from Porter County, Indiana, and opponent of the Indiana Dunes National Lakeshore, drew in 1974. It was his idea of "a perfect National Lakeshore monument."[84] Landgrebe's park was the area between Fifty-fifth Street and Sixty-seventh Street on Chicago's South Side.

A virtually unbroken line of personal, associational and geographical relationships bears witness to the enduring influence of the reformers, artists, and scientists who founded the Dunes movement. A similar situation pertains with regard to the books, art, and scientific literature of the Dunes—what is called here the "Dunes tradition."

By 1917 bibliographies of Dunes literature began to appear in libraries in the Midwest, usually divided into such categories as "Magazine and Newspaper Articles," "History," "Natural History and Geology," and "Belles Lettres." George Brennan's 1923 *Wonders of the Dunes* may be regarded as an attempt to integrate this literature into a unified account of the human and natural history of the region. In 1938 University of Chicago librarian Walter Necker prepared a brief bibliographical essay entitled "A Naturalist's Chicagoana—the Dune Country." In it he wrote that, "There may be no Walden and no Slabsides in the Chicago Region, but the praises of our local area have been equally well sung by many authors, although admittedly in smaller editions. Just as the tramping grounds of Thoreau and Burroughs are more charming in light of their essays, so are the Dunes in the light of their literature—and it is an immense literature."[85]

Necker was correct. The Dunes art and literature *is* immense. There are hundreds of items: novels, histories, children's stories, plays, poems, pageants, masques, travelogues, nature-essays, natural history, speeches, newspaper reports, etchings, watercolors, paintings, sculpture, films, songs, and a seemingly endless number of scientific monographs. The most creative period for the production of this corpus was pre-1930; the dominant themes, symbols, stories, and overall mythic structure were well established by that time.

For several generations the tradition of Dunes art and literature has been influential in forming the characteristic attitudes toward the region held by educated persons locally and in other parts of the nation. Its early expressions, especially, have been repeatedly referenced and quoted as authoritative. An otherwise puzzling example of this occurred in the summer of 1970 when, at a public meeting devoted to the presentation of slides of the Indiana Dunes, the photographer, George Svihla, began by reading aloud the story of "The Dream Jewel" from Earl Reed's 1918 *Sketches in Duneland*.[86]

In part this is an intended result. For not only has the Dunes tradition been passed from person to person, and by means of the ongoing activities of the series of voluntary associations devoted to the enjoyment, study and preservation of the Dunes, but also in the 1920s and 1930s annual "Dunes Summer Camps" and "Summer Schools" were sponsored by the Dunes leadership. At these schools instruction of one and two weeks' duration was offered in the science, art, and religion of the Dunes. In 1922, for example, the Dunes Summer Camp, held at the Prairie Club Beach House, was chaired by Bess Sheehan, with Henry Cowles serving as faculty chairman and Richard Lieber and Philo Read helping in other capacities. Enrollment was selective; an applicant "unknown to the committee must state on the Enrollment Blank his or her occupation and give at least one reference, preferably the name of the President of some organization to which applicant belongs."[87] It was for this camp that Louis J. Bailey prepared his paper, "Literature of the Dunes."

In the 1930s, with the opening of the Indiana Dunes State Park and the abandonment of the Beach House, the camp moved to the Dune Acres Clubhouse where it was sponsored by the Friends of Our Native Landscape. On the evening of June 25, 1938, for example, "The School in the Dunes" began with Jens Jensen speaking on "Nature Study and Spiritual Satisfaction." This was followed by the observation of the moon and stars through 11-inch telescopes. As the week proceeded, the students of the school heard George Fuller speak on plants, May Theilgaard Watts on "The Story of Our Native Landscape," and Frank Dudley on how to paint the Dunes. There were early morning bird walks, group singing sessions, and nightly council fires on the beach. As the publicity brochure stated, to come to the school was to experience a very special landscape whose charm was its friendliness and its perpetual change: "Plant, tree, sky, lake, sand—a blow of wind, a cloud, a shift of shadow; a new color; a new world. A new memory." [88]

THREE

Of Time and Eternity

What do we see here in the sand dunes of the white moon alone
  with our thoughts, Bill,
Alone with our dreams, Bill, soft as the women tying scarves
  around their heads dancing,
Alone with a picture and a picture coming one after the other
  of all the dead,
The dead more than all these grains of sand one by one piled
  here in the moon,
Piled against the sky-line taking shapes like the hand of the
  wind wanted,
What do we see here, Bill, outside of what the wise men beat
  their heads on,
Outside of what the poets cry for and the soldiers drive on
  headlong and leave their skulls in the sun for—what, Bill?

CARL SANDBURG,

"*Dunes,*"
from *Chicago Poems,* 1916

The Chicago Glacial Plain

From *An Annotated Flora of the Chicago Region*, by H. S. Pepoon. Drawing by H. S. Pepoon. Courtesy of the Chicago Academy of Sciences

For those in Chicago who sought a new revelation of the God of democracy in the opening years of the twentieth century, the decisive manifestation of the sacred could be no other than social democracy in the making. In the variegated, ever-changing panorama of the Dunes landscape, they found a place that peculiarly exemplified and enriched their vision of the community-forming Power at the heart of existence. Here, in a remnant of wilderness that felt remote, yet was close by, the ultimate truth of the evolutionary adventure of life seemed dramatically apparent. The end of human striving was to achieve a co-creative human community in partnership with a co-creative world. In the twentieth century, the Dunes became a sacred center for adherents of the religion of democracy in the Midwest.

A REVELATION FOR THE PEOPLE

The revelation of the Dunes was intended for all and accessible to all. This, at least, was the conviction of those who beheld it. The ultimate source and meaning of community was meant to be seen by the whole community, by the common people, and most especially, by the poor. Jensen made this clear from the beginning. "There is a soul in each of us," he testified at the Mather hearing, and when it is awakened there will burst upon everyone a realization of the wonder of the Dune Country.[1] The Dunes, he observed on another occasion, are the right medium for a revelation to the people. "They are more poetical, more free and more joyful, something that appeals more to the average human being, and has a greater influence on him than the more severe, colder, and overwhelming forms of landscape."[2] For this reason, he argued, the proposed Dunes park should be the camping ground for the poor man where he could take his family for weekends at little expense and find spiritual and physical renewal.

Francis Strain's 1936 painting *On the Beach* celebrates Jensen's vision of a Dunes park. Under the influence of the Dunes, "average human beings" themselves become "more poetical, more free and more joyful." The working man's family takes center stage in a lyrical frieze including sand, trees, water, bathers, and even the ubiquitous wire trash basket. Father in rolled-up pants and suspenders, matronly out-of-fashion mother with her Sunday-best hat, the string of children and the family dog—march across the Dunes landscape with the dignity and confidence of royalty.

The perception of the Dunes as a sacred center of the religion of democracy was passed on to succeeding generations. They became a fixed point in the swirling changes of the twentieth century—a point in relation to which the adherents of the new social democratic covenant could take their bearings, a place to turn to for inspiration as they went about the task of founding a more just and fraternal world. The failure of this world to rise into being only increased the value of the Dunes. As most of the native landscape in and near Chicago disappeared, and many of the reforms anticipated in the city failed to materialize, the Dunes became even more precious as a reminder of the original vision.

Most visitors to the Dunes in the nineteenth century experienced them as a vast, inhospitable desert, unfit for human habitation. This was certainly the opinion of John Tipton, who first surveyed the region in 1821, concluding that the sand hills that rimmed Lake Michigan could never sustain settlement or ever be of service to the state. English author Harriet Martineau, who passed through the Dunes a few years later, found the country "so extensive, hot, and dazzling, as to realize very fairly one's conceptions of the middle of the Great Desert. . . . It was as good as being in Arabia."[3] The pioneering motion picture companies of Chicago at the turn of the century agreed. In 1912, while Cowles was busy initiating his botany classes into the mysteries of ecology, one company was filming *Lost in the Desert* nearby.

For the Dune Country patriots, however, the "desert" was the archetypal landscape for a journey to the Promised Land. To undergo the ordeal of ploughing ankle-deep through hot, dazzling sand was part of the trial they expected if they were to reach a new world. The biblical image of the Exodus, and its employment as an interpretative screen for the settlement of America, were deeply impressed in their imaginations. Like Cotton Mather three centuries earlier, they saw themselves in the situation of the Israelites after crossing the Red Sea. Old Testament scholar William Rainey Harper found the beginnings of Israel's history not in the Garden of Eden but in tribes "roaming to and from on the great desert parallelogram of Arabia."[4] Jane Addams saw "the beginnings of a secular religion" coming out of the immigrant experience in Chicago—"this fidelity / Of fellow wanderers in a desert place"—and described her own journey to the settlement as a migration from a life of slavery to one of freedom and community.[5]

Bess Sheehan's account of her arrival in the new "Magic City" of Gary suggests the attitude with which many Dunites approached the native landscape. It was, as she later wrote, the "fascination of building a new city on the sands" (in addition to a fiancé who preceded her) that brought the young Bess Vrooman to the frontier town. Gary was located in the middle of the continent where she believed liberty and equality were born. Her arrival by train encapsulated the immigrant experience. On the day she arrived in 1908, she was the only American-born woman passenger who embarked at Gary. The rest "talked excitedly in many strange languages." She saw sand everywhere—hot, glistening, white sand. In spite of the everyday struggle, Bess Sheehan loved Gary and the Dunes. "There was so much of promise for the future."[6]

The association of the Dunes with the Exodus to the Promised Land was feasible because the Dunes were not, in reality, a desert. Without any periods of prolonged drought, they were more like an oasis in a desert. Those who were willing to plough through the sand found to their surprise a lush landscape of shallow ponds, marshes, streams, lakes, and forests, intermixed with bare mountains of sand. Thomas Allinson confessed that for many years he saw only barren wastes from the railroad car windows as he passed the Dunes, but one day he went down into them, and "like Balboa of old, I felt as if a new world had sprung up before me, something of which I had never dreamed."[7]

In 1913 the art critic W. H. de B. Nelson wrote: "A man must be steeped in imagination, both a poet and a dreamer of dreams, to see themes in such God-forsaken tracts as to most people are these desolate, wind-blown tracts on the southern shores of Lake Michigan."[8]

Earl H. Reed, Sr., was a poet and a dreamer of dreams. The creation myth he invented for the Dunes was the story of the transformation of a desert into a paradise. Entitled "The Dream Jewel," the story begins far in the Northland. For untold ages a stone of ineffable radiance lay embedded in the heart of the great glacier that moved over the region of the Great Lakes. It was of such colors as "may have swept into the heavens on the world's first morning, when the Spirit moved over the face of the waters, or have trembled in the halo at the Creation, when cosmos was evolved out of elemental fires."[9] After many centuries the glacier began to melt and crumble, and the stone, released from its prison, fell like a meteor through the waters of the inland sea. The leader of a school of sturgeon, swimming southward, caught the stone and carried it with him.

Finally, the gray horde reached the southern shore where a roaring surf washed a vast, flat desert of sand, bleak and sterile. Here a few Indians eked out a precarious life at the water's edge. When they saw the radiance of the stone lighting up the waves, they rejoiced, for a prophecy was fulfilled. With eagerness they captured the fish that carried the stone, and then, after much deliberation, gave the dream jewel to the loveliest young woman of the tribe. With an invocation to her gods, she hid it in the sands.

The winds heaped the sand into a mound that covered the stone. As the years went by, the dunes were formed. And on the dunes, trees, grasses, and flowers appeared. The forests teemed with game and were filled with melody, and the community of the Native Americans prospered. Ever afterward, the "holy light" of Beauty shone in the many moods of the Dunes landscape: in twilight afterglows, on the waters of the lake, in star reflections on the wet sands, in the leaves of springtime. "The Country of the Dunes had come into being."[10]

Such was the vision of those who led the Dunes movement throughout the century. Here, in what seemed to be a desert, and what, at one time, as the glacier receded northward, no doubt had been a desert, evolved an abundance of life, a community of being, permeated by a sacred Power whose name was Beauty. "The desert shall rejoice and blossom as the rose" (Isaiah 35:1).

The revelation of the Dunes is the landscape coming into being as a growing whole of lake, sky, sand, forests, ponds, wildlife, and human dwelling. It is the landscape seen as an esthetic whole—not in any passive sense, but as Reed suggests, in the process of transformation, like a painting in the process of composition.

In 1930 Virginia Moe said of the peculiar charm of the Dunes, "One may not single out a particular characteristic and label it as the key. It is all elements of lake, beach, dune and hinterland together, and their endless train of moods and aspects under weather conditions, dawns, sunsets, moon rises, seasonal changes and the passing of time. . . . The restless spirit of the dunes is content with neither color nor contour. It is these changes, this constant creating and tearing down which spells the charm of the dune country." That the tearing down is intrinsic to the process of creation Moe is assured, for she observes that always the dunes' "destruction is a creation beautifully tragic."[11] The material destroyed will be ever used again.

In a similar vein, nearly half a century later, Herbert Read wrote: "The significance of the Indiana Dunes is not vested in one or two of its natural features, but in its combination and wide diversity of features. . . . It's the *totality* that is significant, and at the same time, the most difficult aspect to preserve and protect."[12]

The Dunes as an elementary social democracy, a shared life emerging out of various forms of existence interacting in such a way that their competition is turned to the good of the community, is expressed in various ways in the Dunes tradition. One of the most persistent themes is that in the Dunes all existence is in some sense artistically creative. The Dunes are perceived as a landscape composed of a variety of natural forces and "beings" each of which contributes to the total experience of a vivid and growing world. The analogy between art and nature is pursued with a remarkable consistency. Rarely is there an evocation of a single divine artisan molding matter, as a potter molds clay. Rather, the Dunes are conceived either as nature's own creation, or, most commonly, a democratic society engaged in the construction of the collective work of art that is the whole region.

A favorite image for the Dunes is one of monumental architecture, such as a medieval cathedral, a shared enterprise for the good of the whole community by many artists over many generations. Lorado Taft used this image at the public meeting sponsored by the Dunes Pageant Association in 1917. Theodore Jessup used it in a paper read before the Chicago Literary Club on April 10, 1916, a description frequently quoted in the Dunes literature:

If some one should tell us that thirty miles from where we now are was a Cathedral of Dreams, which had been a thousand years in building, which was a marvel of lofty spires and stone carvings, was adorned with beautiful statues, had windows filled with wonderful glass, chapel walls decorated by the masters of the centuries, and that the whole structure revealed throughout the artistic excellence of a nation long practiced in the making of beautiful things—if, taken altogether it was one of the most precious buildings in the world, and then, if we heard that the worshippers had moved away and no one was left to care for it, and that a stone crushing plant had taken an option on it to use its stone as material out of which to build roads, would we not think all the people hereabouts were barbarians if they did not bestir themselves to raise a fund to preserve so precious a work of art?

But within forty miles of us lies the Dune Country of Indiana, which represents the work of one hundred times one thousand, by such artists as the glaciers, water, wind and sun, until you find there a park perfect, beautiful; a land of solitudes; a land of long beaches; a land on whose frail shore strong waves beat at times with a thunderous roar; a land so fair and fine no city park could be made to equal it by the expenditure of countless millions.[13]

Music is also a favorite analogy for expressing the holy beauty of the Dunes. Like architecture, it lends itself to the communication of a symphonic image. The title of Earl Reed's first book of etchings, *Voices of the Dunes*, suggests a choir. One of the poems he included was by Warren Cheney:

These woods are never silent. In the hush
    Of the high places, solemnly there goes
In endless undertone the stately rush
    Of music—windy melody that grows
And ebbs and changes in uncertain time,
    As if some pensive god tried here apart

> Vague snatches of the harmonies divine
> Before he played them on the human heart.[14]

The most popular musical image in the Dunes tradition is "singing sands." When feet are scuffed or a stick is dragged through a small strip of sand parallel to the water's edge, the beach sometimes strikes up a clear ringing note. The members of the Prairie Club quickly picked up on the experience. "There's a long, long trail a-winding," they sang on their pilgrimages, "Into the land of the dunes / Where the waters gaily sparkle / And from singing sands come tunes."[15] Over time, singing sands became a popular symbol for the Dunes as a whole, and the object of scientific curiosity as well. The *Prairie Club Bulletin* described the phenomenon: "In the glare of sunlight, on a Summer's day, as one walks above the water line along the beach of Old Lake Michigan, there arises from beneath one's feet a curious sound or melody. This is from Nature's Phonograph. For countless years the waves have thundered upon the beach and the ripples have murmured along it. Their music is recorded in the sands. When the true nature lover passes along with ear attuned and soul responsive, from under his feet, from the singing sands, this magic harmony arises."[16]

One essay written in the 1930s describes the Dunes as the "Aeolian sands, ground out under the glaciers, carrying the song of the morning of the world."[17] Here, for "the price of a ten-cent ticket" on the South Shore Railroad, in an intimate paradise, where insects, dragonflies, fireflies, willows, grasses, herons, water snakes, and humans all find sanctuary, may be heard the songs of nature together with the songs of the pageant of human history—the dancing feet of Indian girls, the song of the French fur traders, the march of the feet of the soldiers of the American revolution. The Dunes are alive with the rhythms of the shared adventure of life.

Some called the Dunes the "Garden of the Gods." Others heard voices there that seemed to say, "You do not trespass, you are welcome . . . for this is Utopia."[18] David Sander, in one of his songs, named them "Beulah Land." And as he frequently explained to the audiences at his Saturday's Child Coffee House in Porter, Indiana, during the 1960s: "Beulah Land represents the place you go when you die—a land of milk and honey—and when I moved to the

Dunes nineteen years ago I thought I was indeed moving into that land."[19]

All in all, it seemed the perfect place. A claim repeatedly encountered in the Dunes literature is that they are superlative—the "finest," "most perfect," "most beautiful." Mather's own reference in his report to Secretary of the Interior Lane to these sand dunes as the "finest in the world" is typical.

But the Dunes were not Eden. Seldom, except in sentimental poetry, is there the suggestion in the Dunes tradition that the Dunes are free of struggle or even, paradoxically, tragedy. Again, like the biblical Promised Land, the Dunes are a paradise regained with all the difference of human history and awareness, a wasteland in the process of transformation—a sacred center of redemption as well as creation.

To Earl Reed, the Dunes are home to outcasts and derelicts, as well as beautiful young women and strong warriors. With a sympathy "divinely human," as one critic described it, and an eye for the melancholy, he fills his books with tales of the antagonisms and eccentricities of the lonely dwellers in the Dune country.[20] The "holy light" of the Dunes penetrates the pathos of life as well as its grandeur and promise. The beauty revealed in the Dunes, he writes, "will help us through the twilight."[21] It is a redemptive community-forming Power at work in the midst of struggle and defeat. Like Catfish John who says that Holy Zeke is "part of them that's round us and we ought to get along with him," and Bill Saunders and Old Sipes who sing far into the night "Comrades, comrades, ever since we was boys,—Sharing each other's sorrows, sharing each other's joys,"[22] the Dunes disclose a mutuality born of the acceptance of human differences and limitations. Here the inevitable conflicts and disappointments in existence, which customarily drive persons as well as humanity and nature apart, instead mysteriously bring them together.

Reed would have agreed with Florence Crim's judgment that in the Dunes "Human derelicts they may be, many of them but 'kind of dog-gone Christians' after all."[23] Indeed, according to Crim, the Dune folk, who were content to live in rude huts built of wreckage and driftwood, and eke out a meager existence with their fishnets, game traps, and scanty fruits from the swamps and hills, displayed a more spiritual attitude toward life than their city neighbors. They measured time by the changing seasons, not by human accomplishments, and beneath their uncouth exteriors were unselfish hearts capable of frankness and sincerity in friendship, and profound philosophy.

To the Dune Country patriots, the Dunes were a symbol of America as a home for the homeless, a refuge for the lost and oppressed, where even the criminal could receive a new chance. As if to confirm this symbolism, a Chicago attorney maintained a "House of Refuge" on the Dunes coastline in the early part of the century, a small cabin kept ready with provisions for any lost sailor or traveler who chanced to come along. David Sander remembers his father, a Hyde Park wood engraver, telling him that the Dunes were always a place attractive to people who did not fit. For several generations the Dunes functioned as a de facto public space, or commons, for whomever wished to use them or live there. Although privately owned, mostly by large companies, they were left unguarded. They attracted an odd assortment of squatters and outcasts—those too poor to make it elsewhere, and those who had reason to avoid the law.

The idea of the Dunes as a sanctuary for the persecuted was grounded in nineteenth-century history. Native Americans fled to the wilderness north of the Kankakee River, first after the defeat of Tecumseh in 1811 and then as survivors of the "Trail of Death" in 1835. At the turn of the century, the Pokagon tribe still clung precariously to life in a small reservation on the edge of the Dunes in southwestern Michigan. An underground railway ran fugitive slaves to the Dunes during the Civil War. From here they were taken by boats to Canada. Similarly, as the wild animals of the Midwest were hunted and exterminated, many found for a time refuge in the Dunes. As late as 1906, wolves were sighted in the sand hills, and bald eagles nested there.

Perhaps most important of all, the Dune Country patriots found the Dunes a refuge for themselves. In contrast to the city with its "poisonous smoke, its pomp and vanity, its grasping worldliness," the Dunes offered a precious and pure freedom and an opportunity to rediscover their own best selves. In the Dunes they discovered a "happiness that brings with it forgetfulness of selfish and self-absorbed commercialism."[24] After wandering together among the sand hills for a day or a weekend, the Dune Bugs found they had new strength to board the train for return to their work. They desired this experience for everyone. If they could find renewal here, others might also, and if so, the whole society might be transformed.

Yet, these experiences were not easy to share. Although the Dunes revelation was intended for the salvation of the average human being, and often did "rouse the wonderment of common folks,"[25] not everyone was ready to receive it. Reed, whose sympathies were broad, and who devoted his life to communicating the message of the Dunes to the public, yet felt that the deepest secrets of the Spirit of the Dunes were "kept for those who understand." The revelation of the Dunes was for the dreamer and the poet *in* everyman, in Jensen's view, for his soul. A certain subjective attitude, a faith or love, was prerequisite to experiencing the reality that was there. "If we take beautiful minds and beautiful hearts into the dune country," Reed wrote, "we will find only beauty in it; and if we have not the love of beauty, we walk in darkness."[26]

THE SYMBOLISM OF THE CENTER

Deeply rooted in human nature is the desire to be at the heart of the real, at the Center of the World.

Every religion has its sacred centers—places where the sacred is perceived to be manifest in its totality and with peculiar power. In the Hebrew Bible, for example, Mt. Zion, although in fact a low and undistinguished mound, is nonetheless described as such a sacred space. It is called the tallest mountain in the world, the place Yahweh chose for his dwelling place, the place of battle where the enemies of the Lord will be defeated. And it is declared to be at the center of the world. Similarly, for Christians, Golgotha, the site of the crucifixion of Jesus, and by ancient accounts the site also of the birth and death of Adam, is a sacred center.[27]

Although not customarily recognized as such, for adherents of American civil religion, Capitol Hill and its adjoining shrines and parkways also function as the center of the world. Charles Ferguson, looking out from his window one night in 1900, saw the dome

of the Capitol building "white and magnificent in the moonlight
. . . transfigured . . . like a symbol of the new age and the America
that is in the making. Here is modernity, the age of electricity—
and mystery. Here is the *type* of the longing of the people, the
awe of science, the passion for the eternal, the cosmic fear, the
victorious faith, the contradictions of life, the problems, the poverty, the tragic perplexity, the cry in the night; here steel-clad
battleships and sudden war, the knight-errantry of the Republic,
immense expansion and contraction, the old ethnic hate, the efface-
ment of boundaries, world-wide equality, fraternity, ecumenic
democracy. . . ."[28] Here were concentrated, in other words, the
life and death struggles of the religion of democracy.

The desire for a sacred center is especially acute when a community is intent upon the founding of a new society. It needs to
have a fixed point of orientation. The history of the world's peoples
testifies to the universal need for such a sacred center and the universal methods by which that need is satisfied. Often a sign is given
which establishes a place as sacred. Then the work of building a
new society may commence. At other times, the community taking possession of a territory is required to construct the sacred
center by elaborate rituals of consecration. In any event, no community is free to choose randomly the sacred site. It must be
sought. It must be in some way *revealed*.

All sacred centers, once discovered, share certain features.

A sacred center is saturated with sacred Power. All the attributes
of the numinous experience, the emotions associated with an en-
counter with the Other, are focused there. It is a place of awe,
wonder, mystery, majesty. Simultaneously, it is a place of comfort,
solace, quiet, intimacy. To be at the sacred center is to be in touch
with fullness of being. It is to experience the potency and immen-
sity of the Unknown, and to be unified and healed, to be at ease
in paradise. As long as the community is in contact with the center,
its life has purpose and significance; its existence is fully human.
In contrast, outside the center everything seems ordinary, homogeneous, profane.

To approach the sacred center is to participate in a paradox. On
the one hand, the center is remote and the way is hard to find. To
journey there can be arduous, even perilous. Nonetheless, the diffi-

culty of obtaining entry to the center is worth the labor and risk, for arrival at the center is a matter of merit, and only a few are so initiated. On the other hand, the road to the center is plain and open. The center is close by and it is available to everyone. In either case, going to the sacred center is a creative experience, a source of joy and renewal.

Every sacred center is consecrated by a manifestation of the sacred in some part of the natural order. A tree, a stone, a person, a book, a moral commandment—some aspect of the ordinary world becomes the vehicle for a decisive revelation of the sacred. When this occurs, the object, person, or event functions as a symbol of reality beyond itself. It remains what it is as a part of the natural order, but at the same time, it points to and shares in an underlying structure of the world. In this way, each manifestation of the sacred serves as a paradigm of the nature of the universe. A tree, for example, when experienced as a manifestation of the sacred, discloses the world as a living totality, forever regenerating itself. The sky reveals the infinite distance, the transcendence of the truly real. Every sacred center is built around a particular symbolic apprehension of the absolute.

A sacred center may be identified by the presence of a certain structure of spatial symbolism. This symbolism has two aspects. In the first place, a sacred center is located at the center of the world conceived of as a cosmos. This means the center is perceived as a microcosm, a miniature reproduction of the universe, what Mircea Eliade calls an *imago mundi*. Within the microcosm, often symbolized by a circle, a cross, or a square, lies the space of unity and harmony. Beyond the microcosm lies the uninhabited territory, the abode of chaos.

Frequently, sacred centers appear in the form of a series of world images repeated on larger and larger scales. Thus the sanctuary of the Temple in Jerusalem represented a microcosm of the cosmos, as did the city of Jerusalem in which it stood, and the entire country of Palestine, which surrounded it, as well. Whatever the extent of the territory—sanctuary, city, country—the cosmos represented is perfect. Just as the *imago mundi* may be repeated in a series of larger and larger concentric circles, so there may also be a multiplicity of sacred centers for any one microcosm. When this is the case, such a series will present parallel manifestations of sacred Power. For example, each of the cosmic mountains of ancient Palestine was the dwelling place of Yahweh, yet each such center was still *the* center of the world! As Eliade explains, the symbolism of the center is a matter not of scientific geometry, but of mythic geography.

In the second place, a sacred center is located at the point at which an invisible *axis* intersects the three cosmic levels of earth, heaven, and underworld. Eliade calls such an axis the *axis mundi*. Around this axis lies the microcosm. The axis appears therefore as the fixed point at the center of the world, or as some religions claim, at the "navel of the earth." Here the sacred has effected a breakthrough. An opening has been made, both upward from the world of the living to the divine world, the world of the gods, and downward from the world of the living to the underworld, the world of the dead. As a result, communication between these three realms is possible. Often this takes the form of vertical movement. Thus, to "ascend" the *axis mundi* means to enter the pure realm of heaven and immortality. To descend the *axis mundi* means to enter the lower regions of formlessness and latency, of all that precedes and follows life.

Several archetypal symbols are associated with the *axis mundi*. The most common is a mountain, a tree, or a column. Any one or combination of these may mark a passage among the three planes of existence. For example, frequently the summit of a mountain is considered the point of intersection with the divine world. Here the experience of the sacred is most intense and tangible. Here life is lived most fully. To emphasize this, such a mountain top is often called the "highest point on earth." One widely diffused symbol of the sacred center is a mountain rising from a body of water or surrounded by a desert. In Taoism, for example, a mountain in the midst of the sea symbolized the Isles of the Blessed, at once a world apart and the perfect place.

But the need of a community to orient itself to the source of absolute reality is a need to structure its temporal as well as its spatial relationships. It is not surprising, therefore, that when human beings take up a position at a sacred center, they conceive themselves standing at the place where the world began and where its history and future are most fully represented.

It is at the sacred center that the act of creation occurred in the primordial time before the present race of human beings appeared on the earth. This was the strong time, the time as it was in the beginning, when, as Eliade says, everything which is now of importance came, as it were, fresh from the creator's hands. And here the founding act of creation continues to recur, either of its own accord, or by ritual reenactment, or both.

From the standpoint of the sacred center, the universe is conceived of as a living unity. Time and space are homologous, and both the spatial and temporal orders of existence are manifest in the structure of the center itself. Thus, just as the Temple at Jerusalem was an *imago mundi*, or microcosm of cosmic space, it was also a microcosm of cosmic time. It contained in one integrated symbolism the four points of the compass and the twelve months of the year. In general, the sanctuary that stands at the center of the world reproduces in miniature whatever is held to be the duration of sacred time. It reproduces the universe in its totality.

The pilgrimages to the sacred center engaged in by the community are for the purpose of reentering the zone of the sacred and recontacting the generative Power of existence. By ritually reenacting the cosmogonic myth, the myth of creation, the community is projected back into the time of beginnings and is spiritually reborn. New members are initiated into the community by means of symbolic death and rebirth in conformity with the pattern of the primordial act of creation. They die to their past and are recreated as new persons with a new world and a new identity. In the same way, the society's own founding as a collectivity is renewed. It is enabled to begin again, as the world itself perpetually begins again at the ever-replenished center of fertility and life.

Because the sacred center is the place of fullness of being and of never-diminishing creativity, the community inevitably seeks to live in as close conformity to it as possible. When it builds its dwellings and its towns, for example, it does so in accord with the divine plan and action that established the cosmos itself. The temple, as each home, becomes a replica of the gods' revelatory work, an *imitatio dei.* Everything about the society—its art, its ethics, its styles of life—tends to be congruent with the structure of sacred creativity decisively manifested at the center.

The center also becomes a repository of the sacred history of the people. A narrative tradition emerges that is closely identified with the history of the center and tells the story of crucial persons and events in the community's collective struggle for fulfillment. Through the sacred story, the center contains an ability to prophesy the nature and outcome of the conflicts that will ensue within the society and between the society and its enemies. It is at the center that the struggle between the powers of good and evil continues to be symbolically manifest, and where the final end of that contest will be realized. The believer identifies with the sacred story and sees him- or herself in its victims and heroes. The story provides the believer with a sense of divine destiny, a sense of being chosen. Its narrative is the framework in terms of which the believer's actions in the profane world attain significance.

Obviously, any particular sacred center, once established, occupies a peculiarly cherished position a society will go to any length to defend. The community's continued existence as a community is tied to the continued existence of the center and to the continued existence of other centers like it. No wonder that for those who leave the center and wander afield to new lands and adventures, there is ever a feeling of nostalgia, a feeling that leads many to return time and again in quest of the primal source of their being.

THREE ARTISTS OF THE DUNES

The artists Earl H. Reed, Sr., Frank V. Dudley, and Emil Armin perceived the Dunes as a sacred center. They saw there a vision of the world as an evolving whole unified by reciprocal relationships among all forms of existence. They also shared the conviction that this was a landscape whose revelation was meant to be received by ordinary people. Each emphasized a distinctive aspect of the vision. In Reed's work the *mystery* of the creative Power manifest in the Dunes is predominant. In Dudley's work the *luminous quality* of the vision is communicated. And in Armin's work the *transcending of suffering* in a higher synthesis is most apparent.

Earl Reed felt deeply the drama of existence revealed in the Dune Country. His etchings portray a place pregnant with the creative emergence of life out of non-life. Wind, water, sand, sun yield sparse waving grasses, flights of birds, gaunt sky-thrusting trees, and houses hugging the sand hills as if they had roots down into the earth itself. Through his eyes the viewer is persuaded to see a dynamic, cyclic unification of existence into a single composition and destiny.

By the delicate use of the etcher's art, Reed elaborates the story he told in "The Dream Jewel." The bleakness and desolation of the Dunes are continuously redeemed by a creative Power inherent in nature, which reconciles random and opposing forces. As Lena McCauley, fellow Dunite and Chicago art critic, noted, in Reed's pictures the winds do not blow, but *sweep* across the world. The waves writhe on the beach "as if seeking to drown the whole world and to sink it in the depths of the inland sea." The hills of singing sands rise in peaks like rugged mountains, and are surmounted by ancient pines.[29] Everything is exaggerated because everything is ultimately alive and moving and growing in concert. The titles of Reed's etchings suggest the excitement of the shared adventure of life: *The Heralds of the Storm, The Troopers of the Sky, The Spirit Upon the Face of the Waters.*

This is true whether Reed is drawing the exposed shorelines or the secluded ponds behind the dunes—two of his favorite scenes. In both he is intensely aware of the Other that involves the viewer in its orbit of influence, yet is somehow remote and untouchable. In *The Voices of the Dunes*, it is the height of the numinous experience—the glorious, realized quality of the sacred, the full promise of tomorrow, which is celebrated. In *The Moon in the Marsh*, it is the depth of the numinous—the ripe fecundity of a primordial place that, like the rhythms of the moon, ever changes yet ever remains the same, which is sounded. Reed finds the approaching storm as apt a metaphor as the Dream Jewel for the elemental Power that is perpetually transforming the shifting sands.

But Reed would be misunderstood if his vision of the divine were characterized as limited to the image of an approaching storm or to any other metaphor drawn from the inorganic universe. He was sensitive to the gentle, almost whimsical, quality of sacredness revealed in the Dunes—equally mysterious but not as remote. One unusual etching, *A Vision of Galilee*, shows a glowing white figure standing alone on the shore of the Dunes. Here the super-imposition of a sacred center of Christianity upon the sacred center of the Dunes suggests the lonely presence of divine love. More typical is Reed's use of small delicate creatures—butterflies, rabbits, turtles—set within a dunes scene to suggest a symbolic equation be-tween the "Spirit of the dunes" and the Holy Spirit of Christian tradition.

In Lena McCauley's estimate, "There are many who can sketch the visible, and but few that can convey the force of the unseen." Earl Reed was one of the few. In all of his Dunes etchings, how-ever true their rendering of the world as we ordinarily know it, the "invisible yet dominates, the things never to be seen but ever there."[30]

Frank Dudley was almost obsessed with the revelation of the Dunes. Like Reed, he experienced their mystery, but what was most important for him was what the Dunes showed forth. He found the Dunes "irresistible," and sought to "create canvases great enough to be worthy to carry the message of the spirit of the dunes to the world." The fact that, as he worded it, the Dunes were "pos-sibly too new a subject—a type of landscape almost unknown and perhaps without seeing, hard to understand," only made his task more urgent.[31] In his creed written in 1936, he declared: "I believe the artist through his study and close contact with the landscape, is enabled to see more and feel more the joyous messages of nature, and that his real mission in life should be to interpret and reveal these truths that all may see and experience the same emotional reactions as does the artist himself."[32]

Dudley took his creed seriously. In addition to his canvases, he repeatedly performed in public, seeking to bring the audience into the orbit of his own subjective experience. As he painted a picture of the Dunes, his wife sang songs to evoke the proper mood. In 1933 he created a life-size working model of a dunes blowout for the Chicago World's Fair, so that thousands of Americans could experience them vicariously. More than any other artist, Dudley gave the public its permanent image of the Dunes.

It is indicative of Dudley's concern for what the Dunes revealed that he painted the *View from Mount Tom* repeatedly, and that his largest canvas is devoted to this scene. There was no point in the sacred center with greater access to divine Power than the top of the highest sand dune, where all of Duneland stretched out below and the sun shone strong above.

In this scene the two basic techniques of Dudley's work are evident. The first is his use of light. The second is his way of typifying what is literally present. The purpose of both is to grasp as directly as possible the essence of what he perceives to be the Dunes revelation and make it accessible to everyone.

In all of Dudley's paintings, the light in the picture is noticed first. To walk into a room of Dudley paintings is to be surrounded with light: mostly sunlight, but twilight and moonlight as well. It is to *be* in the Dunes where *Sun and Shadows Meet.* Dudley's paintings recreate the vivid experience of a Dunes day. Even his storm and night scenes are bright. Describing the pictures as much as the fact, the critic for the *Chicago Tribune* wrote on the occasion of Dudley's first exhibit of Dunes paintings in 1918: "When the blue of Lake Michigan shows bluer in the sun, when the winds blow freer and the dome of the sky is flecked with smokeless clouds—there lie the dunes." [33]

The use of light in Dudley's pictures suggests a permanent sacredness permeating the Dunes landscape. Each picture has the effect of capturing an eternal moment. In *View From Mount Tom*, it is the sparkling quality of light, the atmosphere of radiant energy, the rays of sunlight concentrated upon the crown of the dune. There is no hint that the dunescape itself is frozen, that it is not alive and in the process of change. Indeed, everything about Dudley's style, his quick spontaneous brush strokes, his blending and contrasting colors and masses, suggests a reality in process. Yet the picture has found it, stopped it, so that the viewer may see it.

It is through his use of composition that Dudley communicates a feeling for the communal dimension of the Dunes revelation. For Reed the co-creativity of the Dunes is mystically apprehended, and threatens at times to disappear altogether into the divine life; for Dudley co-creativity is experienced through a fundamental sense of belonging in which artist, viewer, and landscape actively participate. This impression is derived, in part, from Dudley's habit of gently idealizing his subject matter. In real life the view from Mount Tom is not quite as grand, and the dunes in the distance are not quite as high, and the scene is not quite as panoramic as Dudley makes it. The impression is also derived from Dudley's decorative simplification, his omission of nonessentials and his repetition of large and simple masses of color, so that relationships are tight and transparent. But most important, the impression is due to the fact that the experience he seeks to reproduce is the experience of the people. The titles Dudley gave his paintings suggest this. He related them to ordinary human feelings about the landscape—*The Magic Hour* for a sunset, *Guardians of the Dunes* for tall pines. There is a faintly posterlike quality to his paintings. The visual perspective is that of the typical viewer and the scene itself is a typical scene. For example, the view from a dune top is one of a half-dozen distinct locales everyone who visits the Dunes quickly comes to recognize. Others, to which Dudley returned, include the beach, moving dunes, blowouts, woodlands, and swamps. Dudley painted these scenes "person-size" as it were. In *View from Mount Tom*, the picture is waiting for someone to walk into it, to climb to the top of the dune. The observer is already there, looking at the scene. He or she belongs.

J. Z. Jacobson in his book *Thirty-five Saints and Emil Armin* called Armin an "unresting pilgrim . . . in search of a spiritual passage to a spiritual India," a "peasant-dreamer" who was an insatiable adventurer.[34] Armin arrived in Chicago in 1905 as a poor Jewish immigrant. Out of his own painful family history, he carried to the land of his adoption an appreciation for the faith of the Jewish people and an identification with the suffering of all people. He was intensely religious, although not conventionally so, and he channeled his religious impulse into his art. He later wrote: "Art is slow in developing. Its roots are always religious. I do not mean creeds. Independent souls are entitled to worship unknown gods."[35]

One unknown god was the God of democracy in America, where he came to live without fear and create without restraint. He embraced America, and especially Chicago, painting the city and its environs with jubilation. Historical continuity was important to Armin, and Jewish themes and symbols recur in his work. But his greatest enthusiasm was reserved for the creativity of the

age of electricity, his own age, and the twentieth-century "peasants" who were its agents, and who ought to be its chief benefactors. In one watercolor, he placed a kiosk, surrounded by people
and resembling a temple, at street level in the center of a fanciful
Chicago skyline. In another he drew the figure of Uncle Sam in
Solomon's Temple. The biblical quest for community was—could
be—answered *here!*

Probably as early as 1914, Armin began making trips to the
Dunes. After 1930, when he met his future wife, Hilda Rose Dia-
mond, a social worker for the Jewish Family and Community Service, he spent almost every weekend and most of the summers at her
cottage outside Chesterton, and later, at their cottage on the beach
in the Central Dunes. Armin loved to walk in the dunes with his
friends. Climbing Mount Tom was always a favorite. Over the years
devotion to the Dunes and devotion to his friends grew hand in hand.
Armin took the same passion to the Dunes as to the desert landscape
and Native American culture of Santa Fe and Taos, but his love
for the Dunes was more enduring. In later life he drew pictures of
the Dunes in profusion—watercolors, oils, woodcuts, silk screen
prints—and sold them, usually for a small sum, at the annual Fifty-
seventh Street Art Fair in Hyde Park. In these works the Dunes
were portrayed as a spiritual landscape, a place where everything
that seemed ordinary to others was extraordinary.

Armin painted *Crescendo* in the early 1920s. It is a scene at
Waverly Beach. Dune Creek is in the foreground, Lake Michigan
to the left with Michigan City marked by a stream of smoke in the
distance. At the upper right is Mount Tom. Armin portrays the
Dunes as forming the sides of a great triangle whose base is at the
feet of the spectator. Everything zigzags upward toward the hidden summit of Mount Tom. The creek courses upward as though
seeking its source in the sandhills. The singing ripples of sand point
forward. The groups of marionette peasant-like figures lead the eye
toward the mountain. The houses, boats, trees, and smoke are so
placed as to reinforce the upward, converging motion.

Triangles are the recurring geometric shapes in Armin's paintings. He acknowledged that they were a symbol of life for him, a
metaphor for the spiritual quest upward from the earth toward the

heavens. In *Crescendo* Armin used the architecture of interlocking triangles and rhythmic angular lines to communicate his naive perception of the Dunes as a sacred center toward which all forms of existence move. The elements in the scene are given equal weight, none higher or grander than any other, all incorporated in the same forward movement of life climbing toward the synthesis of an organic unity. In the foreground, where the viewer stands, the tension is greatest. The figures are bent forward, trudging through the sand. Near the dunes, however, the lines become curved. One group of figures seems running for joy. There is the comic note of an automobile, itself a modern symbol of transcendence, the vehicle that carried them to the Dunes. Higher in the sands hills is the resting point, the ultimate symbiosis.

It is as if Armin is saying that in the Dunes one sees that beyond the ceaseless travail of everyday experience, all existence flows together toward the same end. Human creativity is rooted in an indestructible rhythm of nature that redeems the pain and contradictions of the world.

WHERE ALL THINGS MEET

A seventy-five-mile crescent of beach and sand hills greeted the first European explorers to the southwestern coast of Lake Michigan. Beginning within the present limits of Evanston, Illinois, the sand belt ran south and east, widened to a depth of over two miles at the Chicago River, which originally ran into the lake, and then gradually broadened again to the south where it entered the region of high dunes in the present state of Indiana. Behind the wave-lapped beach lay the drainage basin of glacial Lake Chicago. Except for a series of slightly higher crescents of sand surmounted by black oak forest, ancient beach lines deposited in circles as the great finger of ice that created Lake Michigan melted millennia ago, the plain was flat. Its prairies and marshes teemed with birds and wildflowers. Stands of northern white pine intermixed with hawthorn and cottonwood, and buffalo, bear, and lynx roamed the sand ridges. At the outermost edge of the plain, transcribing a great half-circle around the drainage basin, and marking the farthest penetration of the last ice age into Illinois and Indiana, was the highest and oldest ridgeline, the Valparaiso Moraine.[36]

By the late nineteenth century, a fast-growing industrial civilization had obliterated most of the lakeshore and begun to fill the Chicago glacial plain. In 1870 author and explorer John Dean Caton reminisced: "There are some who hear me now, who remember the lake beach, with its conical sand-hills covered over by the evergreen juniper, whose fragrance loaded with a rich aroma the soft breeze as it quietly crept in from the rippling waters of the lake."[37] By the turn of the century, the native coastline was reduced to the alluvial plain of the Little Calumet River in northern Indiana and remnants of sand dunes and marshland on the far South Side of Chicago. With the founding of Gary in 1906, of the original beach, only the twenty-five miles running east of Gary to Michigan City remained relatively intact.

The remnant that remained in Indiana was one of the most dramatic and interesting portions of the native landscape. In this region the prevailing northwesterly winds and lake currents had been at work piling the lake shore sands into an irregular line of high dunes for centuries. When the Chicago reformers, artists, and scientists discovered them, the shore dunes were larger and more active than those that remain today. They were climaxed, as they still are, by lofty Mount Tom, rising 192 feet above the lake, but there were other dunes of similar height. While many of the shore dunes, like Mount Tom, were more or less stationary, and covered with trees to their summits, others were great masses of constantly moving sand advancing sometimes as much as sixty feet per year on the low-lying interior.

Behind the shore dunes lay the forested peaks and ridges of the more well-established dunes, formed on the earlier beaches of Lake Michigan. The farther from the lake, the older the dunes. Between these waves of sand hills was a series of valleys, containing everything from small hidden ponds to elongated sloughs, rivers, lakes, marshlands, and land-locked fens and bogs. Within a width of a mile and a half, the character of the Dunes region ranged from the lake and storm beach, to the stark landscape of active dunes, to stable sandhills covered with vegetation, and finally to shallow lakes and marshy sinks on the outer perimeter.

The Dunes were home to a diverse, often rare, flora and fauna. Several factors were responsible for this. One was the variety of topography in the Dunes region, which offered a corresponding variety of habitat. Another was that the Dunes lie on the boundaries of two climatic variables. Due principally to rainfall patterns, northern Indiana is on the east-west boundary between deciduous forest and prairie; due to temperature patterns, it is on the north-south boundary between cool- and warm-climate plant and animal species. A third factor was that the region underwent constant formation since the retreat of the Wisconsin Glacier. In the Dunes there were unusual outliers of northern species, such as tamarack, jack pine, and arctic bearberry, remnants from the colder climate after the last glaciation. There were also many southeastern species, such as the tulip tree, black gum, and sassafras, which had advanced during the subsequent warming period. The post-glacial, hot-dry period had brought western prairie and meadow vegetation types such as certain grasses, cactus, and many wildflowers. Later, eastern woodland plants, such as sugar maple, beech, and trillium, had penetrated the moister, protected areas of the Dunes. University of Chicago botanist and geologist Jerry Olson concluded in 1951: "Thus the dunes landscape constitutes a microcosm in which elements of many regions and events are juxtaposed."[38]

The perception of the Dunes as a sacred center was grounded in this natural diversity and carried with it a rich geographical symbolism. Each part of the region developed over time a special meaning, in itself and in relation to the rest of the landscape—both extinct and extant. The mythic geography of the Dunes confirmed and expanded the basic experience of the place as a manifestation of the community-forming Power at the heart of existence.

No person better articulated the perception of the Dunes as the image and axis of the world than A. F. Knotts. Since boyhood, he had hiked over the Dunes, searching out historical artifacts, and taking an especially keen interest in their geography. He became, in the early years of the Dunes movement, along with George Brennan, one of the principal bearers of the legendary wisdom of the tribe. The vision he expounded as president of the National Dunes Park Association was a synthesis of his own perceptions with those of the reformers, artists, and scientists whom he met—

an amalgamation of fact and imaginative commentary. To hear Knotts talk about the Dunes, wrote one contemporary, "is like walking in a new, old world."[39]

When Knotts climbed to the top of Mount Tom, as he frequently did on his excursions into the Dunes, he perceived himself standing in the middle of the cosmos. "Here is the center, all things considered," he declared in 1916, "of the North American continent. *Here the north, south, east and west meet geologically, botanically, zoologically, historically, socially, industrially, commercially.*"[40] For Knotts, the Dunes were a microcosm of Populism, the place where the sacred history of participatory democracy was symbolically represented in the landscape.

Looking first at the horizon that encircled him, Knotts began by facing north. There he beheld the inspiring sight of the "great lake," sometimes "lazily lapping the white sands . . . inviting one to wade or paddle the canoe," sometimes tossing high the white caps and rolling out over the beach." In the distance he saw steamers "carrying their merry crowds of people, pursuing business or seeking pleasure, possibly laden with grain from the golden fields or . . . finished products of the busy mills and factories" nearby. Next facing west, he saw on the horizon the "great Chicago that says 'I Will,' and does," and nearer, the Calumet region, "all the happiest, busiest, most vigorous and most determined, and soon to be, the largest family on earth." Then, turning south and east, his eyes settled upon the series of hills at the horizon's edge, the Valparaiso Moraine, so named "because the city of Valparaiso (vale of Paradise) is situated on its crest, fifteen miles south of the dunes." Along the top of the moraine once ran the Sauk Trail, the "great east and west highway of the red men, and now the Lincoln highway of the white man."[41]

Then, looking at the more proximate landscape, Knotts again rotated in a circle around the axis of the world. Immediately before him to the north, at the foot of Mount Tom, was LaSalle's reputed camping site of 1680, and the presumed spot where the loving companions of Father Marquette helped him ashore to rest. To the west, just beyond Dune Creek, was the greatest of the moving dunes, close to where the "Indians came in their canoes from the great lakes and beyond to the head of the lake and there met the

Indians from the east, south and west for a thousand miles or more at the old council grove." To the southwest was the great Dunes Tamarack Swamp where there could be found the "greatest variety of rare trees, shrubs, ferns, mosses, lichens, orchids, grasses and flowers and the densest and most impenetrable forest for many hundreds of miles around." And finally, to the east, was the place where "immortal" Tom Bradley, "leader by divine right of the first revolutionary army west of the Alleghenies," performed his daring exploits. In Knotts's opinion, Mount Tom was a fit monument to Bradley's patriotism. Knotts concluded his tour of the sacred center by pointing out that he stood on a little spot of nature unchanged by the hand of man, and here "we propose to establish and preserve a national park *for all mankind.*"[42]

Knotts saw in 1916 what most of his fellow members in the Dunes movement saw whenever they climbed to the top of their sacred hills, and what, in various ways, the Dunes movement continued to see as the reality of the place down to the 1970s. In the Dunes tradition there is a recurring litany of references to the perception that the Dunes are located at the epicenter of the nation, and constitute a microcosm of the continent. They are the point where the four points of the compass converge. The implication is that in their natural and historical diversity, the Dunes show how all forms of existence have the capacity to live together in co-creative harmony.

This "fact" was confirmed by experts on each realm of being. Each authority added his distinct voice to the litany.

In this "vast garden of mid-America," began landscape architect Jensen, with characteristic eloquence, "the North, the South, the East, and the West meet in cheerful rivalry, each selecting as its own, the place to which it is adapted. . . . High above the Dune woods loom the gray heads of the Dune giants, where the west wind and the sand play tag over carpets of bearberry, among gnarled oaks centuries old. Farther down, in the blowouts and on the Dune meadows, friends of pleasanter climes, like the cactus, have found shelter and protection far away from their ancestral homes." The Dunes are "the common meeting ground of friends from all parts of the land."[43]

So too "there are found animals there as neighbors that represent the desert conditions of the Southwest and the pine barrens of the North," zoologist Elliot Downing said. The Dunes are home to a "group of animals naturally foreign to this latitude but brought here by plants they inhabit."[44]

"These Dunes of ours know the birds of the four winds," responded ornithologist Edward Ford. "Out of the North in winter the redpolls and crossbills drive; from the East soar with summer the prairie warbler and the acadian flycatcher; up from the South on wings of leisure drift the Bewick's wren and titmouse; from the broad west, flying far, come the willet and the Henslow's sparrow."[45]

"From the dawn of history," historian George Brennan declared, "the Dune region of Lake Michigan has been one of the centers of interest to the peoples who inhabited America. Its commanding position on the southern shores of Lake Michigan, the center where the trails from the North and South crossed those from the East and the West . . . gave it a preeminence that made it a well-known center over all the continent."[46]

"Mt. Tom has served as a landmark for Indians, explorers, Americans, and foreigners," Gary journalist William Lester noted. "Armies of many nations, including those of Spain, France, England, and America have marched by its base. Battles have been fought on its sides."[47]

"When the White men made their first advent in the Calumet region," attorney John O. Bowers added, "doubtless the prophets or seers saw, or fancied that they saw, Destiny pointing her finger toward the land at the southerly end of the great inland sea as the future home of a great aggregation of people, for was not this land fore-ordained by Nature to be the crossroads of the continent? Was not this the heart from which would radiate the arteries of trade?"[48]

"The Dunes are readily accessible to approximately five million people," stated public official Stephen Mather in 1916. "They are ideally located with respect to the center of population, which, when last determined, was in the State of Indiana."[49]

"The Dunes are waiting to be the playground of one hundred and seventy million Americans," declared public relations expert Downing Mann in the movie she and John Nelson made for the

Save the Dunes Council forty years later. Here at the southern tip of Lake Michigan, where the four climates of North America meet, the beaches are vast enough for all the crowds.[50]

No wonder after years of hearing this litany that William Ormond Wallace, newspaperman and presumed author of an unpublished mystery novel set in the Dunes, could recall the 1917 Dunes Pageant as an event of mammoth proportions which enacted the migrations of all the peoples of the earth, and especially the poor and oppressed, to this one place. Into the amphitheater from the east, he wrote in 1956, came actors representing the *voyageurs, courier de bois*, the Miamis and the Algonquins, the Iroquois, the frontiersmen like Daniel Boone. From the north came Canadians with their piraguas and Indians by canoe. From the west came the Potawatomi, Black Hawk, and the refugees from the Fort Dearborn massacre; and from the south, the trappers and home seekers from the National Pike. "The more prosperous came in wagons . . . the women and children riding and the men plodding along behind in the dust driving herds of cattle, pigs, or sheep."[51] The less prosperous came afoot, pushing wheelbarrows. Behind them were freed slaves, and slave fugitives, and groups of broad-hatted Quakers, who helped the fleeing Negroes on their way to the underground railway that led through the Dunes up to Canada. All the world found sanctuary in the Dunes.

To grasp the vision of the Dunes as a microcosm is to hold the key to the complex geographical symbolism with which the Dunes movement endowed the Chicago region. The Dune Country of northern Indiana was a sacred center. But it was not the only sacred center. It manifested in especially vivid fashion characteristics also found in smaller or larger compass elsewhere. For many midwestern Progressives, there was a series of sacred centers, each embodying the world image of an inclusive social democracy in parallel fashion, and each symbolically identified with the sacred center of the Indiana Dunes.

The Dune Country itself had a multiplicity of centers. In the early part of the century, there were four such places, each perceived as a microcosm of the Dunes as a whole. The first was the area surrounding Mount Tom, Waverly Beach, and Dune Creek north of Chesterton, the site of the great Dunes Pageant of 1917.

After the construction of the South Shore interurban line and the Prairie Club Beach House, this was the most popular center within the Dunes. With numerous historical associations and a fine bathing beach, it is not surprising that it was preserved first as the chief attraction of the Indiana Dunes State Park.

The second area lay west of Tremont and northeast of the Dune Park Station, a restricted freight stop on the New York Central Railroad. This was where the Dune Country reached its greatest depth. There were immense moving dunes along the shore, and a large inland lake, variously called Mud or Goose Lake. The Friends of Our Native Landscape built their Dune Shelter in the midst of this wildest area of the Dunes. Botanists agreed that the maximum scale and diversity of plant life occurred here. Midway between Dune Park Station and Tremont, and directly north of Mineral Springs Station on the South Shore electric line, lay a large tamarack swamp, a portion of which, Cowles or Mineral Springs Bog, became an important part of the mythic geography of the Dunes. This area will be referred to as the "Central Dunes" in subsequent discussion.

Farther west was a third area, Miller Woods—so named because it was adjacent to the town of Miller (now a part of Gary). This was where Stevens built his Japanese shack; the scene of walks by Masters and Sandburg; and the objective of frequent field trips led by Cowles and Fuller. United States Steel built its plant immediately to the west of this area.

A fourth area, which played an important part in the history of the Dunes movement but which was not part of the region of high dunes most closely identified with the "Dune Country" proper, lay between Hammond and Gary. It was composed of an extensive series of dune ridges and ponds, intermixed with prairie, running for some miles inland from the lakeshore. This was where Victor Shelford pioneered the science of animal ecology and Donald Culross Peattie learned his love for botany. It was also the area most vulnerable to industrial and urban development. Only remnants of the second, third, and fourth areas were successfully preserved at the end of the century.

The Dune Country occupied the southeastern edge of the Chicago glacial plain. From Mount Tom one had a view of this plain, as well as a view of three states—Michigan, Indiana, and Illinois.

The Dunes occupied a position that readily confirmed their status as a sacred center for the whole inhabited region. This status was frequently referred to by comparing the Dunes to the Grand Canyon, Yellowstone, or Yosemite. Each of these places was a sacred place for a particular region. "Those dunes are to the Midwest what the Grand Canyon is to Arizona and the Yosemite to California," wrote Carl Sandburg to Paul Douglas in 1958, well aware that he had a long tradition behind him.[52]

The adoption of this regional mythic perspective had an important consequence. It meant that the division of the Chicago glacial plain by a state line was purely incidental. The Dunes were a remnant of the shoreline that once encircled Chicago. The real region was ecologically and socially—not politically—defined. The leaders of the Dunes movement insisted on the validity of this viewpoint throughout the century. For example, Dwight Perkins declared at the Mather hearings that the Chicago region is "that group of people that extends from Michigan City to Waukegan. . . . *That* is Chicago. It is a state of mind, a state of activity, and it is *one community*."[53] The Dunes belonged to the community with which it had the most direct, internal relations. This community was graphically apparent to the members of the Dunes movement whenever they looked from Hyde Park across the lake to the low bright crest of dunes on the horizon to the south, or stood in the Dunes and looked north across the lake to the silhouette of Chicago: city and pristine dunescape—one interdependent whole.

Another consequence of this mythic geography was that the sacred center of the Dunes was linked symbolically to other sacred centers of the religion of democracy within Chicago, and other parts of the country. Allinson's settlement house, where, as he said, a sand mountain once stood, became in effect another "Dune Country" in the midst of the city, just as the Dunes were a "settlement house" in the country. Hull House, Jackson Park near the University of Chicago, Springfield, Indianapolis, Washington, D.C.—these and other places were linked together in this way.

The same global hope, therefore, which the Chicago reformers projected upon the settlement houses, or upon the city or nation, was projected upon the Dunes. Graham Taylor articulated this hope clearly: "We have one of the most cosmopolitan populations on the face of the earth," he said of Chicago at the Mather hearings. By establishing a Dunes park as a "great, common playground of the people," a "patch of Mother Earth to which we all have common rights, we will make a *center* for the getting together and unifying of the *cosmopolitan people of the world*, gathered together in this international citizenship *such as nothing else can accomplish*."[54]

Taylor would have appreciated the proposal made by Indiana senator Raymond Willis thirty years later that the United Nations be built in the Indiana Dunes.[55] He also would have understood the symbolism implicit in Illinois senator Paul Douglas's oft-quoted confession that while in his early life he wanted to save the world, and in his middle years his country, at life's end he would be satisfied to save the Dunes.

MOVING MOUNTAINS

The Dunes are "our mountains, the only mountains that we of Chicago will ever have," Jensen explained.[56] The Chicago plain is flat, Dudley noted, but "waves have carried sand to make a miniature mountain range along the shore."[57] Standing on Mount Tom, Reuben Strong remembered, "I had sensations similar to what one gets on a mountain top even though the mountains would be many times higher."[58] Throughout the annals of the Dunes tradition, the Dunes are named mountains, called mountains, compared to mountains. They are painted and drawn to resemble mountains. Earl Reed's and J. Howard Euston's etchings of Mount Tom suggest a high, snow-capped mountain rising in the far distance. When Dudley hung thirty Dunes paintings at the Art Institute in 1918, he simply called them *Western Scenes* and invited visitors to "guess where." The Rocky Mountains and Pacific coast were favored in the guessing.[59]

But for the members of the Dunes movement, the Dunes were more than ordinary mountains. They were cosmic mountains. "The hills around seem like symbols of eternity," wrote Edgar Lee Masters.[60] To follow in the footsteps of A. F. Knotts, and climb Mount Tom, or one of the other high dunes, was to ascend into the upperworld. Louella Chapin describes a day's pilgrimage to the

Central Dunes in 1907; climbing to the top of a dune, she encounters a scene "so intense and vivid that by its very purity it grasps you and lifts you up, *out of yourself*."[61] Like the cosmic mountains of the ancient Near Eastern religions, the high dunes, and especially Mount Tom, were the loci of ecstatic revelations of the perfect order of the world.

Yet, the Dunes were a different kind of mountain and a different kind of cosmic symbol. While many lovers of the Dunes, such as Stephen Mather and Harriet Monroe, shared the monumental esthetic of the American wilderness movement, frequently touring the West and exulting in spectacular mountain grandeur, they were keenly aware of the uniqueness of their own sacred hills. The great rock-hewn mountains of the West appeared as embodiments of permanence. The sacred Power they manifested was transcendent, Wholly Other. In contrast, the Dunes were *moving mountains*, creating a landscape of intimate beauty. "Thus we see the Dunes are not fixed, but moving, slowly, silently, irresistibly, mysteriously."[62]

Numerous individuals have struggled to put their finger on this unique dimension of the Dunes revelation. It remained for Carl Sandburg to find the right image. In 1958, at the time of the Dunes' greatest peril, he put a new twist on Masters's "symbols of eternity" and wrote to Paul Douglas: "They constitute a signature of time and eternity: once lost the loss would be irrevocable."[63] It was the genius of Sandburg to see in the moving mountains of sand a coincidence of opposites, and to recognize that the opposites unified were the very ones religion ever seeks to reconcile—time and eternity. For thousands since, these simple words—"signature of time and eternity"—have epitomized the meaning of the Dunes.

Sandburg's image is more complex than at first appears. Its power derives from the connotations of the metaphor "signature," the double subject "time and eternity," and the multiple meanings implied by the dialectic between them. There are at least four polarities suggested by the image—each a subspecies of time/eternity. These are mortality/immortality, movement/rest, imperfect/perfect, and growth/law.

The notion of a signature is a peculiarly apt analogy for the Dunes. In the first place, it is an analogy drawn from human experience, confirming what many have felt about the moving dunes, that precisely because they are in some sense mortal, they are also approachable. Analogies from human life are frequently used to describe the Dunes. Sandburg himself, in his children's stories of the 1930s, called the Dunes "sand hills which walked wandering now and then."[64] The Dunes are "moving pictures of land in the making" reported the *Chicago Herald* in 1914.[65] "Dunes are not dumb-bells," declared Bess Sheehan in her talk before the wives and legislators of the Indiana Assembly in 1923. "They are intensely human. They organize, mobilize, get together, decide to move, and overnight they are gone."[66]

In the second place, a signature suggests the meaning of time and eternity as movement and rest. Time is in the process of being written into the landscape while eternity is forever written there. "Infinite movement—infinite repose!" exclaimed Irwin St. John Tucker in his 1920 poem "On the Sand Dunes."[67] The Dunes are a "changeless yet ever changing plain" wrote E. Stillman Bailey in his book, *The Sand Dunes of Indiana*. He explained that "Some day you may happen at the dunes when the silence will be the charm. . . . The calm at the dunes is to be felt; it cannot be spoken. The sky, the water, and the land meet and proclaim the peace of heaven and earth and sea. The next day it may be the fury of the wind that will cast its spell upon you . . . both storm and calm are but echoes of your own self; you acquiesce when all is still, and you thrill when all is moving."[68]

The Dunes are also a signature of time and eternity because they symbolize the polarity of the imperfect and perfect. "Mt. Tom," said Jesse Smith at the founding of the National Dunes Park Association on Waverly Beach, "is a sand dune that is one of the most finished pieces of landscape in America. Logically speaking, it is a specimen of the past, present and future. . . . You will find land centuries old and beside it land which was made only yesterday or perhaps is in the making as you look at it."[69]

According to historian of religions G. van der Leeuw, the cosmic mountain is a "primal and permanent element of the world: out of the waters of chaos rose the primeval hill from which rose all life."[70] The Dunes—

Climbing up from out the sea,
And building, row on row . . .[71]

disclose the moment of the cosmic mountain's creation, not as a
once-and-for-all event, first manifest in the primordial past and
evoked now only by ritual imitation, but as a recurring present
reality. It is as though the Dunes were an Isle of the Blessed continually emerging out of the waves of the sea, a creation at once
perfect and incomplete.

The meaning of the polarity of time and eternity most important
to the Dunes tradition is that of growth and law. In this variation,
the moving dunes embody the generative principle of cosmic evolution. Wrote James Russell Price in his poem "The Live Sand
Dunes": "Moving sand, like flowing water, ever purifying self."[72]

Vince Hannell's painting *Pine in the Dunes* is a strong symbolic
statement of the revelation of the Dunes as moving mountains. The
abstract character of the painting suggests a mythic landscape that
is almost a fairyland. The sand dunes, drawn in three dimensions,
show the sculpturing effect of the winds. At the summit of the
sand hills is an evergreen tree whose rhythmic, uplifted limbs identify it as a tree of life, a universal symbol of world regeneration. In
the foreground and distance are other trees or shrubs painted as
though surrounded by halos. The impression of the picture is that
the Dunes are the center of life's eternal capacity for growth
rooted in the ever-changing, yet enduring currents of the physical
universe. Hannell's landscape symbolizes the apprehension that
reality is self-transforming and that at every moment in the process
of creative transformation there is found fullness of life.[73]

Reuben Strong recognized the symbolism of the moving mountains as growth and law when in 1953, in a report to his fellow members of Friends of Our Native Landscape, he included a quotation
from the *Michigan Conservationist*: "One need not be a scientist to
see the beauty of the DUNES, to sense the drama that is taking place,
to feel the surge of some creative force beyond his ken. The Dunes
are more than sun and wind and sand; they are symbolic of the
struggle which all living things endure in order to fulfill their
destiny."[74]

It is not much of a step from the insight that the Dunes manifest some creative force beyond human ken to an attempt to delineate the structure of the divine creativity with greater specificity. This step leads either to philosophy or to science. It was a step Cowles and his colleagues took when they decided to map empirically the evolutionary progression of natural communities they believed to be better represented in the Dunes than in any other place in the world. But it is a step many others have taken also, whenever they have speculated upon the meaning of the evolutionary story of the Dunes on the basis of their original experience and observation. An assumption has underlain all of these efforts: that there is a universal principle or law of world evolution to be discerned in the Dunes landscape.

The comments Edgar Lee Masters's friend "Old Sam" made as the two stood waiting for a train to take them back to Chicago in 1917, summarizes the native philosophy of several generations of Dune Bugs:

"You see," he says, "the wind blows the sand and piles it up, and makes domes and spires of it, and keeps changing it until it gets too far back from the lake for the wind to affect it. In its travels back it may bury some previous generation of trees. But what's the difference? Creepers come along, growing up from wind-driven seeds, and make a first assault and begin to anchor the sand by a great weaving of roots. Then you will see the tamaracks, by and by the pines, and then the oaks. The oaks hold it and make it land. You see, *it's all growth and law.*" [75]

The universal story of evolution many have perceived in the Dunes begins in the primordial past, in the waters of the lake, in the winds, in the elementary particles of sand created by glaciers and by the erosion of rock over eons of time, in the ancient ponds and marshes. It continues in the struggle of life to gain a foothold on land and to survive and to flourish, in the passage of generation after generation, each passing on to the next a bit more to build on, a few more resources in the groping quest for a rich, stable community. And it finds its culmination in the future presaged in all that has gone before and is here now, in the capacity of life, and especially the human imagination, to contain the struggle of existence within the bonds of more gentle and persuasive modes of shared life.

Each of the three great phases of the evolutionary drama—past, present, and future—is *now present in the Dunes* for all to see, perpetually repeated over and over. Each part of the Dunes landscape tells part of the evolutionary story, but to understand the meaning of the story one must see the landscape as a whole, especially its horizontal progression from lake inland. For here, spatially, the past, present, and future are visible as succeeding moments in the life of one interdependent and enduring community.

CREATION

The beginning of the evolutionary drama is experienced as happening now in the Dunes. In the Dunes tradition, this has taken two closely related forms. The primordial *act of creation* goes on continually in the Dunes. The earliest *beginnings* of the evolutionary drama are there still to see. "There is a mystery about untouched places, fresh as it were from God's hand," declared Edward W. Osann, Jr., at an address before the Save the Dunes Council in 1957. "These Indiana dunes possess this breathtaking primal freshness."[76]

It is at the water's edge, where lake and sand meet, that generations of Dunites have found the continuing miracle of creation most vividly reenacted. Here the four great elements of air, water, fire, and earth combine with pioneering plants to create the dunes. It is a simple story in the telling. "The rolling waves of Lake Michigan constantly are tossing the yellow sand upon the beach," where the sun dries them, and the wind "swirls them about until they find a resting place and there, when aided by growing vegetation, they form a dune." The very act of creation in the Dunes is perceived to be social in form.[77]

"There is no history of the dunes," wrote Marjorie Hill Allee in the Foreword to one of her novels of the 1930s, "but there are stories, beginning with the time when Grasshopper danced at the wedding of the Manitou and whirled up the first dunes with the wind of his dancing, and coming down to those of the girls and boys who walk its singing sands today."[78]

Sand—an infinite number of particles of sand—the most elemental and primordial of democracies! One picks up thousands of them in a single handful. Yet each grain is unique, as is each configuration they make together. Each ripple, mound, hillock, and dune is different from every other. And each day each dune is different from the day before. Sometimes, in a strong wind, the dunes change their shapes in muintes. They are endless variations on the theme of unity in variety.

This was a story as old as the earth. "The sand was older than man's most ancient ancestors," reflected Arnold Mulder in his novel *The Sand Doctor*. "It had been there, or somewhere, ten million years ago," he wrote, "and it would be there, or somewhere, ten million years hence. And what a history! It had perhaps been spewed up as metal-like rock by a volcanic outburst from the bowels of the earth. It had been ground and powdered by a million years of glacier action. The rivers of ice covering a continent had rolled it along, grinding it finer and finer. It had wandered as sediment in strange, muddy streams, carried along in the swift current. It had been swept far out into lakes long since extinct whose outlines no human eye had ever seen. It had been tossed about and buffeted, and at last it had been piled up here, clean with a million years of washing, pigmented with a thousand combinations of color, hard, impersonal, 'real'!"[79]

Throughout the Dunes tradition there is an uncanny association of the Dunes beaches with the most elementary processes of the universe. Enrico Fermi, who led the team that achieved the first successful atomic chain reaction at the University of Chicago in 1942, vividly remembered discussing the experiment in the spring of that year when for the first time he saw the Indiana Dunes. "I liked the dunes," he afterwards reminisced with his wife, "it was a clear day, with no fog to dim colors. . . . I like to swim in the lake. . . . We came out of the water, and we walked along the beach and I talked about the experiment with Professor Stearns."[80]

To walk along the beach with the sun bright overhead, to immerse oneself in the fresh waters of the lake, to stretch full length upon the slope of the foredunes, to let thousands of grains of sand fall through one's fingers—for those who have loved the Dunes, these experiences have evoked feelings and symbols of rebirth. Like Enrico Fermi, emerging from a swim in the lake, or Paul Douglas, running barefoot through the surf on one of his trips back to the

Dunes in the 1960s, visiting the Dunes has meant recontact with the regenerative powers of the universe. This is one basis for identifying the Dunes as the place where those who are physically or spiritually sick may be healed, where those who are weak may become strong. Samuel Harper wrote that standing on the beach "one feels an emancipation of spirit which suddenly and involuntarily expands one's chest, straightens one's shoulders, and raises one's forehead to the sky!"[81]

This is also a reason why sexual symbols and experiences are associated with the Dunes beaches, to the point that they constitute one of the major themes in the total structure of symbolism surrounding the perception of the Dunes as a sacred center. Sherwood Anderson's nude bathing parties in the Dunes may have been "all quite innocent enough," but they were nevertheless decidedly sexual. Surely, too, much of the energy that infused the romantic plays and masques of the Prairie Club in its early years, as well as its free and gay rambles through the Dunes, was sexual in origin. Two of the club's members, Arthur E. Anderson and his wife, were married on the top of Mount Tom, and ever afterwards wore gold wedding rings showing the tree under which the ceremony took place. Later, their ashes were thrown to eight points of the compass from the same spot.[82]

From that day in the late 1910s when Webb Waldron, walking along the beach, discovered a "Dune-Faun, innocent of clothes, burned to a mahogany tint,"[83] to Meyer Levin's novel of 1937, *The Old Bunch*, in which he recounted the amorous adventures of a group of Jewish young people in the Dunes, to 1980, when Thomas Rogers told the story of Jerry Engels's adolescent rite of passage in his novel *At the Shores*, the literature of the Dunes has testified to a strong symbolic identification between the Dunes as the place of beginnings and the Dunes as the scene of initiation into the mysteries of erotic experience.

For Waldron, it was "a virgin world" of "empty lake, dazzling sand, sky" that he entered as he hiked along the beach east of Mount Tom, a fitting setting to come across a man in the buff camping as though he were a thousand miles distant from Chicago's Loop. Only after Waldron had shed his own clothes, climbed to the top of one of the dunes and tobogganed joyously down, and then plunged into the lake, did he understand what the place was about. "I've never felt more alive in my life."[84]

For Levin, the Dunes were that clean place beyond the limits of the city where young couples escaped the authority of their parents and the dying traditions of the past, where friends walking together on the beach stood "on the verge of something deep, something incredibly inapprehensible." "Going out to the dunes with some of the bunch, driving the lizzie, and the two of them getting lost accidentally on purpose on some deep waste hollow of sand, and doing it there. Oh, do it again!"[85]

For Rogers, who grew up in Hyde Park and the Indiana Dunes, to be an adolescent in the Dunes was to be drunk with the pleasure of swimming in an inland sea of fresh water ("'Michigan' *meant* fresh water"), flinging oneself onto hot sand, running along a deserted beach, feeling a dune moving beneath one's feet on windy days. It was to be an "erotic pantheist or a pantheistic eroticist." Jerry Engels saw the landscape as a great sprawled body of a woman. Everything was curved and alive in the Dunes, "the whole world—lake, sky, and shore—was alive," and women were everywhere—in the water through which he swam and in the warm sand on which he rolled.[86] Most of all, however, to be an adolescent in the Dunes was to be initiated into the secrets of the procreative act, at once both terrible and transforming. Jerry hides his contraceptives in a tree near the place where he and Rosalind, his first girl friend, make love. Then, one night swimming nude far out in the lake, he discovers there is a "Something" in the depths which is primal and alien. Shortly thereafter, his affair with Rosalind ends abruptly and with such pain that he attempts suicide. Yet he emerges from the experience with a new sense of power, although he knows he will never again love a woman as beautiful as Rosalind.

These stories suggest that to participate in the creative Power of the Dunes is to participate in the act of creation, the first, primal act, at once social, procreative, and sacred. Indeed, the very formation of the dunes is a symbolic hierogamy—a joining of aggressive masculine (wind, sun) and fertile feminine (water, earth) elements. It is the paradigmatic act of reciprocity. It is not, however, an unambiguous experience. As Rogers emphasizes, to be initiated into the fertility rites of the Dunes is also to discover that terrible double knowledge of fulfillment and mortality inherent in humanity's role in the evolutionary drama.

Probably no person was more attracted to the elemental quality of the Dunes, or symbolized it more to others, than Alice Gray. In 1915, at the age of thirty-four, she left her job as an editor for an astronomy magazine at her alma mater, the University of Chicago, and outfitted with only a knife, spoon, blanket, jelly glass, and two guns, lived as a hermit in the Dunes. She came, she once told a reporter, because "I wanted to live my own life—a free life. The life of a salary earner in the cities is slavery."[87] But she kept alive an active intellectual life as well, borrowing books from nearby libraries, and writing manuscripts on Dunes history and ecology. Because she was reputed to make a habit of swimming nude in the lake, she became the center of unwanted publicity, and the real-life subject of the legendary "Diana of the Dunes."

One of her essays, entitled "Chicago's Kinland," reprinted by Margery Currey in the 1917 *Prairie Club Bulletin*, shows a profound grasp of the mythic dimension of the Dunes landscape, especially the symbolic role of Lake Michigan. Arguing that Chicagoans should form myths on the basis of their geological knowledge, she presented a capsule account of the glacial origin of the lake and the Chicago plain. She concluded by suggesting that Chicagoans think of their city and the Dunes as equally children of Lake Michigan and the Northwest Wind, as bound by a family tie. "To see the Dunes destroyed would be for Chicago the sacrilegious sin which is not forgiven."

> As a dower for her sons and her daughters
>   The heedless young city shall take
> This gift of the wind and the waters
>   From her mother, her lake.[88]

Although the public hounded her and she died a premature death in 1925, Alice Gray became a personal symbol to many members of the Dunes movement. Gary Nabhan, in his poem "Diana-Gone-Driftwood Dune Woman," was so inspired by her "radical sense of place," her quest for freedom through identification with the birth and rebirth of the Lake Michigan landscape, that he sought to imaginatively reconstruct her personal sense of cosmic mother-hood. He imagines her swimming,

> pulled on
> by some aquaspheric force
> too strong just to be called *current*.

He sees her dreaming on a Dune Country winter night of taking a walk three hundred miles north to where she finds glaciers moving southward; only after freeing wailing moose from icy traps and sending them to new feeding and breeding grounds does she decide

> to return to the Land of Sacred Reeds and Sand
> to rest as the ice floes crackle
> dissolve into a cool spring lake.[89]

Lake Michigan symbolizes how the Dunes are the place of be-ginnings in two senses—the ever-recurring miracle of creation is manifest here; the genesis of the evolutionary history of the world appears here. This double meaning, implicit in the experience of the Dunes as moving cosmic mountains, is also evident in the sym-bolism associated with the bogs and swamps of the Dunes. In the Dunes tradition, this symbolism is focused most intensely upon Cowles Bog (also called Mineral Springs Bog) and the large Tama-rack Swamp that once surrounded it on all sides.

A relic of the Ice Age, Cowles Bog began its life thousands of years ago as the landlocked lagoon of an ancient river plain. Over the millennia, the lagoon was slowly filled by vegetation, becoming a thick, floating mat strong enough to walk on and fertile enough in places to support trees and a rich assemblage of plants. The flora of the bog is unique and varied—a combination of species such as tamarack and sphagnum moss pushed south by the glacier and left behind as the region warmed, and later arrivals, pushed north as the continent warmed, finding shelter in the sandy soil when the earth cooled again. Because of the attraction of the flora, especially the rare wildflowers, and the thrill of venturing out on the dome-shaped "quaking" mat and exploring the "island" of tamarack and cedar trees that rise at the center, Dunes enthusiasts have made frequent visits to Cowles Bog throughout the century.

Wrote Charles Robinson, retired editor of the *Western Review*, who discovered a rare thirteen-petal variety of rose in the Dunes:

> The Tamarack Swamp is dark and dank;
> Its thickets dense, and its Ivy rank,
>   But its flowers are rich and rare.
> Tamaracks fringe its southern side;
> Through marshgrass tall, with glist'ning hide
> In the bog beyond the serpents glide,
>   But Orchids flourish there.[90]

The bog became the symbol of a "Lost World." As an isolated remnant of one of the earliest stages in the postglacial evolution of the Chicago plain, it suggested to those with imagination a place where one could still come into contact with the beginnings of the evolution of life. Here the primordial chaos, evident in the dark brown waters underneath the floating mat covering the bog, was perceived to yield wild and exotic creatures, some dangerous—snakes, poison sumac, mosquitoes, carnivorous plants ready for the unwary. Peril befitted the boundary between order and chaos. Other plants, like the ferns that George Pinneo claimed grew six to eight feet high and made the bog look like a "section cut from the jungles of a tropical country," showed how the earth may have been millions of years ago during the Paleozoic Era when ferns dominated the landscape.[91] Still others, such as the black orchid, which was reputed to exist in the bog but did not, and the white lady's slipper orchid, which did, were expressions of life's capacity to create rare beauty. No tour of the Dunes, such as the one J. William Lester imagined that Alice Gray once conducted, was complete without a visit to Cowles Bog. In Lester's fictious account, after crossing the trembling ground, Alice's party found "in a setting of black muck and decayed vegetation," a bed of orchids—"so dainty and yet in such dismal surroundings—like a burst of sunshine on a gloomy day."[92]

Through the years, the Dunes movement has found on the beaches and in the swamps and bogs testimony that "In the Dunes the Prologue to the great Drama of Creation is being spoken—whispered—sung!"[93]

THE EVOLUTIONARY DRAMA OF THE DUNES

"The Dunes," one observer suggested, "have an almost mystical capacity for taking to their bosoms the transitory activities of living creatures and preserving traces of them."[94] The story of life's evolutionary unfolding is waiting to be read in the "everlasting making and unmaking and remaking of the dunes," not merely the chronological sequence, but the inner meaning and purpose of the whole evolutionary adventure.[95]

The evolutionary drama is visible as one walks, following the movement of the "living dunes," from the beach inland. First, one is aware only of the ripples made by the wind on the open beach. Then one sees the first signs of plant life—hardy annuals such as the sea rocket, doomed, however, to be wiped out with the coming of winter. Beyond are the first real dunes, small hillocks of sand held against the wind by pioneer plants such as marram grass and wormwood. After these one is greeted by larger mounds, some held by sand cherry and willow, others, higher yet, by cottonwoods and jack pine. The foredunes protect the dunes behind them from the wind. Eventually there is a sheltering forest where many plants and animals live. Sometimes one sees places where the wind has carved a blowout. Typically, the dunes with blowouts on their slopes are the highest of the dunes. The sand from the blowout is thrown up and over the crest where it slowly buries the forest growing in the protected hollow on the other side. Farthest from the lake are dunes covered with black oak and blueberry, maple and beech, with lush ferns and teeming animal and plant life. Ten thousand or more years ago these dunes were foredunes on the shore of the lake. Always the sand is moving inland, and always the plants are seeking to grab hold and create the conditions for a successful and diverse community of life.

Or, as Old Sam put it, "you see, it's all growth and law."

The evolutionary drama is a drama of brute force gradually yielding to the gentle but persistent power of living things. Wilhelm Miller articulated this insight at the Mather hearings in 1916:

How eagerly people from all parts of the country come to see this great revelation of the Infinite.

The dunes are a world wonder because they are a dramatic presen-

tation of the *infinite power of wind.* Think of the north wind, sweeping three hundred miles down this lake and piling up that enormous
area of sand!

You remember Kipling's story about "Letting in the Jungle." It is
an uncanny and fearsome revelation of nature's power; but the dunes
tell a lovelier story—the story of wild and shifting sand, captured, and
brought to life, expressing its soul through many of nature's finest
shrubs and fairest flowers. *This subtle transformation of brute force has
much to do with the charm of the dunes.*[96]

Miller was building on a tradition already well established. The
earliest extant poem on the Dunes, published by Thomas Wood
Stevens in 1901, makes precisely Miller's point. "The Spirit of the
Dunes" is a spirit of power and change:

> Thy fingers twining in the wind
> As lovers' hands with tresses play
> Remould thine empire in the night
> And bring new states to greet the day:
> *New hills—yea, mortal hills shall rise*
> *To boast before the changing skies.*

It is also a spirit of "bleak defiance," shifting with the gale and
drinking the sun, a spirit like "The ghost of Death that Time hath
sired" which "Still brooding guards the undesired." Yet "all is not
wrath":

> For though thy voice doth wail in woe,
> The cedars dare thy heart to find,
> And, nestling to thy barren breast,
> The humbler shrubs still call thee kind.[97]

What Stevens and Miller felt about the struggle of life in the
Dunes to tame the senseless onrush of the physical universe, and in
that taming, to draw sustenance from it, was also felt by others.
For art critic Arietta Towne, the Dunes are pregnant with a Spirit
that calls "Come! Come!" It does not coerce; it persuades; it extends gestures of hospitality rather than commands.[98] For geologist
William Blatchley to "literally watch the growing of the hills" is
to see "how the slow, unceasing action of some of nature's milder
forces have modified to so great an extent the surface of the
earth."[99] For Gary settlement worker and poet Jeannette Vaughn

Konley, it is a "synchronizing grace" that fashions the Dunes.[100] For some it is their "healing power, a listening attitude" that makes the gray old dunes so companionable.[101]

Hyde Park poet Charles G. Bell speaks of a "love like a vine" which "works round and attaches here." Bell begins his 1953 poem, "These Winter Dunes," with the lines:

I sit over the lake on a hill of sand;
Gold light and purple shadows, the playing forms,
Weave on the swift shuttles and are withdrawn.
Other hills are carved in rock, these mounds of the wind
Continually melt and change, wakening
The sweet tenderness of impermanent things.[102]

The moving dunes are imbued with a gentle but dynamic power, which patiently effects a transformation from one extreme to another. From a situation physically and emotionally alien to the appearance of life, the dunes gradually evolve to be supportive of life, and in that change is unlocked the soul of nature. Like the contrast frequently drawn between the abrading power of the driving sand and its softness to the touch, the Dunes reveal how, at the heart of the most hostile environment, a sacred Power works to transform the brute forces of nature into a medium of nourishment for the most fragile of life forms.

Arnold Mulder captured this seemingly paradoxical double nature of the Dunes—their awesome and yet nurturing power:

And the dunes they could always depend upon, because the spirit of the hills was in their hearts—the hills, always changing, yet always the same; constant in all their mutability; beautiful with the unconscious artistry of a million years of sun and storm; luminous with the unassuming splendor of all things true and genuine; unheedful of the hopes and fears, the loves and hates of men; regarding not the lives of the plants growing joyously on their slopes, or the cries of the birds wheeling about their crowns, or the hunger of the little animals roaming over them in their prowling search for food; going onward in their course with blind and unfeeling inexorability, *yet having somehow for those who understand, the warm, living spirit of the earth itself at the heart of them.*[103]

This fundamental lesson is expressed most vividly, however, in the ceaseless struggle between the plant life and the elements. The Dunes are "nature's battleground," [104] yet, in the words of one writer, "Sometimes the weak things of earth are chosen to confound the mighty." [105] Dunes literature abounds with descriptions of how, in face of the fact that advancing dunes overthrow and destroy whole forests, small and tender plants, like the wild grapevine, offer successful resistance. The most symbol-laden pit the epitome of beauty and fragility, wildflowers, directly against the naked sands. In one account the Dunes are imagined as the place where the "fairy threads of wildflower roots" have anchored the flying particles of sand to the earth. "Each tiny fiber has fought for years against the fierce Kabibonokka, the north wind, leaping over the great gray lake and pouncing upon the unhappy, restless sands." But like the fight of the Lion and the Mouse, the "fragile wildflowers have won." What they have won is not only security but community. For nowhere else is there "a haven where so many different families dwell together." [106]

The lesson the moving dunes teach is not, on the whole, as happy an affair as the wildflowers would seem to indicate. Their success is precarious. Most Dunes writers have conceived the evolutionary drama of the Dunes in more tragic terms. Stevens's sober "All is not wrath" more closely reflects their mature assessment of its course to date. There has been, indeed, a movement toward the cooperative unity for which the whole of creation yearns. The forests of oak and maple and beech have taken root. And of course in the most fundamental sense, the Power of transformative mutuality is perceived as active in every stage of dune succession. Yet community is far from realized. It is at least as much a hope, a trajectory from the past into the future, as a fact in the present.

The portion of the Dunes landscape that has most powerfully symbolized the tragic dimension of the evolutionary struggle is the Dunes blowouts. In the blowouts, where the wind has eroded the sand, whole forests, bones of animals, and relics of past cultures, buried by advancing dunes in the past, are sometimes uncovered and exposed to view. Dunes photographers commonly entitle pictures of the dead trees "Resurrection." The blowouts themselves are called the "graveyards" of the Dunes. Frank Dudley's painting *Sun and Shadows Meet* typifies a blowout scene.

In his book *The Lost Woods*, Edwin Way Teale wrote of returning to the Great Blowout, east of Mount Tom, on an August evening. It is a silent scene he has surveyed many times before—a place in which time and eternity meet. Especially at this transitional hour, as day passes into night, the blowout evokes a sense of the past as a present reality. Teale imagines himself sitting in the same spot a thousand years earlier: "In this ancient stillness, so like the setting of another time, I half expect to see a wolf or a deer or a redman rise in silhouette along the horizon."[107]

What he does see are the skeleton trunks of trees fifty feet and more in height, a ghost forest that tells the story of first the victory and then the defeat of life centuries ago. The two sounds he hears—the lisp of lightly blowing sand and the rustle of the plumes of grass—confirm that a "battle without an armistice, without an end" still goes on.[108] He realizes that the plants are using the dead tree trunks as anchors around which to begin the struggle anew. The rhythm of birth, death, and rebirth continues. The wind's victory, like that of the now dead forest, was only temporary. Yet neither side has won a clear-cut victory.

As day fades, the great amphitheater becomes for a while completely black. Then a full moon mounts in the eastern sky and Teale experiences the scene of Sandburg's poem, "Dunes." He has a sensation of being in a world of expanding space. In the moonlight the exposed roots of the ghost forests seem about ready to move. Teale is overwhelmed with a feeling of smallness, "of being a child wandering on some stilled battlefield of the giants."[109]

In the great inverted bowl above him, fitting the rim of the bowl in which he sits, like two cups joined together, stars appear. Teale seems to be standing at the center of a perfect microcosm of the cosmos, "on the very outer skin of the earth, on the shoreline of the cosmic sea."[110] Passage between underworld and upperworld, between time past and time future, between the local and global, is now possible through the medium of the sacred space of the blowout. As if to symbolize the meeting of past and future, down from the stars falls the sound of a throbbing engine, and the red and green lights of a plane heading for Chicago crosses the sky. Landward, to the south, Teale is aware of the distant rattle of a train. Human invention and history take their place within the cosmic venture.

Teale's experience of the Dunes blowout suggests that a new stage has appeared in the evolutionary drama of the Dunes—the struggle of humanity for its place in the universe. But like the wandering dunes themselves, human beings mirror a peculiar freedom. They may take hold like pioneering plants, or they may identify with the brute forces of the universe and destroy the precarious victories of life. Pointing out that the "conspicuous and outstanding fact about the whole southeastern dune region is the element of change," Hermann Pepoon, in striking image, compared humanity's razing of the dunes and draining of the marshes with the destructive impact of the treeless, advancing dunes themselves. Each is "slowly but remorselessly changing the landscape."[111]

In the meantime, the lesson of the moving mountains is patience, endurance and faith.

Jensen believed that in the Dunes, God had shown the development of plant life from the simplest cell structure on upward. He also conceived of the coming of social democracy in terms of the great lesson of ecological succession taught by the Dunes. When in 1940, at the age of eighty, Jensen returned for a walk through the Indiana Dunes State Park, he found to his amazement growing in the same place the same partridge berry plant he first discovered there forty years earlier. And nearby were the same three sycamores, and a great tulip tree that had stood there in 1900. Addressing the tulip tree, Jensen exclaimed: "How many centuries of life have made you. How many of the bodies of your fellows are food under your bark now. . . . All of time is in you. Life is continuity and it cannot be stopped."[112] Afterward, reflecting on the implications of all this for human evolution, he said: "We feed from all our companions and we grow from the shoulders of all the generations that went before us, just like trees. Democracy. Yes, it is slow. It is hard to wait for it. . . . But things can only come when the ground is ready. It must grow on what has come before like the forest. Democracy is the religion of government."[113]

In his children's book *Moving Hills of Sand*, Julian May, like Jensen and Teale, blends the natural history of the Dunes with the advent of modern history.[114] But modernity is fraught with a qualitatively different kind of conflict on this ancient battleground of nature. The Dunes are threatened in their entirety by spreading urbanization. Only a new kind of struggle will permit the evolutionary drama to continue, and that is the struggle to preserve the Dunes as a "park." By implication, this is the authentically human stage in the story of dunes succession. John Hawkinson, in his illustrations for the book, envisages an even more beautiful community beyond the forests of beech and maple—a community constituted by human society in harmony with the moving mountains of sand.

Julian May's 1969 vision of the Dunes drama is not new. It is simply a retelling of the evolutionary schema presented by George Brennan in *Wonders of the Dunes* in 1923, and by other Dunes writers both before and after.[115] Carl Sandburg told it best. A half-century after "Dunes," he set down in another poem, "Timesweep," his most mature statement of the meaning of the cosmic drama he so closely identified with the Dunes landscape.

"Timesweep" is a long evocation of humanity's kinship with all the natural forces and creatures that preceded it and now journey with it through space and time. Sandburg stresses the victories, like love, and the limitations, like ignorance and selfishness, which humanity shares with its animal kin. Beneath and beyond all the bloodshed and terror, a purpose is nonetheless at work. It is seen in the wind carving the sand into an endless variety of new designs, and in the patience beyond human understanding of wind and ice as they together mold the landscape. It is seen most clearly in the striving of the world's creatures for community of being. Sandburg's vision of the meaning of the evolutionary drama reaches a climax with the affirmation:

> There is only one bird in the air
>   and his name is All Wings.
> There is only one fish in the sea
>   and his name is All Fins.
> There is only one man in the world
>   and his name is All Men.
> There is only one woman in the world
>   and her name is All Women.
> There is only one child in the world
>   and the child's name is All Children.[116]

FOUR

The Birthplace of Ecology

Chicago is the center of a region of quiet but varied beauty. He who limits his excursion to the city parks or the immediate vicinity of the city sees only a monotonously level plain, but to him who wanders along the North Shore, explores the Dunes, or rambles over the wooded hills of the nearby moraine country there are presented bits of landscape that charm even the casual observer with their wealth of form and color. The encircling horizon line shrouded in the shimmering haze of the lake or broken by the billowy hills, the nearby woodlands, the cloud shadows that play among them . . . all are sources of exquisite pleasure. Poet and painter fairly astound us with the revelation of beauty which they, with fine sensitiveness, perceive in even so commonplace an outlook. Science too is a revealer. It adds a third dimension to the landscape; it gives depth. It delves below the surface to the foundation. It gives the perspective of time. To the thoughtful man the outstretched view is not alone a beautiful prospect; it is a voice from the past and speaks of history as eventful as do the care-wrought furrows of the human face.

ELLIOTT ROWLAND DOWNING,

from *A Naturalist in the Great Lakes Region*, 1922

H enry Chandler Cowles. His students remembered him years afterwards—a short, stocky man with twinkling eyes and a wide, puckish grin. Paul Voth recalled how Cowles began each year's course in physiographic ecology. He would step briskly to the front of the lecture room in the Hull botanical laboratory, one of the gray gothic buildings on the University of Chicago quadrangle, quote from memory several classical allusions to the "everlasting hills," and then proceed to talk about the evolving hills of the Indiana Dunes.[1]

AMERICA'S FIRST PROFESSIONAL ECOLOGIST

The claim, identified with the figure of Cowles, that the Indiana Dunes are the "birthplace of ecology" is true with qualifications.[2] The Indiana Dunes share the honor with landscapes in other parts of the world that contributed to the emergence of ecology in the late nineteenth century; especially, in the United States, with the sandhills and grasslands of Nebraska, where independently of Cowles, botanist Frederic E. Clements also worked out the dynamics of ecological succession.[3] While Cowles is justifiably considered "America's first professional ecologist,"[4] he shares the honor of pioneering the field not only with Clements, but with men and women bridging several disciplines and working at the geographical center for the genesis of self-conscious ecology—the Middle West.

Yet the fact remains that this genial free spirit, who could quote from Latin masters or tramp for hours "reading the landscape" of the Chicago glacial plain, played the pivotal role in making the Indiana Dunes the symbol of the dynamic viewpoint of American ecology.[5]

At the Mather hearings in 1916, Cowles confessed, "For twenty years I have been studying the dunes more than anything else, more than everything else combined. In fact, that has been my chief reason for existence, perhaps, for those twenty years." Cowles had studied "nearly all the dunes of the world, having personally visited most of them and read about the others," but those he knew and loved best were the dunes that encircled the southern coast of Lake Michigan—in his estimate "much the grandest in the entire world."[6]

The reputation of the Indiana Dunes as a classic landscape for the study of ecological succession was Cowles's achievement. Another midwestern pioneer of ecology, H. A. Gleason, wrote in 1935 that as a result of Cowles's work, "throughout the country, young ecologists, of whom I was one, descended on the dunes, the shores, the marshes, and the bogs and presently returned to the laboratories to write voluminous accounts of their observations."[7] The Oxford ecologist A. G. Tansley appraised his contribution: "It is to Henry Chandler Cowles that we owe, not indeed the first recognition or even the first study of succession, but certainly the first thorough working out of a strikingly complete and beautiful successional series (1899), which together with later and more comprehensive studies (1901, 1911) brought before the minds of ecologists the reality and the universality of the process in so vivid a manner as to stimulate everywhere—at least in the English-speaking world—that interest and enthusiasm for the subject which has led and is leading to such great results."[8]

In 1895, at the age of twenty-six, Cowles was studying the glacial geology of the Midwest with Thomas C. Chamberlin and Rollin D. Salisbury and botany with John Merle Coulter. Raised in Hanover, Indiana, Coulter had begun his botanical career as a member of the 1872 Hayden Survey of Yellowstone Park. He early came to the attention of Asa Gray, establishing a lifelong friendship that culminated in his production, with Sereno Watson, of the sixth edition of Gray's *Manual of Botany*. In 1875 Coulter founded the *Botanical Gazette* as a four-page leaflet. Under his editorship it became the leading botanical periodical in the country. Although he was originally a taxonomist, and later specialized in morphology, Coulter ably fostered work among his students in plant physiology, paleobotany, and phytopathology.[9]

Coulter decided to share with his class the treatise on "oecological plant geography" by the Danish botanist Eugenius Warming, which had just been published. Years later, Charles J. Chamberlain, one of the Cowles's fellow students, recalled the excitement of this event: "None of us could read Danish except a Danish student, who would translate a couple of chapters, and the next day Coulter would give a wonderful lecture on Ecology. . . . While we heard the translation, none of us knew what it was all about until Coulter lectured. Cowles, with his superior knowledge of taxonomy and his geology, understood more than the rest of us, and became so interested that he studied Danish and, long before any translation appeared, could read the book in the original." [10]

Warming's epochal work (revised and republished in 1909 as *The Oecology of Plants: An Introduction to the Study of Plant Communities*) was the crucial synthesis that stimulated the rapid development of the science of ecology in American academic circles at the turn of the century. Defining the new field as the study of "the manifold and complex relations subsisting between the plants and animals that form one community," he devoted the major portion of his treatise to describing the various modes of interdependence found in the social worlds of plants and animals. [11] For example, the most commonplace of these modes was "commensalism," in which different kinds of plants and animals, such as insects and flowers, benefit from the activities of one another without taking anything from the other's life. A more intense mode of mutualism was "symbiosis," illustrated in the partnership of alga and fungus in the lichen. Warming pointed out that in contrast to the lichen diverse species of plants interacting in a common habitat form only a very loose society, and that the emergence of patterns of community life in which there is "cooperation for the commonweal" depended on the appearance of higher organisms. Warming insisted that virtually no species lives without help from other species, and that reciprocal relations frequently join organisms widely separated from one another in the scale of evolution.

Warming's emphasis on interdependence had import for philosophy and religion as well as science. He showed that there was not only competition between individuals for survival in the natural world, but also mutual aid.

In the last section of his work, Warming pointed out that communities do not typically remain the same over long periods of time. He contended that in every habitat there was an ordered transition from one kind of community to another as the relationships within and outside the community underwent disruption and readjustment. This process moved in the direction of a "climax" formation. Donald Worster, in his account of Warming's treatise, concludes: "The ultimate goal of nature, in other words, is nothing less than the most diverse, stable, well-balanced, self-perpetuating society that can be devised to meet the requirements of each habitat."[12]

Well before Warming, of course, the process of plant succession was observed in various parts of the world. It was well known that an undrained pond tends to become first a bog and then a dry forest. Water-loving plants (hydrophytes) invade the water and eventually modify the environment to one more suited to those requiring more moderate amounts of water (mesophytes), or even those requiring very little water (xerophytes). In the far north, lichen and mosses create the thin soil necessary for the invasion of the plants and animals of the tundra. The most striking example of succession is the slow reappearance of life on volcanic islands after an eruption. Warming took these observations and with a genius for system, subsumed them all under the notion of a general law—the evolution of communities of life toward a climax equilibrium. He placed this progressive evolutionary law squarely at the center of the new science of "oecology."

These were formidable new tools for the Darwinian age. They were transported across the Atlantic and transferred into the hands of the Chicago scientists at precisely the opportune moment. In 1895 the notion of progressive social evolution permeated the atmosphere of Harper's University; so did its corollary, the notion of an orderly universe hospitable to human development and imbued with moral law and purpose. Ecologist Jerry S. Olson wrote in retrospect of this period that, "Probably the spark that made the *idea* of succession catch fire so rapidly was its extension of the concept of orderly development of natural systems. Not only the life-cycle of the individual and the evolution of the species but the transformation of the biological community and its habitat—what Tansley later called the ecosystem—at last seemed to fall within the domain of natural law. Cowles . . . wove the physical and biological threads together into a fabric showing orderly design."[13]

Coulter fostered Cowles's interest in Warming's ideas, and suggested that in Warming's theory of ecological succession, Cowles had a way to combine his earlier study in dynamic physiography, or the history of land-forms, with plant geography. Warming had studied vegetational succession in the sand dunes on the coast of Denmark in 1891, and Coulter encouraged Cowles to explore the plant communities of the nearby Indiana Dunes. Perhaps his findings would correspond to Warming's.

Since the 1870s, Coulter himself had felt the lure of the Dunes. The first scientific notice of the flora of the Indiana Dunes was the account written by Coulter for the *Botanical Gazette* in 1879:

> Having been occupied mostly with the flora of that part of Indiana bordering upon the Ohio river, I have often looked longingly upon the map of the state at the northern tier of counties, bordering upon Michigan lake and state, and well filled with small lakes and tamarack swamps. It seemed as if some of our best plants must be found there, and in my preparation for publishing a catalogue of the flora of the state, I could find no report or no working botanist from that region. Last summer an opportunity presented itself of making a hasty survey for myself and the result was most encouraging. . . . Accompanied by my enthusiastic pupil and assistant, Mr. Chas. R. Barnes, I spent three or four weeks along the line of the Lake Shore and Michigan Southern Railroad. . . . The Kankakee river forms a natural boundary on the south side of the northwestern corner of this region. . . . The wildest, most unfrequented part of it we did not even reach, as they were too inaccessible for our limited time, but what we heard of them made us expect great things.

Coulter divided the flora of the Dune Country into five geographical classes: the flora of the sand hills bordering Lake Michigan, the "wet grassy meadows and choked up swamps," the lakes, the tamarack and sphagnous swamps, and the prairie.[14]

Bradley M. Davis, a native Chicagoan who had just joined the faculty and commenced teaching comparative plant morphology, and Coulter went with Cowles on his first field trips to the Dunes. But because of a damaged knee, Coulter stayed behind as Cowles and Davis pushed into more remote regions. The father of Chicago botanists, the Reverend E. J. Hill, occasionally joined them. Cowles later said of Hill that he "studied the dune floras about Lake Michigan for many years, and although he has not written a great deal along ecological lines, he has had the ecological standpoint thoroughly in mind."[15]

Cowles first saw the Indiana Dunes when he alighted from a Michigan Southern Railroad train at the Dune Park Station in early 1896. North and east lay the Central Dunes, the most extensive area of dune activity at the southern end of Lake Michigan. As Cowles noted in his dissertation, east of Dune Park, within an area of about one thousand hectares, moving dunes were active up to two kilometers inland, and established dunes extended southward as far as eight kilometers from the shore. In the late 1890s, the dunes here were rapidly advancing on the marshes, swamps, and forests of the interior. In November, 1897, Cowles drove a stake into the ground at the base of an advancing dune to measure its movement. When he checked it in May, it was almost covered, and by July it had completely disappeared. Although Cowles extended his research into other parts of the lakeshore, at times arranging with the railroad to transport his equipment and material to distant points by freight train, he went back time and again in all seasons to the dunes near Dune Park, the principal site of his studies.

By 1900 Cowles was well acquainted with the high Dune Country throughout its entire twenty- to thirty-mile circumference, as well as with the dunes of the Michigan coast as far north as the Sleeping Bear dune northwest of Traverse City and the dunes on North Manitou Island, Beaver Island, and Mackinac. By this time, too, he had identified the three principal centers east of Gary, each accessible by stations on the Michigan Southern Railroad—the environs of Miller, Dune Park, and Chesterton.[16]

PLANT SUCCESSION IN THE DUNES

In 1898 Cowles completed his dissertation, "An Ecological Study of the Sand Dune Flora of Nothern Indiana"; a year later it was published in the *Botanical Gazette*. In 1901, in a second article, "The Physiographic Ecology of Chicago and Vicinity: A Study of the Origin, Development, and Classification of Plant Societies," he applied his study of succession in the Dunes to the rest of the Chicago glacial plain. A decade later, in "The Causes of Vegetative Cycles," he formulated a general theory of succession for the continent as a whole.[17] The overall effect of these three classic papers was to present to the scientific community the view that the Indiana Dunes were a world-model for the study of the evolution of land-forms and plant communities in interaction with one another.

Cowles began his 1899 monograph with the assertion, following Warming, that "the province of ecology is to consider the mutual relations between plants and their environment." He moved to one of his distinctive contributions to the science, an emphasis on the dynamic physiographic component in the relationship. Physiography, he noted, "studies landscapes in their making." Ecology adopts the physiographic viewpoint and sees the flora of a landscape as a "panorama, never twice alike." "The ecologist, then, must study the order of succession of the plant societies in the development of a region, and he must endeavor to discover the laws which govern the panoramic changes."[18]

An ecologist needs, Cowles observed, to find plant formations "rapidly passing into other types by reason of a changing environment." Empirical investigation of such formations held the key to the developmental principles the ecologist sought to grasp. This need is met "*par excellence* in a region of sand dunes." Perhaps no topographic form is less stable than a dune. In the dune landscape it is not the past but the present that shapes the floras; the present is open to investigation. "By burying the past, the dune offers to plant life a world for conquest, subject almost entirely to existing physical conditions. . . . The advance of a dune makes all things new." The conclusion readily followed. "The primary motive, then, which prompted this present study was the feeling that nowhere else could many of the living problems of ecology be solved more clearly; that nowhere else could ecological principles be subjected to a more rigid test."[19]

In the first few pages of his first article, Cowles thus bluntly sets forth his conviction that by studying "the progressive changes that take place and the factors in the environment which cause these changes" in sand dunes, one had the best access available on the surface of the earth to the "laws which govern the panoramic changes" of plant communities. He was to make this claim even more specific. One conclusion of Cowles's research was that the overall order of succession of the Lake Michigan dunes was the same Warming had noted in the Danish dunes, except that in the Danish landscape "there appears to be less diversity of conditions, and the features appear to be developed on a smaller scale."[20] The implication was that in the Indiana Dunes the laws of ecologic succession are written in larger letters and with heavier impress on the landscape.

Cowles devoted the body of his 1899 paper to the order of development of plant societies in the Lake Michigan dunes in the conviction that this order faithfully expressed genetic relationships. The sequence was the same others had observed earlier in rougher outline as they walked inland from the beach toward the stable forested dunes of the interior. As one walked inland *in space*, one walked backward *in time*. By putting the progressive stages of this spatial sequence together, one could reconstruct the development of the land and its plant communities. In effect, one could reconstruct the life history of a single dune—the evolution of the archetypal landscape. Cowles contributed to the emerging perception of the Dunes as the sacred center of the evolution of natural communities a more precise scientific description of the successive plant societies in the sequence, correlated with the physiographic transformations in the dunes themselves, and most important, an elementary analysis of the reciprocal relationships between vegetation and topography at each stage.

Cowles divided the process of dune succession into five major stages: (1) the primitive formation of the beach, (2) the embryonic or stationary beach dunes, (3) the active or wandering dunes, (4) the arrested or transitional dunes, and (5) the passive or established dunes. The overall genetic development was characterized by two laws: the first, that more rapid changes at the outset yield to slower changes as the plant societies approach the climax type for the region; the second, that "Speaking broadly, the conditions for plant life become less and less severe through all these stages, until there is reached the most genial of all conditions in our climate, that which results in the production of a diversified deciduous forest."[21] This was a way of stating that the course of succession begins on the beach under extreme xerophytic conditions and moves over time toward mesophytic conditions on the established inland dunes.

Cowles subdivided each of the five major stages. For example, the beach includes three principal zones—the extremely xerophytic lower beach, washed by the waves of summer storms; the middle beach, where succulent annuals take root, washed by the waves of winter storms; and the upper beach, beyond the reach of waves, where a group of hardy annuals, biennials and perennials grow.

Critical turning points in the evolution of the landscape occur at the beginning of each of the four subsequent stages. The embryonic dunes appear as a result of perennial plants, such as marram grass, willows, and sand cherry, capturing blowing sand. The growth of these beach dunes and their builders was described by Cowles as "symbiotic" in nature. However, there is a limit to the capacity of the dune-formers to survive as the level of the dune rises above the water table. This marks the transition of the stationary shoreline dunes into wandering dunes.

At this point, as the wind increasingly fashions the hills of sand, they become asymmetrical. The wind sweeps up the gradual windward slopes (almost always ten degrees) and deposits sand on the steep leeward slopes (almost always thirty-two degrees). If unimpeded, the dunes slowly "move" in this fashion across the landscape. Cowles was quick to note that a wandering dune neatly marching inland was an exception. More typically, sand is blown in many directions, and it was more accurate, therefore, to speak of a "dune-complex." At Dune Park, "while there is a general advance of the complex as a whole in the direction of the prevailing winds, individual portions are advancing in all directions in which winds ever blow. It is not at all uncommon to find small dunes advancing over the dune-complex back toward the lake."[22]

Of all stages in the life history of the dunes landscape, the advancing dune complex was of greatest interest to Cowles, and it served, in turn, to qualify any gradualist interpretation of succession to which he might have been prone. The most striking features of the advancing dunes are topographic diversity and restlessness. Needless to say, only scanty life is possible on the dry, blowing surface. The phenomenon of the wandering dunes constitutes, therefore, an interruption in the progressive development of the land and its plant communities toward a climax formation. The symbiosis of the stationary beach dunes is broken. As the dunes advance upon the interior, they display tremendous power to destroy all vegetation in their path. They have the capacity to bury whole forests. This is evident both at the advancing front of the dune complex as it covers living vegetation, and in its rear as previously buried forests become uncovered and a graveyard of tree trunks is exposed to view. The only conspicuous example of the survival of a preexisting flora Cowles found was in the swamps where certain plants, such as willows and dogwoods, adapted to the radically new conditions that encroached on them.

Eventually, the advancing dunes are captured as the effect of the wind is diminished inland from the lake, and plants have an opportunity to survive in protected areas. At this turning point, many kinds of plants "contribute together to the common end" of stabilizing the moving dunes.[23]

The capture of the advancing dunes is the fourth stage in the process of succession. With the improvement of the soil on more established dunes begins the fifth stage, subdivided by Cowles into several successional series, each dominated by a particular sequence of trees. One of these series is initially settled by the basswood, which gradually yields, under increasingly mesophytic conditions, to red oak, and then to sugar maple and beech. Cowles regarded this series as the culmination of the progression that begins at the lower beach. There is also the evergreen series, which grows on the windward north slopes of established dunes, a formation peculiarly susceptible to destruction from rejuvenated moving dunes; it tends to be replaced by the black oak series on the south leeward slopes free of destructive sand-laden winds. Cowles speculated that the oldest black oak dunes might also develop eventually into a beech and maple forest with further soil improvement.

Cowles's account cannot be construed as a rigid theory of convergence of ecological succession to a uniform mesophytic climax. He believed that the maple and beech forest was the "ultimate" outcome of the development of the Dunes region, but his data showed there were other relatively stable outcomes as well. The dunes were constantly being made and unmade and remade. The very circumstance that allowed the student of nature to go back to beginnings and see how life and land evolved together encouraged a concern for process as much as end-products. Furthermore, the Dunes were the meeting point of eastern deciduous forest and western grasslands. The landscape Cowles described was more open-ended than the general law he inherited from Warming seemed to suggest.

In his second paper, published in 1901, Cowles restated the definition of ecology, and refined the fundamental law of succession on the basis of the evidence gathered from his studies throughout the Chicago area. He emphasized his dynamic bias. "Ecology is essentially a study of origins and life histories." For a plant classification to be true, it must be "genetic and dynamic"; it must take account of multiple factors working together over time. Succession is not a straight-line process. Its stages may be slow or rapid, direct or tortuous, and often they are retrogressive. Overall, however, "the great mesophytic tendency is clearly seen." Yet because of the multiple factors involved, "the condition of equilibrium is never reached and when we say that there is an approach to the mesophytic forest, we speak only roughly and approximately. *As a matter of fact, we have a variable approaching a variable rather than a constant.*" [24]

In his third paper, published in 1911, Cowles carried his multiple-factor analysis further by bringing together the results of research on plant succession of the last decade and integrating them within a theory of vegetative cycles, discriminating three interrelated levels at which succession occurs. Each level is associated with a different agency that acts at a different rate, and although they all grade into one another, they nonetheless are independent factors. The broadest and slowest agency is climate, which institutes vegetative cycles of such length that the stages in succession can be grasped only by examination of the record of the rocks. A geographically more limited and faster agency of change is topographic erosion and deposition, which may be studied by comparing its manifestations in various locales. Each cycle of topographic erosion carries with it a correlative cycle of vegetative succession. Finally, there is the most limited and yet fastest agency of change which is the biotic factors themselves. Plant communities produce and reform their own conditions of evolution. Cowles also devoted a short section to the human influence on biotic succession and noted that the "influence of man, almost without exception, is retrogressive" from the mesophytic stage.[25]

Although the overall tendency at all of these levels, with the exception of man, is toward the most mesophytic plant formation the climate of a particular region is able to support (in the United States, this embraced deciduous and coniferous forests, grassland, and desert), the landscape can never be expected to be uniform because of the varying rates and interactions of these various levels.

"Each climatic cycle has its vegetative cycle," Cowles wrote. "Each erosive cycle within the climatic cycles in turn has its vegetative cycle; and biotic factors institute other cycles, quite independently of climatic or topographic change. It is small wonder that within this complex of cycle within cycle, each moving independently of the others and at times in different directions, dynamic plant geography has accomplished so little in unraveling the mysteries of succession."[26]

The distinctive emphases in Cowles's approach to the new science of communities contrasts with the perspective of Frederic Clements. The principal metaphors that informed Cowles's and Clements's interpretations of ecological interdependence were as different as the cultural and physical environments they inhabited. Clements used an organismic metaphor. He compared plant succession to the maturation process of an individual plant or animal organism: "As an organism, the formation arises, grows, matures, and dies. . . . The climax formation is the adult organism, the fully developed community, of which all initial and medial stages are but stages of development. Succession is the process of the reproduction of a formation, and this reproductive process can no more fail to terminate in the adult form in vegetation than it can in the case of the individual."[27] Behind his thought lay the organismic philosophy of Herbert Spencer, best known in the United States for its defense of Social Darwinism. Spencer argued that reformers ought not to intrude on the self-evolving social organism. The reason he gave for opposing deliberate social planning was that social equilibrium was an outcome of a struggle for existence *between* members of society—not the shared struggle *among* members of society for more cooperative modes of life. Similarly, Clements argued that competition between organisms was the governing factor in succession. As Worster, in his account of Clements's thought, concludes: "It was the paradoxical belief of [Clements and Spencer] that the war of each against all for the essentials of life results in a more harmonious social or ecological organism."[28]

Cowles used the metaphor of society. In the textbook on botany he wrote with Coulter and Barnes, he defined physiographic ecology as "plant sociology," and after rejecting the teleological implications of an organic metaphor, discussed the principal mechanism of plant behavior in terms of stimulus-response interactions.[29] Although he was less systematic in his theory than Clements, his descriptions of plant communities undergoing succession read like human societies undergoing varying rates of social evolution and reform. For Cowles, who was taught at Oberlin College, and encouraged at the University of Chicago to keep the liberal arts and the sciences together, the struggle for community in the world of plants was like the struggle for community in the world at large. The engine of progress was not so much competition between individuals as experiments by pioneering associations of organisms (such as the dune-builders) in more adaptive reciprocal relationships with one another and their environment. Behind his thought lay the experimental, social democratic paradigm of the Chicago pragmatists.

Clements's milieu was the grasslands and conifer forests of the West where climatic influences had high visibility: "The net effect was to lead him to broad generalizations, particularly about the 'true prairie,' that were somewhat difficult for his colleagues" farther east to swallow.[30] Cowles, in contrast, had the challenge of the dynamic physical geography of the Chicago Dunes. Clements insisted on a convergence to a single organismic equilibrium as the permanent end-point of succession; Cowles spoke more empirically of a "variable approaching a variable," and noted that diversity of plant life was reduced in converging climax formations, not increased. Clements saw competitive individualism in society and in nature as the means whereby societal equilibrium was more or less automatically achieved; Cowles saw daring experiments in cooperation and adaptation being pushed unpredictably forward as well as set back over the course of history. Clements's model allowed human society only two options—opposition to nature or conformity to the climax form; Cowles's emphasis on pluralism opened the way to a more creative role for human beings in nature's evolutionary adventure.

After the publication of his three classic papers, Cowles's research on the ecology of the Dunes was carried forward by his students in work for their doctorates, and by his colleague George Fuller.[31] William S. Cooper developed one implication of Cowles's ecological theory when he deduced that "succession is a continuous never-ending process, that successional series, instead of representing stages in the genesis of the climax, are merely evidence of a more rapidly changing environment, and that the fundamental feature of all vegetation is . . . the universality of change."[32] No substantial reform of Cowles's account of plant succession in the Dunes occurred, however, until almost exactly a half-century after his first studies.

In the mid-1940s, Jerry S. Olson was first introduced to Cowles's papers by Charles Olmsted, who was then teaching the course begun by Cowles, "Elementary Physiographic Ecology."[33] Olson was only eighteen at the time, a precocious science major, but he was already familiar with the Indiana Dunes. His family spent weekends there. On Saturdays Olmsted took his class on field trips to the Dunes. After the term was over, Olson and a classmate, Floyd Swink (later naturalist with the Morton Arboretum), continued to take trips to the Dunes on the South Shore Railroad. Over the next six years, Olson found himself retracing Cowles's early career—pursuing a joint degree in botany and geology at the University of Chicago, and using the best tools of scientific analysis available to track the dynamics of plant succession in the Dunes.

Like Cowles, Olson approached the dunes as "nature's experiments," the perfect landscape in which to understand, in holistic fashion, how variables like climate and availability of plants and soil influence the emergence of a highly integrated ecosystem from bare sand: "The sand dunes thus show how the ecosystem concept means more than just a name for the biological community and its habitat. The concept of a dynamic, physical-biological system was clearly involved in the interaction of vegetation and physical forces which built the dune."[34]

One of the chief outcomes of Olson's research was confirmation of those tendencies in Cowles's work that cast doubt on the theory of rigid convergence to a uniform climax. More specifically, Olson identified two major routes of plant succession in the Dunes—the first, from dune grass to jack pine to a black oak–blueberry community; the second, found in damp protected pockets, from dune grass to basswood to red oak to sugar maple and beech. Cowles's speculation that better soil conditions and a richer mesophytic forest would emerge with time in all successional series was shown to be ill-founded. In fact, Olson discovered that some soil conditions may actually get worse instead of better for most plants.

Olson's work was a sophisticated scientific updating of Cowles's original research. After two World Wars, it was also an updating of the social perspective with which most Dunes ecologists approached the landscape. Olson took note of the change: "It is necessary to consider the possibility that the limit for some variables might even decline in time. The optimistic American spirit has perhaps given this possibility less attention than it deserves, although the idea has long been commonplace in European studies. Instead of rigid *convergence* to a single climax and a mature zonal soil, one might find a *divergence* of different ecosystems on different sites as a natural outcome of ecological succession."[35]

AN ECOLOGICAL SOCIAL GOSPEL

As a "final thought" in one of his last published essays on plant ecology, Cowles called attention to the "fact" that "all organic nature is a vast and complicated symbiosis." He pointed to the dependence of green plants on other organisms. For their nitrogen they depend on bacteria; for their pollination they may depend on insects; and some of their food may come from dead organic matter. The symbiotic relationship is even more pronounced in the animal world because animals, devoid of chlorophyll, are necessarily less independent. "It is obvious," he concluded, "that evolution has resulted in the general interdependence of organisms, a universal symbiosis."[36]

Cowles spoke with confidence of symbiosis as the primary "fact" of life, yet it is evident that it is as much an ideal as an actuality. Cowles, who repeatedly stressed the struggle for survival and for community, knew this well. That he chose to lift up the principle of universal symbiosis as the first principle of ecology was a token not so much of his science as of the ecological social gospel that informed it.

Cowles communicated his conception of community primarily through his teaching. He taught in the classroom, in the field, among his colleagues in professional forums, and in numerous civic and associational contexts. In spite of the resentment venerable universities felt toward the shift of biological influence from the East to the "barbarian institutions of the Middle West,"[37] and gibes by biologists such as Harvard's William Morton Wheeler concerning the "silo and saleratus belt ecologists" whose primary concern was with the physical environment,[38] Cowles persisted. Through his teaching, he founded a "school" that bore the imprint of his thought and that prepared the ground for the implementation of his ideas in public policy. This would not have happened if Cowles had not brought to his teaching an evangelical fervor for the message of ecology that he saw incarnate in the Indiana Dunes—a personal identification with the panorama of the earth, and a sense of trusteeship for its living landscapes.[39] The gospel he preached was neither primitivist nor managerial, but rather democratic in style, spirit, and principle.

Cowles was a popular and inspiring teacher.[40] It was said that he never forgot a name. With his infectious enthusiasm, he had no trouble holding the students' attention as he led them, in kaleidoscopic fashion, through the hundreds of lantern slides Fuller prepared to depict the evolving landscape of the Chicago glacial plain. But everyone who enrolled knew his heart was in his field trips. Cowles and Fuller took their classes on frequent excursions throughout the Chicago area—north to the clay bluffs near Waukegan, west to the river valley of the Des Plaines, southwest to the sandstone cliffs at Starved Rock—but most often southeast to the Dunes. The class would take a train to the station nearest its destination, and then hike in, carrying cooking and camping supplies. In the summer months Cowles took his advanced classes far afield— to northern Michigan, Maine, the Rockies, Arizona, and one summer, to Oregon and Alaska.

The rapport that grew between the members of the small groups

THE BIRTHPLACE OF ECOLOGY 153

who hiked, cooked, and camped together, sometimes for weeks at a time, was a major factor in Cowles's influence on his students. Cowles was well known for his ability to organize these trips, and for the self-sacrifice and esprit with which he conducted them. Even on a day's outing, he never failed to build a fire and brew a pot of coffee, or tell a good story. One photograph in the botany department archives shows Cowles standing in a field with a cake on his head and on top a single candle burning. Before him are a young man and woman, hands clasped, apparently celebrating a first wedding or engagement anniversary. In Paul Sear's estimation, it was Cowles's sense of the comic that kept him from becoming doctrinaire, allowing him to engage so effectively in the give and take of academic criticism. But beneath his keen wit and good humor was "a fundamental seriousness, and a desire to have the people around him forget their pettiness and pull together."[41]

In 1911 and in 1913, Cowles participated in an international exchange that brought his work in the Dunes directly to the center of discussion among the leading plant ecologists of the time. In the summer of 1911, A. G. Tansley and the British Vegetation Committee invited Cowles and Clements from the United States and various continental scholars, among them Oscar Drude, to join an International Phytogeographic Excursion of the British Isles. After touring England and Scotland, the trip concluded with the meetings of the British Association for the Advancement of Science where Cowles presented a paper on his fifteen-year study of advancing sand dunes.[42] Cowles reflected afterward that as much as he enjoyed seeing the flora of the British Isles, even more important was the fact that "close companionship has made us more sympathetic with opposing viewpoints, and more ready to see at least some truth in views we thought were wholly wrong."[43] He and Clements set about planning an International Phytogeographic Excursion in America.

Cowles asked the Europeans what areas of the United States they would like to visit. The four sites on nearly every list were the Grand Canyon, Yosemite, Yellowstone Park, and the Lake Michigan Dunes. At the end of July 1913, Cowles met the ten foreign scientists in New York. They visited the New Jersey pine barrens and other local attractions, then boarded a train to Chicago. They awoke the next morning to find themselves crossing the Valparaiso Moraine at Michigan City and entering the Chicago plain, with a glimpse of the Dunes. For the next few days, Cowles was in his glory. With the help of Fuller (who had prepared a special guide to the plant associations of the Chicago region), E. J. Hill, Coulter, and Victor Shelford, he shared with some of the leading ecologists of the world his beloved Dune Country.[44]

A. G. Tansley later wrote that following Cowles's opening lectures on the physiographic and geological features of the Chicago region, he was "amused by a remark made to him by an American botanist to the effect that whatever part of the United States one visited one was always told by the local botanist that this was a specially interesting region, because it was the meeting-point of two floras, the eastern and the western—or perhaps the northern and the southern." Everyone, in other words, claimed for their locality the status of an *imago mundi*. Cowles, however, convinced Tansley that he had at last come to the center of the continent: "There can be no doubt, however, as Professor Cowles insisted, that the Chicago region is, in a very real sense, the meeting-place of a northern and southern flora, and of an eastern and western vegetation," Tansley wrote. "This means, of course, that there are actually a large number of species characteristic of the north or of the south which are found intermingled in this region, and that in Illinois and neighbouring States, the great eastern deciduous forest begins to give way to prairie."[45]

The party spent the majority of its time tramping the Dunes. Old photographs show a genial group, many of the men with impressive beards and baggy clothing. On August 2 Cowles took them to Miller Woods where they walked across the dunes to Lake Michigan in reverse order of development, and then to the Central Dunes, where they were impressed by the sight of moving dunes encroaching on a forest. On Sunday they were back to Mineral Springs Bog, and then on to Michigan City to observe an eroding shoreline. Their tour of the Dune Country was climaxed the next day by a visit to Mr. Warren's virgin beech-maple forest near Three Oaks, Michigan. On August 8 the group resumed its journey west to Nebraska and the Rockies.

Cowles was an indefatigable organizer—not only of field trips, but of professional and environmental associations. With his "blithe disregard for boundaries and barriers," he overcame the tension he felt between scientific theory and practice.[46] Cowles never forgot the man who, in 1899, after he showed him with youthful pride his first published article, asked, "Well, what of it?"[47]

Cowles was active in the founding and leadership of some of the twentieth century's most important scientific organizations, among them the Botanical Society of America, the Association of American Geographers, the Ecological Society of America, and various international congresses.[48] Locally, he was active in the Illinois Academy of Science, the Geographic Society of Chicago, and the Chicago Academy of Sciences. He participated vigorously in conservation associations for the preservation of the midwestern landscape. He also spoke frequently on the importance of ecology for conservation and for economic botany—the development of plant resources for human use. He tried to plot an alternative to the exploitation of unbridled private interests, on the one hand, and hyper-sentimental attitudes of urban dwellers who had no direct experience of the land, on the other. In this respect, he regarded himself as a "rational conservationist."[49]

Many long and powerful chains of influence run outward across the United States from Henry Cowles and the Indiana Dunes. One of these chains runs to Cowles's student William Cooper, who as professor of ecology at the University of Minnesota advanced Cowles's work through his twenty-five-year study of the dunes of the Pacific Coast. From Cooper strands lead out to Henry J. Oosting and W. Dwight Billings at Duke University, and to John W. Marr, founder of the Arctic and Alpine Research Center at the University of Colorado. Another chain runs to Cowles's student Paul B. Sears, whose book *Deserts on the March*, written in response to the dustbowl of the 1930s, was one of the first comprehensive attempts to alert the public to environmental issues. Other chains run to Cowles's student Stanley A. Cain, the first ecologist to serve in a subcabinet position in federal government; to the geographers Carl O. Sauer and Gilbert White; to Charles Adams, Victor Shelford, W. C. Allee, Robert Park and the field of animal and human ecology; to Stephen Mather, Richard Lieber, and Cowles's many friends and students among midwestern conservationists and ecologists; to James D. Watson who began his studies in biology in the Indiana Dunes and at the University of Chicago and later discovered the double helix structure of DNA. A map of the "pedagogical genealogy" of American plant ecologists prepared by Douglas G. Sprugel places Cowles at the center and shows lines of influence spreading out from him to leading ecologists throughout the United States—to Edgar N. Transeau (Ohio State), Emma Lucy Braun (Cincinnati), Ralph W. Chaney (California), Elbert L. Little (U.S. Forest Service), Walter P. Cottam (Utah), George E. Nichols (Yale), and Arthur G. Vestal (Illinois). In the judgment of ecologist Beatrice Willard, member of the Council on Environmental Quality in the 1970s, these many chains converged with the passage of the National Environmental Policy Act in 1969 in which the nation was mandated to "create and maintain conditions under which man and nature can exist in productive harmony."[50]

For Cowles personally, the ever-renewing source of his ecological social gospel was the living landscape of the Indiana Dunes. Speaking at the Mather hearings in 1916, Cowles colorfully wove social democratic analogies throughout his argument for the preservation of the Dunes as the ecological microcosm of the world. Cowles began by gently chiding Mather for working for a department that might be better named the "Department of the Exterior" because of its establishment of so many parks on the periphery, rather than the interior, of the country. He eagerly recalled the summer, only three years previous, when, as he said, "I had the great privilege of conducting through our continent . . . men representing all the countries which are now at war with one another."[51] Of the three or four things all mentioned worth seeing, one was the Indiana Dunes. Why? For two reasons, Cowles replied.

First, because in the Dunes is an utterly unique community of life, the "common meeting ground of trees and wild flowers from all directions . . . a marvelous cosmopolitan preserve, a veritable floral melting pot."

There are few places on our continent where so many species of plants are found in so small compass as within the area suggested for conservation. This is in part because of the wide diversity of conditions prevailing there. Within a stone's throw of almost any spot one may find plants of the desert and plants of rich woodlands, plants of the pine woods, and plants of swamps, plants of oak woods and plants of the prairies. . . . Here one may find the prickly pear cactus of the southwestern desert hobnobbing with the bearberry of the arctic and alpine regions. . . . Many of these species are found nowhere for many miles outside of the dune region, so that the failure to conserve the dunes would result in the extinction of this wonderful flora for all time.[52]

In the Dunes, Cowles urged, we see the struggle that creates community: "The struggle for existence always interests because our life is such a struggle. Nowhere perhaps in the entire world of plants does the struggle for life take on such dramatic and spectacular phases as in the dunes." Indeed, there is probably nothing in all nature except a volcano with its lava flow that can be compared with a moving dune. Yet although these moving dunes show the great destructive power of nature, the plants "do not yield supinely." Some species might give up quickly, but others "display an astonishing resistance" with the result that "to almost every condition, no matter how severe, some plants are found adapted." This is the dynamic power of the Dunes revelation. "No other dunes than ours show such bewildering displays of dune movement and struggle for existence, such labyrinths of motion, form, and life. . . ."[53]

The gospel was clear. Wise men from a war-torn Old World make common pilgrimage to the heartland of the New World to see how the struggle for community may be won, how the differences of life may be reconciled. The United States has the obligation to preserve this sacred center so that its vision may continue to renew the earth.

Precisely when and how that portion of the Indiana Dunes which today is designated "Cowles Bog" first received its name is not known. There is no mention of the tamarack swamp or bog north of Mineral Springs in any of Cowles's early papers. The first printed references to the wetland appear around 1913. In the Phytogeographic Excursion Program Cowles wrote for August 3:

After lunch we go to Mineral Springs, traversing an ancient river valley (possibly a former valley of the Calumet River), now characterized chiefly by fen vegetation. . . .

The Mineral Springs bog is on one edge of this ancient valley, representing, probably, a former deep hole in the river which persisted long as a pond. There will be seen the stages in bog development.[54]

Once at the site, the party observed stages in bog succession from reed swamp through xerophytic shrubs to tamaracks and pine-birch climax forest. Despite the occasional appearance of bog plants such as pitcher plant and sundew, the Europeans concluded that the swamp was closest to an English fen.

The location was well known by 1917. In April of that year, John O. Bowers wrote about a fire which had recently invaded the "celebrated tamarack bog,"[55] and E. Stillman Bailey described the "wonderful tamarack swamp" reached by a trail leading west from Mineral Springs Road.[56] The earliest printed references to "Cowles Tamarack Swamp" and "Cowles Bog" date from 1923. George Brennan wrote of "the Cowles Tamarack Swamp—named after the eminent botanist and leading authority on the plants of the Dunes, Doctor Henry W. [sic] Cowles, of the University of Chicago, who had done so much to make it famous."[57] It is apparent that sometime before 1913, in the course of his many field trips to the Dunes, Cowles discovered the bog and began to take his students to visit it. For many generations of students afterward, one of the most fascinating parts of a trip to the Dunes was the walk over the quaking dome-shaped mattress of water-soaked vegetation. At its center was a raised island of tamarack and cedar surrounded by a sea of cattails and sedges. The island seemed like the center of creation itself. Cowles called the bog "a history book with a flexible cover."[58]

The wonder with which Cowles approached this relic of a glacial river valley can be surmised from the legend that grew up after him. According to the story, Cowles was on his way to Chicago for a meeting when he happened to look out of his train window and see an unusually diverse and rare mixture of plants growing together in a nearby swamp. With great excitement he got off the train at Gary, hired a horse and buggy, and rode back to examine the area! He became so enamored of the place that he broke his eastern connections, joined the faculty of the University of Chicago, and devoted the rest of his life to research there.[59]

Although, as Richard Lieber wrote him in 1929, "We have not the money to buy another acre and I don't know anyone who would be willing to give it to the State," by that time Cowles was busy at work trying to save the bog.[60]

A NEW EARTH

In a summary of Cowles's research, George Fuller observed that it was the great desire of the student of nature to want "a new earth" so that he might "watch it to see how the plants come in upon it, how the vegetation develops" to the end that he might "know how the world came into being." "Such an opportunity," Fuller declared, "has been given on the shores of Lake Michigan, where for centuries new land has been continually in process of formation and new plant communities have been developing."[61]

Twenty thousand years ago, the head of Lake Michigan was covered by a great ice sheet that blotted out all vegetation and wiped the surface clean. With the retreat of the ice, the evolution of the land and its communities of life began all over again. The winds and waves went to work on the rocky shores of the glacial lake, and soon tons of sand were piling up. "Century after century this went on," Fuller wrote, "until the new earth measured many square miles spread out as a crescent about the southern end of the lake."[62] While the outer edge of the crescent was twenty thousand years old, the inner ring was built up yesterday. Between the outer and inner rims lay a living panorama of the natural history of twenty thousand years—and through it, the story of the earth itself.

In the period 1875–1925, geologists from throughout the Midwest unraveled the glacial and postglacial geography of the Upper Mississippi Valley and the Chicago glacial plain—the "stage" for the twenty-thousand-year evolutionary drama of the Dunes. Of these, the person most responsible for the view of the Dunes as a "new earth" was Cowles's teacher, Thomas Chrowder Chamberlin.

Chamberlin's epochal studies in glacial geology, cosmogony, and the dynamics of the earth's land-forms permeated the natural sciences of the University of Chicago from the time he came to the school in 1892 until his death in 1928—in the Department of Geology and the *Journal of Geology* which he founded; in the Department of Geography (the first in the country) which his intimate friend, student, and colleague, Rollin Salisbury, founded in 1903; in the Department of Astronomy through his collaborator, Forest Ray Moulton; in the new field of physiographic ecology pursued by Cowles, Fuller, Shelford, and Allee; and in the School of Education, where Zonia Baber and Elliot Downing carried forward his lifelong concern to make science integral to citizenship. Through these and other intermediaries, as well as his own extensive public involvements, Chamberlin became the major architect of the mythico-scientific perspective shared by many members of the Dunes movement toward the physical landscape.[63]

It was not that Chamberlin based his geological studies on the Dunes—although by 1916, he, too, was to view them as a preeminent revelation of the inner meaning of the earth's evolution—but that the world view he developed on the basis of his studies of the glacial history of the Midwest was repeatedly utilized as the foundation for geological studies in the Chicago area, and in this fashion, became associated with the Dunes landscape itself. Chamberlin's idealist interpretation of the progressive evolution of the earth readily confirmed the geopiety with which the members of the Dunes movement approached the geography of their region.[64]

Chamberlin was born on the Illinois prairie in 1843, son of a pioneer mother who loved the wilderness, and a circuit-riding Methodist preacher who came west because he hated slavery. In later life Chamberlin wrote that on the prairie "the skies came down equally on all sides," and as a boy he lived at the center.[65]

After college Chamberlin became head geologist of the Wisconsin Geological Survey (1873–1882). Beginning with field studies in the kettle moraine of southeastern Wisconsin, he early assumed intellectual leadership in the analysis and mapping of the glacial drift sheets of the Upper Mississippi Valley. With his appointment as chief of the new glacial division of the United States Geological Survey (1881–1904), he expanded his study to include most of North America. Chamberlin boldly hypothesized that certain domelike structures in southeastern Wisconsin were ancient coral reefs, which meant that the central United States was once covered by a salt-water sea. He argued that the weight of the glaciers, in addition to erosion, was responsible for the basins of the Great Lakes, thus anticipating his later elastico-solid theory of the earth's surface. In 1894 he published the first formal attempt to define and name the multiple glaciations of North America during the Pleistocene period.[66]

At this point Chamberlin's interest spread beyond glacial geology proper to the larger scientific implications of glaciation. He became concerned for the causes of the glacial climates, a step that led to considerations of cosmogony and "fundamental geological philosophy."[67] As he wrote in retrospect: "If it shall seem strange to anyone that a student of the story of the rocks should turn aside from a field so solid and congenial to venture wantonly into the nebulous wilds of cosmogony, I can only plead in defense the urgent necessities of the scientific chase. It came to be clear that only by close pursuit along the trail that led into the cosmogonic fens and fogs was there any hope of overhauling the quarry that had awakened my instincts of pursuit."[68] Chamberlin undertook a journey, in other words, that led him below and above—from the center of the continent to the origins of the earth in the stellar skies.

At the end of the nineteenth century belief was nearly universal that the earth had gradually cooled from an original molten state—the so-called Laplacian nebular hypothesis. The implication of this view was that the earth would eventually become unfit for human habitation. Chamberlin's studies indicated that there were no radical differences between the atmosphere of the Paleozoic and more recent ages. In place of the nebular hypothesis, he proposed a theory of atmospheric changes that made them dependent on the interplay of a large number of variable factors involved with movements of the earth's surface. These movements oscillated between diastrophic revolutions when lands were raised and base-leveling when shallow seas spread over the continents. The model with which he worked conceived of the earth as maintaining a general equilibrium, with temperature and climate fluctuating between comparatively narrow limits. The implication of his model was that the earth would remain an abode fit for human habitation for eons to come.[69]

The study of ancient geological climates also disclosed facts which seemed to Chamberlin inconsistent with the Laplacian hypothesis regarding the origin of the earth. More plausible, in his view, was the possibility that the earth arose from the condensation of molecules or particles revolving in planetoid fashion. In 1900 Chamberlin revived a notion Buffon had advanced earlier, and suggested that a star had passed close to our sun, that matter had been raised from both stars by tidal forces, and that these cooled into small fragments (planetesimals) which further coalesced into planets. This became his famed "planetesimal hypothesis" of the origin of the earth and solar system.

Chamberlin's cosmogony assigned to the earth a double parentage; it also gave it very different environmental conditions during its formative stages than previous theories. Chamberlin devoted the rest of his life to working out the ramifications of this new starting point for the general theory of geology and organic evolution. In the textbook on geology that he wrote with Salisbury in 1904–06, he traced the evolution of the earth through its volcanic, atmospheric, hydrospheric, and life stages. Later, he argued that in the early stages of the earth's development, the planetesimal infall brought together the appropriate chemical elements under conditions singularly favorable for organic synthesis.

The import of Chamberlin's geological philosophy for the Dunes movement was not in the specifics of his theories, many of which were later superseded. Rather, it lay in the imaginative connections it made between the Chicago glacial plain and the earth's origins, and in the confirmation it provided for what Chamberlin personally referred to as the "honesty" and "fidelity" of the cosmos.[70] Chamberlin spoke with authority about how the earth would continue to endure for hundreds of millions of years as a self-regulated, balanced system on which life may continue to depend. As a result of his work, many saw the degree to which human civilization was a child of the earth's evolution, and how much the progress of civilization depended on maintaining reciprocity with the land.

Chamberlin's influence is readily apparent in Elliot Downing's popular natural history of Chicago and the Dunes. Not only does Downing devote a full third of his text to the "world in the making," recounting Chamberlin's planetesimal hypothesis and tracing the glacial origins of the Midwest and their effect on the distribution of flora and fauna, but he reflects throughout Chamberlin's attitude toward the physical landscape as a causal factor in human history:

> It is interesting to note how human affairs are determined by events that transpired . . . thousands of years ago, long before man had even appeared on the earth. . . . When the Valparaiso Moraine happened to so deposit that the portage from the Chicago River to the Des Plaines was fixed within the present city limits, Chicago's site was practically settled. Even the locations of our fashionable residence sections, streets, railroad approaches, recreation parks, and sewage system was more or less completely settled by the deposits of moraines, locations of old beach lines, sand spits, and dunes of the old glacial lake.[71]

In 1916 Chamberlin carried his own version of an ecological social gospel to the Mather hearings. "To the geologist," he began, "the most important public interest lies in convincing as many of our citizens as possible that this earth of ours, this planet, on whose existence and on whose activities we depend, is not a dead planet, passed on to us from the past, but is a living, active organism. . . ." It is essential to the well-being of the race that the cooperative processes of the earth, such as those that produce our soils, be clearly understood, for only on the basis of such understanding can the citizenry make informed judgments. This is a matter of scientific, moral, and spiritual education. The great cooperative processes of the earth's land, water, and air prepare the earth for our utilization and, at the same time, instruct "us in the duties of the ways of creation." And where can the public gain this instruction? "Now, the dunes furnish one of the best bases for gathering this general impression that is presented by nature that there is."[72]

What Chamberlin (with the help of Salisbury) achieved on a grand scale for the Midwest generally, Salisbury (with the help of W. C. Alden) achieved on a more limited scale for the Chicago glacial plain. In 1899 Salisbury and Alden published *The Geography of Chicago and Its Environs*, the first work to describe in clear, readable fashion the topographic features of the city's physical environment and explain, on the basis of the geological evidence, their origin and history. The book began: "The topography of a region is always significant of its history."[73] Salisbury's and Alden's aim, in other words, was to do locally what Chamberlin had done on the macroscopic scale. It was another study in succession, in "how the world came into being."

The topography of the Chicago region, they explained, is a low, strikingly flat plain roughly crescentic on the southwest side of the head of Lake Michigan. The plain runs from Winnetka on the north, south and east around the lake to the Indiana Dunes, and west to the Des Plaines river valley at Lemont. From the shore of the lake, about 581 feet above mean tide level in New York Harbor, the plain rises very gradually until it reaches the elevation of 60 feet above the lake, and then it becomes rolling and rises abruptly to 200 feet in a great arc, the Valparaiso Moraine. Examination of the plain shows that it is composed of two geological formations—glacial drift (boulders, clay and sand, vegetable mold and peat), lying on top of slopes and valleys of limestone which include fossils of sea life.

These two formations determine the geography of Chicago. By examining their make-up, the development of the present geography may be induced. First the limestone was deposited by ancient seas, after which the land was exposed to erosion for vast geologic periods. Then a great change occurred with the appearance of arctic climatic conditions and the ice sheets of several glacial epochs passed over the area. They ground down previous elevations. They also deposited, in their retreat, a mantle of glacial drift, sometimes, as in the Valparaiso Moraine, a thick belt at the point where the glacier was stationary for a time. The last ice sheet was especially important because as it melted, it created a lake in the depression between the Valparaiso Moraine and the retreating ice front. When the water level reached a certain height, it overflowed to the west along the line of the present Des Plaines river valley.

This was the beginning of Lake Chicago, the ancestor of present Lake Michigan. There were several more or less distinct stages in the history of Lake Chicago, marked by the ridges of beach sand and gravel deposited when the waters of the lake were stationary. Salisbury and Alden identified three major stages: the Glenwood, when the water stood about sixty feet above the level of Lake Michigan, the Calumet, at thirty-five or so feet, and the Tolleston, at twenty feet. After the Tolleston stage, a new outlet was opened to the north, the lake fell to its present level, and the history of Lake Michigan began.

Between the Tolleston and recent stages, deposits of sand and gravel were brought to the head of the lake by the southward drift of the littoral currents. This development is still in process. From Evanston northward, the waves are cutting into the bluffs. The eroded material is constantly shifted southward, creating sand bars across river mouths and new beach lines. The transfer of material reaches its climax in the blowing up of the fine sand of the beach into the ridges and hills of the Indiana Dunes. The Dunes provide the best picture of the geological processes still active in the formation of the geography of the Chicago glacial plain. Salisbury and Alden devoted a major section of their 1899 monograph to describing dune formation and migration, and in the 1920 edition this was expanded to include an account of the succession of plant life on the dunes, based on the work of Cowles.

What Salisbury and Alden achieved for the Chicago glacial plain, George Babcock Cressey set about to do for the Dunes themselves. Before his death in 1922, Salisbury suggested the problem to Cressey and directed his field research. The completed work, *The Indiana Sand Dunes and Shore Lines of the Lake Michigan Basin*, was published by the Geographic Society of Chicago in 1928.

Cressey picked up the story from Salisbury by emphasizing the origin of the present dunes and investigating the principles of aeolian activity—not the activity of ice or water. But his interest in beginnings, in the genetic principles of dune formation, arrived at by examination of the "new earth" before him, were the same. "Since the dunes are but a geologic formation in the making . . ." he wrote.[74] He believed the best place to discover the principles of dune creation was in the Central Dunes between Dune Park Station and Waverly Beach.

Cressey developed a minute phenomenology of the activity of sand particles and sand dunes. Sand jumps rather than rolls (except downhill); its movement assumes the form of either ripples or streamers; and it can accumulate into a dune as smaller ripples overtake larger ones. Sand grains have "had a long and complex history." They have been "handled" by wind and waves and glaciers and rivers, "hurled" and "dragged," and alternately "left stranded" and "blown about."[75] They have been purified, sorted, and selected so that in the sand that reaches the Indiana Dunes, only the quartz grains remain. Cressey calculated wind velocities, constructed a five-tier mechanical sifter on the beach to sort sand by size, and submitted seventy-five samples of sand to microscopic examination in order to arrive at six classes of grains. Disagreeing with W. D. Richardson, who suggested that the explanation for "singing sands" lay in chemical deposits around the grains, he proposed that the sound occurs at the interface of dry and moist layers. Indirect evidence to this effect was provided by the Bureau of Soils, which shipped a sample of "singing sand" back to Washington in a sack. When it was examined there some months later, the musical quality had disappeared.

Perhaps Cressey's most important discovery was that the migration of the dunes was not nearly as extensive as previously supposed. The active blowout dunes, which Cowles described in such detail, while striking topographic features, only involved 1 or 2 percent of the entire area. Salisbury and others had assumed that dunes far inland (subsequent to the Tolleston beach line) were moved there by the gradual transfer of sand from their windward to their leeward side, but stratification studies showed that the inland dunes were formed as foredunes on earlier lake beaches. Cressey painted a more stable and orderly picture of dune development than previous writers had done.

The effect of the work of Chamberlin, Salisbury, Alden, Cressey, and their colleagues in geology and geography, was to map the cosmic space surrounding the sacred center. Theirs was the realm of the spheres—the orderly process of the earth's origin and evolution—the stage on which the struggle for community in the Midwest was being played.

In 1917 Frank M. Woodruff, curator of the Chicago Academy of Sciences, conceived the idea of building a temple to house this cosmic vision. Laverne Noyes, president of the academy, announced the project at the Mather hearings. A large amount of money has been appropriated, he said, "for the purpose of constructing an immense and wonderfully realistic representation of the region surrounding Chicago, starting with the sand dunes, extending west through the marshes, rivers, and lakes, north through the great natural forests, east to the bluffs of the north shore, and thence to the lake again."[76] What Noyes was describing was the great diorama of the Chicago plain which Woodruff spent the next five years building on the second floor of the academy.

Woodruff's effort was painstaking. Deciding that the "background ought to be just a picture, like the backdrop of a stage," he proceeded to project lantern slides on huge pieces of photographic paper. These enormous photographs were then developed in a tank of acid. "Some pictures were so large that I had to get in the tank with rubber boots and sweep the developer over the paper with a big swab!"[77] Reportedly, the largest photograph was of Miller Beach—10 feet high and 168 feet long. The photographs, totaling 265 feet in length, were mounted in a panoramic circle around the sides of the hall and painted over in color. In front of the diorama, Woodruff placed lifelike wax reproductions of trees and plants, and preserved specimens of animals and birds. The impressions of the plants and leaves were first taken in plaster of Paris in the field. Since one tree alone contained hundreds of leaves, and only a few could be made each day, the labor involved was immense.

The result, however, was a marvel to behold: an iconographic replica of the economy of nature of the Chicago glacial plain, with the major portion devoted to the Dunes. During the 1920s Cowles served as president of the academy, and Ragna Eskil remembered that frequently during that period the Friends of Our Native Landscape held its winter meetings there. On one occasion Cowles, carrying a large tray of roast beef, led a grand procession of the members around the circumference of the diorama and then to the dinner tables that awaited them at the center.[78]

After Woodruff's retirement, the new curator, ornithologist William J. Beecher, continued to update the diorama, and by 1982 the full implications of the originator's conception were manifest. After passing panels illustrating the glacial history of the Upper Mississippi Valley, the "Ecology of the Primeval Great Lakes," and the inscription, "Chicago's Past is the Key to Its Present," one enters the darkened second floor hall. To the left (southeast), the native Dunes landscape stretches out bright and glistening in the sun. On the overhung ceiling is written, "North American ecology had its birth in the Indiana Dunes. Prof. H. C. Cowles of the University of Chicago in 1900 noted that dunes farther inland . . ." Above the diorama itself one reads, "This diorama is a study of ecology in the sand dunes at Miller, Indiana. Starting with the physics of sand movement, it shows how certain plants arrest the sand and in time . . ." A little farther on the legend reads, "Professor Victor Shelford added to the work of Dr. Cowles by showing that certain animals . . ." Displayed are interdunal ponds and streams. Then the scene changes to the "Tamarack Bog—an Arctic Remnant," the "Sand Ridges of the Calumet," and "Life on the Tolleston Beach of Ancient Lake Michigan."

The visitor who turns at this point toward the center of the hall wanders through a cave that opens onto a trail crossing the floor of the Chicago plain. Below are seashells. Above are the great black stellar spaces and the constellations of stars. Around the sides of the hall, between the diorama of the Chicago landscape below and the universe above, are depictions of the "Origin of the Earth," and the "Pageant of Life." Here one stands at the still-point, at the *axis mundi* of sacred space and time.

THE BEGINNINGS OF ANIMAL ECOLOGY

In the course of their description of the closing stages of the history of Lake Chicago subsequent to the Tolleston shoreline, and the gradual transition to the earliest stages of Lake Michigan, Salisbury and Alden noted a "remarkable series of parallel ridges, so closely set that they cannot all be separately represented on the map" running north and east of Hammond, Indiana. They identified ninety such ridges, ranging from three to ten feet in height, and separated in most cases by narrow, marshy belts. Taken together, they constituted a "great dispositional terrace" which had been built up under water and exposed by degrees as the lake fell to its present level.[79]

In 1903 Victor Shelford, a graduate student working under the guidance of C. M. Child in the zoology department of the University of Chicago, began to make field excursions in the Chicago area. It was not long before he recognized the potentialities of the sand ridges and ponds at the south end of the lake for the study of the relation of plant and animal succession. As he noted a few years later in one of the first papers published in the United States describing the role of animals in succession, "the selection and analysis of the place of study is the most important step in the whole investigation. Indeed there are only a few suitable localities in North America."[80]

Shelford's first paper (1907) was elegant in conception. His object was to correlate the distribution of various species of the "graceful, predatory, swift-flying" tiger beetle (genus *Cicindela*) with various stages in plant succession.[81] He began with laboratory studies that showed the physiological key to local differences in distribution to be differences in egg-laying instincts. The adults of the various species required different kinds of soil in which to dig small vertical holes and deposit their eggs. He then drew on the order of plant societies worked out for the Dunes by Cowles, showing that with each stage in plant succession there was a corresponding change in species of tiger beetle. These changes were caused by the changing soil conditions created by the succeeding plant associations. Thus, while the copper tiger beetle was abundant on the sandy strip next to the water's edge, the larvae of the white tiger beetle were found principally among young cottonwoods farther back on the lakeward side of the first ridge. In the transitional zone between cottonwood and pine associations, the large tiger, *C. formosa generosa*, made its appearance, yet it was displaced in the pine association proper by the bronze tiger. The green tiger beetle, which thrived in the oak-hickory forest, could not reproduce in the beech and maple association because it could not deposit eggs in pure humus. Shelford concluded his article by suggesting that similar correspondences existed with respect to the fauna in general.

Four years later Shelford's work in animal ecology bore further fruit in a study that contrasted fish succession in streams with that in ponds.[82] In the former, he drew on data collected in streams north of Chicago and showed that in this environment physiographic erosion was the most important factor in succession. In the latter, he drew on his ongoing studies in the interdunal ponds and marshes at the south end of the lake; here succession was conditioned largely by biotic factors making over the habitat. This study, especially its second phase based in the Dunes, had great influence on the growth of animal ecology.

By careful study of the differences between the youngest ponds nearest the lakeshore and the increasingly older ponds farther inland—a progression that spanned several thousand years—Shelford concluded that ponds undergo succession from the bottom upward, that this aging is the consequence of the activities of the plants and animals themselves, and results in the step by step replacement of those plants and animals that cannot tolerate the changed conditions by those that can. The outcome is the elimination of the ponds altogether and their replacement by climax prairie or forest.

Shelford stressed changes in the amount of humus on the floor of the ponds and in the amount of vegetation in the water. For example, the youngest ponds had a bare, sandy bottom without shrubs at the edge, and they were populated by pioneering fish, such as black bass and sunfish, which make their nests in sand. Soon, the bottoms of the ponds became covered with *Chara*, a plant that does not reach the surface of the water, and the bass and sunfish were replaced by fish such as perch, chub sucker, and speckled bullhead, which tolerate dense vegetation and lower oxygen content. The next stage showed the appearance of plants, such as water lilies, which grow in the soil made by *Chara* and reach to the surface. With this change, only muck-loving mud minnows, pickerel, and black bullhead were able to survive. Shelford found that the amount of life per unit volume increased as the ponds grew older, and that the presence or absence of particular species of fish was dependent, not on food supply, but on breeding conditions and breeding activities. That is to say, succession was primarily a matter of changing animal behaviors correlated with changing plant formations.

In 1913 Shelford published a systematic statement of animal ecology, *Animal Communities in Temperate America*, based on field studies at seventy-six stations within a hundred miles of Chicago, the majority at the southern end of the lake. The book was principally a study of the succession of the animal communities of various major habitats—streams, lakes, ponds, swamps, forests, prairie. Of the several lines of thought along which Shelford proposed to organize his data, two were of special significance for those who followed him in the field of animal ecology at Chicago.

The first revolved around the notion of "mores" as the "central problem of ecology."[83] In his work on pond fishes, Shelford had concluded that "ecological succession is based upon physiology, habits, behavior, mode of life, and the like, which I have proposed to call *mores* (opposed to the term form)."[84] The kind of mores important in his work on the tiger beetle and pond fishes was breeding behavior. In these studies Shelford had shown that the changing character of mores defined the different stages of the successional order, and most closely correlated communities of animal organisms with changing environmental conditions. In his 1913 work, Shelford defined "mores" as "physiological life histories in relation to natural environments together with that of the relations of organisms in communities."[85] This was an attempt to bring together under a unified concept the autecological and synecological aspects of the new field.

The second line of thought pushed Shelford in the direction of Clements's general theory of succession.[86] Shelford opened his book with the assertion that the first step in any adequate understanding of nature was the recognition that the state of nature was a struggle for survival among competing individual organisms. To make this point especially vivid, he quoted a long passage from Theodore Roosevelt describing the "hideous horror" that was the everyday life of wild creatures and preliterate man.[87] Later in the book, he developed the notion that the primary engine of ecological succession was the deleterious effects of each organism's particular mores:

The biological causes of succession lie chiefly in the fact that organisms frequently so affect their environment that neither they themselves nor their offspring can continue to live at the point where they are now living. Every organism adds certain poisonous substances to its surroundings, and takes away certain substances needed by itself. It frequently thus so changes conditions that its offspring cannot live and grow to maturity in the same locality as the parents. However, by these same processes it prepares the way for other organisms which can live and grow in the conditions thus produced.[88]

It was through these negative mechanisms—the war of all against all, and the self-elimination of species from their own habitat—that the various sequences of plant and animal succession inexorably converged on the permanent equilibrium of the climax beech and sugar maple forest in the eastern United States.

Shelford's studies on succession in the Dunes were brilliant, but his interpretation of the process of succession went against the grain of the Cowles school of ecology. Nor was his interpretation congenial to most members of the Dunes movement, who saw some form of cooperation intrinsic to all stages in the evolution of the landscape. A more positive interpretation of the struggle for community among animals awaited the appearance of another Dunes ecologist.

In 1908 Warder Clyde Allee, recently graduated from Earlham College, began graduate studies in zoology at the University of Chicago.[89] He quickly became one of Shelford's favorite students, and it was not long before he was in the field helping him map the ponds and ridges west of Gary. In 1911 Allee published his first paper, a study of seasonal succession in the ninety-third depression back from the lake. It was one of the first on the subject in ecological literature. He concluded that "seasonal succession may be regarded as the cyclic or slightly spiral process, by means of which ecological succession is carried on. It therefore presents a minute unit for the study of the general succession problem."[90]

The dominant species in the ponds throughout most of the year was a fresh water crustacean, the isopod *Asellus communis* Say. Over the course of the next two decades, Allee was to devote the major portion of his experimental research to this little creature. These studies were to serve, in turn, as the groundwork for his construction of a general theory of social cooperation in animals—perhaps the most comprehensive and ethically sensitive theory of the century.

In 1912 Allee, still following in Shelford's footsteps, completed a dissertation comparing the mores of stream and pond *Asellus*. Gathering his stream specimens from north of the city, and his pond specimens from the marshes near Gary, Allee submitted them to laboratory analysis to test their tendencies to swim against the current. Allee found a marked difference between the two when physical conditions were such as to duplicate those found in the natural environment. Stream isopods swam strongly against the current, while the response of pond isopods was indefinite. Further experimentation indicated that the difference was most likely due to the amount of oxygen in their respective habitats. Allee concluded that "we are dealing with the pond *mores* and the stream *mores* of *Asellus communis*, which depend on environmental rather than on hereditary differences for their distinctive features."[91]

The most pregnant observation Allee made in the course of his doctoral studies received only slight mention in his dissertation. Many years later Allee recalled the sunny April day when, in the midst of his laboratory experiments, he went out to check the behavior of freshly collected isopods in a brook. To his surprise, the stream isopods, instead of going against the current, cut across it at any angle in order to reach other nearby isopods. "When I used five or ten individuals at a time, as I had done in the laboratory, they piled together in small clusters that rolled over and over in the gentle current."[92] This bunching, he later discerned, was primarily related to the onset of the breeding season, but it was apt to occur at any time during the year if environmental conditions became unfavorable, as with a sudden drop in temperature.[93] Wrote Allee in 1938: "That was the beginning of the road that I have followed from that April day to this time, continuing to be increasingly absorbed in the problems of group behavior and other mass reactions, not only of isopods, but of all kinds of animals, man included."[94]

Allee was married in 1912, an event of more than incidental importance for traveling the road on which he had just embarked. Marjorie Hill was graduated from the University of Chicago College in 1912 with a major in writing and English literature. She, like Clyde, was a committed Quaker, and a native of Indiana. Her writing ability was to be an asset to her husband in the preparation of papers and books, but she was to help him most through the shared life she helped make possible in the face of great personal hardship.[95]

Between 1925 and 1945 Marjorie Allee wrote a series of novels for girls. These popular books, built out of the experiences of the Allee household in Chicago and its travels to other parts of the world, were vehicles for the expression of the liberal social ideals she and her husband shared. Often, Clyde appeared as one of the older professorial characters in her adventures, as did others among their mutual friends at the university. The backdrop to the books was the social issues of the day, often racial relationships and conflicts, and their connection, both personal and symbolic, with biological ideas and research. In several of her books, Marjorie Allee placed these relationships in the setting of a landscape she especially loved—the Indiana Dunes.

The 1937 novel *The Great Tradition* tells the story of a young woman by the name of Merritt who arrives at the University of Chicago for graduate study in zoology. Soon she is enmeshed in a series of relationships—with her professor, Dr. Overman, who is doing work on isopods; with a young handicapped girl by the name of Hilda; and with several fellow students: a black woman, Delinea; an attractive, but self-centered girl, Charlotte; and an advanced student, Gordon, with whom she falls in love. Merritt displays a set of exemplary social virtues. She takes responsibility for her friends, especially caring for the needs of Hilda; she has great respect for Delinea and helps her in every way she can; and she tries to show Charlotte what a mutually supportive family can be. Merritt is assigned the problem of repeating Dr. Overman's first experiment with *Asellus communis* Say: "Hour after hour she had stirred relays of isopods, small flat grayish crustaceans . . . round and round in a blue crockery jar half full of water, observing closely how they righted themselves to face upstream as soon as they had got on their eight pairs of legs again."[96]

One day Gordon takes Merritt and Hilda (whom Merritt wishes to get some fresh air and sun) on their first trip to the Dunes. "Miles and miles they drove through traffic past a monotony of houses and mills. . . . It was an hour before they had actually come into the country where the sky was a clear blue instead of dingy as if seen through smoked glass." Finally, they cross a series of railroad tracks and stop at a spring marsh. The purpose of the trip is to collect isopods. "Slip your dip-net down into the clearer places and shovel in under the dead leaves in the bottom," Gordon tells Merritt. "Then drain it. And see if you can tell which are isopods and which are rotten leaves." Merritt is surprised how closely the sluggish isopods resemble the decaying leaves they live among, and soon she is immersed in the mud with the isopods, amphipods, and flatworms. Afterward, she, Gordon, and Hilda ("with an appetite that would have astounded her mother") enjoy the communion of a great picnic feast under the hot noon sun.[97]

W. C. Allee continued his experiments on the physiological reactions of *Asellus* throughout the 1910s. His 1918–1921 work at Woods Hole impressed him with the distinctive character of biotic communities as social entities. The war also made a deep impression. In articles for the *Quaker,* Allee called attention to the biological causes of international conflict and peace.[98] Soon after receiving a permanent appointment at the University of Chicago, he announced that his studies were focusing on the bases for cooperation in animals, and that, contrary to the accepted theory that derived organized society from the family by way of the clan, he was interested in the emergence of community by means of the consociation of adult individuals.[99] In 1926 the first of a long series of research papers under the title "Animal Aggregation" appeared.[100] These papers stressed the importance of the phenomenon of bunching in *Asellus* as an example of proto-cooperation in a wide diversity of animal forms. In work with land isopods, which congregated into dense bunches when their habitat became dry, Allee discovered that the phenomenon had definite survival value.

Christmas, 1926, C. M. Child reported to Allee that he had discovered a great aggregation of *Asellus communis* Say in the Indiana Dune Country. Allee immediately drove out to observe it. The aggregation had formed on either side of a roadway recently thrown across a cattail swamp at the headwaters of Dune Creek, about two miles southeast of Waverly Beach. Under the ice Allee could see tens of thousands of isopods, all swimming against the current upstream; thousands more were resting on the bottom in protected places, and still others were being swept downstream. Marjorie Hill Allee described the event in *The Great Tradition:*

"Has it occurred to you," [Professor Overman] asked, "how difficult it would be to watch the behavior of an isopod in his native watercress swamp? . . . One winter I heard of a great mass of isopods imprisoned in a clean sandy-bottomed pool under the ice forty miles out of the city, and once a week I drove out there to look at them until the spring thaw set in and washed them away. The ice was as clear as glass. I could lie down flat and watch how they moved about against the current or downstream. I analyzed samples of the water. I had a fine time.[101]

Allee was given a rare opportunity to test his laboratory findings in the field. As he wrote, "Great aggregations of these animals in nature have hitherto escaped attention." His conclusion was that for the most part the aggregations could be explained on the basis of individual tropistic reactions to environmental stimuli. "The main social trait exhibited appears to be that of tolerance for the presence of many other individuals in a limited space where they have collected. . . . The same idea can be expressed by saying that almost the sole social trait exhibited is the immunity to injurious effects resulting from the presence of many others in a limited amount of space."[102] In particular, they were able to tolerate the low oxygen tension and high concentration of carbon dioxide resulting from the aggregation.

These findings in themselves would not appear to be startling. But placed within the context of a general theory of sociality in animals, they took on large significance. In 1931 Allee published *Animal Aggregations, A Study in General Sociology.* The purpose of the book was to provide a unified account of recent discoveries of the beneficial effects of relatively unorganized crowds of animals. Allee again reported at length on his studies in 1927 at Dune Creek and asserted that the aggregations observed represented a major advance toward social life among nonvertebrates, that they were the first step in the evolution of social integration among animals. "So far as I am aware," he wrote, "no other great natural aggregation at the low level of group organization here existing has been analyzed. . . ."[103] Although he had no proof, it was likely that in the long run the aggregation was an adaptive reaction for the species.

What Allee believed he saw in the Dunes Christmas 1926 was the primal society. Its defining characteristic was tolerance.

In the final chapter of *Animal Aggregations*, Allee summed up the implications of his discussion by positing what was in effect a first principle of existence. This principle he named variously "unconscious cooperation," "automatic mutual interdependence," or simply, "the principle of cooperation." The principle of cooperation was manifest when the first living molecules so conditioned their immediate environment that as other particles of living matter appeared in the same niche, they had a better chance of survival. "These first living particles were probably dependent on each other for the final adaptation of their physical environment so that they could continue to live." Cooperation has survival value. It is therefore a "fundamental trait of living matter," one of the fundamental qualities of protoplasm in general.[104] Furthermore, the principle of cooperation is rooted in similar but simpler forms of interdependence in antecedent nonliving matter. Thus, it is a principle of existence as such.

It is not an exaggeration to say that in aggregations of organisms, such as *Asellus communis* Say at Dune Creek, Allee felt he had found the key to organic, if not cosmic, evolution. Previous to his studies, he pointed out, unconscious cooperation was virtually unrecognized. Those few, such as Kropotkin, Espinas, or Wheeler, who were concerned with building a case for mutual aid as a basic evolutionary tendency, appealed exclusively to the evidences of cooperation among insects and the larger animals. But these were all evolutionarily advanced societies. Now, with the discovery that "general cooperation exists among loosely organized, or among apparently unorganized, groups of animals living even temporarily in the same region," evidence is available that cooperation was operative at the beginnings of integrated social activity.[105]

By 1931 Allee had transmuted the first principle of plant and animal succession, reciprocity, into a principle of the evolution of life in relation to the physical environment as a whole, a movement that had always lain implicit in the imaginative margins of the new ecological science. Beginning, with the help of Cowles, Fuller, and Shelford, in the exploration of seasonal succession in the ridges and ponds west of Gary, a mere "unit" in the larger sequence of topographic and climatic succession, Allee had moved twenty years later to a hypothesis whereby the study of ecology and evolution were one. Allee's synthesis befitted the vision held by many members of the "Chicago School," laden as it was with cosmogonic insights concerning ultimate origins and ends.

Allee concluded *Animal Aggregations* with a brief discussion of the implications of his theory for the current conflict between national and international organization. "Now, as in each stage of the social evolution of man, the proponents of the narrower organization maintain that the type of groupings they advocate satisfies the natural instinctive and traditional drives of man, while the more inclusive grouping is an abnormal desire for an idealistic utopia. So might the conservative primitive-living molecules, the protozoans, flatworms, isopods, or ants have argued, had they wit, at each stage of their cooperative evolution."[106] The principle of cooperation is the first principle of existence and it is universal in its application and in its tendings. It is, therefore, going with the current of evolution to move toward an increasingly more inclusive and cooperative world order.

Allee, too, had an ecological social gospel, and after 1931, as he became increasingly preoccupied with the problem of the evolution of human social ethics out of lower social forms, he rapidly developed it. In this project he received considerable mutual aid from his colleagues in Chicago.

Over the years the custom grew up for a meeting of an Ecology Seminar as a biweekly Monday evening event in the Allee home. The group was drawn from the Department of Zoology, students interested in ecology, and invited persons from other departments and nearby institutions. Books and publications of interest were reviewed, and current research presented for discussion and criticism. With the help of this group, Allee produced in 1938 *The Social Life of Animals*. In 1939 the six principal members of the group, Allee, Ralph Buchsbaum, Alfred E. Emerson, Thomas and Orlando Park, and Karl Patterson Schmidt (Buchsbaum later withdrew because of army duty) began the ambitious project of writing a comprehensive textbook of animal ecology. A decade later the magisterial *Principles of Ecology* appeared. Noting the changes in the study of ecology in the half-century since its beginnings in the Midwest, it concluded: "In present day ecology succession no longer occupies so prominent a place. It is studied, but the emphasis is on the total community, with succession essentially a developmental phase of that total unity."[107]

The point of view represented by the "AEPPS Group," as it was called, was shared by a wide spectrum of natural and social scientists associated in various ways with the University of Chicago from the 1920s through the 1930s. James Tufts and George Herbert Mead in philosophy, Paul Douglas in economics, T. V. Smith in political thought, Robert Park and Ernest Burgess in sociology, Robert Redfield in anthropology, Ralph Gerard and C. M. Child in biology were only a few of those at the University who pursued the quest for a "science of community."[108] Charles C. Adams was an example of those who carried the mainstream viewpoint of animal ecology at Chicago to other scientific centers of the country.[109]

In September, 1941 on the occasion of the university's fiftieth anniversary, the Ecology Group sponsored a symposium on "Levels of Integration in Biological and Social Systems."[110] Participants included Allee, Redfield, Gerard, Robert Park, and A. L. Kroeber. The participants found general agreement in the proposition that the competitive aspects of developing social integration were overstressed at the expense of the cooperative. However, Robert Park was most concerned for the freedom of the individual, while Gerard argued for a greater subordination of the individual to the larger group. One way of resolving these differences, Redfield suggested, was to discriminate two different levels of interaction in human societies: the ecological-economic-symbiotic and the moral and religious, and the modes of cooperation and competition appropriate to each.

The influence of the Ecology Group was also apparent at the Fifth Symposium of the Conference on Science, Philosophy and Religion held in 1945. In his paper Allee pointed out that human beings are unique among animals because when they accept subordinate social status, they often retain a consciousness of an inner compensation. They *"know* that the dominance gradient of true merit is quite different from the one that actually exists."[111] Human

beings are aware that when the principle of cooperation is interpreted as a democratic principle—as a principle of cooperation
among equals—it has the status of an "unseen" reality ontologically
prior to the seen.

The most concise and far-ranging statement of Allee's mature
thought appeared in an essay published in 1943, "Where Angels
Fear to Tread: A Contribution from General Sociology to Human
Ethics." Allee begins with "the problems imposed by the present
war and by thoughts of the coming post-war world."[112] He then
posits a fundamental dialectic, the resolution of which constitutes
the light the study of biology throws on the social behavior of
human beings.

One side of the dialectic is represented in the first of two experimental approaches to the phenomena of biological sociology. An
example of this approach is the research Allee pursued for over a
decade on the dominance-subordination relations characteristic of
many social groups, for example, the nip-orders in fish. These social
orders appear to be an expression of crude, individual-versus-indi-
vidual competition for social status and privilege. They furnish
ample illustration of the individualistic, egocentric phase of group
biology. In other words, they are an aspect of the individual
struggle for existence closely associated with the Darwinian theory
of evolution. If the premises and conclusions of this kind of study
are accepted as the whole truth of social evolution it is evident that
human altruism is connected with the mass of animal behavior by a
"very slender stalk."[113] In the absence of biological foundations on
which to base the idea of a natural drive toward altruism, such
drives are readily interpreted as some sort of enlightened selfishness.

This first perspective, Allee takes pains to point out, is what the
ordinary biologist still thinks of as the sum of natural selection, and
the man in the street cannot be blamed if he shares the same point
of view. "Personally," he adds, "I was well and thoroughly trained
in this orthodox biological doctrine. For example, it was clearly
stated in the first chapter of a book published in 1913 by my stimu-
lating friend and former teacher, Professor V. E. Shelford."[114]
Needless to say this first perspective offers little incentive to humankind to move toward more inclusive forms of international cooperation, and insofar as the scientist represents it as the whole

truth, he is morally culpable. Yet it is part of the truth. The human vices of pride, covetousness, lust, anger, gluttony, envy, and sloth are real and they have natural roots in infrahuman behavior.

The other side of the dialectic is represented in the experimentation Allee pursued for twenty-five years in unconscious forms of cooperation among lower organisms. Allee summarizes briefly the evidence for the existence of such cooperation. In his list he turns Shelford's interpretation of the dynamics of succession on its head: "Both plants and animals are able so to condition an unfavorable medium that others following or associated with them can survive better and thrive when they could not do so in a raw, unconditioned medium." Further evidence for the interdependence of organisms is the repeated observation that all living things, from the simplest to the most complex, live in ecological communities. Moreover, the evolution of social animals in widely separated divisions of the animal kingdom would not have occurred apart from a strong substratum of generalized natural cooperation. Allee notes that pursuit of "group-centered, more or less altruistic drives that lead to the preservation of the group or of some members of it perhaps at the sacrifice of many others" was also recognized by Darwin when he argued that natural selection acts on the family as well as on the individual.[115]

Both egoistic and group-centered forces exist in nature, and both may be scientifically investigated. The question is their relationship. Any group organization may be helpful under some conditions, even if, like the pecking orders, it is attained by individual competition. But the question persists as to which is more fundamental and potent. Allee's conclusion is that while the "balance between the cooperative, altruistic tendencies and those which are disoperative and egoistic is relatively close," and under many conditions the cooperative forces lose, "in the long run the group-centered, more altruistic drives are slightly stronger."[116] Allee was a provisional pessimist and an ultimate optimist.

Allee believed he had grounds for healing the tragic division between science and religion—the twin bases of civilization. "God," he suggests, following John Dewey, "is a possible permissible name for the personification of all the best that the human race has been able to think and do and of all the beauty we have created, together with all the natural beauty we can appreciate."[117] The essence of "God" so defined is the social doctrine of the world's ethical religions: behave toward all others as you would have all others behave toward you. Ecological science now provides objective evidence for the age-old religious insight that a just and enduring peace can only be found in a positive application of this rule.

Allee's lifelong quest for the ecological and evolutionary bases of cooperation was motivated by his ethical and religious commitments. These commitments were apparent in his concern for peace, in his regular attendance, along with Paul Douglas, at the meetings of the Hyde Park Society of Friends, in his chairmanship of the Chicago area American Friends Service Committee, and in his active participation in the Wildflower Preservation Society. In this respect, he was no different from most of the members of the "Chicago School" of ecology in the first half of the century. The same concerns that motivated the Allees also motivated Zonia Baber to work with the Hyde Park Council of Churches to better racial relations, and to participate with Jane Addams in the Women's League for International Peace and Freedom. The same concerns motivated Thomas Chamberlin to develop an elaborate proposal for an "omninational confederation" after the First World War as a way of offsetting the thirst of "feudal castes" for greater possessions.[118]

The ecological studies pursued at the University of Chicago, and focused so intensely upon the Indiana Dunes, appeared as part of a larger movement among Progressive intellectuals in the Midwest for a more thoroughly democratic social order. There is something fitting about the fact that the science of ecology, which must, as Paul Sears argues, "operate for the general welfare,"[119] and which represents a point of view as well as a scientific field, should be indebted to those who acted out a concern for the general welfare in practical life, and identified their vision of community with the plants, animals, and soil of a particular landscape. The perceptions scientists have of nature are not isolated from the rest of their mental lives—least of all from the cultural metaphors and experiences shaping the presuppositions of their worldview. It is an exemplification of the first principle of ecology itself that natural science, social ethics, and religious myth and symbol should be so interdependent.

FIVE

Hearth Fires

From the dry stick
Is born Flame;
No man may careless be
With this most sacred rite.
Perpetual lamps
Burn to the gods,
Who burns in wanton waste
Destroys our hearth.
Let fire be thy constant care,
Leave it not to its own will,
It serves with faithfulness the true
But devastates with cruel lips
The leas and fields when flung astray.

MARY LARNED,

from "*The Voices of the Dunes, a Masque*," 1918

Daily the hearth owner celebrates the greatest of all discoveries—that of fire. . . . For fire is man's secret uniquely; no other animal can make or use it, though we can see the hearthside cat or dog worship it with shining eyes. For ourselves, the hearth has become the family altar.

For untold time, millions have known like joys and associations with the hearth; indeed, the first hearth-stones mark the beginning of civilization. For, unlike the wandering beasts, man knew now a spot so dear that he would die defending it, and seeing the smoke of other hearths arise he first learned the meaning of neighbor.

DONALD CULROSS PEATTIE,

from *A Cup of Sky*, 1947

The sun has gone below the horizon and put the heavens afire. . . . More and more young and old gather around the camp fire for play and inspiration. It is the most democratic gathering on earth, one man is no more than the other, they all are on the same level. It is a distinct message for us, for it brings back to our minds the struggles and the life of all mankind from all times.

JENS JENSEN,

from "*The Campfire or Council Fire*," in *Outdoors with the Prairie Club*, 1941

According to the myth of the 1917 Pageant, the Dunes were the dwelling place of the High Manitou, Nanabozho, at the beginning of time. They were

. . . the place his fires made bare, the place
Where his great lodge was standing in the time
Before he first created men.[1]

By implication Nanabozho's hearth fire was the first altar. The Dunes today are the site of the original home, the first temple, the house of God.

AT HOME IN THE UNIVERSE

A recurring image in the life and work of those who participated in the Dunes movement is the image of building a fire and constructing a home at the center of the Dunes. The creation of a place for human dwelling is an archetypal ritual in the history of religions. The model for the ritual is the myth of the god's creation of the world, and the temple or house is conceived as an *imago mundi*, or microcosm of the universe. As Eliade explains, "Religious man wants his own house to be at the center—to reproduce the universe, near the sanctuary."[2] By means of the fire symbolism associated with the ritual, religious communities dramatize their view of how human beings are to use the primal energy of the universe—the sun on earth. The ritual provides a pattern for the construction of towns and cities. It is a paradigm for the distinctly human way of life.

There is a remarkable similarity among the "pictures" of the various camps, huts, cottages, lodges, and houses that the leaders of the Dunes movement have established (or imagined establishing) over the years in the Dunes. They suggest a shared image of the nature of Nanabozho's original lodge—a consensus on how human beings ought to live in the world. For the Dune Country patriots, the ideal home in the Dunes has not served as a blueprint for society so much as a transcendent model in terms of which judgment may be brought against an industrial civilization out of the control of its citizens.

George Brennan introduces his book, *Wonders of the Dunes*, with a photograph by Indianapolis photographer Frank Hohenberger entitled "The Camp Guardian."[3] It illustrates the prophetic ideal of human dwelling in the Dunes experience. On the high knoll of a dune a clearing for a camp has been made. A tree bough arches over the camp's firepit, and together they frame the distant view. In the background, foredunes run down to the beach; beyond, the lake stretches out to the horizon. The closed space of tree and camp and the open space of foredunes, beach, and horizon, center and periphery, evoke a feeling of the vitality and intimacy of human dwelling with nature in the midst of an infinite universe.[4]

A camp is no one's exclusive possession, but rather a setting in which many persons come to share a common experience. By omitting any particular human figure in the clearing, the photograph suggests the presence of many persons—including potentially the viewer. The wind-blown tree is like Hannell's cosmic tree, symbolic of all organisms striving for life in the ever-changing, yet peculiarly sustaining environment of the Dunes. The shape of the tree shows that it lives only through the medium of sun, wind, rain, and sand; it exists by grace of its surroundings even as it asserts itself over against them.

Earl Reed's popular story "A Romance of Mt. Tom" confirms this association of the camp with the cosmic mountain, and the interdependence of humanity and nature. It makes explicit an additional element—the association of love and faithfulness between persons with the sacred fire at the Dunes' center.

Reed places his story in the time when a Potawatomi village flourished near the monarch of the sand hills—what the Indians called *Wud-ju-na-gow*, or "Sand Mountain." A period of great famine comes to the Dune Country. Wa-be-no-je, a young brave, sets out on a long journey in quest of food. During his absence a fire is built every night on the top of the sand mountain, as a beacon to guide the brave during his journey. Wa-be-no-je meets with tragedy and dies in the quicksand of one of the great Dunes bogs. Meanwhile, Taheta, a young woman who loves him, night after night faithfully climbs to the summit of the Sand Mountain and kindles the fire. One night, in the dead of winter in a snowstorm, she dies huddled in a blanket. Reed concludes: "Today the Fireweed, that ever haunts the burnt places, lifts its slender stalk above the spot, and it may be that the soul of faithful Taheta lurks among the tender pink blossoms—a halo that may be seen from the dark waters of the distant marsh."[5]

On May 17, 1924, Samuel Harper left Chicago and set out on a ten-day pilgrimage through the Dune Country, a walk that he later described in *A Hoosier Tramp*. Leaving the first morning train at Tremont, he followed the trail north to the Prairie Club Beach House. After a series of detours, including a walk along Dune Creek where he encountered a magnificent cluster of eighteen giant white trilliums, he arrived at the Duneland Studio of Frank Dudley and his wife Maida. For many, including Harper, the life the Dudleys made for themselves in the Dunes was "the stuff that dreams are made of."[6] Harper's description of his visit is a classic account of the image of sacred dwelling in the Dunes tradition.

Harper and the Dudleys spent the afternoon walking together, enjoying the beauties of the landscape, with Dudley occasionally stopping and making observations for painting the next day. Toward evening, they returned to the Duneland Studio. Like Brennan's camp, it "stood upon the first ledge of the sand hills, its rustic porches reaching out toward the watery horizons to the north." It was both home and artist's workshop. Here Dudley painted and he and Maida held weekly open house. "The glow in the large open fireplace in the studio softened the chill in the evening air," and the light from candles placed around the walls filled the room with a "twilight atmosphere of golden tranquillity which brought rest and peace for every weariness." Harper and his hosts talked before the fire far into the night. One story Dudley told was of a pet cowbird who became a member of the family. The evening ended around midnight with a walk along the shore to a blowout nearby. "Reclining in the white sand on the dune crest with this magnificent panorama about us silvered by the soft light of the moon we talked in quiet tones of the mysteries of life and the great cosmic purposes of Nature."[7]

Walking in fellowship with those who share an appreciation of the beauty of the landscape; returning to a house on the summit of a sand mountain, built for serious work and for an open community of friends; the power of fire controlled for warmth and light; the kinship of other creatures; the joy of shared experience; communion with the whole of existence—these define the image of human fulfillment in the Dunes. The image implies human beings as artists in community—each using creative individual capacities to build a cooperative social order and an artifactual world in harmony with the natural environment. The Dudleys endured financial hardship to realize that vision at the Duneland Studio. In the 1960s, after Frank Dudley's death, members of the Dunes movement tried—but failed—to preserve the studio as an historical monument in the Indiana Dunes State Park.[8]

The Dunes experience of harmonious dwelling with nature is typically less obvious and less accessible than this brief account of Harper's trip makes it appear. There is usually a noticeable qualitative break between the experience of ordinary life and the experience of the Dunes. In Harper's story, the break is communicated by the train ride to the Dunes, like the car in Armin's painting *Crescendo*, a modern symbol of transcendence. The home in the Dunes is at the sacred center. It is something that has to be sought; it is something that can be easily lost. More often than not, the image appears in the Dunes literature as a precious memory and lasting hope—something experienced once upon a time and never forgotten.

Irma R. Frankenstein's story *The Chronicle of the Befogged Dune Bugs* conveys the elusive quality of the experience and the complex symbolism associated with it. Frankenstein's essay was written to be read aloud at one of the "Monday Evenings" of George Burman Foster, Professor of Comparative Religions at the University of Chicago. Earl H. Reed, who was often present at these gatherings, added illustrations and Emily Chapman, a friend of Paul and Emily Douglas, published her mother's story in a 1958 Save the Dunes Council pamphlet to explain why "EVERY man, woman and child" loves the Dunes.[9] At one level the story is simply a humorous account of a trip one fall Sunday in the company of several friends. At another level it is an allegory of a spiritual pilgrimage to the temple in the Dunes. Appropriately enough, the guide for the day's pilgrimage was Captain Charles Robinson, care-taker in his retirement of the Prairie Club Beach House.

Leaving Hyde Park in Chicago by daylight saving time on the Illinois Central Railroad, the party of "Dune Bugs" (an entomological thing which sees marvelous effects of color and line where an ordinary bug sees sand and more sand")[10] travels to Port Chester and thence by foot to the Geraldine cottage, nestled in the sand hills by the lake. They spend much of the day in fellowship around the stove; later, some gather wild grapes, and others buy fish from a neighbor. When it is time to leave a dense fog has set in and on the return trip the party becomes hopelessly lost. After everyone pitches in and helps build a fire they discover a dune and climb to its summit, from which they can see the light of the Geraldine cottage. Laden with grapes and fish, they find their way, singing on the long hike to Port Chester Station. Even here they are delayed; the time has changed back to standard time.

The story is a brilliant portrayal of how easily the communion of the temple may be lost, and how only by the repetition of the corporate ritual of fire-building, and struggle up the cosmic mountain, sacred time and space may again be reentered, and the dwelling at the center refound.

Marjorie Hill Allee's 1933 novel *Ann's Surprising Summer* also illustrates this archetype. One spring, her mother seriously ill and the family under heavy financial pressure, Ann accompanies her father and his zoology class from the University of Chicago on a field trip to the Dunes. Ann climbs to the top of Mount Tom and contemplates what it would be like to live there for a summer. Later, while the class is "setting up small apparatus on the beach; thermometers to take the temperature of air and sand and water, a whirligig to measure wind velocity," Ann visits a "little weathered box of a cottage" which belongs to a family friend.[11] Waiting to be torn down because it is within the boundaries of the new State Park, the shack sits on a dune with sand-cherry bushes and a broad beach below and a great hill of yellow sand topped by jack pine above. The only solid part of the house is a wide chimney composed of dozens of different kinds and colors of brick, tile, and stone contributed by friends over the years of its construction. At Ann's urging, and with the unexpected addition of her aunt who has lost everything in the Great Depression, the venture of the family for the summer is to restore the cottage as a place for human dwelling. The story symbolizes how human beings, faced with personal and social adversity, may, by relighting the sacred fire in the Dunes, and recreating a shared life in close relationship to the land, renew their corporate existence and begin again.

A related theme is the Dunes home as a refuge won after a struggle with adversity. David Sander wrote a memorable instance of this theme based on a childhood experience in the 1930s. He remembers looking down the beach during a fierce summer thunderstorm and seeing his father, on his way home from Chicago to spend the weekend, trudging through the rain and down the sand. Afterward, Dave's father stood on a pile of newspapers in the front room of the cottage, his Palm Beach suit and straw hat ruined, his pocketwatch never to run again, his briefcase turned on its end to drain. "But he was wild with excitement. He hugged each of us in his wet clothes, laughing as we pulled away. He did a little dance on the papers and all afternoon he hummed songs to himself. He had battled nature and won, and it was as though he had saved us all from howling wolves or predatory monsters or a gigantic avalanche. He had met with nature triumphantly, at the very ends of the earth. Outside the giant swells of water crashed and boomed on the sand. Wet birds rustled their wings under bushes. Mice stayed dark in their nests. The great hills of the dunes let themselves soak up the moisture slowly. Inside my father hummed and the smell of hot cocoa came from the kerosene stove. It was a day to remember."[12]

Arnold Mulder symbolized the full scope of the cosmic conflict that must be overcome before humanity can be finally "at home" in the Dunes—the conflict within humanity itself. Mulder, who completed an M.A. thesis at the University of Chicago in 1910 on the esthetic socialism of William Morris, wrote *The Sand Doctor* in 1921.[13]

Briar Quentin, Mulder's messiah of the Dunes, discovers his love of the earth and its history while hiking the dunes as a boy. Later, as a medical intern at the University of Chicago, he is so nostalgic for them that he sits on the beach at Jackson Park, closes his eyes, and imagines himself back on the Dunes. Chicago is insubstantial;

the Dunes symbolize "reality"—sand, water, the atmosphere, plants, soil, animals, particular human beings. One Sunday Briar takes the interurban for a day's trip to the sand hills. On the top of the Crowned Monarch, the highest of the dunes, he meets a young woman—seemingly by accident, but actually "ordained that way."[14] They will often return to the Crowned Monarch to dream of the "real" things they will experience together, all associated with a house in the Dunes, a house that will be a true *home*.

After their marriage the two live in a cottage owned by her father in the Dunes, and Briar sets up medical practice in nearby Finley. He refuses to make it a business and the public nurse, who raised him as an orphan, brings Briar patients from the poor sections of town. The climax of the novel is an operation Briar performs on the brain of Barry Larramore, a schizoid personality who alternates between irresponsible adolescence and brooding adulthood. In the most complete operating room in America, created in the Dunes by the patient's father, Briar "saves" humankind. As a dark storm descends on the Dunes, Briar works under a large hooded light—symbol of the redemptive use of fire in the arts and sciences. He is possessed of a special power that "the hills, the lake, and all that kind of thing" have given him. "The emotions that made him exult [in the Dunes] were a part of him as physician; they were involved in the act of healing as much as was his technical knowledge of medicine."[15] Briar is a healing artist, a poet-scientist, a little bit like God, and hence with the ability to re-create the human personality.

Dazed and fatigued after the operation, Briar loses his way in the storm, stumbles into the gully in the sand hills where he has pursued geological researches, and is buried by a moving dune blowing in from the lake. His burial identifies him with the evolution of the earth so that when his wife discovers him, and he is "resurrected" from the dead, the earth is symbolically reborn with him. Afterward, the couple live "at home in the universe" in the Dunes, and the town of Finley is at peace with itself and with nature. The grateful father of the healed patient buys a thousand acres of Dunes and the Big Swamp to preserve it as a public park, and as the setting for a medical institute. The Dunes are the sacred place where, through love and reason, human creativity at long last allies itself with the creativity of the universe and, in the process, re-deems humanity.

In American history fire symbolism is associated most typically either with the Promethean myth or the dream of an escape to a simple life. The image of fire in the Dunes movement is an alternative to these two positions, close to the complex pastoral tradition of Thomas Jefferson. Unlike the Promethean myth, the human use of fire and the subsequent development of the arts and sciences are viewed as parts of the created order. It is natural and good that human beings build fires and construct an artifactual world. Unlike the primitivist myth, the development of technology is conceived as a special human vocation. Only through the rational use of fire may human beings build a civilization in reciprocal relationship to the environment.[16]

But fire is an ambiguous reality. In nature it may manifest the graciousness or the wrath of the sacred. The fire in the heavens, the sun, gives life to the earth; it may also, when too much or too little, bring suffering. Fire on the earth is an important part of the ecological cycle; it may also bring untold devastation. In its natural manifestations, therefore, fire displays both good and evil.

The same ambiguity attends the deliberate human use of fire, and to an even greater degree. Fire is the ancient symbol of the coopera-tion of nature and humanity, "given" by nature but directed by persons. As Eliade notes, by fire humanity may work with amaz-ing swiftness, and create something not found in nature.[17] Fire manifests humanity's magico-religious power to transform the world. By the same token, it is also the means of humanity's lack of cooperation with nature. Carelessness, hatred, greed, pride, igno-rance can lead human beings to use fire against nature as well as against their own species. "Fire," declared W. D. Richardson in 1919, "controlled, is the greatest friend of man, and uncontrolled his most relentless enemy."[18]

In the Dunes tradition, alongside the image of sacred dwelling, in which the fires of the heavens and the earth are ritually contained for the benefit of the community, there is a counterimage. In the counterimage, the fires of the earth are foolishly lit, and their burning causes havoc. If those who seek to live at home in the universe are to achieve their vision of sacred dwelling they must liberate the principalities and powers enthralled by the counterimage; they must enlist in the democratic struggle for the creative use of fire for the good of all.

The image of fire out of control, devastating the landscape and the lives of men and women, assumed various guises in the Dunes experience. At its simplest level, it was visible in brush fires ignited by human carelessness, or from the sparks of coal-fired trains. Writing under the headline "Salvation of Dunes Depends on Action to Prevent More Havoc," John O. Bowers described the extensive damage forest fires were causing in the Dunes in 1917. He noted that in a day a single fire may destroy the timber growth of a century. Local volunteer fire companies were constantly called out to "save the dunes."[19]

But the counterimage of fire was of greatest concern at a much more threatening and complex level. What most disturbed the Dunes apostles was the irrational obsession with fire by industrial civilization; the self-consuming worship of fire; the use of fire for the domination of the many by the few, and the domination of nature by one species; in sum, the childish selfishness of those who refused to stand together with their fellows in equality as artists building a common world.

The Dunes movement has rarely condemned the employment of fire for the industrial arts per se. Indeed, from A. F. Knotts to Paul Douglas, most leaders of the movement have lauded the enterprise of those John O. Bowers once called the "craft-descendants of old Tubal-Cain."[20] The movement *has* condemned, in Harriet Monroe's words, "the world of overgrown children playing with expensive and explosive toys,"[21] and especially what it has conceived to be the biggest and most selfish of these children, the corporations, which often like Tawiskaron, steal the energy of the universe for their own privileged use. It was symbolically pregnant that the corporations most directly threatening the Dunes were engaged in steel production, the most basic modern metallurgical craft. Ancient and so-called primitive peoples were often ambivalent about the metallurgical crafts because of their violation of the earth and the unprecedented power they bestowed on human society.

The word most often used to describe the counterimpulse to democracy was "feudalism." In *Democracy: A Man Search*, Louis Sullivan wrote: "Every man, in every thought, hence in every act, casts a real ballot—the kind that counts and is surely life-counted—either for Feudalism or for Democracy."[22] For him, as for most midwestern Progressives, unbridled capitalism was a new form of feudalism. But as Sullivan insisted, feudalism was more than laissez-faire capitalism; it embraced all totalitarianisms. Donald Peattie later pointed out that racism, war-hungry imperialism, and materialism were the American counterparts to German fascism, all examples of a feudal state of mind.[23]

An incident in the life of a Save the Dunes Council member is symbolic of the struggle of the Dune Country patriots with the feudal mind. Gladys Rizer lived as a child near Tremont. Often she would guide Prairie Club members through the Dunes. When she began to make friends with Hyde Park people, however, especially Jews, she was ostracized. The Ku Klux Klan burned a cross on her father's lawn. One day Gladys and her companions learned that the Klan planned to burn a cross on Mount Tom. Climbing to the top of an old Boy Scout tower at the summit where they could be hidden from view, they saw the Klan members climb the hill, light the cross, and then return to the beach to admire the spectacle. Gladys and her friends descended from the tower, put out the fire with sand, and fled into the woods. They had engaged in a skirmish with the feudal powers at the top of the cosmic mountain.[24]

There are numerous expressions of the feudal counterimage in the Dunes literature.

In direct counterpoint to the old cottage in the State Park that Ann and her family restore for the summer is a pink stucco house in a new subdivision nearby. The pink house is out of place in the Dunes, and the developer, an immigrant to the United States who has come up the hard way, but who has no interest in the land of his adoption, is motivated solely by the profit motive. When Ann's father sees the house standing on land he wanted included in the park, he exclaims: " 'A foolish man built his house upon the sand; and the rain descended, and the floods came, and the winds blew, and smote upon the house; and it fell; and great was the fall thereof.'"[25] A careless match eventually destroys the house and leads, with the help of human love and understanding, to the utopian decision of the developer to deed his land as a public park.

The antagonist of Mulder's sand doctor is the "syndicate," which exploits the townspeople of Finley and defies the Dunes by building a gambling casino behind a seawall on the beach. This incites the denunciations of Reverend Joseph Otley, who walks the streets of Finley like a Hebrew prophet, crying: "The Lord will visit it in his wrath. . . . He will turn the fires of his anger against it."[26] True to Otley's prediction, the storm that engulfs the Dunes while Briar Quentin performs his operation breaks the seawall and destroys the syndicate's resort. At the moment of humanity's salvation, the enemies of the God of democracy are vanquished.

Some of the strongest images of the feudal powers are Sandburg's. If there is greatness in the City of the Big Shoulders, it lies in the people, not the captains of industry. About 1890 the commercial boosters of Chicago unofficially changed the motto of the city from "Urbs in Horto" to "I will." Sandburg answered: "I won't . . . I can't . . . I couldn't."[27] In the *Chicago Poems* he wrote that the worst men could ever say about his city was that it took children away from the sun and the grass and put them to work between walls to die empty-hearted.[28] In 1915 Sandburg took the labor conflicts in Gary as a symbol of the repression of the people by the new American oligarchy in the poem, "The Mayor of Gary," and later, in *Smoke and Steel*, he crafted an image of the Gary steel mills in which women danced like scarves out of the smoke stacks, and the bars of steel were made of smoke and the blood of men.[29] Human lives were being consumed in those mills, along with the dreams of the common people for a humane and just civilization.

Perhaps the most memorable image of the feudal mind was bequeathed to the Dunes movement by Earl Reed in two little-known works—*Sketches in Jacobia* and *The Ghost in the Tower*.[30] In the first, Reed is introduced to a tower that dominates a wealthy friend's estate in the Dunes, built to imitate a famous old tower in Hungary, from which generations of robber barons pillaged the countryside. From the walkway that rings the top of his tower,

Reed's friend Jacobs can survey his feudal kingdom. But inexplicable events have occurred on the estate since the raising of the medieval fortress. For example, the workmen on their way to build a small family chapel "lost" the church steeple.

In the second book, Reed returns to the estate on Christmas Eve, and encounters a wisp of rising vapor in the tower. The smoke turns out to be a ghost, a one-time Hungarian Magyar general, who has recently come from a trip to New York, where he met his modern counterparts—the robber barons of Wall Street. These feudal thieves so outclassed him that he retreated to Jacobs's tower in shame.

Although written tongue-in-cheek, the story, especially in light of Reed's own decision to quit the Chicago Board of Trade, has an undertone of dead seriousness. Hungary was known at the time as the country with the last open remnants of feudalism. In a postscript Reed prints a presumed rejoinder from his friend, who argues that the "hue and cry against 'big business' is the turbulent protest of the untutored mob—the yelp of the Bolshevik," and that "in our modern social structure certain concentrations of wealth are inevitable and seem necessary to our economic life." Reed puts into Jacobs's mouth the slogan of the Englishman Arthur Young, who led the movement to enclose the English commons in the 1750s: "Make two blades of grass grow where one grew before."[31] Reed leaves little doubt that in his opinion Jacobs's obsession with efficiency and laissez-faire industrial growth is a delusion and a rationalization for wealth and privilege.

The smoking ghost in the tower was an imaginative portrayal of the feudal threat to the Dune Country. In the image of a smoking column one could see the smoke stacks, steel furnaces, and steam locomotives that in Reed's lifetime swept with such force across the Chicago glacial plain. The *ghost* in the tower was a perfect symbol for the concept of an enemy within—the feudal mind that governed these deadly expressions of excessively concentrated technological power.

Throughout the twentieth century, the proponents of the religion of democracy who participated in the Dunes movement perceived themselves as engaged in a great struggle. They hoped to master—certainly to reform, at least to repel—the ghost in the tower. It was a struggle they believed they inherited from preceding generations, yet a peculiar responsibility of their own to wage because the very survival of the democratic promise of the nation was at stake.

The struggle was believed to have begun in earnest when the Native Americans were evicted from the land. Many members of the early Dunes movement knew or remembered the last of the Potawatomi chiefs, Simon Pokagon, who had been educated at Notre Dame and Oberlin College.[32] He was an eloquent spokesperson for the view that the Potawatomi knew how to build a fire and construct a human dwelling in such a way as to live at peace with one another and with nature. ("Potawatomi" is variously translated as "guardian of fire," the "nations of fire," and "people blessed with the spirit of building fire in a certain way by the Good Spirit.")[33] He combined outrage at the violence of white civilization with a belief that only if the Indian forgave the past, and adopted Christian virtues, could he survive, and a new democratic civilization, greater than either European or Native American, emerge.

At the opening of the World's Fair in Hyde Park in 1893, six years before his death in 1899, Pokagon appeared on the stage of Chicago public life. After the singing of the "National Anthem," and Harriet Monroe's "Ode to Brotherhood," he rang, with tears running down his cheeks, the newly recast Liberty Bell. He then handed to Mayor Harrison a duplicate of the original deed by which, sixty years before, his father, Leopold Pokagon, had conveyed the land of the Chicago glacial plain to the United States. With dignity he asked for money to sponsor a congress of the Indian race to prove that "we are men and brothers, worthy to be called Americans, and fit for citizenship."[34]

Pokagon spent the rest of his time at the fair handing out birchbark copies of the *Red Man's Greeting*. In it he noted that when the Dune Country was the site of Indian council fires, it was held in common by the members of the tribe, and there was no sin of "mine and thine." Condemning the white man's destruction of the environment—"All our fathers once loved to gaze upon was destroyed, defaced, or marred, except the sun, moon, and starry skies above, which the Great Spirit in his wisdom hung beyond reach"—he left the reader with a memorable image of feudal fires:

In those days that tried our fathers' souls, tradition says: "A crippled gray haired sire told his tribe that in the visions of the night he was lifted high above the Earth, and in great wonder beheld a great spider-web spread out over the land from the Atlantic Ocean toward the setting sun. Its network was made of rods of iron; along its lines in all directions rushed monstrous spiders, greater in strength, and larger far than any beast of earth, clad in brass and iron, dragging after them long rows of wigwams with families therein, outstripping in their course the flight of birds that fled before them. Hissing from their nostrils came forth fire and smoke, striking terror to both fowl and beast. The red men hid themselves in fear, or fled away, while the white men trained these monsters for the warpath, as warriors for battle." [35]

Pokagon's lonely witness was not forgotten by the Dunes movement. Stephen Mather let a Potawatomi representative have the last say at the Sand Dunes National Park hearings in 1916, and although he was embarrassed by the tirade Mr. Cox took the occasion to deliver against the United States government, he let Cox's concluding declaration stand unchallenged: "I will just say, then, that the Indians are in favor of this park, providing that the title is procured as the law provides, from the rightful owners of the property." [36]

In 1926 Stephen Mather's friend Richard Lieber, who believed the Native Americans were the "first and most scrupulous conservationists," named the new Indiana state park on Lake James in honor of Simon Pokagon.[37] In 1960 Edwin Way Teale paused on his "journey into summer" to remember Pokagon's brave words of 1893, and to visit his birthplace in the Dune Country.[38] Teale noted that while Pokagon died in poverty, his spirit was alive in the Indiana country he loved. In 1972 the Reverend Charles Doyle began his invocation at the dedication of the Indiana Dunes National Lakeshore: "Nestled in between these ancient sand dunes, and lulled by the lapping of the same waves that Chief Pokagon loved . . ." [39]

The other nineteenth-century figure remembered for offering resistance to the invading forces of feudal oppression was Joseph Bailly, the first permanent white settler in the Dunes. Bailly is the subject of diverse interpretations, but for Julia Cooley Altrocchi, Chicago author of *Wolves Against the Moon*, and her fellow

Dunites, he was a predecessor of their own quest for a just society in harmony with the rest of nature.[40]

Altrocchi paints Bailly as an enterprising visionary who discards the mask of his French-Canadian aristocratic past to become a man of the people, a seeker of the dream of the ideal society in the wilderness of the Indiana Dune Country. With his wife Marie, part Ottawa Indian, also called the "Wing Woman" because of her legendary kinship with birds, Bailly settles in the Dunes in 1821. There the Bailly Homestead and trading post occupies a position at the center of the geographical and cultural contrasts of the period. Located on the Little Calumet River, at an intersection of the ancient Sauk Trail, it is a point of mediation between Native American and European, past and future, wilderness and civilization, Christian and pagan.

In one incident of the novel, Altrocchi describes a meeting between Bailly and his friend Leopold Pokagon, Simon's father. After they smoke together, Leopold tells Joseph that he is building his homestead on an especially sacred spot in the Dunes and gives Bailly permission to build there, because: "If all white men were like you, Monami Bailly, there would never be any trouble, but the white race and the red race would hunt together and play bagataway together, and sit around the campfire and smoke the pipe of peace forever."[41]

In retrospect, the Bailly Homestead symbolized the potential for a truly democratic society inherent in the time of origins. The potential was far from realized. As increasing numbers of settlers entered the region, Marie finds their cruelty to wildlife unbearable. And at the end of his life, Joseph is forced to watch in horror as the United States cavalry leads the Potawatomi and Ottawa Indians on the infamous "trail of tears" along the Sauk Trail.

But the fires of the frontier civilization Pokagon sought to repel and Bailly to master were modest compared to the fires the Dune Country patriots faced by the late nineteenth century. In 1898 University of Chicago author Robert Herrick observed: "Chicago is an instance of a contemptuous disregard of nature by man."[42] By that date the city had raised itself as much as twelve feet above the lake, and created the most specialized urban space in the nation. Symbol of the new urban fires out of the control of the people was

the Great Chicago Fire of 1871. George Brennan reported that it
burned not only the city but the Dunes as well. It was this fire, in
his view, that first brought the Chicago region to the attention
of the world, and sparked its explosive growth.[43]

JENS JENSEN: THE COUNCIL FIRE

Sometime around the turn of the century, Jens Jensen began the
practice of gathering the members of the groups with which he
was associated into circles around a central firepit for community
dialogue and worship. He called these gatherings "council fires."
Soon he was building permanent council rings into the design of
his public and private parks. These simple structures consisted of
a circular stone bench, about twenty feet in diameter, with a fireplace in the center elevated eight to twelve inches above the
ground. Over the years Jensen developed an elaborate symbolism
for the council fire. It became his personal image of human dwelling on the earth, and the basis of an ideal conception of how a community ought to organize itself and live in harmony with the native
landscape.[44]

Jensen inherited the tradition of the council fire from his forefathers on the seacoast of Denmark, and from the folk high school
he attended as a youth. Once in America, Jensen identified the
idea with the beginnings of civilization, with the council fires of the
Native American, and with the fires of the pioneers. Most of all, the
council fire came to symbolize for him the democratic spirit of the
Midwest.

Jensen stressed that in the council fire ceremony every person,
whether rich or poor, is on an equal level. The council ring creates
a fellowship of equals who can look one another squarely in the
eye and engage in honest give and take. A person who has an idea
can express it freely and openly. Everyone will be understood by
his or her actions, and must speak the truth. In imitation of Native
American practice, Jensen encouraged the speaker to rise and go to
the center of the ring, speak, and then return to his place alongside
his companions. Another can then speak, or silence can reign and
each can then meditate while watching the flames in the center. The
purpose of the council fire is "profound thinking and spiritual com-

munion."[45] It is no wonder Jensen disliked speaker's tables and made a point on formal occasions of sitting randomly with anyone.

The council ring was believed also to encourage the companionship of humanity and nature. In the circle, one is aware of the stars, the smells and the sounds of the woods and flowers, the wind and the earth. In the flame of the leaping fire, uniting heaven and earth, one sees the heat of many summers' suns. Jensen felt an absolute unity emerging from such gatherings, which encompassed the whole of being—"the brotherhood of all living things."[46] This unity was symbolized in the figure of the circle, the strongest and most perfect geometrical form.

The ideal spot for building a council ring in Jensen's view was a high knoll overlooking a vast expanse, on the edge of the prairie or by the edge of the water. There the light of the fire could symbolize the beacon that guides lost wanderers to a place of security and welcome. He landscaped the ring with native plantings, such as hawthorns (his personal signature) around the periphery, and violets, columbine, and wild asters among the rocks.

The finest remaining example of Jensen's architectural implementation of these ideas is the Lincoln Memorial Garden at Springfield, Illinois. In the last great public park he designed, the garden is held together by eight council rings, around which lanes and forests of native trees revolve. The largest of these rings, called by Jensen "the Lincoln Council Ring," is located in a grove of white oak planted from acorns collected throughout the country. Jensen took the commission to design the garden with extreme seriousness and considered the council ring the perfect symbol for the spirit of Lincoln.[47]

Jensen's conception fit the natural experience of fellowship around the campfire that accompanied the early trips of the Prairie Club to the Dunes. As Emma Doeserich remembered years afterward: "The campfire was one of the most enjoyable features of dune life. The hearty greetings as we gathered around the cheery blaze, community singing, stories; the red glow of the fire, and the beating of the waves upon the shore."[48] Jensen sought to press this spontaneous experience into explicitly ritualistic forms. Often, on his trips with the Prairie Club, he gave an inspirational talk on the meaning of nature in human experience at the campfire.

It was with the Friends of Our Native Landscape, which from the time of its founding took as its mission the task of providing the motivational power for a new democratic society, that Jensen most fully developed the ritual symbolism of the council fire. Every year the Friends held four principal meetings: the Annual Meeting in January by an open fire in Chicago; the Pilgrimage to the Crab Apple Blossom in May; the Pilgrimage to the Full Leaf in June, when the Goodman masque was presented in an area worthy of conservation; and the Pilgrimage to the Fallen Leaf, at the height of autumn colors in the Sand Dunes of Indiana. Jensen used some modified form of the ritual of the council fire at all of the meetings. Ragna Eskil remembered one annual meeting in Chicago when Harriet Monroe joined enthusiastically with the other Friends in lighting candles and singing "America the Beautiful" as they followed the son of Ernest Hemingway into the hall![49]

Every fall, on the anniversary of the "discovery" of America, the Friends returned to a little valley in the Central Dunes for the culminating event of their sacred calendar. One such occasion, Sunday, October 14, 1928, began on an overcast day. The group of thirty Friends first warmed themselves by a fire on the beach and drank coffee made by George Hooker from fresh Lake Michigan water, then took a long hike through the Dunes. Jensen pointed out a dune to the east "where the Friends would have a noble setting for their rites dedicatory to the beautiful in nature" if the company that owned it could be dissuaded from commercial despoliation.[50]

As the colors of autumn were "set afire by the last rays of the setting sun," the group reached the site of the evening's council fire. In a clearing beneath the stars, surrounded by the "mystery of the dune lands now in deep shadows," Jensen set the branches of jack pine and scrub oaks ablaze. The time for "open meditation and communion of thought"—the climax of the day's pilgrimage—had come. After a period of silence, Jensen spoke about a conference on state parks he had recently attended with Richard Lieber. Others added their thoughts. Then the Friends in single file circled the fire, laying on fagots in memory of departed members. A few songs were sung, hands were clasped, the fire was extinguished, and the Pilgrimage to the Fallen Leaf was over.[51]

Just as the medieval cathedral had its origins in the image of the

primitive hut in paradise, so there was a more elaborate image of
shared human dwelling implicit in the cosmogonic rite of the council fire. In Jensen's imagination the council fire was the nucleus
for a communitarian ideal inherited also from the Danish folk
school tradition, which he adapted to his new land.

In 1913 Jensen made his first effort to translate this communal
ideal into practice. Early that year he became the chairman of a
committee of the Prairie Club to investigate the possibility of a
permanent camp in the Dunes. Jensen threw himself into the task,
surveyed the coastline from Gary to Michigan City, and recommended a site at the top of a shore dune a short distance east of
Mount Tom. Under Jensen's supervision, money was raised for
leasing the land and a community retreat house was designed and
built in the course of the summer. The Beach House design was
simple and revealing. It was built in the form of a cross, with a
large living room and fireplace at the center, and the four wings
pointing toward the four cardinal points of the compass. On the
east and west sides were the men's and women's dormitories, con-
sisting of locker rooms and sleeping porches, to the south the
kitchen, and in front a broad porch facing the lake. The Beach
House was a replica of the vision of the Dunes as an *imago mundi*,
with the council fire built at the center.

Every Sunday through the summer, special programs were held
on the site, culminating in Jensen's dedication of the building on
October 19. Of such symbolic significance was the first light that
graced the Beach House that a photograph of it was chosen by
Emma Doeserich, Mary Sherburne, and Anna Wey for the frontispiece to their history of the club. And so rich was the community
life in this public temple that ten years later, Columbus Day, 1923,
the dedication service was repeated word for word. When, after the
State Park was established, the club took leave of its retreat, Jensen
designed a Memorial Fountain, which was erected at the entrance
to the Beach House Trail, and dedicated by Allinson, Dudley, and
Robinson on Memorial Day, 1932.

The Beach House became the center of a colony of camps—first
primitive tents, then more elaborate tents with platforms, and finally
shacks and small cottages. They were said to look like a colony of
cliff-swallows from the shore. In Jensen's eyes this meant turning

the Dune Country into a summer resort, which he deplored. The idea of the house in its original purity, as he later explained, was to serve as a shelter so that the members might sleep out of doors and engage together in the pursuit of a disciplined and dedicated communal life close to nature. By the 1920s, the Beach House had, in his view, fallen away from this original ideal.[52]

In 1929 Jensen led the Friends of Our Native Landscape in an attempt to reclaim that ideal. With the generous help of Eames MacVeagh, the Illinois chapter of the Friends built a Shelter in a secluded spot in the Central Dunes. Here Jensen's image of human dwelling was reborn. The simple cabin was one large room dominated by a great fireplace on a raised hearth. There were also lockers, as at the Beach House, and outside, two palisaded stockades for sleeping under the stars. One member of the Friends, arriving for the first time at the Shelter, was greeted by a campfire, a hospitable circle of Friends, and a cup of coffee poured by Mrs. Jensen. Afterward, she wrote: "An idea is housed there, in fitting form, that of a selfless devotion to a world beautiful."[53]

As important as they were for the course of the Dunes movement, and for his personal religious quest, neither of these community centers founded by Jensen in the Dunes was more than a glimpse of the vision of a total, self-sufficient community "at home in the universe" that he saw implicit in the primordial image of the council fire. The radical communitarianism of the Beach House and Dunes Shelter must be set within the context of the organic dream of human settlement he shared with Louis Sullivan and Frank Lloyd Wright. Jensen pursued this dream in a variety of forms, not least in his designs for Chicago parks. One form intensely absorbing to him was his plan for a permanent settlement in the Dunes.

Jensen's original idea of a "Dunes park" was more than a wilderness preserve and camping ground for the common man; it included an outdoor biological and geological laboratory for the University of Chicago, a school of horticulture (teaching forestry, landscaping, and market gardening), a self-sustaining experimental farm, an arboretum of native plants, and facilities for art students and writers. The Dunes park was to be linked to an extensive chain of forest preserves surrounding Chicago, by an interstate park running south of the city around Wolf Lake and along the Grand Calumet River through Gary. Jensen thus envisaged a land-use plan for a major portion of the Chicago glacial plain, combining urban, rural, and wilderness areas. Most significantly, the plan included at the center of the Dunes, in close proximity to the city, a model cultural complex in organic relationship to the native landscape.[54]

After the World War, Jensen's vision became increasingly transcendent. Chicago grew in directions antithetical to those he envisaged, and the Dunes were invaded by the fires of a capitalist economy which divorced ownership and labor. Slowly, reluctantly, and with considerable disillusionment, he disengaged himself from the hope of influencing Chicago's future directly. "Chicago was once called the garden city," he wrote in *Siftings*. "What has become of the gardens?"[55] In his view, the city should have grown to be a prairie Venice, a maze of canals, settlements, islands, lakes, and marshes. Instead, it eliminated any vestige of the native landscape and became a homogeneous, rectangular grid, a profane space without qualitative differentiation. Gradually the idea took form in Jensen's mind of founding a school in an area remote enough from the city that it could serve as a permanent embodiment of his vision. Thus was born "The Clearing," built upon a landscape of solid rock, on the coast of Door County, in northern Wisconsin.

In The Clearing, Jensen's dream of a "Dunes park" came to modest yet concentrated fulfillment. In a letter to a friend and patron in 1932, he described his proposed school near Ellison Bay. Although inspired by the folk high schools of Denmark, it by no means copied them. "We should have something," he wrote, "that fits our Country."[56] For Jensen this meant an exemplary social democracy, one which combined self-discovery with disciplined labor and conceived of human community in terms of a fraternal order of artists in close communion with nature. Everybody would live in dormitories and partake of common meals. Landscape architecture—as Jensen understood it, that is, as a philosophy of life—would be the chief subject, and most of the studies would be out of doors. The evenings would be devoted to art and literature, and in the summer artists of all kinds would be invited and housed in tent colonies with an open hall where they might come together. From 1935, when he was seventy-five years old, until his death in 1951,

Jensen presided over The Clearing, deep in the woods of Wisconsin. At the center of his little settlement, on a bluff overlooking the lake, he built a large stone council ring, the largest of his career.

PEATTIE AND TEALE: NOSTALGIA AMERICANA

Donald Culross Peattie and Edwin Way Teale were contemporaries, born in 1898 and 1899 respectively. They stood self-consciously in the tradition of the nineteenth-century American literary naturalists, but wrote from what they conceived to be a new intellectual position informed by science, specifically ecology. For Peattie and Teale, this meant that nature was not a garden benignantly planted, but a symbiotic whole in which dissimilar organisms survive by mutual interdependence. Nature includes both good and evil, but its order is on the side of life. The place of humanity, standing uniquely apart from the rest of nature, yet indissolubly united to it, is on the side of those adaptive tendencies that increase the likelihood of what Teale once called "moments of brightness and beauty." In Peattie's words, one day "men shall pledge united loyalty to all other men," and humankind shall recognize its fellow creatures as "allies in the long fight of all to live."[57]

The crucial factor that enabled Peattie and Teale to make this leap of faith, allying themselves with what they believed to be an evolutionary adventure making for greater community among all forms of being, was not so much scientific theory as the experience each had as a boy in the Dunes. Underlying their rigorous allegiance to scientific inquiry, and their full-blooded humanistic conviction of humanity's capacity to go beyond nature's intentions, was their own never-forgotten experience of being at home in the universe in the Dune Country. This experience determined their attitudes and their careers. Through its dialectic, which revolved around the poles of loss and recovery of a sacred center, they came to conceive of their vocations as contributions to the destiny of the nation and the earth. As a result, their works were read as sources of renewal by thousands of their fellow citizens.

It was in terms of "A House That Was Home" that Peattie cast his account of his youth in the Dunes south of Chicago's city limits.[58] Purchased by his grandfather, publisher of the *Hyde Park*

Herald, in 1877, the two-story frame dwelling was the center of his family's life for forty years. As a boy, Peattie could see from the cupola of the house in all directions. Immediately to the east were the bright sandy swells of the dunes and the lake, and sometimes on very clear days, the coast of Michigan. South were the steel mills of Gary. North was the Loop with buildings as high as twenty stories! West was the prairie and the low hills of the Valparaiso Moraine. Peattie grew up with a clear sense of dwelling at the center of the Chicago glacial plain.

As important as the outside of the house was its inside, where proximity to nature was joined with artistic creativity. Both of Peattie's parents were writers, and from the earliest age he remembered the sound of his mother typing her novels and book reviews at night. Books were everywhere. The house served as an informal center for the vibrant literary and reform life of Chicago in the years before the Great War. Writers, agitators, settlement workers, teachers, were constantly coming and going. In such an environment, Peattie recalled, "Conversation had rights of sanctity." The room warmest with family life was the library, which held the widest hearth. The mantelpiece was made of a great beam Peattie's mother had found on the lakeshore. One Christmas Eve Donald watched his brother Roderick stencil above the mantel the words "O Ye Fire and Heat, Praise Ye the Lord." [59]

From the Peattie manse, standing alone by the lakeshore in what is now South Shore, Chicago, Donald commuted first to the University of Chicago Laboratory School, where he met his future wife, Louise Redfield, and her close friend, Emily Taft, and then to the College, where he studied in the botany department under Cowles. He made daily sorties into the dunes and prairie, and fell in love with their flowering plants. By combining the humanistic traditions of his family and the university with the esthetic and ecological wonders of the Dunes, Peattie discovered his vocation as a "heart-naturalist."

In 1916, at the age of seventeen, he published the poem "Night":

I woke in the night and heard the waves
    Lap on the sand,
And cool and sweet, the water breeze
    Blew on the land.

Through quiet hours, while all men slept,
  I lay awake.
And breezes stirred the cottonwoods
  Down by the lake.
It seemed to me, as still I lay,
  That pulses beat,
As if the Earth drew long, deep breaths
  Of night air sweet.
I turned to sleep and journeyed far
  To dreaming lands,
But woke again to hear the waves
  Lap on the sands.[60]

During the same years, not more than forty miles away, near Furnessville, in the Indiana Dunes, Edwin Way Teale was spending every summer and every vacation with his grandparents at their farm of Lone Oak. Until 1914, when Teale was fifteen, his life was divided between his parents' home in what he considered the wearisome city of Joliet, Illinois, and the new world of freedom and adventure on the borderland of the Dunes.[61]

Teale's equivalent of Peattie's cupola was the mossy roof of his grandparents' farmhouse. As he tells the reader in *Dune Boy*, he often climbed there to watch bald eagles and sandhill cranes fly overhead. The farmhouse and its signature, an immense white oak, stood at the precise center of Grandfather Way's ninety-odd acres. From the peak of the roof he could see the orchards and fields of the farm spread around him, while to the south rose the blue hills of the Valparaiso Moraine. To the north, about a mile away, across woods and swamps, lay the crests of the great Indiana dunes. Teale remembers that as a youth his imagination was often stirred by the mystery of those "hills of gold shining in the sun."[62]

Like Gilbert White's English village of Selborne, with which he compares it, Lone Oak seemed a place apart, a miniature universe. As a young boy, Teale had a sense of knowing every one of its citizens—every plant and animal of garden, barnyard, marsh, and woods. The most remarkable inhabitants were his grandparents, who in their advancing years seemed to understand the world of dreams in which Teale lived. With Grandfather Way, Teale recounts, one had the sense that he had always been your friend. He was a person to whom a good joke was worth more than a dollar, and although illiterate, had a keen mind. Grandmother Way read aloud from the classics every evening. She was an "Isaiah in a sunbonnet. Singlehanded, she was a society for the prevention of cruelty to animals and men." [63] An indomitable spirit had kept the Ways at work since 1867 eking out a living and raising a family on the poor soil of the Dune Country.

Teale describes Lone Oak as a self-sufficient society, rich with the bounties of nature and the virtues of common humanity. Within the web of its simple economy, he learned the elementary lessons of ecology, and passed his most formative years. By picking twenty thousand strawberries, he earned the money for his first box camera; by the age of ten, he had completed in pencil a book of twenty-four chapters called "Tails of Lone Oak."

Peattie and Teale abruptly lost their homes in the Dunes, and about the same time. One bitter cold night in January 1915, Grandfather Way left the draft of the great dining-room stove open, a wind came up, and the farmhouse burned to the ground. Three years later, in the midst of the war, Peattie's father, a newspaperman, was transferred to New York, and the Peattie home was closed. In each case the sudden loss accelerated a transformation already underway. No longer realities, the dwelling places in the Dunes became sacred memories. In the transition, the ideal of community, which seemed intrinsic to the two homes, was set free. Thereafter they were not only personal memories, but symbols of the universal as well.

Peattie and Teale each remembered specific instances when their homes in the Dunes became identified with the universe.

At age twenty Peattie was charged with closing the house for the last time. After shutting the door, he walked out into the yard and beneath the tall oaks he had known and loved since childhood. But he had the strange feeling that he did not truly know them. Wishing to salute them one last time, he opened a copy of Gray's *Manual of Botany* he happened to be carrying with him, and identified them as *Quercus velutina*, black oaks. From that moment on they became fixed for him, like stars. "And like a firmament slowly broke over me the grandeur of a system where every oak puts down its roots eternal and unshakable, yes, and every transient flower," he later wrote. "Like stars, I saw each plant, perhaps each animal, had not only its place but its relation with all others, its measurable distances from them, as if, in evolution's slow tremendous course, all exerted pulls of varying strength upon the others." The trees that were Peattie's childhood companions became the symbolic link between the home he was losing and the eternal order of the cosmos. "I closed the book, and walked away from the old address that I would never give again. I had no other, but I had at least a new sense of direction overhead, astronomically sure, and spreading over all the living earth." [64]

The lone oak, after which the Way farm was named, also had cosmic significance for Teale. But the most intense revelation of the universal came unexpectedly one winter morning when he accompanied his grandfather to a distant forest to cut firewood. While his grandfather worked, Teale fearfully explored the surrounding wood, ominous in the early morning light. Suddenly he was overwhelmed with a sense of "standing in a charmed circle where all life paused, enchanted, until we passed on." He perceived the woods to be dreadfully and secretly alive. That morning Teale experienced the *mysterium tremendum*. Afterward, the image of the somber place returned thousands of times to his memory. "It was the starting point of my absorption in the world of Nature," he wrote, "a symbol of all the veiled and fascinating secrets of the out-of-doors." [65]

Peattie and Teale also identified their Dunes homes with America, with the American earth, and with American democracy.

Although, as Peattie wrote in 1943, "the American dream was taught me in the household where I grew up as a child," and "I had it like a religion, as privately and deeply," there were not many people of his faith, or so it seemed to him, in America during the boom of the 1920s. Leaving the United States in disgust, Donald and his wife Louise lived in Europe as expatriates until the rise of fascism. Then "the idea of my country" as an experiment in humanity—interdependence, democracy, "nostalgia Americana"—brought them home. [66] To return to America for Donald Peattie was to return to the Dunes. And just as he had earlier found immortality for the Peattie home by discovering its place in the transcendent order of nature, he now in the same way, in the face

of the increasing destruction of the Dunes by the industrial cities
of the Calumet, went about the work of defending his homeland.
In 1930, drawing on the technical papers on the origin of the Dunes
flora he wrote while a graduate student at Harvard, and years of field
study, Peattie published *The Flora of the Indiana Dunes*.[67] In it he
made sure that every transient Dunes flower put "down its roots
eternal and unshakable."

For Teale, too, the Second World War brought to light deep
associations between the Dunes and America. He published *Dune
Boy* in 1943, in the course of a war in which he lost his son. Writing in a later, revised edition, Teale noted with pride that more
than one hundred thousand copies of the book had been distributed
to servicemen and that he had heard from many men who read it
while engaged in the battle for freedom in all parts of the world.[68]
A United States senator (it was Paul Douglas) had written to tell
him that during vacations in the Dunes, he read the book aloud to
his daughter. Teale apparently recognized that the image of sacred
dwelling in the Dunes he described in *Dune Boy* was a timeless
model of the democratic common life, for many of his country-
men an image of their *real* American homeland.

The Dunes, the universe, America—the identification explains
much about Peattie's and Teale's life journeys. Each was driven by
a nostalgia for his home in the Dunes and for all it symbolically
represented. Each sought to find a way to reenter sacred time.
Their search took several forms. The first was the most personal.
They each sought to find a substitute for the homes they had lost.
For Peattie, this search led to a house on the shore of the Pacific
Ocean at Santa Barbara. For Teale, it led to an eighty-acre farm in
Connecticut located on the same latitude as Lone Oak, on which
he planted roses and peonies from the Dunes, and which had a
corner that reminded him of the woods in which he entered the
sacred circle.[69] Over and over in Teale's later books, he tells of a
return trip to the Dunes. Each time he searches for the "Lost
Woods." When he finally tracks down their physical location in
1950, the woods themselves are gone.[70]

A second means of redemption was through the rhythm of natural recurrences. Teale structures *Dune Boy* around the form of a
liturgical year that begins and ends with Christmas. Peattie believed

that to spend a year experiencing the seasons in a shack in the Dunes was the equivalent to three trips around the world. He offers a loving description of the passing of the seasons in the Dunes where "spring, stepping tardily and shyly, brings hepaticas, anemones, violets, lupine, and phlox; after them troop buttercups, Jack-in-the-pulpit and blue flag. . . ." It is not long before "crab-apple and dogwood flower, and with the coming of early summer an abundance of wild roses bloom, and the strangely beautiful dune cactus appears. Autumn is a triumph of foxglove, of more than a dozen kinds of sunflower, of the stately purple blazing star, of the wild asters that some call 'farewell summer.' "[71] Peattie saw each day's dawn bring renewal to the Chicago glacial plain. Once, after a night of work on a newspaper in the city, he went home at 4 A.M., and "from the east, from over the great cool lake, some mercy, newly sent once more, in spite of all our sorry yesterdays, was coming now to spread in radiance and freshness over all the city. In the waning dark I felt the offer of its purification."[72]

Peattie and Teale each wrote a series of books in which the temporal cycles of nature became so many modes of the sacred ways of recovering the enduring time—the time first fully manifest in the Dunes.[73]

A third source of redemption was memory. For Teale, especially, memory was haunting. Repeatedly in the course of a book he returns to some incident in the Dunes. In the *Circle of the Seasons*, written in 1943, he said, "The universal solvent is memory. It dissolves the past. It eliminates time. A moment ago, as I wandered among the sunflowers of my insect garden, some fragment of sound, some passing emotion, recalled a time in the Indiana Dunes fully forty years ago. For the moment, forty years ago is closer than yesterday."[74]

For Peattie, too, memory was a means to salvation. A steady theme is his call to his fellow citizens to remember their sacred time of origins. Memory was the means to new beginnings, to a new American Revolution; it also was a source of forgiveness. In 1960, in failing health, Peattie wrote in the Chicago newspaper, to which he had contributed so many columns: "Forgive me, Chicago, that I loved and left you. Forget you I do not."[75]

One last source of redemption was active participation in efforts to preserve the native American landscape for future generations. Peattie considered "love of the living world's beauty . . . an unwritten franchise in the rights of man. American nature is a first national principle."[76] Through his columns he aided efforts to implement that principle wherever possible, and he was especially galvanized when the efforts touched on those "communistic" American institutions—the national parks. Teale, equally committed to conservation, was a leader in the movement to preserve Walden Pond, and until his death in 1980, a member of the Save the Dunes Council Advisory Board. He believed that "the long fight to save wild beauty represents democracy at its best. It requires citizens to practice the hardest of virtues—self-restraint."[77]

In 1958 Paul Douglas wrote to Teale for help in the Dunes fight. He said that he considered him and Peattie the best naturalists to come out of the Midwest, and that it was ironic that the east and west coasts pulled them away. "There is something blighting in the effect which the Midwest has upon our writers of talent," he went on. "In order to flourish, they have to go elsewhere. I do not quite know the reason for this, but I wish we could hold on to some of our men like you and Don Peattie because we need you very badly."[78] If Douglas had looked more carefully, he would have seen that the Midwest had held on pretty hard.

THE SANDBURGS:
A HOUSE WITH WINDOWS TO THE WORLD

One evening in late June 1962, as the members of the Save the Dunes Council took their seats in the Crystal Ballroom of Hotel Gary, a large birthday cake with ten glowing candles celebrating the council's tenth anniversary was placed before president Dorothy Buell.[79] She promptly made a wish everyone present could not help but guess and blew the candles out. After dinner the guests sang Pat Walsh's new song "Save the Dunes," and reports were presented on the campaign to halt construction of a deep-water port at Burns Ditch. Florence Broady introduced the speaker for the evening, Helga Sandburg. Sandburg's quiet voice betrayed strong emotion. In her opinion the proposed "ditch port" would

ruin the Dunes and their inspirational value. She read selections from
the Bible, Ovid, Thoreau, and her father's poetry, and between the
readings she sang folk songs, accompanying herself on the guitar.
One poem was from her own work. Entitled "The Visitor," it
began—

> Returned this year to the old tall house
> Where my childhood was,
> Where ever since I've lived my dreams . . .[80]

Not long before, Helga Sandburg had returned for the first time
in many years to the home of her youth in the Dunes.[81] It was not
an easy trip. She loved the Dunes too much, and feared they had
changed. She drove the gravel road from the crossroads town of
Harbert, Michigan, twenty miles north of the Indiana state line,
to Lake Michigan and the three-story house on the top of a great
shoreline dune. At the age of seven she had been brought to this
house, separated by a mile from all but one of its nearest neighbors,
and she had grown to maturity there during the 1930s. Climbing
the path up the back of the dune, she looked out again at the wide
view of lake and beach bending to the north.

"Chickaming Farm," the Sandburgs called it, in honor of the
first Indian settlers, also "Pawpaw Patch," after the little pawpaw
trees with the great drooping leaves. It was a miniature world,
wild, rural, cosmopolitan—all were gathered within its circumference. Before it was the lake whose profound presence qualified
each aspect of the place. Beneath it and on all sides were the shifting sands. The wind kept things in a constant flux—sending the
waves crashing, the sand flying, and the trees bending. Overhead,
the stars and moon shone clear and full. Often, Helga remembered,
she would climb to the crow's nest on top of the roof, where a
telescope was mounted, and learn the names of the stars from her
father.

At the rear of the Sandburg homestead was the farm proper, a
small plot of ground where the family raised fruits and vegetables,
chickens, ducks, geese, rabbits, pigs, a horse or two, and of course,
Lillian Sandburg's prize goat herd. Every day was defined by farm
chores and every year by the rhythm of nature's harvest.

Between lake and farm was the house in which, like a miniature polis, people of all sorts converged, and even the goats, on cold winter nights, were welcome. Often in the evenings Helga listened to the songs of her father mixed with conversation of friends and family around the fireplace. Some of these friends were their poor yet "land-loving" neighbors. Others were summer folk from Chicago, many from the University of Chicago, living in the cottages along the beach. Others were acquaintances of Carl's who descended upon the house from all parts of the country. It was not by accident that Carl Sandburg had said: "I was foolish about windows. . . . I was hungry for windows . . . ," and Lillian Sandburg had designed the house so that it was lined with a multitude of panes facing in all directions.[82]

When Helga Sandburg came to write of those Dunes years, she re-created a world in which a young girl grows to maturity by awakening to her common humanity. In the spring of 1962, Helga had just published her novel *The Owl's Roost,* a book peopled with the same diversity of human personality she knew at Chickaming Farm.[83] In the beginning, her characters share the environment of a summer resort in the Dunes, yet, as the story unfolds, it becomes clear how they also share the human condition: a shared quest for immortality in the face of the certainty of death, and a shared sinfulness, specifically, the betrayal of one another. Each of the main characters of the book embodies these two dimensions of his or her common humanity: Clara Olson's father, a doctor, seeks immortality through his work while betraying his son; her mother, obsessed with the loss of her youth, commits adultery; the Reverend Thwaite, in his mad rush for an otherworldly immortality, betrays everything beautiful and natural in the world around him; Clara herself, in the process of realizing her own emergent sexuality, betrays a companion immediately before his death. Only those who recognize this shared human condition possess sufficient wisdom for forgiveness and only they find freedom to assume responsibility. By the conclusion of the story, Clara and her father feel complete within themselves, whole, precisely because they see the circular pattern of life. They can act on behalf of a universal liberation.

Throughout *The Owl's Roost,* the metaphor for enlightenment is the Dunes themselves. Each creature, even each insect, seeks immortality, and in that seeking preys on the others. Of all the aspects of the Dunes world, it is the lake that most powerfully symbolizes the truth of reality. In the opening scene, the lake on an early summer morning brings both the renewal of life and an unexpected death by drowning. At the conclusion, the lake, which Clara's companion loved like a lost mother, destroys him. Yet it is also the lake that is complete unto itself, a whole that endures. As much as her house, Helga remembered the lake of her childhood in the Dunes:

> Great Lake of my childhood, dangerous and beautiful,
> Will you never let me go?
> Tonight again you come into my dream,
> Churning and foaming, and almost drowning me,
> And hurling me upon the shore . . .
>
> Dear Great Lake, let me go!
> In dreams I walk in sandied bathing suit
> Along your sunsetting shore,
> The pool of the dying orb spreading to make
> A path that follows my progress like a scarlet finger.
> All this in broken-hearted dreams.
> Dear lovely memory, let me go![84]

Years earlier, before her birth, before the star-filled night walks that she took as a girl with her father along the beach near Harbert, Helga Sandburg's parents had associated their deepest commitments with the Lake Michigan coast. In 1894, at the age of sixteen, Carl Sandburg saw Chicago and Lake Michigan for the first time.

> Out from the huddled and ugly walls,
> I came sudden, at the city's edge,
> On a blue burst of lake.[85]

Sixteen years later, in 1908, he met Lillian Steichen in the Social Democratic party headquarters of Milwaukee. They fell in love immediately. In the spring he wrote a letter to her from a small lakeshore town in Wisconsin, where he was working for the party as an organizer:

Back from a long hike again—sand and shore, night and stars and this restless inland sea—Plunging white horses in a forever recoiling Pickett's charge at Gettysburg—On the left a ridge of jaggedly outlined pines, their zigzag jutting up into a steel-grey sky—under me and ahead a long brown swath of sand—to the right the ever-repelled but incessantly charging white horses and beyond an expanse of dark—but over all, sweeping platoons of unguessable stars! Stars everywhere! Blinking, shy-hiding gleams—blazing, effulgent beacons—an infinite, traveling caravanserie—going somewhere! "Hail!" I called. "Hail—do you know? do you know? You veering cotillions of worlds beyond this world—you marching, imperturbable splendors—you serene, everlasting spectators—where are we going? do you know?" And the answer came back, "No, we don't know and what's more, we don't care!" And I called, "You answer well. For you are time and space—you are tomb and cradle. Forever you renew your own origin, shatter to-day and re-shape to-morrow, in a perpetual poem of transformations, knowing no goal, expecting no climax, looking forward to no end, indulging in no conception of a finale, content to move in the eternal drama on which no curtain will be rung. You answer well. I salute you to-night. I will see you again and when I do again I will salute you for you are sincere. I believe you O stars! and I know you! We have met before and met many times. We will meet again and meet many times."—All this time I was striding along at a fast pace, to the music of the merry-men. The merry-men, I forgot to explain, ride the white horses and it is the merrymen who give voice to the ecstasy and anger and varying humor of the sea. The tumultuous rhythms of the merry-men and a steady ozone-laden wind led me to walk fast and when I turned from the sea, there burst on my vision, the garish arc-lamps of the municipality of Two Rivers. So I turned to the sky and said, "Good-by, sweet stars! I have had a good companionship with you to-night but now I must leave star-land, and enter the corporation limits of Two Rivers town. Remember me, O stars! and remember Paula down in Princeton, Illinois! and if any agitators appear in starland, let them agitate—it will be good for them and for all the little stars." And as I plodded down a narrow street fast past the hovels of fishermen and the tenements of factory workers, I quoted from the bare-footed, immortal Athenian, "The gods are on high Olympus—let them stay there." Yes, let the gods who are on high Olympus stay where they belong. And let us turn to the business of rearing on earth a race of gods.[86]

Lillian (Paula) Steichen was uniquely prepared to understand how Carl could link his love for her to a cosmic image of human salvation. A Phi Beta Kappa graduate of the University of Chicago, she was not only an accomplished student of science and literature, but like Sandburg, loved the native landscape and was a sincere convert to socialism.[87]

Sandburg has been called the "poet of the prairie," but he spent most of his life within an area biographers call the "Sandburg range," a reverse J-shaped strip of land encircling Lake Michigan and roughly coterminous with the inside perimeter of the Valparaiso Moraine. For Sandburg this coastal landscape concentrated the social democratic promise of the Midwest. When he settled at Chickaming Farm in the 1920s, he positioned himself so as to live permanently at the center of the sacred cosmos he first vividly evoked in his 1908 letter. Instead of the garish lights of Two Rivers, however, it was the lights of Chicago he saw in the distance, the city which, of all cities, symbolized for him the struggle of the laboring poor for dignity and freedom. As if to confirm this symbolism, Sandburg once wrote that his idea of a suitable suicide was to find a "starlit night on the eastern shore of Lake Michigan, walk out into the black waters, slanting my eyes toward the haze of light over Chicago, and then go walking till my hat floated."[88]

Sandburg called the Dunes a "wonderland for creative art or creative pause."[89] To dwell there meant in his view to create art, and this in turn meant, for his own calling, to carry forward the task of Whitman and create the scriptures of democracy. While living at Harbert, Sandburg wrote two of his most important contributions to the literature of the democratic faith, *Abraham Lincoln: The War Years*, and the epic poem, *The People, Yes*.

Chicago Daily News editor Henry Justin Smith noted in the 1910s that there were two contending images of Lincoln in the Chicago region—represented in two statues by St. Gaudens. The first, in Lincoln Park, was a statue of Lincoln standing, symbol of the self-made man of the new city. The second statue was in Lake Front Park. There Lincoln sat in "accusing loneliness . . . under the shadow of the city skyscrapers, built by those corporations which he warned against as the menace of the future."[90] The struggle for the meaning of Lincoln, the greatest symbol of democracy America had produced, was one that advocates of the religion of democracy, from Jane Addams to Paul Douglas, took up gladly. Carl Sandburg did the most, however, to create the figure and the myth twentieth-century America remembers.

Chickaming Farm was purchased with the royalties from *Abraham Lincoln: The Prairie Years*. For twelve long years Sandburg labored in the Dunes on *The War Years*. So well known, in fact, was the association of Sandburg, Lincoln, and the Dunes that John Steinbeck and a group of friends, intending a practical joke, employed an actor to impersonate Lincoln and confront Sandburg one morning on the beach in front of his home. Sandburg's disarming reply: "Good morning, Mr. President!"[91]

Helga Sandburg remembered how, always at night, when the world was quiet, and the wind blew hard off the lake, a beam speared from the attic window where her father was working. Often she drifted off to sleep to the clacking of her father's typewriter. The typewriter stood on an orange crate. In the corner was a small black stove which Sandburg stoked with driftwood gathered on his walks. Lincoln came back to him on such nights and he typically wrote from midnight to dawn.

In his interpretation of Lincoln as the prophetic keeper of a covenant with the land as well as with the founders of the Republic, Sandburg saw himself retelling a myth that "the people" had already created in their legends and stories. In *The Prairie Years*, especially, did Sandburg take poetic liberty. Lincoln was the son of Nancy Hanks, a woman of mystic affinities, somehow predestined to bear a child who would lead the American people in the time of their greatest trial. Sandburg described how, in their Kentucky wilderness home, she would sit quietly with her son by the Rock Spring and meditate upon the biblical words, "Peace, be still." There in the valley of Knob Creek, Lincoln spent his first seven years. "Birds have made the valley a home," Sandburg wrote, "oncoming civilization has not shut off their hopes; home for all are here. . . ."[92] It happened that later in life, after Abe first shot a wild turkey, he could never shoot a game bird again; in school he refused to join his classmates in torturing a live mud turtle. With such legends Sandburg rewove the story of Lincoln's youth and, by mythic identification, the authentic youth of all builders of

America in the great garden at the center of the continent.

But he was to become even more explicit in his association of Lincoln with the vision of the Dunes. In a passage preceded by a discussion of Lincoln's indebtedness to Emerson, Thoreau, and Whitman—whose ethics of human freedom were grounded in a philosophy of nature—Sandburg describes Lincoln's response to Lake Michigan:

> One summer evening Lincoln had sat on the front porch of the Judd home on Lake Shore Drive in Chicago. The plumes of steamboat smoke and the white canvas of sailboats met the eye as twilight glimmered and failed, and a red rim of a big slow moon pushed up the horizon where the sky line touched the water line on Lake Michigan. The stars came out and a silver sheen glistened on the lake waves breaking and rippling on the beach sand.
>
> The night brought a slow surprise for Mrs. Judd. Something came into the air that evening that set Lincoln to talking to the company on the porch, and his talk was of far things, of man in old times and man in times to come. In the old times of the Bible, and earlier than that, men had looked at the stars and contemplated the mystery of the lighted clusters and forms on the sky.[93]

The question of human destiny lay in the stars and on the lakeshore beach. Sandburg goes on to describe how Lincoln mused upon the possibilities of humankind in the universe, and what it might achieve in the next one thousand years.

In *The War Years*, Lincoln lived to see one such possibility realized—the abolition of slavery. Sandburg's biography also suggests another possibility—a "Union" of the creation itself. But was Sandburg himself aware of all that he was doing? To all appearances he deliberately retold the greatest of the democratic myths to include a covenant with nature so profound that as he wrote in his conclusion, when Lincoln died, "the brown thrush no longer sang."[94]

The People, Yes was Sandburg's most ambitious attempt to use the language of the people as his almost total means of expression and to shape that language into cadences of scriptural quality.[95] Its publication in 1936 was timely. But Sandburg's aims were larger than any particular economic or political crisis. The first section establishes the biblical parallel. Sandburg paraphrases the story of the Tower of Babel and then retells the story in modern idiom. Out of Illinois and Indiana comes the tale of the earth's peoples gathering on a great plain to shout in unison. This time it is not the Lord who confounds them; the people are their own undoing. Everyone is so eager to listen, silence reigns. In Sandburg's new testament of sacramental humanism, the people are not disobedient; they are ignorant. They want to experience life. Most of all, they want to know who they are, what is their next move, and what is their ultimate destiny. These are religious questions, and Sandburg proceeds to give what answers he can—drawn from the tales, proverbs, jokes, anecdotes, wisdom of the people themselves.

Whoever you are, Sandburg asserts, you are a member of "the people." King or beggar, your life follows the same route of birth, trouble, and death. It also has, potentially, the same dignity. But this is not your whole identity. You are also brother and sister to mud and gold, bug and bird, behemoths and constellations. For example, there are two purple martins who live on the shores of Lake Michigan. They are people, too, "people of the air . . . lights of wonder . . . for other children, other people, yes."[96] To ask who and what is the people is not far from asking what is grass, or salt, or the sea.

> Who of the poets equals the music of the sea?
> And where is a symbol of the people unless it is the sea?[97]

Your fullest identity is your membership in the world of land, sea, and sky, the world which all creatures own in common. In this world—

> The sea has fish for every man.
> Every blade of grass has its share of dew.[98]

You have, with the breathing of the earth and the music of the sea, "joined belongings."[99]

Yet pain, injustice, despair plague the human condition. The earth is defaced by the greed of man, and even the law of nature is unfair to the weak. Behind every correctable evil stands someone who commits the unpardonable sin, who separates himself from the rest of his kind, who would be himself a master and make the rest of humankind, and nature itself, his slave. It is hard to understand what the United States of the Earth might look like as long as the privileged munitions and money kings, war lords and bankers, transportation and credit kings, claim title to it. Only a new revolution will put things right. Revolution by the fireborn who are "at home in fire," people like the Chicago railroad engineer who directed in his will that his ashes be thrown from his pet locomotive there at Eighty-seventh Street on Chicago's South Side because that was the place he so often looked out across the prairie to the sky.[100] Those who recognize that the saving covenant of tolerance, patience, and sympathy is borne by a sinful humanity will do the job. They go back to the earth for rootholds, and realize there is no personal salvation apart from the salvation of all.

The saga not yet written is the saga of the people. Books have only begun short, stammering memoranda of the resources and stamina of humankind. The religion of the people has only begun to be formulated and celebrated. The people have a long way to go, and they must carry much grief as they march in the night with "overhead a shovel of stars for keeps."[101]

Looking west across the lake to Gary from his attic retreat in the Dunes, Sandburg saw that—

> The steel mill sky is alive.
> The fire breaks white and zigzag
> shot on a gun-metal gloaming.

In such brilliant display of human inventiveness and power, bespeaking both creativity and destructiveness, lay the promise that someday human beings might fulfill their destiny:

> Man is a long time coming.
> Man will yet win.
> Brother may yet line up with brother.[102]

PAUL DOUGLAS: WHERE ANTAEUS
RETOUCHED THE EARTH

Paul Douglas begins his autobiography, *In the Fullness of Time*, with the Lincolnesque declaration: "I grew up in a log cabin in the heart of the Maine woods."[103] His mother dead at the age of four, his father unable to support him, Douglas lived for eight formative years, from 1898 to 1906, with his stepmother in a wilderness camp near Moosehead Lake, Maine. Here, where a railroad line to Bangor served as the only transportation link with civilization, he grew to know the primitive life of the old frontier. But he came to know it in the context of the resort hotel his uncle ran in the summer and through the eyes of the muckraking publications of the day, especially Joseph Pulitzer's crusading *New York World*, which functioned as his first bible and chief contact with the outside world.

In the winter Douglas shoveled paths of snow, cut wood, and attended an improvised school his stepmother organized for the children of French-Canadian loggers. "Struggling to keep warm, we kept the fireplaces and stoves always burning."[104] In the summer he did chores for the guests who streamed in from Boston and New York, and roamed with his companions the surrounding wilderness.

Two great sympathies contributed to the lasting image of his boyhood home. The first was a strong identification with nature: "Lonely as I was, I gained a certain serenity of spirit from the woods and mountains, along with a basic faith in the goodness of the earth." Several times a year, Douglas climbed Borestone Mountain alongside the lake. The beauty of the forest interspersed with lakes and rivers stretched out before him. Douglas's love for the woods readily translated itself into a love for its creatures and he "resolutely refused" to hunt with his uncles. "I had once killed a porcupine with a club and had been stuck with remorse when I saw its pained and accusing eyes. It seemed to be telling me, 'I have the right to live also.' "[105]

His second sympathy was for "the people." Inseparable from his love for nature was his identification with the common lumbering men on the Maine frontier. It did not take him long to realize that the dominant businesses of the region were prospering at the expense of the poor and ignorant, and he sharply felt the injustice. With this realization went a disdain for the conventionally good, for the church-attending and sanctimonious who exploited others while retaining the facade of self-righteousness, and conversely, respect for those who, while victims of personal vice, fought on the side of public justice. When the section hands of the railroad went out on strike, Douglas was passionately on their side.

Douglas's sympathy for nature and for the people formed the basis of a vision of community that was to remain with him throughout his life as the wellspring of his personal identity and political ambition. In his democratic vision, there was dignity for all, and especially for the least of the creatures of the earth. "I can say in retrospect that the woods were also the home of lost people, and the refuge of those beaten by life." [106]

From Moosehead Lake, Douglas moved to Newport, Maine, where he thrilled to the two great civic events of the year, the town meeting and Memorial Day. In 1909 he entered Bowdoin College, and with the help of the writings of John Stuart Mill, Henry George, John Ruskin, and William Morris, and the 1912 campaign of Eugene Debs, became absorbed in the field of economics. The next years found him in New York, organizing for the ladies' garment workers, and enrolled in the Graduate School of Economics and Political Science at Columbia University. In 1920, after a year at Harvard and teaching stints in Illinois, Oregon, and Washington, he was appointed assistant professor of industrial relations at the University of Chicago. Douglas arrived when the Chicago renaissance was on the wane, but he quickly became a friend of Jane Addams, and found sympathetic colleagues at the university, and among the Amalgamated Clothing Workers and the NAACP. [107]

Douglas was fiercely independent, always preoccupied with questions of personal and public morality. With his special dedication to improving the lot of industrial workers, his theoretical mastery of economics, his prolific pen, and his willingness to expose himself to personal attack on behalf of unpopular causes, he was well qualified to carry the insurgent flag of midwestern social democracy into the fast-shifting battlefields of the mid-twentieth century. [108]

In the 1920s and '30s, Douglas became active, locally and nationally, in a wide variety of progressive causes which sought to improve the status of labor, and to use the power of government to equalize wealth and provide for the welfare of all citizens. In his view, the right direction for American society was between and beyond the extreme right and the extreme left. Economically, this meant a mixed economy including the participation of private enterprise, unions, co-ops, and government, and politically, a reinvigorated democracy returned to the hands of the people. By 1935 Douglas had written eight books on political economy, including the 1934 classic *Theory of Wages*, which made a comprehensive argument for the economic benefits to be derived from redistributing surplus income to the wage-earning class and indigent.[109]

Douglas achieved political visibility in the late 1920s when he emerged as the spokesman for the People's Traction League, organized by Harold Ickes and Charles E. Merriam to challenge Samuel Insull's midwestern utilities empire. In this campaign, newspaper reporter Carl Sandburg and professor-reformer Paul Douglas collaborated for the first time. In 1939 Douglas was elected alderman of Chicago's Fifth Ward with support of Independents and regular Democrats, and for three years, as the "perfessor," played the role of "gadfly," "windmill-tilter," and "nagging conscience" of the Chicago City Council. During this time he focused public attention on the wretched housing conditions of Chicago blacks, instituted New England-style town meetings in Hyde Park, sponsored activities designed to build local community spirit (what he later called "an experiment in 'ecology'"), and earned the friendship and respect of influential members of the Democratic machine.

In 1942, following an unsuccessful bid for the Democratic senatorial nomination, Douglas made the most dramatic move of his career. At the age of fifty, he enlisted as a private in the United States Marines, determined to see front line action. He was discharged four years later with a paralyzed left arm and two Purple Hearts. In Chicago he was quickly noticed by "Boss" Jake Arvey, who was looking for good government candidates to revive the Illinois Democratic organization. Douglas had strong support from labor, veterans organizations, and independent voters, and in 1948 he was slated as the Democratic candidate for United States senator.

In the face of a prevailing defeatism within the Democratic party, Douglas launched himself with vigor into the national political arena. He equipped a Jeep with loudspeakers, and started each morning with handshaking at a factory gate, carrying his campaign directly to the people. Emily Taft Douglas, who had served a term in Congress as Illinois Representative-at-large, was constantly by his side. At the Democratic National Convention in July, he joined Hubert Humphrey and the ADA to push acceptance of a strong civil rights plank and to renominate Truman for the presidency. When the votes were counted in November, Douglas scored an upset. Truman carried Illinois by 31,000; Douglas won by a majority of 407,000.

For eighteen years, from 1948 until his defeat by Charles Percy in 1966, Douglas served in the U.S. Senate. His avowed aims throughout his three terms were: progressive social legislation on the domestic front, collective security on the international scene, economy in government and competition in industry, and a high ethical code among all elected officials. This translated into leadership in support of such policies as public housing and open occupancy, reform of Senate Rule XXII (the cloture rule), civil rights, truth-in-lending, aid to education, reform of Taft-Hartley, minimum wage legislation, social security insurance and medicare, environmental protection and conservation of natural resources, continuation of the Marine Corps, a strong United Nations, defense of South Korea and South Viet Nam, tax reform, attack on the pork barrel rivers and harbors bills, breakup of monopolies, a balanced budget, and congressmen's disclosure of personal finances. During his Senate tenure, Douglas considered himself a distributionist, seeking a broad diffusion of economic and political power, and a liberal, holding to the view that, given the chance, truth had power to establish itself in the arena of public opinion. Among his liberal Democratic colleagues, he was distinguished by his dual program of social reform to help the poor and his opposition to waste in public expenditures.

In retrospect, Douglas's years of struggle for social justice may be seen as an outworking of the elementary democratic faith he first experienced as a youth in the Maine woods. Intertwining the long years of public service and scholarship, there is visible a movement of personal conviction and spiritual self-consciousness, a religious pilgrimage. The direction of this pilgrimage was toward an increasingly explicit adherence to the religion of democracy as the new testament of the Judeo-Christian tradition.

There were several crucial turnings of the soul along the way. The first came when, as a young man, after an early immersion in the literature of the religion of democracy, Douglas was converted to Quakerism. Reading John Woolman's *Journal*, he felt an immediate and powerful attraction to the Christian principle of active suffering love. Although in the 1930s, in the face of aggressive dictatorships, Douglas rejected the belief that spiritual super-resistance could be effective at the collective level, he retained membership in the Society of Friends, and a commitment to ever-affirming love as the way to transform personal opponents into friends. In the Quaker "religion of the Spirit," with its combination of personal mysticism and social reform, Douglas made contact with one of the principal roots of the democratic faith.[110]

A second turning came as a result of his efforts to form a third national Progressive party, first with La Follette in 1924, and then as co-founder with John Dewey of the League for Independent Political Action in 1928. Thinking through the requirements necessary for the success of such a party, Douglas concluded that only a new political faith, in league with economic and political necessity, could generate power sufficient to overturn the feudal control of American society. He was helped to this conclusion by personal observation of the transformations effected in Russian society by the "social religion" of communism.[111]

In 1932 Douglas made a public appeal for a new social democratic faith in *The Coming of a New Party*. Dedicated to Norman Thomas, and with a preface by John Dewey ("If I knew any way to make this book compulsory reading for all citizens . . . I would gladly do so"), Douglas argued that the foremost reason why American workers failed to combine for their collective welfare was the prevailing American philosophy of competitive individualism. This capitalist-inculcated ideology could not be exorcised by vague palaver from the religious establishment about service. Faith with power to transform, like primitive Christianity, or the great art of Michelangelo and Beethoven, convinces men that they are participating in a way of life that leads somewhere—that the eternal is "revealed in the midst of time." In this fundamental religious sense, politics too may be an art. Its vocation is to enable the people to see the eternal at stake in social life. The foundation of a new third party movement must be the perception of transcendent significance in cooperative action for the common good, grounded in a "passionate belief in the worthwhileness of the common man." Those who join in a third party movement dedicated to "faith in the ultimate power of democratic methods" must be ready for heartache, labor, and sacrifice. They will be rewarded by a new-found "fellowship with humble men and women," and by the joy that comes from the greatest adventure conceivable—"as though man had resolved to become a god and to order a happier existence for himself." [112]

Testimony that these were not mere words, but in fact reflected an honest belief that the God of democracy was worthy of one's ultimate devotion, is evident in the public service that defined Douglas's career. Testimony of a different sort came in the course of the Second World War, and with it, a third turning of the soul: the identification of the American nation as the last, best hope of democracy. Since the days of his youth when he thrilled to the view of forests and lakes from Borestone Mountain, and watched the parades on Memorial Day, Douglas had felt a keen love for his native land. But as a Quaker pacifist, and a social and intellectual radical, he had resisted armed conflict and any easy glorification of the virtues of the United States. Yet historically and constitutionally, the United States was founded on principles of freedom, and in the onrush of events it was forced to defend them. The eternal did indeed appear in the midst of time. At the crucial moment, an enlightened patriotism and religious commitment could be one.

Douglas remembered a "deep wave of exaltation" sweeping over him when, on Okinawa, he realized he had "shed blood in defense of my country." [113] After he was wounded, lying on a stretcher in the pouring rain, he found himself discussing with an Episcopalian chaplain the doctrine of the Eucharist and the meaning of Frazer's *Golden Bough*. By sacrificing a portion of his own life for freedom, he had participated in the most potent sacrament of the religion of democracy. Douglas believed his life was mystically joined with countless others who had risked or made the ultimate sacrifice, and with that mysterious Power of death and resurrection, in whose hands the hope for a rebirth of democracy ultimately lay.

It remained for Douglas to find an explicit articulation of the faith that moved him. He found this when he moved to Washington, D.C., in the gospel of democratic universalism preached by A. Powell Davies, minister of All Souls Church, Unitarian. By 1954, the year Paul joined Emily Douglas as a member of All Souls, Davies had attracted a large following among liberal Democrats in the Capitol, including Chief Justice William O. Douglas, and Senators Ernest Gruening and Richard Neuberger. In one of his most popular books, *America's Real Religion*, Davies traced the democratic faith of the United States from its founding by Jefferson upon principles of human equality, freedom, and fraternity ("a turning point in history . . . a turning point in human destiny"), through the life of democracy's greatest incarnation, Abraham Lincoln, and the acts of its many "apostles, heretics, and saints" (among them Woolman, Paine, Emerson, Parker, Whitman, Steffens, Darrow, Addams, Sandburg, and Dewey).[114] Davies corroborated Douglas's belief that the democratic faith was the modern fulfillment of Christianity, that it had universal legitimacy, and that in spite of its many enemies, it was still the basic faith of the majority of Americans. With Davies's help, Douglas likely reached greater awareness of the ritual import of his yearly pilgrimage to the grave of Jane Addams; why, each year, he felt the call to spend a night walking through New Salem with a copy of Sandburg's *Lincoln* under his arm; and how he could feel overwhelmed by a "religious sense of fellowship" during the civil rights march on Washington led by Martin Luther King in 1963.[115]

In the early 1920s, soon after his arrival in Chicago, Douglas began tent-camping with friends in the Dunes. Sometimes he stayed with friends in the shacks of the Prairie Club colony near Mount Tom. Not long after his marriage to Emily Taft in 1931, he built a cottage at Dune Acres in the Central Dunes. Until Paul's enlistment in the service, the Douglas family spent every summer and as many weekends as possible at their Dunes retreat. Later, Douglas remembered these years as the happiest period of his family's life. So did Emily Taft Douglas. Speaking at a Save the Dunes Council dinner in 1972, she recalled, "with a catch in my throat," the fourteen years she and Paul enjoyed their cottage in the Dunes. "We woke at the cardinal's call to freshminted mornings and bedded down with the whip-poor-wills. . . . Our view over-looked the lake, framed like a well known Cezanne painting by the green pine trees on our hill."[116]

To appreciate the meaning of the Indiana Dunes for Paul Douglas, it is necessary to recognize the symbolic associations they came to hold for him. In the Dunes he rediscovered the Maine wilderness home in which he first experienced the goodness of the earth and the worthwhileness of the common man, and first felt sympathy for the persecuted and oppressed. Douglas evoked Greek myth to explain it: "Like Antaeus, I retouched the earth and became the stronger thereby."[117] The image of the Maine camp was the center of his life—the basis for his identification with Progressivism, the source of his love for his country, the motivation for his political and academic career, the personal myth of origins that led to his adherence to a universalistic democratic faith. Now these complex associations were superimposed upon the Dunes, an imaginative act no doubt encouraged by the fact that so many of his Chicago friends within the Dunes movement, not least of all his father-in-law Lorado Taft, had found a similar inclusive vision embodied there.

The events of the war and the 1948 senatorial campaign strengthened these associations. In 1938, on the eve of Munich, Douglas drove in from his cottage in the Dunes to speak to a rally of 30,000 Czechoslovakians in Chicago Stadium. He told those assembled that the world was threatened by tyranny and that the democracies must now stand together in defense of their homelands. Douglas exercised in the Dunes to prepare for combat, once swimming two miles in choppy water to prove that at age fifty he was fit to enlist, and when it came time to ship out as a member of a combat division in the Pacific, he first spent time in "our beloved Dunes." In 1948, before the final engagement of his political campaign, he once more renewed himself in the Dunes. He mortgaged and eventually sold the cottage in order to raise funds for the campaign. Eventually Douglas was to will the capital from his Marine Corps disability pension, as well as the proceeds from his awards for public service, to the Save the Dunes Council for the purchase of park land. The identification of homeland, America, democracy, the Dunes, ran deep.

Another symbol was involved in this rich complex of associations. It was the symbol of fire. Forest fires were the major drama of Douglas's youth in the Maine woods, and one fire in particular stood out in his memory. To fight it, he journeyed nearly to the Canadian border. The fire, ignited by either a locomotive or a careless smoker, was a mile long. "With terror in my heart I fought the fire all that day and night. The heat was scorching, and at times it seemed as though all avenues of escape were being cut." Finally rain removed the danger. "We climbed into the caboose for the return trip, dirty, singed, and hungry, but triumphant and humbled at the same time by what we had endured."[118]

This experience became in retrospect the paradigm for a theory of democratic social action. It taught Douglas in college to mistrust classical theories of social equilibrium. In their place he inserted an awareness of the impetuous forces of history, which, once set in motion, "release latent forces until a cumulative process of change takes place in which the final, unpredictable result is out of all proportion to the initial cause."[119] The fire taught him the role of chance, and of human will, and the importance of deliberate human effort in the outcomes of history. It also showed him the crucial distinction between those who honor a covenant with the land and the people and who participate in a common struggle in their defense, and those who stand by complacently and refuse to help.

Throughout his life Douglas used the image of a forest fire raging out of control to symbolize the feudal enemy with which the cooperative action of democracy must struggle. It was a forest fire out of control that Lincoln faced in the Civil War, and that the Union troops sought to extinguish at Gettysburg. It was a forest fire out of control in the form of capitalist greed that brought the country to its knees in the Depression. It was a forest fire out of control that swept fascism into power in Italy, Germany, and Japan, and finally provoked the resistance of the Allies in the Second World War.

One moonlit evening in the late 1930s, as he stood on the beach in front of his home in the Dunes and surveyed the scene on the western horizon, Douglas saw the fires of the Gary steel mills and the polluting smoke of Chicago as a great onrushing forest fire closing in upon him. "I felt we were in the grip of an almost irreversible force, which would overrun those who loved the Dunes and sweep on to Michigan City and beyond. . . . The worse features of our civilization threatened to invade what had been an earthly paradise."[120] So that night he "took an oath" to fight the feudal fire that was out of control on the border of the Dunes, just as he had fought the forest fires of his youth, if the way ever opened to do so.

SIX

Standing on the Last Acre

The problem of the Dunes is a symbol of the crisis that faces all America. It is as though we are standing on the last acre, faced with a decision as to how it should be used. In actuality, it is the last acre, the last acre of its kind; in essence it foreshadows the time not too far removed when we will, in all truth, be standing on the last unused, unprotected acre, wondering which way to go. Have we the courage to stand up and place physical limits on the constant relentless march of industrialization?

SENATOR PAUL H. DOUGLAS,

U.S. Senate speech, May 26, 1958

Thomas Paine wrote that when the Tory innkeeper said he wanted no war against the Crown because he wanted peace in his lifetime, Paine looked down at the children crawling on the floor and thought, "Were this Tory a man he would say, 'If there must be a conflict with tyranny, let it come in my lifetime. Let there be peace and freedom in my children's time'." That's the answer! If we must fight this slow, creeping, callous encroachment of industry on our sea and lake shores let it be in our time. Let there be physical and mental health-giving breathing space, let

there be freedom for the development through
nature of men's minds, bodies, and souls, in our
children's time. The Bible says, "Where there is no
vision the people perish." This has been the vision of
the Save the Dunes Council. And there we still stand!

DOROTHY R. BUELL,

*Testimony before Committee on Interior and Insular Affairs,
United States Senate,* May 13, 1959

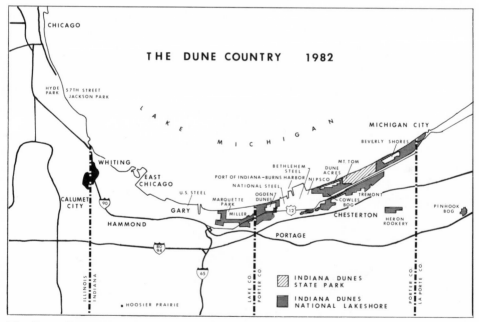

The Dune Country, 1982
Drawing by Joan G. Engel

At the time of their discovery by the first Dune Country patriots, the Dunes constituted a de facto public park—an "everybody's land." For years the South Shore railroad, exploiting this circumstance, advertised and ran excursion trips to the Dunes. At no time, however, were the Dunes immune from the destructive consequences of expanding industry and population. As these consequences became apparent in the succeeding decades of the century, the Dunes movement was repeatedly galvanized to action in defense of its sacred center.

A NEW ACT IN THE DUNES DRAMA

By 1912, the year the first public meetings were held in Henry Booth Settlement House and the City Club to discuss the prospect of saving the Dunes, one dramatic transformation of the native landscape had already occurred. Well before the turn of the century the great virgin forest of white pine and cedar was cut to build Chicago.

Other transformations were underway.

Sandmining, which for years had made inroads into the Dunes, continued apace. Steam shovels were loading railroad cars on sidings built against the dunes, while along the coast sandsuckers were at work transferring sand from the shallow water into barges. The impact of this activity is suggested by the fact that in 1898 alone more than three hundred cars of sand were shipped from Dune Park Station every twenty-four hours. Inevitably, many of the highest and most spectacular of the sand dunes were obliterated. By 1916 a rumor was abroad that Mount Tom itself was to be sold to a Chicago contractor and removed bodily, a fate which had earlier befallen the famous "Hoosier Slide" at Michigan City.[1]

Equally devastating, the wildlife was being trapped and shot in wholesale numbers, and the marshes were being drained. In 1906 R. W. Burns, a Chicago attorney and land speculator, began to build Burns Ditch, a major cut through the Dunes to the west of

Dune Park. By 1926 it was to drain 22,000 acres of marshland fed by the Little Calumet River, and effectively remove most of the waterfowl habitat on the southern rim of the Dune Country. The rapid industrialization of the Calumet region was taking a large toll as well. In 1911 Shelford complained that the ponds and ridges west of Gary were being rapidly destroyed. Two decades later one of Marjorie Allee's scientists commented: "The university will have to buy us an airplane so we can hop out to the mountains if the city keeps on spreading. . . . Can't run a decent field trip within twenty miles."[2]

The increasing popularity of the Dune Country also contributed to its destruction. By 1916 the "House of Refuge" was burned by vandals, and the picking of rare wildflowers by hikers was a serious problem. The Dunes Highway, which paralleled the South Shore railroad between Gary and Michigan City, was opened in 1923. Ostensibly built to link the two cities and make access to the Dunes easier for holiday excursions, it resulted in a real estate boom. In the 1920s three exurban residential developments were platted: Ogden Dunes east of Miller, Dune Acres in the Central Dunes, and Beverly Shores west of Michigan City.

Consequences of the industrial and speculative ownership of large tracts of land in the high Dune Country were evident by 1930. In that year National Steel Corporation and Consumers Company of Chicago announced plans for the construction of a "second Gary" in the heart of the Central Dunes. Covering 5,000 acres, the city of fifty thousand was to be built adjacent to a proposed $50 million steel plant and harbor at Burns Ditch.[3] In 1932 the Northern Indiana Public Service Company (NIPSCO) purchased a 350-acre site a few miles to the east, and two years later, Republican Charles Halleck of Indiana began his long congressional career with the promise that he would obtain federal funds for a deep-water port to serve the planned steel complex.[4]

It is not surprising that as the years progressed the Dune Country patriots beheld a new revelation from Mount Tom. In 1929 George Cottman, an Indiana historian and writer, visited the Dunes to write a description of the new Indiana Dunes State Park, and to pursue the "pervasive indwelling spirit" that he found "stirs the soul" there. He observed that looking out from Mount Tom one saw, in sharp juxtaposition, a primeval wilderness and a "seething civilization." Little more than a mile from where he stood, automobiles were forever scurrying along the Dunes Highway, "looking like lines of swift-moving beetles scuttling in opposite directions." And farther off, out of sight in the misty west, but not out of hearing, were the many factories and mills of the amazing Calumet region. Cottman felt himself poised at the juncture of "Nature versus Civilization."[5] By 1944 Chicago author and Dunite Milo Quaife could describe the new revelation of Mount Tom in even more apocalyptic terms. "In recent decades," he wrote, "the vast industrial development which centers at Chicago has pushed steadily eastward around the lakeshore, overwhelming Duneland as it advances with a congeries of cities whose roaring furnaces and bellowing smokestacks redden the sky by night and blacken it by day. . . . Necessarily, however, as industry advances, primitive life and beauty disappear. *Probably nowhere in the world can a more striking illustration of this truth be seen than in the cities of the Calumet.*"[6]

Few emotions known to humankind are stronger than the fear aroused by a threat to a sacred center, a unique incarnation of universal fact and value. Once it is destroyed, the world to which it points is symbolically destroyed with it. And conversely, once it is saved, the cosmos is saved also. A threat to a sacred center is seen as a threat to the meaning of existence itself.

Paul Douglas, addressing the U.S. Senate in 1958, expressed this fear within the context of a nascent public awareness of ecological limits. The Dunes constitute a unique landscape, "in actuality," the "last acre" of their kind. They are a rare remnant of the original American wilderness. To recognize that the Dunes are in imminent danger of destruction by an industrial and urban society out of the control of its citizenry is to recognize "in essence" that the whole country is under attack and that time to save it is running out. Standing on the last acre of the Dunes we stand symbolically on America's last acre. Therefore, to save the Dunes is to save our native land.

What in the first place was beheld as the story of the creation and redemption of the cosmos became, in light of the new revelation from Mount Tom, the story of saving that cosmos—a new act in the

Dunes drama in which the Dune Country patriots were the heroes and heroines. In addition to participating in the struggle for social democracy in the society at large, they were actors in the life and death struggle of the divine for victory at the sacred center itself.

In Herbert Read's words: "The Indiana Dunes has been a battle-ground from the beginning."[7] The members of the Dunes movement were well prepared by their myth of sacred history for conflict. Indeed, the fact that the Dunes as they knew them were always under siege by some human agency no doubt influenced their perception of the significance of struggle in the natural history of the landscape. At the very least, the two confirmed one another, and nerved the patriots to undertake a campaign in defense of their holy ground against overwhelming odds. Looking out at the marram grasses holding the dunes against the onslaught of storm and wind, they saw by analogy the courage and tenacity required to save the Dunes against the onslaught of the feudal powers. And as the time for action came, they appreciated the existential meaning of Simon Pokagon's saying,

Freedom—the selfsame freedom you adore,
Bade us defend our violated shore.[8]

The martial metaphor pervades the rhetoric of the Dunes movement throughout the century. As the decades passed, it became increasingly relevant. In the first stage of the Dunes struggle, the goal was to save the whole territory. However, as the fires on the borders of the high Dune Country became more threatening, the goal shrank to saving some portion of the sanctuary before it was too late, with the hope that other areas could be added later. When threats to the heart of the sacred center itself appeared, it was necessary simultaneously to repel the invaders and to make a last-ditch stand to save the remainder. Douglas's description of his fire-fighting experience in Maine could serve as well as an account of the last thirty years of the Dunes conflict: "We dug ditches, which the fire leaped over, we felled trees, we tried to create a non-conducting zone, and we started backfires."[9] Thomas Dustin called the Dunes conflict "bitter trench warfare" and identified the lessons of environmental warfare that it taught: "Never give up," "watch for competitive interests," "be alert to the possibilities of peripheral issues and be prepared to capitalize on them," "you will have to win the same fight again, again, and again."[10]

From its inception, the campaign to "save the Dunes" was a prophetic movement. Intrinsic to its sacramental vision of sacred space and time was the apprehension of a universal ethical demand. Orpheus Schantz articulated this imperative when he evoked the natural rights concept of the Enlightenment and declared that saving the Dunes was required in order "to enjoy the things that are the inherent right of both the wild life and the human population."[11] A. F. Knotts used the language of utilitarianism to express the same principle when he argued that the preservation of the Dunes is our sacred duty because "not to do so would be a crime against Mother Earth and a crime against future generations of mankind."[12] The Dunes not only revealed the unifying source and end of existence but prompted the recognition of an environmental social ethic for modern society. In true biblical fashion, the prophets of the Dunes warned of the doom to come were the ethic rejected.

Response to the moral imperative to save the Dunes took the form of a covenant. The Dunes movement began as a distinct political movement when individuals, alone and together, pledged themselves to stand for the "inherent right of both the wild life and the human population" to enjoy the Dunes. The covenant-making process was most explicitly symbolized in the outdoor dramas of the pre–World War I period. The Kenneth Goodman masque, for example, objectified for its audiences the inner meaning of the preservation drive by portraying a ritual exchange of vows between the "citizen" and the "spirit" of the landscape. Earl North's pageant presented at Michigan City in the summer of 1916, like Thomas Wood Stevens's Dunes Pageant of 1917, concluded with a plea for protection by the "Spirit of the Dunes": "We stand here on thy northern coast, a monument high and strong. Gladden our hearts this day, my State, and tell us that thou wilt ever, in beauty and love, our lives maintain on this thy beauteous lake." The "Spirit of Indiana" then gives its pledge: "Heeded will be your request. Indiana needs thy beauty and her strength will preserve thee for the future as well as for the past."[13] Legally, the process of covenant-making was enshrined in the articles of incorporation and bylaws of the several voluntary associations formed to preserve the Dunes.

Perhaps the most determinative moments of promise-making came in times of solitude. At such moments individuals experienced within the Dunes a question that required a personal answer. Most of these intensely private moments are only hinted at in the Dunes literature. Author-naturalist Sigurd Olson recorded one such occasion so similar to the experience of Paul Douglas that it suggests a model of what must have occurred to many. Returning in the early 1960s to the Dunes he knew so well as a student (under Shelford) and as an instructor at the University of Illinois, Olson walked down and stood on the beach at sundown.

He wrote, "Imagine my surprise and delight to stand on the old beach once more watching the surf rolling in from the north just as I remembered. The water was opalescent, the white caps marching in great rows as far as I could see. I looked toward the west and to the smoky concentration of steel mills, transmission lines and factories that was Gary. I looked to the northwest to the twinkling lights and massive skyline of Chicago's loop thirty miles away, all bathed in the rosy light of the sunset. The waves crashed at my feet and the roar of the surf was everywhere. *This was the moment of truth.*" [14]

Richard Lieber would have understood Olson's experience. His diary of 1926 shows that he was "very happy" when the Indiana Dunes State Park was purchased because he had "walked those sandy shores with the moonlight on the dunes and a high sea rolling in." [15]

The covenant to honor the universal rights of nature and of humanity and to enter the battle to save the Dunes was implemented in several ways over the course of the century. First was the attempt to preserve the Dunes through art. The vision could be preserved by means of an esthetic medium. This purpose may have motivated early Dunes artists such as Dudley and Reed. At least others thought they had achieved it. J. Howard Euston wrote of Dudley: "Through his many hundreds of paintings he will keep inviolate the best of the Indiana Duneland against any possible industrial encroachment." [16] But however consoling in the face of tragic destruction, art could not be a substitute for the fullness of concrete, original experience. Politically effective defenses were also necessary.

A second form of protection, most apparent in the early period when the sanctuary functioned as a de facto commons, was the voluntary effort to police the Dunes against increasing vandalism and fire. John O. Bowers and Caroline McIlvaine were among those who urged the appointment of a "guardian" for the Dunes. Warned an early pamphlet: "If one person destroys one flower, the seeds that would bring other plants and flowers next year are absolutely eliminated from performing their part in the plant succession."[17] The response of the Chicago Conservation Council was to post large canvas signs throughout the Dune Country which read: "To be seen taking away from here flowers, foilage or mosses is to be condemned as a barbarian."[18] To enforce this judgment, the Prairie Club organized itself as a private police force. Members of the club pledged themselves to perform "combined police-and-missionary service" by calling offenders to account.[19]

A third and more effective way of preserving the Dunes was private purchase, ownership, and donation of land. The Prairie Club, the Friends of Our Native Landscape, and the Save the Dunes Council each preserved tracts of the sanctuary in this way. Some individuals, for example, Flora and W. D. Richardson, tried to maintain their own homesites as nature preserves; others, like Vin and Hazel Hannell, donated land to the Indiana Dunes State Park or National Lakeshore.[20] (Philo Read explained to his son the transfer of land by the Prairie Club to the state: "Instead of being sole owner of several Dunes acres, you are now part owner of twenty-two hundred acres.")[21] Many Dunities thought the only practicable way of preserving the region as a whole was through private donations. A fund for this purpose was established by the National Dunes Park Association. In the 1920s, John Merle Coulter and the Chicago cartoonist, John T. McCutcheon, sought to raise money by popular subscription to finance the State Park. In the 1950s, the Save the Dunes Council tried to interest foundations in helping to purchase the Central Dunes, and Paul Douglas initiated a campaign to raise $3 million. The Save the Dunes Council today maintains a Presidents Fund, in honor of Dorothy Buell and

Sylvia Troy, for the purchase of land for the National Lakeshore. Private contributions have often come at crucial times in the course of the struggle when exceptionally valuable areas were at stake.

The Dunes movement early recognized that some form of state action was necessary to preserve the sanctuary intact. This was the fourth and most important form of defense. Not only was government action required, it was appropriate. The Dunes were perceived as a revelation of and for a socialized democratic society, and it was therefore fitting that they be preserved by the government of that society for its common good. It was widely presumed that if the people in concert took responsibility for purchase and maintenance of the Dunes they would feel a new sense of shared ownership and participation in the society as a whole. Thanks to Stephen Mather and Richard Lieber, established vehicles for government preservation lay directly at hand. Over the course of the century, federal and state parks became an official system of public shrines memorializing significant events and places in the nation's civil religion. It seemed only right that the midwestern shrine of social democracy also receive government custodianship.

The Dunes patriots pursued a double strategy: to mobilize citizens as public advocates and to gain, principally by legislation, legal protection for the Dunes sanctuary; and to use the courts to stop activities destructive to the native landscape, and to require adherence to law.

For the strategy of advocacy to succeed, "the people," including their elected representatives, must be convinced. The Dunes revelation, meant for all, was yet neither known nor received by all. Richard Lieber noted with dismay, "Teachers and preachers, nature-lovers and artists, social welfare workers and other visionaries and wholly impractical people in season and out of season have worked for the preservation of the Dune Land, while eminently practical men have the meantime been busily at work removing whole hillsides of sand for purposes of track elevation and for cash. During this time the great mass of people has indolently looked on."[22] The voluntary associations dedicated to the defense of the Dunes pursued the massive task of conversion by appeals to experience and reason. Pilgrimages, pageants, testimonials or "hearings," slide shows, movies, photographs, posterettes, poetry, songs, paintings, etchings, stories—all were used as tools of evangelism to persuade the uncommitted to share the Dunes revelation and to join in a covenant for their preservation. Thousands of words were spoken and written to delineate reasons for the preservation of the Dunes. Preservationists appealed to carefully assembled facts and to what they presumed to be shared public assumptions in order to convince nonbelievers that the Dunes had universal significance.

The Dunes apostles and prophets, who began the century as poetic visionaries, became a half century later knowledgeable political strategists. An important part of their self-education was the discovery that common currency in debate on matters of environmental policy was neither poetic intuitions, nor ethical principles, nor (at least before the passage of the National Environmental Protection Act in 1969) ecological understandings. It was quantitative norms, such as benefit-cost ratios, or abstract secularized goals, such as "recreational needs," which only thinly concealed a regnant economic model for determining social policy, and a massive commitment by American society to exploitation and management of nature. The difficulty of translating the language of visionary reason into the reductionist vocabulary appropriate to the technological ethos and interest group politics that dominate the American political process was evident in the course of debate over the Indiana Dunes National Lakeshore. It accounts for the relative paucity of symbolic reference in the literature of the most recent period. Appeals to either experience or reason were difficult to make given the lack of explicit allegiance within American public life to the principles of an ecologically responsible democratic faith.

The focus on citizen advocacy for governmental action led in the course of the Dunes campaign to an unexpected result—increasing dissent from the policies of government, even at times, from those governmental agencies charged with responsibility for the protection of the Dunes. To a degree, such dissent was inevitable. Given the presumed separation of religion and politics in the American system, the implicit religious purpose of preserving inviolate the purity of a sacred space and the explicit political purpose of establishing a state or national park for multiple constituencies and uses were bound to come into conflict.

But there was an even deeper source of conflict. Government

action to preserve the Dunes at state and federal levels came hesitatingly and only after years of heart-breaking labor. This was disillusioning enough. Even more disheartening was the discovery, as the years wore on, that elected officials and governmental agencies frequently acted in service of private, not public, interests. Accustomed to look with favor upon certain forms of governmental intervention and regulation in other arenas of social policy, most Dunes advocates were surprised to discover that the ruling premise in the arena of natural resource policy was that the private economic development of natural resources brings the greatest good to the greatest number and should take priority over competing goals. The close identification of federal agency, state government, industry, local business, and land speculation interests took tangible and personal form in the 1950s and '60s.[23]

This discovery went far to explain one of the most serious concerns of the Dunes movement: the lack of regional, urban-oriented land-use planning in the United States.[24] There were limited opportunities for debate on the pros and cons of environmental preservation, and virtually no regional entity with adequate legal power to make or administer policy. The absence of a national or regional land-use policy, and the antiquity of the federal political system, which delegated zoning responsibility to local units, meant that, with the exception of Congress, the movement had to create its own public forum. The primary reason for the lack of opportunity for debate on matters of regional planning seemed painfully clear. It was to the advantage of the dominant economic and political interests that it *not happen*. Dunes advocates concluded that the "interests" had successfully co-opted the institutions of the people, and in many respects, their minds and hearts as well. In 1969 Peggy Moran completed her history of the struggle for the Indiana Dunes National Lakeshore with the statement: "the philosophy and power of the robber barons is alive, well, and faceless in a hundred panelled conference rooms."[25] In 1982 Charlotte Read, executive director of the Save the Dunes Council, deplored the resurgence of a "new feudalism."

That these failures of American political life should be exposed in the course of a campaign to save one small landscape remnant of such obvious ecological significance, and of such apparent value to the millions of citizens of the nation's second largest metropolitan center, was as it should be. Many intimations of larger importance were gathered up in the perception of the Dunes as a sacred center. One of these intimations was that the struggle to preserve and fulfill the ancient ties that bind human and natural communities in the Dunes was a struggle in microcosm of the global struggle for the liberation of the common world. The radicalization of the Dunes movement over the course of the century was a part of the radicalization of the environmental movement world-wide as the full import of the modern thrust toward domination of the earth became apparent.

INDIANA DUNES STATE PARK

When Jensen, Allinson, Cowles, and their friends decided in 1912 to risk the danger of land speculation, and to go public with their plans for some kind of a Dunes park, attention was immediately focused upon the Indiana political scene, especially upon Indianapolis, the state capital, and Gary, the western gateway to the high Dune Country, and the center of strongest sentiment for Dunes preservation outside of Chicago.

The campaign to preserve the Dunes before 1920 was closely associated with the role Armanis F. Knotts exercised in northern Indiana civic affairs. Knotts was a colorful figure, involved in real estate speculation in Gary and horse racing at Mineral Springs. He was his own man, a self-proclaimed disciple of Tom Paine, and a Progressive Republican, who drove his family each Sunday to Chicago to hear M. M. Mangasarian preach the gospel of democratic humanism at the Independent Religious Society. His avowed aim was to build industrial democracy in the Calumet region. In 1901, while mayor of Hammond, he successfully diversified the city's industrial base after a fire closed the G. H. Hammond meatpacking plant. Soon afterward, he helped persuade Elbert H. Gary to locate United States Steel's new plant in Indiana; he served as agent for the corporation in the purchase of 9,000 acres of Duneland, and, later, as manager of the Gary Land Company. Knott's vision for Gary was a model city in which workers could own their own homes and

determine their own civic destiny. He assumed that he had an understanding with the steel company that the town would be independent and that the company would donate land for a large public
park.[26]

United States Steel built its plant in such a fashion as to mimic
a feudal castle. As Graham Taylor's son Graham R. Taylor
pointed out at the time, the Grand Calumet River served as a con-
venient moat between the plant and the town, and under conditions of industrial siege, strike breakers and supplies could reach
the plant directly from the lake.[27] By 1907, before ground was
broken for the new steel plant, Knotts had resigned from the land
company, and in 1909 he joined hands with his brother Thomas
Knotts, Gary's first mayor, to found the *Gary Evening Post* and
to challenge the power of United States Steel in the management
of Gary's affairs. The vision that Tom Knotts, friend of Eugene
Debs, had for Gary was not to last for long. In 1913, after a stormy
tenure, he was defeated for a second term by a United States Steel-
backed candidate.

When, in 1916, as president of the National Dunes Park Association, A. F. Knotts ascended Mount Tom, he could still interpret,
with a good imagination and in spite of setbacks, the smoke on the
western horizon as a sign of promise for the future. In a long
speech at the Mather hearings, heavily colored by Populist rhetoric, he said that he could not understand why, with proper planning, there should not be ample space for both industry and parks
throughout the region, including a twenty-mile national park between Gary and Michigan City. "The people who want to locate
industries all the time," he declared, "and exploit labor all the time,
had better think a little about the welfare of the laborer." In the
meantime, he argued, it was the responsibility of the laborers' government to preserve the Dunes.[28]

Although the hopes for a national park dimmed in 1917, Knotts
and the National Dunes Park Association doggedly continued their
campaign. In 1918 the American Federation of Labor decided to
organize the steel industry. As tensions mounted in the Calumet
area through the winter and spring of 1919, fanned by the effort of
United States Steel to brand the union organizers "Reds" bent on
the destruction of the American free enterprise system, the associ-

ation was quick to identify the national park project with labor's demands for better working conditions. On March 19, 1919, it issued a manifesto, which read in part:

One of the fundamental obligations and primary duties of a nation founded on the principle of a government of the people, by the people and for the people is the provision of ways and means of national, wholesome and healthful recreation at a cost within the reach of its humblest citizen. . . .

At the present hour the cry has gone out over the world for equal human rights, privileges and opportunities for the masses as well as the classes, and it will be well, indeed, to heed that call from out of the depths of our innermost consciousness. Surging, seething humanity demands an audience.[29]

The hope of resurrecting the idea of a National Sand Dunes Park was short-lived. A few months later the city was in the throes of the great steel strike. By 1921, when Clarence Darrow interrupted a trial in Denver to come to Gary to deliver the funeral eulogy for Tom Knotts, A. F. Knotts had piloted a boat down the Mississippi River and founded a new city in the wilderness—Yankeetown, Florida.

Either because it heeded the call of humanity, or feared competition from the development of industrial sites farther east, in 1919 United States Steel began to take an interest in parks, and the name of William P. Gleason, superintendent of the Gary Steel Works, and president of the Gary Park Board, replaced that of Knotts as president of the National Dunes Park Association. In August of 1919, through the good offices of Gleason, the steel company surprised the city with the donation of 116 acres of lakefront near Miller Woods. Known at first as Lake Front Park, the area was later expanded and renamed Marquette Park. This was the first portion of the Dune Country to pass into public ownership.[30] The Friends of Our Native Landscape dedicated the park on Columbus Day, 1919.

About this time, A. J. Bowser, editor and owner of the *Chesterton Tribune*, made it known that while Porter County was still unwilling to consider a national park, it would be in favor of a Dunes park that covered only a portion of the county. Indeed, on one occasion Bowser told the National Dunes Park Association that Porter County was "prepared to surrender all territory from the

Burns Ditch to LaPorte County" if it could retain the remainder for industrial purposes.[31] This would have permitted a Dunes park of at least fifteen miles. In 1922 the Gary chapter of the association resolved that the "only feasible, just and proper plan of procedure is to create an Indiana Dunes Park which shall be incorporated in the Park System of the Department of Conservation of our State."[32] To this end the 595 members of the association were encouraged to bend their labors.

The idea of a state park was present from the beginning of the Dunes campaign.[33] Prior to the First World War, however, Indiana had no state park system. It took the leadership of Richard Lieber first to motivate the state to found such a system, and then to maneuver a reluctant state assembly into appropriating the money required to purchase a portion of the Dunes.

Lieber was the son of a Prussian army officer. He had emigrated to Indianapolis in 1891 after a year in London, where he was introduced to the traditions of English liberty. His wife later recalled that he also saw that year "for the first time, the poor, which had a deep and lasting effect on his life."[34] Lieber became a thoroughly convinced social democrat, later a staunch LaFollette-style Progressive Republican.

Lieber argued that in the twentieth century the citizens of the United States must put aside an individualist viewpoint and learn that "aversion to socialized democracy" is a dread enemy to a free and self-governing society. Such aversion is found among "those whose knowledge, ability, and influence and wealth make them look on the city not as a communal center but rather as a field of personal exploitation." Socialized democracy requires economic democracy. "Political liberty we have enjoyed since the Declaration of Independence and the French Revolution," he said, "but we are far from, very far from, economic independence." However, to bring economic independence to the masses of the modern city without revolution will require a "public revival of civic virtue" among the favored classes. They will have to think more of their duties and obligations than their rights and privileges, and realize that "the interest of the individual should be centered in the greater interest of the community, and in that sense the majority make up the sum total of the community's interest."[35] If any proof was needed that American society was subject to class rule rather than democratic rule, one had only to look at the cities of Indianapolis and Chicago.

First as art and music critic for the *Indianapolis Journal*, and then as founder of a bottling company, Lieber quickly made friends among the liberal elements of the Indianapolis business community. But his chief interest was municipal reform. As the founding member of the Advisory Commission to the Mayor on Municipal Government, he was instrumental in establishing a civil service system for city employees and in leading a campaign to induce every man to vote. By 1910, when he first began to visit the Indiana Dunes and to share with others his vision of a state park system, he was well prepared to make common cause with the Chicago reformers, and to play an active part in that wing of the midwestern conservation movement for which they were the vital center.

By January 1916 Lieber had the public platform he wanted. He was appointed to the Indiana Historical Commission, charged with oversight of the centennial anniversary of Indiana statehood. At Lieber's urging, the commission voted to inaugurate a movement for state parks. The commission then appointed him chairman of the State Park Memorial Committee. By the end of the year, with funds raised by private subscription, the committee had purchased Indiana's first two state parks: McCormick's Creek Canyon and Turkey Run. Lieber continued as head of the committee until 1919, when the Indiana legislature adopted his proposal for a State Department of Conservation and Republican Governor James P. Goodrich appointed him the department's first director.

Lieber also played a major role in the development of the state conservation movement throughout the United States. Joined by his friend Stephen Mather, who was eager to encourage an integrated system of national and state parks—with "A State Park Every Hundred Miles" so the ordinary citizen could camp every night on his own land—he helped organize the first national meeting of state park personnel in 1921. In 1923, meeting at Turkey Run State Park, the new organization became the National Conference on State Parks. Mather served as its first president and Bess

Sheehan of Gary as its first treasurer; Lieber was elected president in 1932. During these years the Indiana Department of Conservation was widely regarded as a model for other states.

Undergirding Lieber's success as salesman, administrator, statesman, and artisan of the state conservation movement, was a democratic ecological and cultural philosophy. Its premise was the unity of nature. Human beings, as all living creatures, were part of a God-given, interdependent, but finite whole. Participation in this whole for the sake of the good of the entire community of life was the source of all economic wealth and the foundation of cultural and political freedom. But the masses of modern men, caught in the snarls of "whirring million-geared social and economic machinery," and oppressed by the excesses of a disorderly and wasteful society dominated by personal greed, were ignorant of the true "origin and construction" of their civilization. They did not grasp their shared history and the crucial part that the environment played in the American ideal of a better and happier life for citizens of all ranks. It was the crucial function of state parks to educate the people to an "affectionate sympathy" with their fellow citizens and their land—to instill a "New Patriotism."[36]

Lieber advocated the preservation of state parks for civil religious reasons. Parks were to him sacramental instruments by which citizens might come to understand the foundational covenant of the Republic. "A State Park is a typical portion of the State's original domain," Lieber wrote. "It is a physical expression of life, liberty and the pursuit of happiness."[37] Acting on this belief, Lieber was concerned to include in the state park system the sacred spaces associated with the history of democracy in Indiana, including for example, the site of Nancy Hanks's grave and twenty acres of the original land purchased by Thomas Lincoln, Abe's father. He assumed that the parks were primarily for citizens of little economic means and went to great lengths to provide "family dinners" and accommodations almost anyone could afford.

It took sixteen years, from 1916 when the State Park Memorial Committee first advocated the purchase of a portion of the sand dunes, until 1932 when the last acreage was purchased, to establish what Lieber considered "the greatest state park on the American Continent."[38]

Lieber began work on the Dunes project with Governor Goodrich in 1919. In a 1921 speech in the Dunes before a gathering of Republican state newspaper editors, he paraphrased Graham Taylor to the effect that no other site in the Midwest could better offer the masses of industrial laborers a sense of shared participation in the American experiment than this wilderness remnant from revolutionary days. In his third annual report for the Department of Conservation the following year, he noted that since there was no precedent for federal purchase of private property for park purposes, it was now "the privilege and duty of Indiana, with private assistance, to preserve this heritage and God-given spot."[39] Lieber proposed that the Dunes park consist of eight miles of lakeshore and that the legislature appropriate $1 million for its purchase, with an additional $1 million to be subscribed by wealthy benefactors.

Meanwhile, a coalition of voluntary associations, including such diverse constituencies as the Prairie Club, the Daughters of the American Revolution, and the American Federation of Labor, led by the officers of the National Dunes Park Association and Indiana conservationists like M. Stanley Coulter (brother of John Merle Coulter), was hard at work lobbying for the park. Bess Vrooman Sheehan, who for seven years chaired the Dunes Park committee of the Indiana Federation of Women's Clubs, mobilized grass roots support among six hundred local units of the federation scattered over two hundred cities and towns. Her motto was "Dedicate a Day to the Dunes." Soon every Indiana legislator was familiar with the project. Mrs. Sheehan was to say afterward that, although many were opposed to the park, "they couldn't have faced their wives at dinner after a 'no' vote."[40]

On January 4, 1923, Lieber wrote in his diary: "The legislature meets—let us pray!"[41] In the following weeks, H.B. 144, which incorporated Lieber's proposal for combined private and public funding, but limited the park purchase to three miles of lake frontage and two thousand acres, was introduced by representatives of Porter and Lake counties. On the evening of January 26, a special joint session of the members of the state assembly and their wives listened for two hours to a stereopticon lecture by Bess Sheehan. The *Indianapolis News* reported that behind her every sentence was the message that this "changing, shifting, restless, age-old,

ever-new possession of Hoosierland will be gone for good if the
State does not act soon."⁴² With the last-minute help of former
U.S. Senator Thomas Taggart, enough economy-conscious Demo-
cratic votes were gathered to pass the bill in both houses. On
March 6, 1923, Republican Governor Warren T. McCray signed
the legislation authorizing an Indiana Dunes State Park into law.

It would take several years for the state to accumulate sufficient
money to purchase the property; meanwhile the price of acreage
was rising precipitously. Lieber was placed in the painful situation
of having to appeal to the social nature of some of the very capi-
talists who wanted the land for industrial expansion. But he was
hopeful. In a letter to Jensen he wrote: "Our multi-millionaires
have done so many completely foolish things along imaginary philanthropic lines" that perhaps they might support a project that so
obviously benefits their employees.⁴³ Yet after two years of effort
by both Mather and Lieber, no money was forthcoming.

In 1925 Indiana's newly elected governor, Republican Edward
Jackson, broke the stalemate. Lieber predicted that if Jackson once
gave himself over to the winning personality of the Dunes, he would
forever call them friend. Visiting the Dunes for the first time in
late May, Jackson climbed Mount Holden, and then, breaking
away from the rest of the party, scaled Mounts Tom and Green
alone. Afterward, Lieber joked with Jackson about his alpinist feat
and the governor complimented Lieber on his conservation work.
As a result, the governor directed that $200,000 of accumulated
tax money be used to purchase the first acreage immediately, and
by August the boundaries for the new park were set.

On August 29, 1925, the first Duneland deed was delivered to
the state in a simple ceremony on Mount Green—quickly renamed
Mount Jackson. With the Indiana state flag flying aloft, 120 acres
of land, including the larger portion of Mount Tom, became at last
public property. John O. Bowers, Sr., the owner, set the price at
$300 an acre, half market value, in order to establish a precedent for
further purchases. Soon afterward, the Prairie Club sold its 55 acres
at cost. These initiatives by the state and by Dunes supporters
prompted United States Steel chairman Elbert Gary and Sears
Roebuck president Julius Rosenwald to come forward with gifts
of $250,000 and $50,000 respectively.⁴⁴ On July 1, 1926, the first

admission fees were collected, and in the first three months of the park's opening, 62,880 persons passed through the gates. In order to commemorate the continuity of the history of the Dunes campaign, Lieber erected a bronze plaque in honor of Stephen Mather on a stone monument in the center of the new park.

When Lieber turned to the development of the park, he found himself caught between two conflicting aims. He fervently believed that to preserve "spirit of place" was the first law of park selection and management,[45] yet he shared the conviction that ordinary citizens, and especially the poor, ought to have easy access. To make matters more difficult, racial integration of bathing beaches did not come easily to northern Indiana. While Lieber's plans for a recreational center for the state's orphans failed to get off the drawing boards, the rechanneling of historic Dune Creek through a concrete conduit in order to provide parking and hotel accommodations at Waverly Beach brought storms of protest from Dune Country patriots. Virginia Moe accused the Department of Conservation of adding to nature's stationary and living dunes a third type—"the corralled tame dunes, the political pets."[46] In response to Jensen's criticism, Lieber replied with irritation: "You would feel differently if you were holding down my desk to take care of more than a million people in public preserves."[47]

The "improvements" of the Indiana Dunes State Park continued to be an issue in succeeding decades. In 1971 a 1,500-acre Dunes Nature Preserve was established within the 2,220-acre state park. This action assured that two and one-half miles of coastline, including Mount Tom and its environs, would be left henceforth in what Bess Sheehan once aptly called its "Original State."[48]

SAVE THE DUNES COUNCIL

In 1922 Frank Dudley prophesied: "When that portion which lies between Dune Park [Station] and Michigan City is broken into and divided by corporate interests the fate of the dunes will be sealed."[49] In the 1930s Paul Douglas warned his neighbors in Dune Acres of the approaching industrial fires that threatened the Dunes, and Donald Peattie appealed in his columns in the *Chicago Daily News* for expansion of the Indiana Dunes State Park before it was too late. These warnings went unheeded, and when in 1940 the National Dunes Park Association held its last annual meeting, the major order of business was to pass a resolution in memoriam for its deceased members.

By 1949 the figures and events were in place for the denouement of the Dunes drama. Paul Douglas, elected in 1948, was in the Senate. Charles Halleck was in the House. The Corps of Army Engineers had just issued a preliminary report favorable to a deepwater port at Burns Ditch and the proposed St. Lawrence Seaway was promising a boom for Great Lakes industry.[50] The remaining unspoiled portion of the Central Dunes, running for almost five miles between the subdivisions of Ogden Dunes and Dune Acres, was now ripe for development.

In the fall of 1949 Dorothy Richardson Buell experienced her call to save the Dunes. Returning with her husband from a vacation in the Southwest, she visited White Sands National Park, and although she was enthralled by the great stretch of pure white sand, she found its beauty inferior to the duneland surrounding her home in Ogden Dunes. (She once said that in Indiana the color of the sand varied with the time of day, "lavender, deep purple with glints of yellow, tan when the sun was bright in the middle of the day," and the dunes were "bare in majesty, or covered about their shoulders with lacey shawls of vines . . .")[51] "If I feel this way," she thought, "am I supposed to do something about this?" On the way home the Buells stopped at the Gary Hotel for dinner, where, as if by fate, they read a sign in the lobby announcing a meeting that night of a group to save the Dunes. Mrs. Buell said to her husband, "This is what I have been thinking of. Let's go."[52]

With the favorable report by the Corps of Engineers on a deepwater port, a new group anxiously sprang into life in 1949, the Indiana Dunes Preservation Council, sponsor of the meeting Dorothy Buell and her husband attended. University of Chicago student Jerry Olson prepared for the council's use a detailed ecological survey of the undeveloped areas remaining between Gary and the Indiana Dunes State Park and recommended the preservation of approximately seven miles of lakeshore.[53] But the new association had trouble getting started. One afternoon in early 1952, at a meeting of the Chicago Conservation Council, president Reuben Strong pressed the question of how best to proceed. Dorothy Buell, remembering that Bess Sheehan had "gone down in history" for her work in mobilizing support for the State Park, was prompted to suggest, "Maybe the women could do it." After the meeting Strong confronted her: "You spoke out as the woman of Indiana. Would you take it?"[54] She gave it several days' thought and decided yes, she would try.

Dorothy Buell loved drama and was skilled in the use of dramatic effect. Graduated from Lawrence College in 1911 with a Bachelor of Arts and a Bachelor of Oratory, she was schooled in Wisconsin Progressivism through her involvement in the community arts movement. Although she knew little about conservation or politics in 1952, she relished the prospect of a righteous struggle. Once she reflected: "Politics were always a mystery to me and I guess they still are. All I know is that we're right and we have to go through a lot of grief to win."[55] She did know something about organizing groups from her experience in community theater, and she brought to her task a rare sense of personal determination tempered by humor and a lively interest in people.

The first meeting of the Save the Dunes Council was held on June 20, 1952. A group of twenty-one women met in the Buell home and heard Bess Sheehan recount the history of the struggle to preserve the Dunes. The purpose of the council, Mrs. Buell stressed, was not to fight the proposed port but to add the remaining five miles of unspoiled lakeshore—the heart of the Central Dunes—to the Indiana Dunes State Park. Soon afterward, she announced to the press: "We are prepared to spend the rest of our lives, if necessary, to save the Dunes!"[56] For her, as for many of the women who joined with her in the early 1950s, this was no idle pledge.

Within a year the council was well on its way to its eventual membership of more than two thousand, representing every state in the Union, and its purpose had expanded with it. Howard Baker, regional director of the National Park Service, and Conrad Wirth, the director, encouraged the possibility of a national monument in the Central Dunes. In addition, the one mile of lakeshore and 830 acres of land owned by Inland Steel west of Ogden Dunes also came under consideration for preservation.

The scope, imagination, and ambition of the activities initiated that first year were to characterize the functional citizenship of the Save the Dunes Council for the next three decades. These activities ranged from designing stationery, publishing a brochure, "One Dollar for the Dunes," constructing maps, and assembling color slides for programs, to researching land ownership and development plans, contracting newspaper editorials and magazine articles (including some by Edwin Way Teale), and releasing statements to the press. The council provided liaison with national conservation associations, contacted key leaders in every women's club in every city in the state, every state legislator, and every chamber of commerce; it testified against the construction of Markovitch Ditch, which threatened to drain Cowles Bog; members attended national park conventions, exhibited in home and garden shows, traveled to Indianapolis to confer with Governor George Craig and Senator Homer Capehart, and other state officials and civic leaders; they lobbied Ogden Dunes to zone the lakeshore for two miles on all sides, and initiated a "Children's Crusade to Save the Dunes." On June 3, 1953, as a climax to the first year's work, Howard Baker, Kenneth Cougill, director of Indiana State Parks, Reuben Strong, Floyd Swink, and architectural historian Earl H. Reed, Jr., spoke on the occasion of "A Day in the Dunes."

The most dramatic action of the first year was the council's purchase of Cowles Tamarack Bog. Fifty-six acres of the bog were placed on sale by Porter County for delinquent taxes in 1953. To buy it, Bess Sheehan, who continued as secretary of the National Dunes Park Association and custodian of its park fund, donated the park fund's balance, $751.68; Mrs. Norton Barker of Michigan City donated $700; the council had $125 in its treasury; and Mr. Buell advanced the remainder, $153.32. The rare glacial bog, which Henry Cowles visited so many times and personally tried to preserve, was thus finally saved for the grand sum of $1,730. Mrs. Buell, announcing the purchase at the home of Mrs. Sheehan in Gary, noted that the bog was a "Lost World" preserved, and that it constituted the nucleus for a national monument or an addition to the State Park. Later, Maurice Sullivan, who began his studies in botany at the University of Chicago under Cowles, made field trips to Cowles Bog, as well as nearby Pinhook Bog, and recommended both wetlands for inclusion in the national register of Natural Landmarks. On February 26, 1966, the two bogs were dedicated by another student of Cowles, Stanley A. Cain, assistant secretary of the Interior for Fish, Wildlife, and Parks.[57]

In the midst of this multiform activity, the leaders of the Save the Dunes Council immersed themselves in the art, literature and science of the Dunes tradition. Among their teachers were William Beecher, Vin and Hazel Hannell, Charles Olmsted, Walter Necker, Philo Read, Earl H. Reed, Jr., Bess Sheehan and Reuben Strong. Agreement was by no means perfect, and differences were often fiercely debated. Dorothy Buell, for example, was a staunch Republican; others were equally staunch Democrats and Independents. All were individualists. Yet a consensus on the importance of the Dunes' preservation for the public interest, and for the ideals of the Republic, again took shape.

Sylvia Troy, looking back on the early years of the council, concluded that for many it became a way of life, a recovery of the archetypal democratic experience of human dwelling. "I remember the wonderful old Baillytown School where we held Board meetings. It had one room with a pot-bellied stove and high windows. . . . To the north of the school were rolling forested dunes extending to Lake Michigan. It was the best of the dunes, almost like an idyll." In this setting, Troy reflected, it was apparent that democracy could work. The council was a dedicated community of "practical idealists" confident that the fruit of its labors would last for generations.[58]

Dorothy Buell's oratory degree stood her in good stead for the sixteen years she served as president of the Save the Dunes Council. She quickly earned a reputation as a witty, disarming, and eloquent spokesperson for the Dunes cause. In her speeches she repeatedly hammered at four points. First, she never failed to point out that the Dunes movement was not opposed to jobs ("jobs mean bread, and bread is the staff of life"), but only to the tyranny of an economic system that refused to debate the how and wherefore of jobs, and eliminated from consideration other life-giving needs. "Mr. Humphrey [president of National Steel] has said he prefers jobs to picnics," she told the Senate Committee on Interior and Insular Affairs in 1959. "We ask, why is it not possible to have jobs *and* picnics? Surely this is the viewpoint of a humanitarian."[59]

Her second point was that of the many reasons for saving the Dunes—the most important and the most inclusive was the spiritual. The Dunes were "God-given and man-inherited. . . . One of the most beautiful natural shrines in all of America."[60] Artists and writers of the Dunes tradition like Dudley, Teale, Peattie, Reed, and Sandburg, testified to this. Such a supreme manifestation of universal grace belongs by right to the people.

These two points logically led to the third. "Though we share the pride of an advancing, industrial nation, *we would save the inner core of its strength through preservation of its beauty and natural resources.*"[61] Ecologists such as Cowles and Fuller saw in the Dunes landscape a vision of community, of the interdependence of living things with their environment. This vision is of the essence of the Republic. To despoil the Dunes would be a "travesty of the true American spirit."[62]

Dorothy Buell was ready for her culminating appeal. A great drama is being played out in the Dunes. The first act of that drama spanned the centuries from 12,000 B.C. to 1900; it was the drama of plant succession and of human history that did not irreparably disturb ecological relationships. The second act occurred between 1900 and 1952, the years of the first movement to save the Dunes. The third act, which began in 1952 with the formation of the Save the Dunes Council, would not be concluded until the remaining Dunes were preserved. All citizens were invited—indeed, obligated—to participate in that third act.[63]

Within a short time, the council made liaison with other groups concerned about the Dunes, and its membership expanded to include men. One of the first male members was a Dunes resident and Chicago attorney with a history of involvement in public interest law, Edward W. Osann, Jr. At the annual spring dinner of the council in 1957, Osann gave an address, later republished in pamphlet form, in which he evoked Sandburg's great poem *The People, Yes!* because it affirmed "the response to this wonderland of nature in the soul of the ordinary people." The issue of the Dunes, he asserted, was the issue of whether this revelatory landscape, "hint-ing of creation's continuing miracle," which belonged by right to the people of America, should be usurped by private interests. Quoting liberally from Mather, Chamberlin, Cowles, and Taft, he argued that the Dunes belonged to the people because they dramatically demonstrated the processes of geological transformation, because "they provide a common meeting ground of trees and wild flowers from all directions, and present a picturesque battle ground between plant life and the elements," and because they continue to inspire a noble American cultural heritage.[64]

Unlike the 1910s and 1920s, Indiana state administrations and congressional and state representatives, Republican and Democratic alike, were now almost solidly aligned behind the goal of industrial development at Burns Ditch. Shortly after he took office in 1953, Republican governor George Craig began to lobby for a port. Soon afterward, with the release of a favorable engineering report financed jointly by National Steel, the New York Central Railroad, and the Consumers Company of Chicago, which owned a large block of acreage in the Central Dunes, the Indiana Legislative Advisory Commission recommended that the state appropriate $3.5 million to buy 1,500 acres for a harbor at Burns Ditch. In 1957 John Van Ness, state senator from Porter County and president of the Indiana State Assembly, successfully steered an appropriation of $2 million for the port through the state assembly. The appropriation had but one provision—the U.S. Army Corps of Engineers must give final approval to the project, a vital first step in the proposed acquisition of $25 million in federal funds. State officials were taking initiative in the development of the area before public debate on alternative uses for the land or selection of the site by a legally established board.[65]

From her visits to Indianapolis, Dorothy Buell got the impression that for most Hoosiers a tacit agreement had been reached that the southern part of the state was to be kept for farmers and the affluent, and the northern part for blacks and other workers. The industrialized Lake Michigan shoreline was to provide the tax base for the rest of the state. General opinion throughout Indiana held that industrialization was inevitable. Governor-elect Harold Handley expressed the latter view in 1956: "There is nothing anyone can do, that I can see, to stop the industrial progress of the state. It's explosive. In ten years, this could be the nation's greatest steel producing area."[66] Mrs. Buell and other members of the conncil heard some of their neighbors declaim that they preferred a blast furnace to having poor blacks from Gary and Chicago use the land as a park.[67]

The low point in the history of the Save the Dunes Council came in 1957 when Bethlehem Steel verified that it had acquired land in the Central Dunes through its undisclosed land-buying agent, Lake Shore Development Corporation. The second largest steel producer in the nation was now committed to the development at Burns Ditch. Land values in the Central Dunes rose to $2,750 an acre. This not only made it impossible for the council to acquire further tracts but called into question the capacity of any government agency to purchase the area. To make matters worse, there were allegations that some state officials were financially involved in land speculation and stood to benefit from the port development, charges that confirmed the council's belief that it was involved in a righteous struggle against the hidden powers of darkness.[68]

One day the secretary of the Prairie Club told Mrs. Buell: "There is one man who loves the Dunes and who has power to do something about it. We have written him and tried to get him interested. Senator Paul Douglas. He lived there and loved it."[69]

Paul Douglas loved the Dunes but was reluctant to inject himself into a land-use controversy in another state, and so Dorothy Buell's first letters brought only polite regrets. Mrs. Buell was not to be discouraged. She learned that Donald and Louise Peattie were long-time friends of Paul and Emily Douglas. Twice she wrote to the Peatties in California, asking for an interview, and twice she was turned down because of Donald Peattie's ill health. Yet there she was, in the spring of 1958, 5 A.M. in the morning, in the Santa Barbara railway station, suitcase in hand. "It took nerve," she later reflected, "and I still don't know how I had it."[70] She had breakfast, then took a cab to the Peattie home. She was graciously received and left with the assurance that Paul Douglas would respond to her next letter.

On Easter evening, 1958, the Buells' telephone rang. It was Paul Douglas, saying that he intended to introduce a bill to establish an Indiana Dunes National Monument. He had tried to interest Indiana senator Homer Capehart in assuming leadership of the Dunes fight and had failed, but the fact that the council had developed visible public support within Indiana made it possible for him to act. Dorothy Buell was to say of Paul Douglas: "This man had the 'vision' and plunged into the fight."[71] The assessment of the director of the Indiana Izaak Walton League, Thomas Dustin, was more sober: "Until this time it had been an impossible campaign."[72]

THE BATTLE FOR THE CENTRAL DUNES

True to his word, on May 26, 1958, Douglas introduced a bill (S. 3898) to establish an Indiana Dunes National Monument of 3,800 acres in the unspoiled Central Dunes. On the same day, Representative John P. Saylor of Pennsylvania defied his powerful constituent, Bethlehem Steel, and introduced a bill for the same purpose in the House (H.R. 12689). Thus began one of the most prolonged legislative efforts to save a particular landscape in the history of the nation, an effort which was to run by 1982 to nearly one hundred separate bills proposed for passage by Congress.[73]

Douglas's decision to "take up the fight in the eleventh hour and the fifty-ninth minute" brought new life to the Dunes movement.[74] Within two weeks Alderman Leon Despres of Hyde Park introduced in the Chicago City Council a resolution, passed unanimously, memorializing Congress to enact the Dunes bill. Within twelve months the Save the Dunes Council had assembled more than a quarter million signatures, some from foreign countries, on petitions favoring the park. Herbert Read described these petitions as "grease stained, having passed through machine shops, some were sent in by boy scouts after house to house campaigns, church groups and schools, and from neighborhood people." He reflected: "When I think of all the unpaid and donated manhours dedicated to this cause, I get new hope for success."[75] A number of national environmental associations, such as the Izaak Walton League, joined the cause, and Earl H. Reed, Jr., secured the unqualified endorsement of the advisory board of the National Park Service, on which he served.

Many Dunes lovers of past years wrote Douglas to offer their support. Horace M. Albright, former director of the National Park

Service, wrote that he still vividly recalled the beauty of the Dunes forty-two years after he first visited them as assistant to Stephen Mather. Another correspondent remembered how Jens Jensen always said the Dunes were predestined to be preserved for the soul in order to foster a high patriotism. Still another correspondent asked if there could be anything more fitting than for a Chicagoan to come to the defense of the very area that for years was lumbered and sandmined to build the Illinois metropolis. In one way or another, all said that they considered the preservation of the Dunes a sacred duty.[76]

But any expectation the council and its allies might have had of a quick victory now that Douglas was their champion soon died. While the Douglas and Saylor bills languished in committee, the industrial and political interests intent upon the development of the Burns Ditch site exploited the customary advantage of private industry over conservationists in Congress—they simply proceeded to develop the land.

In 1959 the town of Portage was incorporated to surround Ogden Dunes on three sides, and the entire shoreline within its limits was zoned for industry by Porter County.[77] In the spring of the year, concurrent with the opening of the St. Lawrence Seaway, George Humphrey, president of National Steel, sharing a shovel with Governor Handley, turned the first sand for the construction of a $103 million finishing plant on the 750 acres owned by National Steel straddling Burns Ditch. Soon afterward, NIPSCO began to clear its Z-shaped 350-acre tract immediately to the west of Dune Acres. A coal-fired generating plant would be constructed there. The council alleged that NIPSCO deliberately destroyed as much of the dunes as possible in order to weaken the argument for saving them. Whether intentional or not, weaken the argument it inevitably did. The last wild section of the high Dune Country was finally being broken into and there was nothing the Dunes movement could do to stop it.

Protested David Sander in his song, "Beulah Land":

Well I want my lake and I want my shore.
I want them now for evermore.
The lake is mine, the land is mine
Despite their damn No Trespass sign.

Oh Beulah Land, Oh Beulah Land
Among my hills I want to stand.[78]

Yet the major section of the Central Dunes remained untouched: the very heart of the tract lying between NIPSCO on the east and National Steel on the west. This was the section owned in large part by Bethlehem Steel, which in 1959 had still not made its plans public. Consequently, the destruction of the Central Dunes was by no means an accomplished fact. For the next several years, Douglas and his allies fought to save every inch that remained undisturbed.[79]

The principal weapon Douglas and the council had was persuasion. And the first and most effective form of persuasion, they agreed, was the persuasion of experience. When on May 13, 1959, hearings began before the public lands subcommittee of the Senate Committee on Interior and Insular Affairs on the second expanded bill for an Indiana Dunes National Monument, Douglas tried to waive his time for oral statement. He invited the committee to join the fifty members of the council, who had come to Washington, in watching their new 16mm color and sound film, "Indiana Dunes: Playground of Mid-America." "Right now power shovels are in there tearing the dunes down, rapidly eating into them," Douglas told the committee. "The most eloquent testimony that we have for why they should be saved is on this film."[80]

The committee did not accept Douglas's invitation, but a month later, on June 13–14, Senators Ernest Gruening of Alaska and Frank Moss of Idaho joined Douglas to tour the Dunes by jeep and helicopter and to hold hearings in the field. On July 1 they issued a joint statement in support of S. 1001.

Another kind of appeal to experience was through science. "Let me call my witnesses," Warder Clyde Allee's former student William Beecher told the Senate Interior subcommittee in 1959:

They are the thousands of naturalists, scientists, and ordinary outdoor Americans whose brushwood fires have burned at night atop a low foredune. Many of these loved the dunes, fought the good fight to save them, and are now at the end of a lifetime of struggle only in a small way successful in preserving them.
Scientists come from all over the world to see the Indiana Dunes. . . . What makes them unique in the entire world is that nature has

by happenstance carried on here a controlled experiment where no man could have done so. This experiment has taken at least ten thousand years to perform, yet . . . today . . . we can show any group of youngsters or adults who know nothing of natural history how a complicated plant-animal community grows, starting on nothing but plain sand.[81]

Jerry Olson emphasized the continuing importance of the Dunes for scientific research. In a speech at the State Park in 1959, he suggested that empirical studies in the Dunes might yield the knowledge needed by the atomic age. For illustration, he cited his own research at Oak Ridge on the fate and dangers of radioactive isotopes that contaminate the environment. In order to predict the movement of such isotopes, it is necessary to understand the movements of chemicals normally circulating from soil to plant to animal and back to soil. Now, with radiocarbon dating techniques, ecological succession in the Dunes can be described in quantitative terms. This means that concentrations and rates of movement of chemicals through the environment over extended time periods may be traced with accuracy there.[82]

The Dunes advocates were not the only ones to appeal to experience during this period. The opposition claimed that the Dunes were a wasteland of no use except for industrialization. Representative Halleck and Senator Capehart were quoted to the effect that the Dunes were good only to get sand in one's shoes, and Governor Handley went so far as to say that "There are no dunes left up there; they've all been hauled away to fill Chicago beaches."[83] On the Gruening-Moss tour in the summer of 1959 a local reporter accompanied the party and repeatedly harassed Douglas with the question: "Are you really serious about saving these dunes? I don't see anything here worth saving!"[84] And in order to present its own version of testimony by experience, the Duneland Junior Chamber of Commerce sold sand from the Dunes in a box with the explanation: "Enclosed is a box of virgin sand, disturbed only by the blade of a bulldozer. It is a portion of the sand that Illinois Senator Paul Douglas and his fellow bird watchers are trying to conserve as a bird sanctuary."[85]

Two years later, with a third bill before the Senate Committee on Interior and Insular Affairs, this time for an 8,000-acre "Indiana

Dunes National Scientific Landmark," Douglas succeeded in persuading the committee's chairman, Senator Alan Bible, along with Secretary of the Interior Stewart Udall, to accompany him to Indiana to see the Dunes for themselves.[86]

The pilgrimage to the Dunes on July 23, 1961, was one of the high points of Douglas's legislative campaign. In the early afternoon the Washington party arrived in jeeps at the entrance to the Bethlehem Steel property in the Central Dunes. By this time the party had swelled to include National Park Service director Conrad Wirth, Representative Ray Madden of Lake County, Indiana, Mayor Daley of Chicago, and the mayors of Gary, Whiting, East Chicago, and Hammond, Indiana. The caravan drove cross-country around bogs and marshes and past Mud Lake to the beach, where it was joined by members of the Save the Dunes Council for a hike along the shore. One member of the council carried a placard which read: "World at brink of War—Save the Dunes!" Another read "Save the World—Save the U.S.—Save the Dunes." It was an emotion-filled afternoon for Douglas because this was part of the beach on which he had rambled so many afternoons with his family in the 1930s. Although the sky was overcast and there was occasional rain, Douglas and Mayor George Chacharis of Gary waded into the lake to the delight of newspaper reporters and friends. At one point Douglas and Earl Reed, Jr., broke away from the party and climbed Howling Hill, a high dune not far from the beach. At the conclusion of the hike, at about the site of the proposed port, the entourage stopped to inspect a large blowout and to hear brief discourses on the ecology of the Dunes from members of the council.[87]

Both Bible and Udall were converted by the trip. A month later Udall and Douglas appeared on television to show films of the Central Dunes and to discuss the pending legislation. Douglas told how the Dunes formed a highway through the history of the United States, and Udall read from the writings of Cowles and Chamberlin. By this time Congress had established two national seashores, Cape Cod and Cape Hatteras on the East Coast, and the Department of the Interior was in the process of reviewing five more areas, including the Dunes, for shoreline protection.

It was of the essence of the Dunes advocates' democratic faith that matters of public policy be decided only after full and informed public discussion. In 1958 Emily Chapman, Emily Douglas's childhood friend from the University of Chicago, wrote to Senator Douglas that John Milton's classic defense of freedom of speech in his *Areopagitica* was what the Dunes movement was all about.[88] As the destruction of the Central Dunes began, the Save the Dunes Council issued a "Policy Statement":

> We are unalterably opposed to LEGISLATION BY BULLDOZER. The current destruction of this irreplaceable land before suitable compromises or adjustments can be made or considered is inexcusable. It is bulldozer legislation, both literally and figuratively; it is immoral and a direct attack on the American principles of fair hearing and fair play. It has substituted the law of the 'Cat' for the law of man and society. The Save the Dunes Council and the private citizens of which it is composed will fight efforts to undermine the *American process* with all legal means at its disposal.[89]

Given a fair hearing, Douglas and the council were as confident that they could win in debate as they were that, once seen, the Dunes would win the support of anyone with a glimmer of love for beauty in his soul. They believed that they could demonstrate to most people's satisfaction that this last remnant of native coastal landscape on the Lake Michigan crescent ought to be preserved for its recreational, inspirational, and scientific values.

It was reasonable to assume, they argued, that if further steel development in Indiana was justified, space could be found for it in developed areas east or west of the Dunes, or that new steel plants could be located inland with access provided by canal. If space could not be found for National and Bethlehem Steel, the several firms already producing steel in the Calumet region were ready to expand and create new jobs. Furthermore, a national park would also create new jobs, and have the advantage of diversifying the economic base of the region. The destruction of the irreplaceable Dunes was too high a price to pay simply to add two new competitors to the already tightly managed steel industry of the Midwest.[90]

The problem, they quickly discovered, was in getting the opposition to debate the issue and to debate it in terms of the public interest—namely, in terms of the good of the region as a whole, and in terms of the variety of values involved.

That the corporations were not disposed to debate the issue was obvious from the fact that National Steel and NIPSCO were proceeding to construct new plants prior to a decision by Congress. In 1961 Bethlehem announced that it now owned 4,350 acres in the Dunes. Asked about the purpose of the large acquisition, Bethlehem chairman Eugene Grace was quoted as replying, "We certainly aren't planning to put up a bird sanctuary."[91] After this announcement the officials of Bethlehem refused to confer with Douglas and other pro-park members of Congress. With the exception of one occasion when Governor Handley agreed to a verbal exchange with Douglas, the state administration appeared just as closemouthed as the corporations. So did the U.S. Army Corps of Engineers, the crucial federal agency charged with responsibility for evaluating the port project. At one point the secrecy of the corps provoked Herbert Read to denounce them scathingly as the "totalitarian shock troops running interference for big industrialists allied with politicians with eyes on the pork barrel."[92] Considerable energy was devoted by Douglas and the Save the Dunes Council to try to get the so-called port versus park issue debated publicly and on its true merits by these various agencies. Sometimes members of the council dramatically debated an empty chair at community meetings.

The port and the steel complex were linked by virtue of the fact that a deep-water port was required for a fully integrated (basic) steel mill. It was primarily for this reason that Porter County business interests had been anticipating a port at Burns Ditch since 1908 and lobbying the federal government for a port subsidy since 1929. It did not seem to Douglas and the Save the Dunes Council, however, that a harbor should be built with public monies for the almost exclusive use of two corporations. United States Steel and Inland Steel had earlier constructed their own harbors. Douglas and his allies tried to disentangle the proposal for a public port from the industrial development at Burns Ditch; they argued that other port sites were equally satisfactory. Indeed, they pointed out that Indiana already had two public ports, at Indiana Harbor and at Michigan City; they noted that the former handled more general

cargo than Illinois facilities, and that both were capable of considerable expansion. The hope was that without a publicly subsidized port, the steel companies would be discouraged from further
developing the Central Dunes.

The Dune Country patriots soon discovered that behind the
single-minded pursuit of the Burns Ditch port by the state and by
local businessmen was not only the lure of new revenues, profits, and
jobs, but a dedication born of years of struggle to build a "metropolis of the West" on the Porter County, Indiana coastline. As
Lawrence M. Preston noted in his "official" 1969 Indiana history
of Burns Harbor, for many Hoosiers the very geography of the
state seemed to demand a gateway to world commerce at the southernmost tip of the lake. In his view the Burns Waterway Harbor,
as it came to be known, was the fulfillment of a 150-year expan-
sionary dream that began with Joseph Bailly's plan for a harbor at
Dune Creek in 1832.[93] That this sense of historic destiny inspired
the zeal with which many Porter County citizens pursued the goal
of a port is indicated by a report issued in 1939 by the Northern
Indiana Industrial Development Association. What is at stake in the
Burns Harbor project, the pro-port report said, is the "public heritage" of land won from the Potawatomi Indians in 1833. "We bring
this out so that you may have your memory refreshed that the fight
to preserve [i.e., develop] our shoreline is not new but as old as the
state itself."[94]

While bulldozers went to work on the properties of National
Steel and NIPSCO, the state left no stone unturned in its effort to
assure the construction of a port. A law passed in 1959 by the Indiana General Assembly restricted the proposed public harbor to
the Burns Ditch area without survey of alternative sites. Further
legislation established the Indiana Port Commission with the power
to issue bonds and acquire land for the construction of harbor facilities. The commission was prohibited by law from selecting any
existing harbor for the site of the new port. Soon afterward, the
commission signed agreements with National Steel and Bethlehem
Steel for the purchase of land for the port and in return granted to
the corporations free, perpetual, and exclusive rights to the entire
western and eastern sides of the port. Only after these agreements

were signed did the commission formally announce, on May 18, 1961, that the Burns Harbor site was its choice for the new port.

Meanwhile, in October 1960, Colonel J. A. Smedile, the Chicago district engineer for the Corps of Engineers, submitted a long-awaited report to the Board of Engineers for Rivers and Harbors that gave the Burns harbor project a 5.7:1 benefit-cost ratio. Smedile's report made no judgment on whether Burns Ditch Harbor was more in the public interest than a park or whether another site was as suitable. When the board, at Douglas's urging, returned the report with a request for information about possible alternate harbor locations, Governor-elect Matthew Welsh countered with the declaration that "If for any reason the Federal government does not move with reasonable dispatch to provide the initial construction, as it has customarily done for other similar facilities around the nation, Indiana will undertake the entire job itself."[95] Senator Vance Hartke went a step further and said that if neither the federal nor state governments built the port, the steel companies undoubtedly would build their own. In retort Douglas thundered, "I am declaring war on any deep water Indiana harbor at Burns Ditch. . . . The steel companies are declaring war on the people of the Midwest by seeking to destroy the priceless Indiana Dunes."[96]

In February, 1962, hearings were held in Washington on the fourth Douglas bill (S. 1797 amended) by the Senate Interior Subcommittee on Parks and Recreation. The National Park Service and Department of the Interior strongly endorsed the proposed park. Sixty-nine members of the council paid their way to the Capitol to attend and testify. They brought with them original Dudley and Templeton oil paintings and placed them around the walls of the hearing room. The recently released report of the Outdoor Resources Review Commission added fuel to the Dunes proposal by its urgent call for the preservation of shoreline areas near urban centers.

Much of the hearing was devoted, however, to the pros and cons of the Burns Ditch Harbor project, and to the newly released second report of the Army Corps of Engineers. By this time it was apparent to the Dunes advocates that there were serious inaccuracies in the report's figures. Thomas Dustin pointed out, for example, that the benefit-cost ratio, now revised downward to 1.5:1, took into account all the presumed benefits, but only the estimated federal cost of $25 million, not the state's portion of $38 million. He also claimed that the Indiana Port Commission did not have commitments from business firms planning to make use of the port.

At the same time, it was evident at the hearings that there was growing support for a new or expanded harbor in the Lake County region. Urban planners such as Harold Mayer of the University of Chicago geography department testified in favor of a Lake County port, and the Democratic chairman of Lake County, Mayor Jeorse of East Chicago, joined Mayor Chacharis of Gary, and Representative Madden, to add some political muscle to this possibility. In the course of the hearings, the subcommittee asked the backers of the Burns Ditch project to produce detailed surveys of alternative sites. They were not forthcoming. Subsequently, Congress passed an appropriation for study of the Tri-City Port alternative—a new artificial port of potentially 8,000 acres that could be built lakeward of existing shoreline and port facilities between the Illinois state line and East Chicago, Indiana.

It was evident in the winter of 1962 that if the debate was allowed to continue, the remaining Central Dunes might yet be spared.

But on March 30, 1962, the final blow fell. The Indiana Port Commission announced that Bethlehem Steel had contracted for the removal of 2½ million cubic yards of sand from the Central Dunes. A dredging company was to take the sand from the Bethlehem property across the lake to Evanston, Illinois, where it was to be used as fill for Northwestern University's campus expansion. The news came as a great shock to Douglas and the council. The next day Thomas Dustin called it "an infamous Pearl Harbor for conservationists everywhere."[97] Douglas and his allies insisted that Northwestern could not escape moral responsibility for the deed. But protests were to no avail. On December 2, with personal assurances from Senator-elect Birch Bayh that he would join Senator Hartke in seeking federal appropriations for Burns Harbor, Bethlehem announced plans for the first stage of its Burns Harbor plant. It then began clearing the land. Dorothy Buell remembered how in early winter 1962, as the bulldozers went to work, "Senator Douglas stood beside me, watching, with tears running down his cheeks."[98]

In a desperate last attempt to save the Central Dunes, Douglas introduced S. 650 in the opening days of the new Congress in 1963. "The bulldozers are poised, Mr. President, but the Dunes still remain and can be rescued."[99] But it was no use. Within the year, the heart of the Central Dunes was gone. The wildest and largest area of the Dunes outside the Indiana Dunes State Park, the center of maximum ecological diversity, the landscape of moving dunes where Cowles did his first research on plant succession—was no more.

THE INDIANA DUNES NATIONAL LAKESHORE

The battle for the Indiana Dunes involved two national political coalitions.

On the one side stood Democrat Paul Douglas, Senator of Illinois, labeled by his opponents "Indiana's third senator." Allied with him from the beginning were Senators Alan Bible, Ernest Gruening, Ted Moss, Wayne Morse and Richard Neuberger, and Representatives John Dingell, Barratt O'Hara, Mel Price, Ralph Rivers, John Saylor, and Morris Udall; Congressman Ray Madden and several mayors from the Calumet region; the Secretary of the Interior, Stewart Udall, and the National Park Service; the Save the Dunes Council, and a network of local and national conservation and civic associations, such as the Sierra Club, the National Parks and Conservation Association, Nature Conservancy, and the American Planning and Civic Association; a list of several hundred distinguished scientists and educators (180 from Indiana alone); the national and state leadership of the United Steelworkers of America and the United Auto Workers, and building trades unions in Lake County, Indiana; and a string of prestigious newspapers, including the *New York Times, Washington Post, Christian Science Monitor, San Francisco Chronicle, Milwaukee Journal, Saint-Louis Post-Dispatch,* and *Louisville Courier-Journal.* After the initial expression of enthusiasm by the Chicago City Council in 1958, the Democratic party of Chicago, as well as the Chicago press, adopted a neutral stance.

The Douglas coalition was thus chiefly composed of mid-twentieth century descendants of the Progressive movement and the New Deal, and local urban leaders in Lake County, Indiana concerned for continued economic development in their own area and recreational opportunities for their citizens. By most indications the Douglas coalition also represented the mass of voter sympathy throughout the country.

Douglas pursued the Dunes cause at every opportunity—inside and outside the halls of Congress. He carried a worn packet of dune photographs wherever he went. He assigned Kenneth Gray, one of his special assistants, to work on the Dunes legislation half time for six years. Douglas's perception of the coalition he led contributed to his zeal; in his view, the proponents of the Dunes were "the common people and a few of us politicians." [100] At the end of the campaign, he paid tribute to those who "by their fight to save the dunes, held high the banner of a civilized and humane society." In particular, he singled out the Save the Dunes Council: "This group is the most remarkable citizens organization I have ever had the privilege of working with. . . . They have always kept the hope that our form of democratic government permits the people to be heard if their hope is matched by faith in the people as citizens and by vast quantities of intelligent work." [101] It is apparent that the Dunes movement embodied Douglas's dream for a new social democratic party, and reincarnated the camaraderie that he first experienced as a youth with the lumberjacks of Maine.

When Douglas fought the forest fire in Maine, he fought it alongside hard-working anonymous men of private vices who were nevertheless devoted to the common good. Nothing delighted Douglas more in his portrayal of the Dunes campaign than exposing the betrayals of the ostensibly good (the church-attending hypocrites of his youth) and praising the loyalty of supposedly disreputable allies. Douglas goes out of his way in his autobiography to register his opinion that National Park Service Director Conrad Wirth buckled under fire from Indiana Senator Capehart. He praised George Chacharis, on the other hand, although in the course of the Dunes battle Chacharis was convicted by the Department of Justice and sent to prison. "Since George would not run out on the Dunes question, I would not run out on George."

When Chacharis, fresh out of prison, showed up at Douglas's office in Washington, "shame-faced and teary-eyed lest he embarrass me," Douglas insisted that he come in and join Dick Daley (who "was also disapproved of by many of the conventionally good") for a good talk over coffee.[102] It was faithfulness to the covenant of the people and the land, not one's private weaknesses, that counted for something in Douglas's ideal of democratic fraternity.

Also of importance to Douglas, and of significant help in the final passage of Dunes legislation, was the support of labor. Douglas noted with pride that, at a large Democratic dinner in Chicago, union leader Joseph Germano demanded of President John F. Kennedy, "I want you to help Paul Douglas to save the Dunes!"[103]

On the other side stood Charles Halleck, minority leader of the Republican party in the House of Representatives, and Representative of the Indiana Congressional District that included most of the Dunes. With him at the beginning stood nearly every one of the elected officials of both parties in local, state, and federal offices of Indiana, including Senators Capehart and Hartke; conservative colleagues in the United States Senate and House; the U.S. Army Corps of Engineers and the U.S. Department of Commerce; financial interests of Porter County and much of the Midwest, including Chicago; Bethlehem Steel, National Steel, Inland Steel, the New York Central Railroad, NIPSCO, and other regional and national corporations; local building and trade unions in Porter County; and the vast preponderance of the Indiana press. The coalition was largely between those Hoosiers seeking the quickest route to new economic development in northern Indiana and a network of financial interests spread throughout the country.

Halleck's coalition included a number of Douglas's old foes. Douglas had fought the Northern Indiana Public Service Company and the Chicago, South Shore, and South Bend railroad when they were controlled by Samuel Insull; National Steel president George Humphrey when he was Secretary of the Treasury under Eisenhower; Indiana Republicans Halleck, Capehart and ex-Senator William Jenner in Congress; and various sponsors of the rivers and harbors pork-barrel throughout his Senate career. But the exact nature and extent of the Halleck coalition remained baffling to Douglas even at the height of the campaign. "I do not pretend to be able to give the full story," he said. "The tangled web of conspiracy associated with the attempt to get a federally financed harbor built in the midst of the most valuable and unspoiled dunes would defy the combined investigative talents of Perry Mason, James Bond, J. Edgar Hoover, and Senator John L. McClellan. The vast interests involved and the information withheld from the public can only be guessed at." [104]

The legislative outcome of the Dunes conflict depended on the relative influence of the Douglas and Halleck coalitions within the Congress and on the president of the United States.

During the 1958–1963 period, neither side had the votes necessary to pass the legislation it desired. Each year Douglas's bills met the same fate in both chambers—referral to the respective committees on interior affairs and then stagnation. The Senate was unwilling to pass a Dunes park bill without the agreement of the Indiana senators, and Halleck was able to control the House. On the other hand, Douglas and his allies were able to thwart the passage of port legislation in the public works committees of each house and block legislation in the Senate. The stalemate between the contending parties reflected in part the cleavage in the federal government between parks and public works projects. It also raised the possibility of a compromise.

The two coalitions were fairly well balanced in their influence on the White House. Although Douglas suspected that President Kennedy had made an agreement with Governor Welsh, a Democrat, that Indiana would get a port, the president recommended a Dunes park in his March, 1961 "Conservation Message to Congress." On one occasion Douglas made a direct personal appeal to Kennedy. He showed him his folio of photographs and told him that the Dunes were the Midwest equivalent of the president's beloved Cape Cod. However, at the point at which the Dunes bill had the greatest chance for passage, following the 1962 hearings, the administration dropped it from its list of legislative priorities. Douglas later commented that the Kennedy staff did not really believe the Midwest had anything worth preserving. Halleck, minority leader of the House, with the key to virtually the entire Indiana congressional delegation in his pocket, had strong influence in the White House. At one point it was alleged that the Indiana delegation had informed the president that it would withhold support of his civil rights legislation if he actively supported the park.

Although the Halleck coalition had won the battle for the possession of the Central Dunes, it did not in 1963 have the federally subsidized harbor it desired for the most intensive development of the site. Without a harbor, National and Bethlehem would be restricted to the production of finished steel products. The alternative was for the state of Indiana or the companies to finance the harbor by themselves, and neither seemed ready to make such an investment. At the same time, with the basic direction of industrial development established, the way was open for some shifts in the political alliances that had so far kept Congress in deadlock. Indiana politicians who wanted a park in addition to a port could now more easily come forward. As early as 1961, Senator Hartke proposed legislation to establish both a park and a port (S. 2317). In 1963 Senator Bayh and Representative J. Edward Roush of Fort Wayne, Indiana, were both ready to work for a compromise. On Douglas's side, Congressman Madden was eventually prepared to support a port of sufficient size to benefit Lake as well as Porter County. Between 1958 and 1963, as the heart of the Central Dunes was destroyed, Douglas bit by bit expanded the Dunes bills to include areas east of Dune Acres and west of Ogden Dunes. He was thus in a position by 1963 to also consider the compromise that double-edged political reality appeared to make necessary: no park, no harbor; no harbor, no park.

In the spring of 1962, the revised report of the Corps of Engineers was approved by the Board for Rivers and Harbors and then by the Chief of Army Engineers. Denying Douglas's requests for fair procedure, the board sent the report to the U.S. Bureau of the Budget, which has responsibility for coordinating the program of the president and, specifically, of clearing public works proposals on behalf of the president for submission to Congress. Had not Douglas again made a personal plea to President Kennedy, final administration approval for Burns Ditch Harbor would have then gone to Congress in the closing weeks of 1962.

Kennedy responded by ordering a full study by the Bureau of the Budget of the economic feasibility of the harbor and of ways in which a compromise might be reached to establish a national lakeshore. In September, 1963 the bureau concluded its study and, bow-ing to pressures from Indiana, permitted the Army Corps of Engi-neers' positive recommendation to go forward for congressional action. Yet the study agreed with many of the objections that the Save the Dunes Council raised; it laid down a series of economic and environmental conditions to be met before federal funds could be spent. The bureau recommended to the Congress creation of an 11,700-acre Indiana Dunes National Lakeshore. The compromise administration bill drafted by the National Park Service excluded most of the Central Dunes. It included Inland Steel's property west of Ogden Dunes, a large area of inland marsh and woods around Dune Acres and south of Indiana Route 12, most of the (largely un-developed) town of Beverly Shores, some isolated nature preserves, and subject to donation, the Indiana Dunes State Park. Douglas agreed to this compromise and it was understood that the Halleck coalition did likewise.

In October, 1963, at Douglas's request, Senator Henry Jackson, chairman of the Senate Committee on Interior and Insular Affairs, introduced the new proposal (S. 2249) with Douglas and twenty-five senators as cosponsors, including Senators Hartke and Bayh. Simultaneously, Representative Morris Udall of Arizona introduced a similar bill into the House (H.R. 8927). The Kennedy assassi-nation interrupted further legislative progress, but early in 1964 Jackson reintroduced the legislation (S. 360) and extensive hear-ings were held by the Senate Interior committee in March. The Senate passed the bill and in July Representative Roush intro-duced a companion bill in the House (H.R. 12096). Then the supposed bargain disintegrated. Halleck said he had not agreed to any bargain and Douglas could not produce evidence to the con-trary. Inland Steel broke into strong opposition and began an in-tensive lobbying campaign against the Lakeshore through Wash-ington attorney J. Edward Day. The Roush bill died in the House Interior committee at the end of the year.

In early 1965 Roush reintroduced the compromise bill (H.R. 51). Fearful of being outmaneuvered again, Douglas persuaded the Senate Public Works Committee to incorporate into the omni-bus rivers and harbors bill, which included the Burns Harbor proj-ect, a contingency provision to prevent the harbor from being funded until the Lakeshore had been approved. But Halleck convinced the House Public Works Committee to insert in its version of the omnibus rivers and harbors bill language that divorced the port and Lakeshore. At this point Senator Bayh stepped in and renegotiated the compromise agreement. The final omnibus bill as passed by both houses included approval for construction of Burns Waterway Harbor (P.L. 89–298), but made the appropriation of funds for the harbor contingent upon both chambers having a chance to vote on a Dunes bill before the end of the 89th Congress in 1966.

Nineteen sixty-six was an election year. As the second session of Congress opened, Douglas made personal calls upon the leading members of the House Interior committee. In addition, the effects of the contingency provision attached to the approval of Burns Harbor were soon apparent. Indiana's Democratic delegation to the House petitioned Representative Wayne Aspinall, chairman of the Interior committee, to report an Indiana Dunes bill out of committee by the end of the session. Aspinall's committee held extensive hearings in Valparaiso, Indiana, and Washington, D.C., and with Representative Udall's help, issued a favorable report in July, 1966. By this time, Democrat Roger Branigan, governor of Indiana, had joined Hartke, Bayh, and at least five Indiana congressmen in support of park legislation. In the meantime, President Lyndon B. Johnson reaffirmed the administration's support of the compromise bill and with the help of Senator Bible, head of the Senate Interior committee, the Lakeshore bill (S. 360), now cosponsored by thirty-two senators from twenty-two states, passed the Senate on June 21.

By early October, however, no action had been taken in the House. Time was running out. Douglas's defeat by Charles Percy in November was widely forecast. At this crucial stage, Vice-President Hubert H. Humphrey called Speaker of the House John McCormack and members of the Rules Committee for help on the bill, and President Johnson personally told McCormack of his support. Save the Dunes Council members flew to Washington to visit every congressman who would listen. Members of the liberal, civil rights, and labor lobbying groups put in extra hours on the Rules Committee and lobbied in the House. Douglas later wrote that although McCormack owed him nothing, the Speaker knew "that of all my legislative work the Dunes park was closest to my heart."[105] Representative Madden successfully brought the bill through the House Rules Committee; then McCormack scheduled consideration on the floor despite competing demands for time.

On Tuesday, October 11, McCormack brought the Dunes bill up for consideration in the Committee of the Whole. Debate began on the evening of October 11 and continued the next day. Charles Halleck took the floor repeatedly to argue against the legislation. His points were simply put: the people in favor of the park are from outside the state of Indiana; their purpose is "roadblocking Indiana's opportunity and potential for an industrial development"; the dunes worth conserving are in the State Park that Indiana plans to expand in the future, and what is left is worthless—"I am telling you right now that most of it is 'puckerbrush' and you would not be caught dead on it."[106] Halleck was joined in his arguments against the legislation by Republicans Joe Skubitz of Kansas and Rogers Morton of Maryland.

Morris Udall was the aggressive floor leader for the bill; Representatives Brademas, Madden, and Roush of Indiana, Saylor of Pennsylvania, and Pucinski and Yates of Illinois made impassioned speeches on its behalf. The propark speakers pointed out that the present debate was the culmination of sixty-five years of debate over the fate of the Indiana Dunes and that the initial proposal for a national park had been made by many of the country's greatest scientists and writers. They noted that the Chicago metropolitan region had the lowest recreational acreage of any major metropolis in the country: eleven acres for every 1,000 people as compared to seventeen acres for New York and 167 acres for Los Angeles. Representative Madden countered Halleck's claim that the state would take care of the Dunes by asserting that "for the benefit of my colleagues here who are not familiar with Indiana, for the past many years I know of the northern part of Indiana, whether the administration was Democratic or Republican, has generally been looked upon as a stepchild or an orphan child. They do not seem to be interested in the development, from the State angle, up in the northern part of Indiana." Madden charged that the state's sudden interest in the Indiana Dunes State Park was a "case of deathbed religion."[107] John Brademas, whose Indiana congressional district abutted Halleck's on the east, said that in a recent poll 73 percent of his constituents were in favor of the Lakeshore.

Representative Sidney Yates of Chicago said that he could not "believe that we as a nation have learned the lesson of conservation so poorly that we will let our present opportunity slip through our fingers, as the sands of the Indiana dunes slipped so lazily through my own fingers as a boy." "Yes, Mr. Chairman," he went on, "I know the worth and wonder of the Indiana dunes from personal experience. My birthplace was Chicago, my home has always been Chicago, and man and boy I have spent some of the happiest days of my life on those dunes."[108] Representative Roman Pucinski, also of Chicago, added that he too "grew up on the sand dunes of Indiana. As a matter of fact, the first job I ever had in my life was down at the sand dunes at a hot dog stand many years ago." Pucinski noted that his colleague, Mr. Halleck, "talks about this project as if the area only belonged to the people of Porter County." The fact of the matter, he declared, was that the Dunes belong to the Midwest and to the "metropolitan Chicago-Gary area, stretching from Waukegan clear around to St. Joseph, Michigan."[109] At one point Udall expressed exasperation with the opposition: "Only 5 percent of all the Indiana land on Lake Michigan is available for the public. I cannot understand—I simply cannot understand— why some of the people of Indiana—they are a minority I am sure—when the Federal Government is willing to come in here and spend up to $26 or $27 million to save one of the really choice and beautiful areas of this country and provide them with really gorgeous lakeshore bathing beaches, would come in here and fight the bill. I will never know quite why they have fought the bill as hard as they have."[110]

With only a few days left in session, many congressmen were at home campaigning. Especially troublesome was the absence of the favorable New York delegation, which was due to meet with President Johnson in its home state on October 13. As the debate wore on, faced with the possible loss of the vote, McCormack suggested to Halleck that they postpone the decision on the Dunes bill until later in the week. Halleck, forgetting that the House had postponed consideration of the Demonstration Cities and Metropolitan Development Act (Model Cities) to the end of the week, agreed, and at the end of debate on October 11 the House by unanimous consent rescheduled the vote for Friday noon. Douglas himself had introduced the Model Cities bill in the Senate some months earlier at the request of the president; it was one of the most important pieces of Great Society legislation of the year and there was sure to be a large number of liberal urban congressmen present to vote for it.

Douglas was told afterwards that even with victory almost certain, the Speaker nevertheless lobbied for the bill. "I am told that his appeal was simple. In the professional's term of loyalty he merely said, 'Paul is in trouble. We have to help!'"[111]

On Friday, October 14, 1966, H.R. 51 passed 204–141, and on October 18 the Senate accepted the House amendments and sent the bill to the president. H.R. 50 authorizing an appropriation for the Burns Waterway Harbor also passed. On November 5 President Johnson signed the Indiana Dunes National Lakeshore Act (PL 89–761). The acquisition cost for the Lakeshore was initially set at $28 million.

The passage was not without cost. There were several last-minute deletions and changes in H.R. 51 as it passed the House. The final version of the Indiana Dunes National Lakeshore authorized only 8,330 acres, including the Indiana Dunes State Park, and most of its shoreline lay in front of residential communities in Porter County. It consisted of several noncontiguous sections of land divided among three zones. The Shoreline zone, bordered on the south by Route 12, included an East Beach unit surrounding the town of Beverly Shores, a Cowles Bog unit surrounding Dune Acres, and a West Beach unit of one mile of Inland Steel frontage and one mile of beach in front of Ogden Dunes. The Inland zone, lying between Route 12 and Route 20, included the Bailly Homestead, a small portion of the floodplain of the Little Calumet River south of Cowles Bog, and an area south of the State Park in the vicinity of Tremont and Furnessville. In addition there was the 165-acre Pinhook Bog in La Porte County.

On November 8 Douglas was defeated for reelection to the Senate. The Dunes bill was passed at the fifty-ninth second of the fifty-ninth minute of the eleventh hour. And it was passed in large measure as a personal tribute to Paul H. Douglas. That it was passed on the same day as the Model Cities bill was totally fitting. Whether those who voted for the two pieces of legislation thought of it this way or not, by voting for Douglas and the Indiana Dunes, they were also voting for a progressive vision that had sought for three quarters of a century to join human and environmental welfare in a single cause.

Four years later the Port of Indiana was officially opened. A Goodyear blimp floated in the twilight above the South Side of Chicago flashing cartoons of ships, trains, and trucks, alternating with the words "Port of Indiana, July 16, 1970." The blimp had not accidentally wandered across the state line. It was a deliberately commissioned symbol of triumph. In the meantime, outside the gates of the Burns Waterway Harbor, Indiana national guardsmen stood with raised bayonets ready to repel any possible attack by the several dozen picketing members of the Save the Dunes Council. Joseph Thomas, chairman of the Indiana Port Commission, later said that the port was the "state's most important contribution to our free enterprise system."[112]

The Indiana Dunes National Lakeshore was dedicated the eighth of September, 1972—the centennial year of the world's first national park, Yellowstone. It was not an unambiguous occasion. William L. Lieber, grandson of Richard Lieber, and chairman of the Indiana Dunes National Lakeshore Commission, was master of ceremonies, and Dorothy Buell was flown back from California to sit on the speaker's platform. The Special Guest of the Day was Julie Nixon Eisenhower, who spoke of her father's program to bring parks to the people. There was little mention, except by Reverend Charles Doyle in his invocation, of the years of struggle by the Save the Dunes Council and its predecessors to bring parks to the people, and there was no mention of the sacrifice of the heart of the Central Dunes—the area whose preservation alone would have given the Lakeshore irrefutable national status. Nor was there any acknowledgment that the lands finally preserved were those of least value to industry and quite vulnerable ecologically. Yet, in spite of its small size and patchwork pattern, administration officials seemed convinced of the Lakeshore's importance as one of the first urban parks in the nation, and spoke of the Indiana Dunes as a proto-type for the mission of the National Park Service in its second century.[113]

NEW BORDERS TO DEFEND

After 1966 the Dune Country patriots learned the truth of Edward Osann's observation that eternal vigilance is the price of conservation as well as of liberty. Led by Sylvia Troy, second president of the Save the Dunes Council, and later by Ruth H. Osann, who succeeded her in 1978, they tried to meet the difficult problems that faced the vulnerable new park. These problems began at once with a permit issued to Bethlehem Steel in 1966 by the U.S. Army Corps of Engineers for a 300-acre industrial landfill to project one-half mile into Lake Michigan. Although the permit was challenged by the council, the United States Public Health Service, the U.S. Department of the Interior, and former Senator Douglas and was for a brief period rescinded, it was supported by Senator Bayh and reissued. Bethlehem proceeded to build a landfill and complex of blast furnaces visible along the entire beach from Gary to Michigan City.

Erosion of the Lakeshore's eastern beach was stimulated by harbor structures at Michigan City. Air, water, and noise pollution were a constant threat. The Park Service, unable to patrol its widely scattered areas, had difficulty controlling vandalism. Proposals for a jet airport to service the new industrial area and plans for a railroad marshalling yard within the Lakeshore posed new dangers. Seepage from NIPSCO fly ash disposal ponds entered Cowles Bog. There were continual hassles with Congress for appropriations and fights over a comprehensive plan for the Lakeshore to assure preservation of ecologically delicate areas. The National Park Service faced zoning difficulties on the borders. The threats to the new park were legion.

Reflecting on these and similar problems, James R. Whitehouse, the Lakeshore's first superintendent, concluded that the new park was a "good example of man at war with himself." He considered the Indiana Dunes a laboratory to test whether "technical man" and "natural man" could coexist.[114]

Two campaigns dominated the post-1966 period. The first was the effort initiated by the Save the Dunes Council to expand the Lakeshore to a size and shape capable of meeting recreational demands while preserving the ecology of the several remnants of native landscape. In large measure this meant reclaiming areas deleted in the "compromised compromise" of 1966. As it happened, Paul Douglas played a crucial role in this struggle also.

In the summer of 1971, Congressman Roush of Indiana led a "walk" through the Dunes to publicize his bill to expand the Indiana Dunes National Lakeshore by 7,023 acres (H.R. 10209). Senators Hartke and Bayh introduced similar legislation in the Senate (S. 2380), and Mayor Richard Hatcher of Gary, and numerous civic and labor organizations, strongly endorsed the proposal. But soon Bethlehem Steel, Republican Governor Edgar Whitcomb, and the Indiana Great Lakes Commission denounced it. Earl Landgrebe, who had succeeded Charles Halleck in Congress, and who had introduced legislation *to cut* the size of the park, also opposed the measure. It was the Dunes battle rejoined.

The breakthrough came three years and eighteen bills later in 1974, when Floyd Fithian, a former history professor at Purdue University, defeated Landgrebe and was elected the first Democrat since 1932 from the Second Congressional District of Indiana. Soon after taking office, Fithian conducted extensive hearings and introduced a revised Lakeshore expansion bill (H.R. 11455) comprised of 5,230 acres. Fithian worked hard and long to achieve a bill that had support of the Save the Dunes Council, the state administration, and even Bethlehem Steel. Fithian's bill included a remarkably unspoiled 330-acre section of beaches, lagoons, ponds, and black oak–blueberry forest within the city limits of Gary—part of the original Miller Woods retained by United States Steel for future expansion; a 700-acre tract south of West Beach, the so-called Burns Bog area, which displayed successive stages of old lake bottom and shorelines, owned in large part by Inland Steel; a blue heron rookery along the Little Calumet river; the still largely undeveloped town of Beverly Shores; and the Hoosier Prairie, Indiana's sole remnant of original prairie large enough to be considered a landscape type. In contrast, the Nixon administration and the National Park Service recommended the addition of only 1,152 acres. In a reversal of previous legislative history, a compromised version of the bill totaling 4,300 acres passed the House in early 1976 but stalled in the Senate. It was widely feared that any expansion bill to pass both houses of Congress would be vetoed by President Gerald Ford, who had voted as a congressman against the original 1966 legislation.

On September 24, 1976, a further compromised expansion bill of 3,663 acres, sponsored by Bayh, Hartke, Percy and Adlai Stevenson III, came up for vote in the Senate. In the middle of the debate Senator Percy announced that it was his "extremely sad duty to inform the Senate of the passing today of our beloved former colleague, Senator Paul H. Douglas." Percy went on to say that "Senator Douglas had a rare gift—the gift of vision—that made him a towering figure in the U.S. Senate," and that Percy had pledged, at the time of his election, "to work diligently on behalf of two particular pieces of legislation that were especially important to Senator Douglas—the truth in lending bill to protect consumers and the bill to preserve the Indiana Dunes."[115] Immediately following Percy's speech, Senator Strom Thurmond of South Carolina rose to say that although he and Douglas differed on many matters, "I admired him because he went to World War II when he was entirely too old to be drafted."[116] Senator Stevenson then took the floor and said that "for all his long life, which ended this morning, [Douglas] had fought the hard fight—for the underprivileged and for the equal rights of all citizens," and that he "championed the threatened environment long before the word 'ecology' came into our popular vocabulary."[117]

The expansion bill passed 74–0. The association of Douglas's death with the new bill made it almost impossible for President Ford to veto; on October 21, 1976, he signed the bill into law. Once again it was the reputation of Paul Douglas that helped save the Dunes.

By 1982 further additions had brought the total size of the Indiana Dunes National Lakeshore (inclusive of the Indiana Dunes State Park) to 13,023 acres. The federal land acquisition program had expended close to $60 million in the acquisition of 8,220 acres. Yet the expansion and acquisition of the Lakeshore were still issues. Not only did the purchase of the remaining authorized acreage need to be completed, but the continued exclusion of the 660-acre tract known as the Beverly Shores "island" raised the spectre of an enclave of high-rise buildings appearing someday in the middle of the eastern section of the park.

Also by 1982 two small remnants of the series of dune ridges and ponds interspersed with prairie west and south of Gary had been preserved. The first of these, the 300-acre tract known as the Schererville, or "Hoosier Prairie," owed its preservation to the foresight and determination of Save the Dunes Council member Irene Herlocher.[118] For more than a decade, beginning in the late 1960s, Herlocher led the campaign to save this rare reminder of the original "Grand Prairie" that at one time stretched from northwest Indiana across Illinois into Iowa and westward, the southernmost portion of the area studied by Shelford 1907–1911. The Indiana Department of Natural Resources and the United States Department of Interior cooperated in its purchase and protection. The second remnant, a forty-acre tract closer to Lake Michigan, home of one of the richest single collections of plant species in Indiana, a portion of the native landscape also associated with the names of Shelford, Allee and Peattie, was preserved by the Indiana Department of Natural Resources, with the aid of the Indiana office of Nature Conservancy.

This meant that by 1982 at least a fragment was saved of each of the four principal sacred centers visited by the Dune Country patriots before World War I. The most intact region was south and east of Mount Tom and Dune Creek, preserved in the 1,500-acre nature sanctuary of the Indiana Dunes State Park. Segments of the original Central Dunes, south and west of Dune Acres, including Cowles Bog and the Bailly Homestead, were part of the Indiana Dunes National Lakeshore. The expansion of the Lakeshore in 1976 added a portion of Miller Woods between United States Steel and the community of Miller in Gary. The two purchases by the Indiana Department of Natural Resources preserved tiny fragments of the landscape of ridges, ponds and prairie west and south of Gary.

After Douglas's death, the Wooded Island in Chicago's Jackson Park, part of the mythic geography of Hyde Park Progressives since the 1893 World's Fair, was renamed the Paul H. Douglas Nature Sanctuary and his ashes were spread there. Chicago congressman Sidney Yates, who was elected with Douglas in the Truman upset of 1948, called for the Lakeshore to be named in his honor also. Several bills were introduced in both houses of Congress to that end. They did not pass. But legislation dedicating the Indiana Dunes National Lakeshore to the memory of Paul Douglas did pass, and eventually his bust will be permanently housed at West Beach, along with a plaque that reads:

> In gratitude for his courage, his vision, and his leadership in the effort to preserve this unique landscape, Indiana Dunes National Lakeshore is dedicated to the memory of Senator Paul Howard Douglas, 1892–1976.
>
> Through careers in teaching and government that spanned half a century, he spoke for the poor and the old, workers and the unemployed, and for citizens denied the full rights of citizenship because of race or creed or color.
>
> Paul Douglas believed in open space as a source of spiritual renewal, especially for those who spent their working lives, as he did, in cities. He said that he came often to the Indiana Dunes because, in doing so, "like Antaeus, I retouched the earth and became stronger thereby." He felt that all citizens, rich and poor, should have access to that same source of strength and worked for the last twenty years of his life that here, at least, it might be so.[119]

The second important campaign of the post-1966 period was the movement to halt construction by NIPSCO of a 685-megawatt reactor close to its fossil-fuel Bailly Generating Station at Burns Harbor. Application for the reactor, to be built 800 feet from the western edge of the Lakeshore, and in similar proximity to the eastern boundary of the Bethlehem Steel plant, was filed with the Atomic Energy Commission in 1970. By the end of the decade, Bailly Nuclear-1 was to be the target of an extensive coalition of environmentalists, labor activists, and antinuclear groups in the Midwest.[120]

Assistant Secretary of the Interior for Fish, Wildlife, and Parks Nathaniel P. Reed took a dim view of NIPSCO's plans. However, only after he threatened Secretary Rogers Morton with his resignation was he allowed to testify before the AEC in 1973.[121] Reed cited a long list of potential environmental hazards: among them, impairment to the esthetic quality of the Lakeshore from the 450-foot cooling tower; defoliation of vegetation by salt from the cooling tower plume; damage to plant and animal life from acid misting produced by the mixing of cooling tower vapors with sulphur dioxide from the coal-fired unit; seepage from waste holding basins; and lowering of the water table during excavation. Reed argued that neither the Indiana Dunes National Lakeshore nor any park should be required to serve as a buffer for a nuclear plant.

Other testimony before the AEC raised questions about the design of the reactor, the safety of the workers at the Bethlehem and National Steel plants, and the proximity of the plant to Chicago and adjacent Indiana towns.

Without settling the issue of the peaceful use of nuclear energy per se, members of the Dunes movement judged a nuclear plant at this location to be a particularly careless use of fire—perhaps the ultimate "ghost in the tower." Furthermore, its physical juxtaposition to Cowles Bog—"the evolutionary treasure, the time machine of the plant kingdom"—added apocalyptic overtones.[122] The Bailly reactor soon became a symbol of two major post–World War II environmental threats—nuclear annihilation and contamination of the earth by chemicals.

A construction permit was granted to NIPSCO by the AEC in 1974. Efforts to halt construction continued in the form of legal suits brought by Robert Vollen, Edward Osann, Jr., and others on behalf of the Business and Professional People for the Public Interest and the Izaak Walton League, and by the state of Illinois and the city of Gary. In the course of his investigations as technical and environmental consultant to the interveners, Herbert Read discovered that NIPSCO's maps incorrectly stated the population densities near the site. In April, 1975 the Seventh Circuit Court of Appeals agreed and ordered construction stopped. This was the first time environmentalists had won a court battle to halt construction of a nuclear plant. The victory was short-lived. In November, 1975 the Supreme Court reversed the decision on the grounds that the AEC had a right to make and interpret its own rules. In its subsequent reconsideration of the case, the Appeals Court appeared to invite the Department of the Interior to seek judicial relief. Although ex-Senator Douglas, Senators Percy and Stevenson, and Representative Yates urged legal action, the department merely reiterated its previous objections.

In the mid-70s the anti-Bailly movement began to mushroom. Save the Dunes Council members were joined by activists from the civil rights and peace movements, and Chicago-based antinuclear groups began to pick up support in Indiana. The American Friends Service Committee gave active leadership in both states. Of special importance for the future of the campaign was the interest of Joe Frantz and the environmental committee of the United Steelworkers Local 1010 (representing eighteen thousand workers at Inland Steel). A coalition called the Bailly Alliance took shape.

In 1978 "An Energy Policy Briefing for Northwest Indiana" was cosponsored by Mayor Hatcher of Gary, USWA 1010, and the Save the Dunes Council. Barry Commoner, the featured speaker, argued that not only were conservation and cogeneration the safest energy strategies for northern Indiana, but they were also the source of the largest number of jobs. Later he commented that he had seldom seen such a mixture of environmentalists and unionists in the same room.

This activity stimulated members of USWA Local 6787 at Bethlehem Steel to check the proposed evacuation plans for their mill. They discovered that, in the case of a radiation emergency at the NIPSCO plant, the Bethlehem management expected 170 workers to stay in the plant to save the equipment. The union also learned that for purposes of calculating population density the six thousand workers of Bethlehem were not technically considered "residents," and therefore not "people," by the Nuclear Regulatory Agency. Later the Bailly campaign picked up additional support from NIPSCO's own striking workers.

In 1977, in the midst of its excavation, the utility was again forced to halt construction when it discovered that it could not reach bedrock and thereby ensure that the plant would not sink. Further delays were caused by suits and testimony before the NRC by the interveners as new problems with the project appeared. The result was that by 1981, although NIPSCO had spent $200 million, only 1 percent of the site work was completed. Estimates of the total cost of Bailly Nuclear-1 (originally set at $187 million) now ran to $1.81 billion. In April 1981, after NRC again gave NIPSCO permission to build, a massive protest was staged by the Bailly Alliance at the construction site at Burns Harbor. A few months later the company decided to cancel the project. This decision marked the first time in United States history a nuclear plant under construction was abandoned.

As the controversy neared its climax, certain local newspapers described the Bailly Alliance as "outsiders," "counter-culture people," rich people who did not care for the working class. In fact, wrote Brenda Frantz, it was composed of "steelworkers, journalists, a mechanic, housewives, professors, an architect, secretaries, all working people . . . living in the industrial heartland of the country."[123] Robin Rich, a steward in USWA Local 6787, observed, "We were a solid community coalition."[124] This was precisely the kind of coalition that had been the promise of the Dunes movement since its beginnings in the early twentieth century. The purpose of the Bailly Alliance, like its predecessors, was justice for the people and preservation of the land.

Epilogue

Again it was late May in the Dune Country. But on this particular Memorial Day weekend in 1969, the skies were clear and it was warm and still as families packed picnic lunches and headed in cars from Chicago and various points throughout northern Indiana toward the Dunes. On this day's pilgrimage, the Gary police force was not on hand to help the visitors to their destination as it had been in 1917. Instead, a phalanx of Bethlehem Steel guards, armed with pistols, white hard hats, and radios, were waiting at the plant's main gate to guide the visitors past the railroad yards and rolling mills, which, in a fit of boardroom whimsy, the corporation had painted a two-toned sand color to match the dunes that were no longer there. Nor this time did the pilgrims have to trudge a half mile through deep sand to reach their destination. They had only to walk a few hundred feet from where they parked their cars a mile or so deep inside the property of Bethlehem Steel.[1]

If Thomas Wood Stevens had been present in 1969, he might well have appreciated the discordant pageantry of the day, although he would not have recognized the landscape. If Thomas Allinson had been present, he would have been pleased to see so many children. Cowles, once he got the spirit to come, might have brought his vasculum just in order to have the fun of brandishing it in front of the Bethlehem guards. Jensen would have applauded the Save the Dunes Council for choosing a great festive council fire as the way of celebrating the last trip to the last two acres at the heart of the Central Dunes.

In 1969 "Hawk's Island" was the last private inholding on the Bethlehem Steel tract. John Hawkinson was offered $45,000 for the land, but he refused to sell. Every few months the Bethlehem realty agent stopped at his home in Hyde Park, but Hawkinson wouldn't budge. Once he was told to name his own price. Other members of the council had also held their land and refused large profits—$100,000 for ten acres in the Reuterskiolds' case.² But in 1969, about the time Bethlehem's rolling mills began to turn, Hawkinson alone remained. Lee Botts, who worked with the Open Lands Project of Chicago, had decided the council should invite the public for one last trip to the Central Dunes. "Happening on Hawk's Island," she called it, or "A Trip to Bethlehem Steel's Bird Sanctuary."

John Hawkinson discovered the Dunes in the 1920s as a member of a Hyde Park scout troop. In 1950 he purchased for the grand total of $400 a two-acre plot not far from Mud Lake. The land had its own small pond and there were tall dunes to the north to ski. To reach it Hawkinson hiked in about a quarter mile from Barking Dog Road along a path believed to be the original Pota-watomi portage trail from the southernmost tip of the lake to the Little Calumet River, the same trail Bailly used when he arrived in 1822. Hawkinson built himself a small shack, gathering the lumber and sliding it in to his land on a homemade sled during the winter. His policy was to leave the cabin open for anyone who wanted to use it. "The key was in the tree."³

Not long after he bought the property, Hawkinson began to take racially mixed groups of children from the South Side of Chicago for trips to the Dunes. His objective, as he put it, was "to touch kids to the land and bring them together."⁴ On one of the last of these trips, he was accompanied by a *Chicago Daily News* reporter who recorded the following exchange: "'Is this all yours?' asked one youngster. 'Any time my foot touches the ground, it's mine for that instant,' replied the fifty-seven-year-old naturalist, plunging ahead." Hawkinson was also quoted as saying, "You can't confuse progress with civilization. If we're not civilized, it doesn't make any difference whether you've got progress. It's either Gen-ghis Khan or a steel company. Who wants to be a winner?"⁵

Hawkinson was, and is, a Dunes artist. He knew Emil Armin and James Gilbert and the poet Charles G. Bell, who frequented shacks not far from his own. Although he attended the Art Institute of Chicago, Hawkinson says that he learned how to paint in the Dunes; he went there with his easel in all seasons and in all kinds of weather. As he learned to imitate with his brush the natural flow of the dunes, he came to know and love them with ever greater intensity. He believes that his watercolors are a cross of oriental and occidental styles because this is the way the Dunes are, and this is where the world is now.

The gray-haired man defending a tree from a worker with a chain saw on the mural under the Fifty-seventh Street viaduct is also John Hawkinson. The painting celebrates an incident when Hyde Parkers were protesting city plans to run a new expressway through Jackson Park. Hawkinson, along with Paul Douglas and the Allees, was a member of the Hyde Park Society of Friends, but during World War II, he was no more of a pacifist than Douglas was. He never made more than Private First Class, and the Jackson Park incident, he says with a wry smile, was his chance to be a sergeant. Hawkinson had another chance to be a sergeant as the bulldozers of Bethlehem Steel began to clear the Central Dunes surrounding his two-acre retreat in the early 1960s. Stubbornly, he continued to visit his land, and with Edward Osann, Jr., went to court to force Bethlehem to grant him access. The steel company in turn designed its plant in such a way as to work around Hawk's Island.

By Memorial Day Weekend, 1969, Hawk's Island rose like a mirage on the desert of the industrial landscape. There were sharp cuts separating its boundaries from the flattened and mangled sandy plain that encircled it. Under constant surveillance by the Bethlehem guards, the picnickers left their cars and headed toward the small group of hills. There they followed the path along the sand ridges. From the crest they could look out to the north to the lake and the Bethlehem Steel landfill, to the west to National Steel and the Port of Indiana taking shape alongside it, to the south to the Valparaiso Moraine, and to the east where, beyond the NIPSCO disposal ponds, the oasis of Cowles Bog was still visible. Mud Lake was gone as were Howling Hill and the other old landmarks of the Central Dunes.

But for that one afternoon the Central Dunes lived on. Although Hawkinson's little pond had dried up, at the site of the cabin the pilgrims were enveloped once again in a space that seemed remote from everything around it. A great bonfire was lit. Food was prepared. Hawkinson encouraged the children to write haiku verses and to bring them to him for impromptu illustrations as he sat on the ground against a tree. Someone had brought a guitar and the group gathered to sing songs. A festive spirit prevailed. If the adults had heavy hearts they did not show it.

In 1969, in the midst of widespread social turmoil, the national environmental movement was beginning to build momentum. The little band that gathered at Hawk's Island could not help but wonder what might have happened if the "Age of Ecology" had dawned a decade earlier, just as their predecessors must have wondered what might have been had World War I not intervened. But such wonderings were, and could only be, wistful speculations. The truth was that by 1969 a public drama worthy of respect had taken place in the Dunes, and they had played their parts in its most recent act.

Three quarters of a century after the first pilgrimages to the Dune Country, new meanings had been added to the symbol "Dunes park." To the foundational meaning, the Dunes as the sacred center of the religion of democracy, where the community-forming and redeeming Power of the universe is manifest, there were now added—the Dunes as the shrine of midwestern Progressivism, the Dunes as the birthplace of ecology, the Dunes as an invitation to a shared, artistic way of life, the Dunes as a battleground in the struggle for social justice and environmental preservation. In the closing decades of the twentieth century, the fragmented, vulnerable, yet ever-renewing Dunes landscape was an apt metaphor of the struggle for community in the midst of a divided society and a broken land.

Notes

PROLOGUE

1. Rutherford H. Platt, *The Open Space Decision Process: Spatial Allocation of Costs and Benefits* (Chicago: University of Chicago, Department of Geography, 1972), p. 138.
2. *Chicago Sun-Times*, August 4, 1964.
3. Thomas Dustin, "The Indiana Dunes: A Symbol," in *Twelve Celebrations*, Unitarian Universalist Association, Boston, Massachusetts, 1963.
4. *Chicago Tribune*, November 13, 1966.
5. U.S. Congress, Senate, Committee on Interior and Insular Affairs, *Indiana Dunes National Lakeshore: Hearings on S. 2249*, March 5, 6, and 7, 1964, p. 124.

CHAPTER ONE: THE GREAT DUNES PAGEANT

Memorial Day, 1917
1. The following description of the 1917 Dunes Pageant is drawn from Thomas Wood Stevens, script for the "Historical Pageant of the Dunes," Newberry Library, Chicago, Illinois; Thomas Wood Stevens, *Book of the Historical Pageant of the Dunes* (Chicago: The Dunes Pageant Association, 1917); correspondence and papers in the Thomas Wood Stevens Collection, University of Arizona Library, Tucson, Arizona; William R. Rambin, Jr., "Thomas Wood Stevens: American Pageant Master," (Ph.D. diss., The Louisiana State University and Agricultural and Mechanical College, 1977); and observers' accounts. For the latter, see George A. Brennan, *Wonders of the Dunes* (Indianapolis: Bobbs-Merrill Co., 1923), pp. 163–173; Emma Doeserich, Mary Sherburne, Anna B. Wey, *Outdoors with the Prairie Club* (Chicago: The Prairie Club, 1941), pp. 110–112; Mary Kelly Graves, "The Dunes Pageant," *The Club Messenger* 1 (April 1917): 1–3, 11; *Chicago Daily Journal*, May 27, 31, 1917; *Chicago Daily News*, May 30, 1917; *Chicago Daily Tribune*, May 31 and June 4, 1917; *Chicago Herald*, May 31, 1917; *Fashion of the Hour*, May, 1917, p. 8; *Gary Post*, May 5, 15, 18, 31, and June 4, 1917; *Gary Tribune*, May 11, 15, 29, and June 1, 4, 1917; *Indianapolis News*, March 14 and June 4, 1917; *Indianapolis Star*, May 20 and June 4, 1917; *Michigan City Evening News*, May 28, 29, 1917.
2. *Chicago Daily News*, May 30, 1917.
3. Ibid.
4. Other prominent Chicagoans among the sponsors were John D. Shoop of the Public Schools, Charles L. Hutchinson, foremost Chicago cultural philanthropist, Eames MacVeagh, philanthropist with a special interest in the

preservation of natural scenery, and Everett L. Millard, president of the Municipal Art League.

5. *The Dunes Pageant Association Announces for Production May 30 and June 3, 1917, an Historical Pageant and Masque* (Chicago: The Dunes Pageant Association, 1917).

6. There were several sources for the strained relations between Stevens and the pageant association: the association was late in employing Donald Robertson, who had worked with Stevens on previous pageants, as narrator and pageant master; Stevens was late in delivering the completed manuscript, which led to a forfeiture of a portion of his fee; the original agreement between the association and Stevens that the masque be a night performance with special lighting and music was broken by the trustees, leading Stevens to refuse to turn over his script for the masque, and his forfeiture of another portion of his fee. Due to these problems, the association did not request Stevens's presence at the rehearsals and performances of the pageant, and depended entirely upon Donald Robertson to pull the show together. See Rambin, "Thomas Wood Stevens," pp. 170-175.

7. *Chicago Tribune*, May 31, 1917.

8. Brennan, *Wonders of the Dunes*, p. 169.

9. Ibid. See also *Chicago Herald*, May 31, 1917, for an almost identical account.

10. However, the number of paid spectators numbered only 5,000. Houston to Stevens, June 16, 1917, Stevens Collection, University of Arizona, Tucson, Arizona. The Dunes Pageant fell far short of being the largest outdoor drama in American history.

11. Stevens, *Historical Pageant of the Dunes*, p. 34

12. Ibid., p. 35. Stevens's original plan for the masque was far more elaborate than this, but the misunderstandings with the pageant association led to its abandonment. Stevens had developed sophisticated techniques for staging masque performances at night with multicolored artificial lighting and he intended to use these techniques with the Dunes masque. As his original manuscript indicates, he also intended the masque to portray an elaborate symbolic interpretation of the Dunes, in keeping with his theory that the pageant should present the historical *facts* and the masque should interpret these facts through *symbol and allegory*. The advance publicity for the Dunes Pageant and masque included references to Stevens's original plan, for example, photographs of a "priestess of the dunes" who would symbolize "their mystic lure, their wreathing mutability, their secrets of the centuries." (*Fashion of the Hour*, May 1917, p. 8.) Stevens intended to use an elaborate pantheon of symbolic figures, including Artemis, Proteus, Evil Manitous, The Dreamer, Wild Nature, and so on. The masque as presented consisted of a series of dances, choreographed by Mary Hinman, director of a school of dance in Chicago. James Houston requested Stevens to let the association stage the original masque the following fall. It is probable that once the association, due largely to financial difficulties, dropped its support for a night performance of the masque, Stevens lost his original motivation for the project. What had excited him from the beginning was the prospect of doing poetic justice to the Dunes landscape.

13. Brennan, *Wonders of the Dunes*, pp. 171–172.

"The Pageant of Big Purpose in the Sand Dunes"
14. See Dudley to Mrs. Shoemaker, March 30, 1945, Dudley files, Lafayette Art Center, Lafayette, Indiana; Maude I. G. Oliver, "Advertising with a Purpose," *The Poster*, June, 1926, p. 15.
15. *Exhibition of Paintings of Frank V. Dudley: The Sand Dunes of Indiana and Vicinity* (Chicago: catalog of Art Institute of Chicago, May 9–June 7, 1918).
16. Mabel McIlvaine Baker, "Early Years in Chicago," *Educational Theatre Journal* 3 (December 1951): 312.
17. Jeannette Vaughn Konley acknowledged her indebtedness to Thomas Wood Stevens for inspiration for her poem, "The Saga of the Dunes," in *Cradled in Dunelands* (Parkville, Missouri: Park College Press, 1956).
18. See Robert Shankland, *Steve Mather of the National Parks* (New York: Alfred A. Knopf, 1954); Donald C. Swain, "The Passage of the National Park Service Act of 1916," *Wisconsin Magazine of History* 50 (1966): 4–17.
19. Stephen T. Mather, *Report on Sand Dunes National Park, Indiana* (Washington, D.C.: Government Printing Office, 1917), p. 5.
20. *Gary Tribune*, May 15, 1917.
21. *New York Evening Post*, June 5, 1917.
22. *Chicago Tribune*, February 27, 1917. Italics added.
23. Caroline McIlvaine, "The Memorable Inaugural Pageant on the Dunes," *Chicago Commerce*, June 8, 1917, p. 20.
24. *Fashion of the Hour*, May, 1917, p. 8.
25. *Gary Post*, May 15, 1917.
26. *Gary Post*, June 4, 1917.
27. *Gary Tribune*, June 4, 1917.
28. *Chicago Herald*, May 1, 1916.
29. Mary Kelly Graves, "The Dunes Pageant," *Prairie Club Bulletin*, April 1917.
30. *Chicago Tribune*, June 4, 1917.
31. Stevens, *Historical Pageant of the Dunes*, p. 6.
32. Brennan, *Wonders of the Dunes*, p. 172.
33. John Dewey, *A Common Faith* (New Haven: Yale University Press, 1934), p. 27. Cultural anthropologist Clifford Geertz defines a religion as "(1) a system of symbols which acts to (2) establish powerful, pervasive, and long-lasting moods and motivations in men by (3) formulating conceptions of a general order of existence and (4) clothing these conceptions with such an aura of factuality that (5) the moods and motivations seem uniquely realistic." (Clifford Geertz, "Religion as a Cultural System," *The Interpretation of Cultures* [New York: Basic Books, 1973], p. 87.) Geertz considers rituals as the primary means by which religious symbols and correlative conceptions of a general order of existence are used to create "such an aura of factuality" that "powerful, pervasive, and long-lasting moods and motivations" are induced in persons.

Pilgrimage into Sacred Space and Time
34. McIlvaine, "Memorable Pageant," p. 20.
35. Such terms are used in the *Gary Tribune*, June 4, 1917; the special edi-

tion of the *Gary Dune Park Post,* published by the College Club of Gary, April 16, 1917; *Chicago Herald,* May 31, 1917; and Graves, "The Dunes Pageant."

36. John O. Bowers, "History of the Dunes Park (Indiana)," unpublished typewritten manuscript in Gary Public Library, Gary, Indiana.

37. Edgar Lee Masters, "Perpetuating America's Strangest Work of Nature," *Chicago Herald,* May 27, 1917.

38. Mather, *Report,* p. 24.

39. Amalia Hofer Jerome, "The Beginning of the Saturday Walks," *Prairie Club Bulletin,* March, 1973. Also see account in Doeserich, *Outdoors with the Prairie Club,* pp. 24–38.

40. Ibid.

41. See Hugh D. Duncan, *Culture and Democracy* (Totowa, N.J.: *The Bedminster Press,* 1965), pp. 14–26.

42. See Doerserich, *Outdoors with the Prairie Club,* pp. 77–123; Brennan, *Wonder of the Dunes,* pp. 163–180; Mrs. Jacob J. Abt, "The Spirit of the Dunes," unpublished typewritten manuscript in Indiana State Library, Indianapolis, Indiana. "The Spirit of the Dunes" was presented again on October 19, 1923, on the occasion of the rededication of the Beach House. See *Chicago Daily News,* October 20, 1923.

43. *Chesterton Tribune,* June 3, 1915.

44. Prairie Club, *Anniversary Exercises and Spring Festival,* program, May 30, 1916. The last recorded new production of the Prairie Club was "Voices of the Dunes," written by Mary Larned, and performed on Memorial Day, 1918. No doubt the success of another pageant, given by Michigan City on August 25, 1916, also contributed to the decision to hold the 1917 pageant. Written by the chaplain at Indiana State Prison, it included local members of the Prairie Club in its cast of several hundred. Its re-creation of the history of the region, including the Sun Dance of the Indians, the first explorations of Father Marquette, the visits of Harriet Martineau and Daniel Webster, the sending of volunteers to the Civil War, and its symbolization of the Dune Country in dance and song, prefigured the even more ambitious Dunes Pageant of 1917. See Earl Roswell North, *The Spirit of the Dunes: A Pageant* (Michigan City, Indiana, 1916).

45. See Karen Hermassi, *Polity and Theatre in Historical Perspective* (Berkeley: University of California Press, 1977).

46. See Mircea Eliade, *Myths, Rites, Symbols: A Mircea Eliade Reader,* eds., Wendell Beane and William Doty, vol. 1 (New York: Harper and Row, 1975), pp. 137–257. Eliade stresses the ahistorical, or archetypal character of the myth that informs the collective memory invoked by the cosmogonic ritual. In contrast, Hermassi notes that Greek drama performed the same function of societal recollection without a derogation of human experience, or a denial of the irreversible character of human history. The myth of the Dunes Pageant, like the myth of Greek drama, assisted the recollection of the past for the sake of constructive action in the present.

47. Stevens, *Historical Pageant of the Dunes,* p. 29.

48. *Chicago Daily News,* May 30, 1917.

49. Brennan, *Wonders of the Dunes,* p. 172. Italics added.

50. See unidentified newspaper clipping, Dunes Miscellaneous Clippings,

1917–1965, Chicago Historical Society Library, Chicago, Illinois; *Chicago Tribune*, May 31, 1917; *Chicago Herald*, May 31, 1917.

51. Stevens, *Historical Pageant of the Dunes*, p. 29.

Landscape and Imagination

52. Margery Currey, *Prairie Club Bulletin*, May 1917.

53. Sherwood Anderson, *Mid-American Chants* (New York: B.W. Huebsch, Inc., 1923), pp. 70–71.

54. Louis Sullivan, *The Testament of Stone*, ed. Maurice English (Chicago: Northwestern University Press, 1963), p. 149.

55. Harriet Monroe contributed several plays and masques to the literature of outdoor drama, one of which was the occasion for John Muir's July 4, 1908, experiment in theater. See Linnie Marsh Wolfe, *Son of the Wilderness: The Life of John Muir* (Madison: University of Wisconsin Press, 1978), p. 317. She also wrote in admiration of the Apache dances and other ceremonials she saw in Arizona, remnants of the Native American civilization lost at great spiritual cost. See "Arizona," *The Atlantic Monthly* 89 (1902): 780–789. In 1916, Jens Jensen designed a "players green" as part of his famed Columbus Park on the West Side of Chicago. In explanation he wrote: "The American drama is still in the making. The writer believes that its early expression will be in the out-of-doors, and he sincerely hopes that this simple but poetic place will become an inspiration that will help to create the great American drama." (Malcolm Collier, "Jens Jensen and Columbus Park," *Chicago History* 4 [Winter, 1975–1976]: 234.) Jensen also did the landscaping for some of Stevens's historical pageants.

56. Lorado Taft, "Pageant at the Dunes," typewritten manuscript in the Taft Archives, University of Illinois at Urbana, Urbana, Illinois. This speech was a variation of the one Taft delivered October 30, 1916, at the Mather hearings. The quotations are found in Mather, *Report on Sand Dunes Park*, pp. 52, 54.

57. Quoted in William Lewis, "Lorado Taft: American Sculptor and Art Missionary," (Ph.D. diss., University of Chicago, 1958), pp. 50, 109.

58. Quotations from Genevieve Richardson, "Lorado Taft and Theatre," (M.A. thesis, University of Illinois at Urbana, 1948), p. 20. In addition to a concern for the preservation of distinctiveness of place, Taft had an avid interest in public theater, evident in the dramatic motifs of his sculpture, his support of civic theater, such as Donald Robertson's Drama Players, and his use and enjoyment of pageantry in his Midway studios and summer colony at Oregon, Illinois. In his view, much of the art of Europe was founded upon pageantry. Taft's plan for statues of the world's great humanists, from Moses to Whitman, to range along the length of the Midway from the "The Fountain of Creation" to the "Fountain of Time," was a vision of the pageant of human history frozen in stone. See Peter B. Wright, "Apotheosis of the Midway Plaisance," *Architectural Record* 28 (November 1910): 335–349.

59. See Thomas H. Dickinson, with cooperation of Thomas W. Stevens and Kenneth Sawyer Goodman, "The Open-Air Theatre," *Play-book* 1 (June 1913): 3–14; George McCalmon and Christian Moe, *Creating Historical Drama* (Carbondale: University of Southern Illinois, 1965). The masque is one of the oldest forms of human drama, its origins closely associated with

the fertility rite. One of its definitive features is an impromptu dance or *komos* in which both spectators and performers engage. In the Middle Ages the masque told an allegorical story in which characters were personifications of ideas or ideals. Akin to the medieval morality play, the masque presented universal truths through dramatic development, music, and pantomimic dancing. Noted the *Prairie Club Bulletin*, February 1918: "The festive spirit is the PRAIRIE CLUB SPIRIT. After all the parts have been assigned it is hoped that there will be enough Dune-bugs left to act as audience. It takes the right spirit to be an audient and a beholder, no less than to take part."

60. See Claude E. Dierolf, "The Pageant Drama and American Pageantry," (Ph.D. diss., University of Pennsylvania, 1953); Frederick George Walsh, "Outdoor Commemorative Drama in the United States 1900–1950," (Ph.D. diss., Western Reserve University, Cleveland, 1952); Helen L. Horowitz, *Culture and the City: Cultural Philanthropy in Chicago from the 1880's to 1917* (Lexington: University Press of Kentucky, 1976), p. 218; Frank C. Brown, "The American Pageant Association," *The Drama Magazine*, January 1913, pp. 178–91. Jane Addams considered the new community theater a "pioneer teacher of social righteousness." (Jane Addams, *Twenty Years at Hull House* [New York: Macmillan, 1938], p. 391). Like other members of the Dunes movement, she was impressed by the capacity of peasants to re-create a living religious drama in the outdoor Passion Play at Oberammergau.

61. Stephen T. Mather and William C. Langdon, "Historical Pageants in America," *The City Club Bulletin* 6 (1913): 288.

62. Charles Dickinson, *The Case of American Drama* (Boston: Houghton Mifflin, 1915), pp. 86, 131. Dickinson considered the community drama movement a citizen's movement organically associated with the spirit of LaFollette Progressivism. See Robert Gard, *Grassroots Theatre: A Search for Regional Arts in America* (Madison: University of Wisconsin Press, 1955).

63. For biographical and critical studies of Thomas Wood Stevens, see: Thomas H. Dickinson, *The Insurgent Theatre* (New York: B. W. Huebsch, 1917); Stevens Commemorative Issue, *Educational Theatre Journal* 3 (December, 1951); Rambin, "Thomas Wood Stevens"; Dierolf, "The Pageant Drama." Dierolf ranks Stevens second only to Percy MacKaye as a pageant writer and producer 1914–1920. In 1912–1913 Stevens was lecturer in art history at the University of Wisconsin and worked closely with Thomas Dickinson.

64. Kenneth Sawyer Goodman, "A Masque," *The Morton Aboretum Quarterly* 7 (Spring and Summer, 1971): 15.

65. Ragna B. Eskil, "Notes on the Masque," *Friends of Our Native Landscape Bulletin* 5 (Winter, 1948): 2. Eskil, a student of Henry Cowles and freelance writer in Chicago, wrote several masques for the Friends in the same vein as the Goodman masque, among them "Fire-Light and Lantern Light," and "The Jensen Masque." See Jens Jensen Papers, Morton Arboretum Library, Chicago, Illinois. Among the places where the masque was performed and which were later set aside as public preserves, were White Pines, Starved Rock, Nauvoo, Apple River Canyon, and Funk's Grove in Illinois, the Wisconsin Dells and Devil's Lake in Wisconsin, and Luddington in Michigan. See Carol Doty, "About the Masque," *The Morton Arboretum Quarterly* 7 (Spring and Summer 1971): 8, 16–17.

The Drama of Democracy

66. Gail Gehrig, "The American Civil Religion Debate: A Source for Theory Construction," *Journal for the Scientific Study of Religion* 20 (1981): 51. See Phillip E. Hammond, "The Sociology of American Civil Religion: A Bibliographic Essay," *Sociological Analysis* 2 (1976): 169–182; Donald G. Jones and Russell Richey, *American Civil Religion* (New York: Harper and Row, 1974); Robert N. Bellah, *The Broken Covenant* (New York: Seabury Press, 1975); Catherine Albanese, *Sons of the Fathers* (Philadelphia: Temple University Press, 1976).

67. For discussion of Memorial Day as a civic religious ritual see W. Lloyd Warner, *American Life: Dream and Reality* (Chicago: University of Chicago Press, 1953); Conrad Cherry, "American Sacred Ceremonies," in Phillip E. Hammond and Benton Johnson, eds., *American Mosaic* (New York: Random House, 1970), pp. 303–316.

68. *Chicago Daily Journal*, May 27, 1917.

69. Much of the confusion and debate surrounding the concept of American civil religion in recent years is due to the fact that, like all religious traditions, it assumes various related forms—one, a folk religion, found in the popular culture, another, Protestant civic piety through which the civil religion becomes a vehicle for the legitimation of specifically Protestant values in the national life. Still another form, religious nationalism, is the most troubling, for in this manifestation, the American nation itself is glorified, and the transcendent dimension is perverted by the idolatrous self-worship of the particular economic, social, and political institutions of the American people. However, a fourth form, civil religion as the *transcendent universal religion of the nation*, a cluster of inclusive ideals and practices by which the society is both affirmed, unified, and judged, is the most significant expression of public faith in America. It was this form, a synthesis of prophetic biblical and deist themes, that found expression in the Declaration of Independence. Sidney E. Mead holds that at their best, Americans have given their supreme allegiance to a "universal principle which is thought to transcend and include all the national and religious particularities brought to it by the people who come from all over the world to be 'Americanized.'" (Sidney E. Mead, *Nation with the Soul of a Church* [New York: Harper and Row, 1975], p. 63.) It was a revitalization and reform of civil religion understood as the transcendent universal religion of the Republic that found expression through the pen of Thomas Wood Stevens in the Dunes Pageant of 1917.

70. Graves, "The Dunes Pageant."

71. The symbol of the Indian Prophet also played the central role in Stevens's previous attempts to write a regional myth for the Midwest. He used the figure of White Cloud, one of the last of the Indian prophets, in "An Historical Pageant of Illinois," Northwestern University, 1919, "Madison County Historical Pageant," 1912, and the "Pageant of St. Louis," 1914. In each case Donald Robertson played the role.

72. Stevens, *Historical Pageant of the Dunes*, p. 34. In order to underscore the combination of human fraternity and communion with nature, the *Book* of the pageant included two poems to accompany the ritual of the Calumet: a selection from Longfellow's "Hiawatha" in which Hiawatha appeals to his people to "as brothers live hence forward," and lines by Mary Austin which

link the hearth fires of men with the stars above and the forest of the hunter at rest. (Stevens, *Historical Pageant of the Dunes*, p. 35.)

73. Stevens drew upon the same source for his myth of Nanabozho as Longfellow for his poem of "Hiawatha": Henry R. Schoolcraft, *The Myth of Hiawatha and other Oral Legends of the North American Indians* (Philadelphia: J. B. Lippincott, 1856).

74. Eliade, Mircea *The Sacred and the Profane* (New York: Harcourt, Brace & World, 1959), p. 140.

75. This analysis agrees with those who argue that much of the romanticized history of the turn of the century was not an escape from industrial civilization, but an attempt to use the past to shape the society. See David Glassberg, "Restoring a 'Forgotten Childhood': American Play and the Progressive Era's Elizabethan Past," *American Quarterly* 32 (Fall 1980): 351–368.

76. Kenneth S. Goodman and Thomas W. Stevens, *A Pageant for Independence Day* (Chicago: The Stage Guild, 1912).

77. Unidentified newspaper clipping, April 7, 1917, Dunes Scrapbook, Gary Public Library, Gary, Indiana. In fact, those who staged the Dunes Pageant took a most exalted view of civil ritual. By writing "lyric dramas," for the "great patriotic and religious festivals," they saw themselves adding "new religious festivals to the great chorus of divine worship." (William Langdon, "Compass Points in the Festal Drama," *The Drama Magazine* 5 [August 1971]: 405.) Wilhelm Miller, landscape architect and member of the Dunes movement, advocated a ritual in which each citizen of Illinois, on coming of age, would take the "Illinois Citizen's Oath" on the town commons. See Wilhelm Miller, *The Prairie Spirit in Landscape Gardening* (Urbana, Illinois: University of Illinois, 1915).

78. *Chesterton Tribune*, June 7, 1917.

79. Mather, *Report*, p. 89.

80. William L. Chenery, "The Guide Post," *The Chicago Herald*, March 23, 1917.

81. *Gary Tribune*, July 17, 1916.

82. Thomas Wood Stevens, *A Pageant of Victory and Peace* (Boston: C.C. Birchard and Co., 1919).

CHAPTER TWO: DUNE COUNTRY PATRIOTS

Apostles of the Dunes, Prophets of Democracy

1. *Chicago Herald*, May 31, 1917.

2. Theodore Jessup, *Illinois State Parks* (Chicago: Chicago Literary Club, 1916), p. 15.

3. Peter S. Goodman, *Rand McNally Map of Indiana Dunes, The Wonder Region of the Middle West*, 1st ed. (Chicago: Rand McNally Co., 1920). The now rare 2d edition caused the greatest furor.

4. *Gary Post*, June 18, 1921.

5. Ibid.

6. *Gary Post*, June 20, 1921.

7. *Gary Daily Tribune*, July 6, 1914.

8. *Chicago Daily Tribune* editorial, May 31, 1917.

9. In the view of some historians of American religion, the dedication to the "humane values and ideals of equality, freedom, and justice without necessary dependence on a transcendent deity or a spiritualized nation represent civil religion at its best in American experience. To some extent the American creed of Gunnar Myrdal, the common faith of John Dewey, the vision of America discerned in progressive era historiography and the democracy-as-religion of J. Paul Williams, encompass this concept of civil religion." (Donald G. Jones and Russell Richey, *American Civil Religion* [New York: Harper and Row, 1974], p. 17.) The religion of democracy has not received the treatment accorded such early nineteenth-century revitalization movements of the civil religion as Transcendentalism and Christian evangelicalism. See, however, Ralph Gabriel, *The Course of American Democratic Thought*, 2d ed. (New York: The Ronald Press, 1956); Herbert W. Schneider, *A History of American Philosophy*, 2d ed. (New York: Columbia University Press, 1963).

10. Unidentified newspaper editorial, Jensen Papers, Morton Arboretum Library archives, Chicago, Illinois.

11. Charles Ferguson, *The Religion of Democracy* (New York: Funk and Wagnalls Company, 1900), pp. 55, 56.

12. For the significance of the democratic faith to the Progressive conservation movement, see J. Leonard Bates, "Fulfilling American Democracy: The Conservation Movement, 1907–1921," *Mississippi Valley Historical Review* 44 (1957–1958): 29–57; Grant McConnell, "The Conservation Movement—Past and Present," *The Western Political Quarterly* 7 (September 1954): 463–478.

13. Thomas Allinson, in Emma Doeserich, Mary Sherburne, Anna B. Wey, *Outdoors with the Prairie Club* (Chicago: The Prairie Club, 1941), p. 21; Allinson, as quoted in *The Survey* 38 (June 30, 1917): 287.

14. Caroline McIlvaine, "The Memorable Inaugural Pageant on the Dunes," *Chicago Commerce*, June 8, 1917, p. 20.

15. Stephen T. Mather, *Report on Sand Dunes National Park, Indiana* (Washington, D.C.: Government Printing Office, 1917), p. 6.

Midwestern Reform

16. For the Progressive era as a whole, and its aim of perpetuating democracy into the urban society of the twentieth century, see Arthur Mann, *The Progressive Era, Major Issues in Interpretation*, 2d ed. (Hinsdale, Illinois: The Dryden Press, 1975). The distinctiveness of the midwestern emphasis upon the *community of humanity and nature* is apparent when it is contrasted to the other two major directions within the Progressive conservation movement. Gifford Pinchot, director of the Bureau of Forestry under Theodore Roosevelt, advocated economic development of the environment within the context of an amended utilitarianism—the greatest good of the greatest number for the longest time. Pinchot's concern was for *equality and efficiency in the use* of natural resources. His position confirmed tendencies toward scientific management and the corporate welfare state. John Muir, founder of the California Sierra Club, took a divergent position. His emphasis on wilderness preservation for its own sake was rooted in a mystic appreciation of the divinity pervading all the wild things in the democracy of creation. For him the democratic faith meant the opportunity of each individual to experience

the *freedom of spiritual renewal* in the wilderness. This was to lead to increasingly radical dissent from the prevailing technological and managerial ethos of American society. Midwestern Progressivism as exemplified in the Dunes movement included aspects of both these positions within its own distinctive social democratic or ecological perspective. For Pinchot and the dominant direction of Progressive conservation, see Samuel P. Hays, *Conservation and the Gospel of Efficiency* (Cambridge, Mass.: Harvard University Press, 1959); for Muir and the wilderness preservation movement, see Roderick Nash, *Wilderness and the American Mind* (New Haven: Yale University Press, 1967).

17. Quoted in George S. Cottman, *Indiana Dunes State Park, A History and Description* (Indianapolis: State of Indiana, Department of Conservation, 1930), p. 46.

18. Opie Read, *The Colossus* (Chicago: Laird and Lee, 1893), p. 55.

19. "The rural village—the basic, stable unity of social life throughout most of human history—was being destroyed in the nineteenth century by the competition of agriculture in the New World, by manufacturing, by migration. . . . If social life were to become sound again, the sense of belonging to a community would have to be restored to the people who had been uprooted. Reformers who felt this way put community at the center of their plans . . . *a community;* that is to say, a group of men and women few enough in number to know each other well, sympathetic enough to work together, idealistic enough to strive for a better world than the one stretching out before them." (Arthur J. Bestor, "The Search for Utopia," in John J. Murray, *The Heritage of the Middle West* [Norman, Oklahoma: University of Oklahoma Press, 1958], p. 101.)

20. In the view of Leo Marx, what Jim and Huck discover as they travel down the Mississippi on their raft is a bond of caring. Clemens "joins the pastoral ideal with the revolutionary doctrine of human fraternity." (Leo Marx, *The Machine in the Garden* [New York: Oxford University Press, 1974], p. 332.)

21. See Chester MacArthur Destler, *American Radicalism 1865–1901* (New London, Connecticut: Connecticut College Monograph 3, 1946); Lawrence Goodwyn, *Democratic Promise, The Populist Moment in America* (New York: Oxford University Press, 1976): Russell B. Nye, *Midwestern Progressive Politics* (East Lansing: Michigan State College Press, 1951).

22. Murray, *Heritage of the Middle West,* p. 27.

23. *Prairie Club Bulletin,* February 1918.

24. Paul H. Douglas, *In the Fullness of Time* (New York: Harcourt Brace Jovanovich, 1971), p. 149.

Settlement Houses

25. For the Chicago settlement house movement, see Allen F. Davis, *Spearheads for Reform* (New York: Oxford University Press, 1967); Perry Duis, *Chicago, Creating New Traditions* (Chicago: Chicago Historical Society, 1976); Daniel Levine, *Jane Addams and the Liberal Tradition* (Madison: State Historical Society of Wisconsin, 1971); Louise C. Wade, *Graham Taylor, Pioneer for Social Justice, 1851–1938* (Chicago: University of Chicago Press, 1964).

26. Mildred Marshall Scouller, *Women Who Man Our Clubs*, Gary, Indiana, n.d., p. 179. See Bess Sheehan, *History of Campbell Friendship House, Gary, Indiana, 1912–1940* (Gary, Indiana: Campbell Friendship House, 1943).

27. Quoted in Davis, *Spearheads for Reform*, p. 9.

28. Stanton Coit, *The Church of the Republic, Preliminary Manifesto*, 1914, n.p., archives of the Chicago Ethical Humanist Society, University of Illinois Library Special Collections, Circle Campus, Chicago.

29. See Woods and Kennedy, *Handbook of Settlements* (New York: Russell Sage Foundation, 1911), pp. 52–53; Thomas Allinson, "Annual Report," *Henry Booth House*, 1907, 1912, 1916, University of Illinois Library Special Collections, Circle Campus, Chicago.

30. William Wilder, "The Functions of a Settlement," *Henry Booth House*, September 1917.

31. Quoted in Davis, *Spearheads for Reform*, p. 15.

32. Jane Addams, *Twenty Years at Hull House* (New York: Macmillan Co., 1938), p. 115.

33. Graham Taylor, "The Settlement Name," *Chicago Commons* 1 (April 1896): 6.

34. Ibid.

The Chicago Renaissance

35. See Bernard Duffey, *The Chicago Renaissance in American Letters* (Westport, Conn.: Greenwood Press, 1972); Dale Dramer, *Chicago Renaissance* (New York: Appleton Century, 1966); Duis, *Chicago, Creating New Traditions;* Ethel Joyce Hammer, "Attitudes Toward Art in the Nineteen Twenties in Chicago" (Ph.D. diss., University of Chicago, 1975); Ralph Fletcher Seymour, *Some Went This Way, A Forty Year Pilgrimage Among Artists, Bookmen and Printers* (Chicago: Ralph Fletcher Seymour, 1945).

36. Jensen wrote of first visiting the Dunes in 1889 in "Wild Flowers in the Dunes," *The Club Messenger* 1 (June 1917): 3–4. For his life and work in Chicago, see Leonard K. Eaton, *Landscape Artist in America, the Life and Work of Jens Jensen* (Chicago: University of Chicago Press, 1964); Malcolm Collier, "Jens Jensen and Columbus Park," *Chicago History* 4 (Winter, 1975–1976): 225–234; Stephen F. Christy, "The Metamorphosis of an Artist," *Landscape Architecture* (January 1976), pp. 60–66; Ragna Eskil, "Jens Jensen: Landscape Architect," *The American Scandinavian Review*, May 20, 1918, pp. 140–144. Wilhelm Miller defined the Prairie School of landscape architecture as "an American mode of design based upon the practical needs of the middle-western people and characterized by preservation of typical western scenery, by restoration of local color, and by repetition of the horizontal line of land or sky which is the strongest feature of prairie scenery." (Wilhelm Miller, *The Prairie Spirit in Landscape Gardening* [Urbana, Illinois: University of Illinois, 1915], p. 5.)

37. See J. Howard Euston, "Notes on Earl Reed, Etcher of the Dunes, 1865–1931," lecture at Duneland Historical Society, April 1953, archives, Westchester Public Library, Chesterton, Indiana; John Drury, "Artist-Author 'Discovered' the Dunes," *Gary Post-Tribune*, April 22, 1956.

38. Webb Waldron and Marion Patton Waldron, *We Explore the Great Lakes* (New York: Century Publishing Co., 1923), p. 247.

39. Dudley to Mrs. Shoemaker, March 30, 1945, Dudley Files, Lafayette

Art Center, Lafayette, Indiana; C. J. Bulliet, "Artists of Chicago Past and Present—Frank V. Dudley," *Chicago Daily News*, March 28, 1936.

40. Quoted in Duffey, *Chicago Renaissance*, p. 215.

41. Helga Sandburg, *The Owl's Roost* (New York: Dial Press, 1962).

42. Books by Earl Howell Reed, Sr., include: *Voices of the Dunes*, Chicago: Aldebrink Press, 1912); *Sketches in Jacobia* (Privately Printed, Chicago, 1919); *Tales of a Vanishing River* (New York: John Lane and Company, 1920); *The Ghost in the Tower* (Privately Printed, Chicago, 1921); *The Silver Arrow, and other Indian Romances of the Dune Country* (Chicago: Reilly and Lee, 1926).

43. Mather's tour is described in "At Federal Hearing Chicago Pleads That Indiana's Matchless Sand Dunes Be Created National Park," *Chicago Commerce*, September 3, 1916. See "An Exhibit of the Dune Country," *Chicago Public Library Book Bulletin* 7 (1917): 2–3; "Pictures of Our Country Assembled by The Friends of Our Native Landscape," *Catalog of First Annual Exhibition*, Art Institute, Chicago, 1919.

44. Donald Culross Peattie, *Flora of the Indiana Dunes* (Chicago: Field Museum of Natural History, 1930); Edwin Way Teale, *Dune Boy: The Early Years of a Naturalist* (New York: Dodd, Mead and Company, 1943).

45. See J. Z. Jacobson, *Art of Today* (Chicago: L. M. Stein Co., 1929); Esther Sparks, "A Biographical Dictionary of Painters and Sculptors in Illinois, 1808–1945" (Ph.D. diss., Northwestern University, Evanston, Illinois, 1971); Helen Ruth Huber, "Fred Biesel Led the Way: Porter County Artists Find Inspiration in the Dunes," *Gary Post Tribune*, November 13, 1955; Helen Ruth Huber, "Vince Hannell . . . Wood Sculpture Brings Fame to Porter County," *The Gary Post-Tribune*, September 26, 1956; C. V. Bulliet, "Artists of Chicago Past and Present—Frances Strain," *Chicago Daily News*, March 21, 1936; David Sander, "The Unique Vision of V. M. S. Hannell," *Dune Country Magazine* 3 (Winter, 1979–1980): 25–26.

46. See Marjorie Hill Allee, *Ann's Surprising Summer* (Boston: Houghton Mifflin, 1933), and *The Great Tradition* (Boston: Houghton Mifflin, 1937); Julia Cooley Altrocchi, *Wolves Against the Moon* (New York: Macmillan Company, 1940); Meyer Levin, *The Old Bunch* (New York: Viking Press, 1937); Elma K. Lobaugh, *She Never Reached the Top* (New York: Doubleday, Doran and Co., 1945); Arnold Mulder, *The Sand Doctor* (Boston: Houghton Mifflin, 1921); Thomas Rogers, *At the Shores* (New York: Simon and Schuster, 1980); Seymour Fleishman, *Where's Kit?* (Chicago: Albert Whitman and Company, 1962); Julian May, *Moving Hills of Sand* (New York: Hawthorn Books, 1969); Charles G. Bell, *Songs for a New America* (Bloomington: Indiana University Press, 1953); Galway Kinnell, *The Avenue Bearing the Initial of Christ into the New World* (Boston: Houghton Mifflin, 1974); Jeannette Konley, *Cradled in the Dunelands* (Parkville, Missouri: Park College Press, 1956); Samuel A. Harper, *A Hoosier Tramp* (Chicago: The Prairie Club, 1928); E. Stillman Bailey, *The Sand Dunes of Indiana: The Story of an American Wonderland* (Chicago: A. C. McClurg and Co., 1917); Kathlee M. Lynch, "Steelman Preserves Dunes' Glory: The Life and Work of John Cowan Templeton," (M.S. thesis, Purdue University, Lafayette, Indiana, 1959).

47. David Sander, "The Dunes, a Personal Reminiscence," *The Northern Indiana Dunes Review* I (April 1966): 3.

48. See Elia Peattie, *The Precipice* (New York: Houghton Mifflin, 1914); Lennox Bouton Grey, "Chicago and the Great American Novel: A Critical Approach to the American Epic" (Ph.D. diss., University of Chicago, 1935).

49. Seymour, *Some Went This Way*, p. 3.

50. William Dean Howells, "Certain of the Chicago School of Fiction," *North American Review* 176 (1903): 739.

51. Duffey, *Chicago Renaissance*, p. 261.

52. See Helen Horowitz, *Culture and the City: Cultural Philanthropy in Chicago from the 1880s to 1917* (Lexington: University of Kentucky Press, 1976).

53. Quoted in Eugene Tesler, "Carl Sandburg, Journalist and Critic" (M.A. thesis, University of Chicago, 1950), p. 61.

54. Harriet Monroe, *Poets and Their Art* (New York: Macmillan Company, 1926), pp. 234, 242. See Hugh D. Duncan, *Culture and Democracy* (Totowa, N.J.: Bedminster Press, 1965).

55. For an excellent discussion of these impulses, see Hammer, "Attitudes Toward Art in Chicago."

56. Seymour, *Some Went This Way*, p. 164.

57. Sherwood Anderson, *Sherwood Anderson's Memoirs* (New York: Harcourt, Brace and Company, 1942), pp. 248, 249.

Harper's University

58. See Richard J. Storr, *Harper's University* (Chicago: University of Chicago Press, 1966); Darnell Rucker, *The Chicago Pragmatists* (Minneapolis: University of Minnesota Press, 1969).

59. William Rainey Harper, *The University and Democracy* (Chicago: University of Chicago Press, 1970), pp. 27, 17. Harper's address was given as the Charter Day address at the University of California in 1899, and first published in *The Trend in Higher Education* (Chicago: University of Chicago Press, 1906).

60. Harper, *The University and Democracy*, pp. 5, 4, 12, 42.

61. Storr, *Harper's University*, p. 99.

62. Quoted in Rucker, *Chicago Pragmatists*, p. 3.

63. Thomas C. Chamberlin, "Religious Work in Connection with the University," *Educational Papers*, vol. 3, pp. 11, 9, 9, 8, 20.

64. John M. Coulter and Merle C. Coulter, *Where Evolution and Religion Meet* (New York: Macmillan Co., 1926), pp. 3, 6.

65. Harriet Monroe, *John Wellborn Root: A Study of His Life and Work* (New York: Houghton, Mifflin, 1896), p. 244; See Harriet Monroe, *Ode for the Opening of the World's Fair, Chicago, 1892* (Cincinnati: John Church Co., 1892).

66. Louis Sullivan, *The Autobiography of an Idea* (New York: Press of American Institute of Architects), p. 319.

67. See Sarah Gibbard Cook, "Cowles Bog, Indiana, and Henry Chandler Cowles (1869–1939)," Indiana Dunes National Lakeshore, Chesterton, Indiana, 1980.

68. Thomas Wood Stevens, script for "Historical Pageant of the Dunes," Newberry Library, Chicago, Illinois.

69. "Minutes of Board of Trustees, University of Chicago," volume 4 (May 19, 1903), p. 258. Papers of the Board of Trustees, University of Chicago, Regenstein Library, Chicago, Illinois. Jens Jensen reported that in 1900 Harper asked him to lead a committee to investigate an area of about three thousand acres for purchase by the university as an outdoor laboratory and sanctuary. See Doerserich, Sherburne, and Wey, *Outdoors with the Prairie Club*, p. 96.

70. See Rollin D. Salisbury and William C. Alden, *The Geography of Chicago and Its Environs* (Chicago: University of Chicago Press, 1899); Reuben M. Strong, "Indiana's Unspoiled Dunes," *National Parks Magazine*, August 1959, pp. 5–6; Frank M. Woodruff, *The Birds of the Chicago Area* (Chicago: Chicago Academy of Sciences, 1907); Victor E. Shelford, *Animal Communities in Temperate America, as Illustrated in the Chicago Region: A Study in Animal Ecology* (Chicago: University of Chicago Press, 1913); Charles C. Adams, *Guide to the Study of Animal Ecology* (New York: Macmillan and Co., 1913); Warder Clyde Allee, "An Experimental Analysis of the Relations Between Physiological States and Rheotaxis in Isopoda," *Journal of Experimental Zoology* 13 (1912): 269–344; W. C. Allee, A. E. Emerson, O. Park, T. Park, and K. P. Schmidt, *Principles of Animal Ecology* (New York: W. B. Saunders Co., 1949). Most were students of Cowles before becoming colleagues.

71. A classic of the Cowles school of ecology is May Theilgaard Watts, *Reading the Landscape: An Adventure in Ecology* (New York: Macmillan Co., 1957). Other members of the Dunes movement influenced by the Chicago ecologists while students at the university include: William Beecher, Ragna Eskil, Irma Frankenstein, Marjorie Hill (who married W. C. Allee), Walter Necker, Donald Culross Peattie, W. D. Richardson, Lillian Steichen (who married Carl Sandburg), Floyd Swink, Hazel Wiggins (who married Charles Olmsted).

72. John Dewey, "The Relation of Philosophy to Theology," in *The Early Works: 1882–1898*, ed. Jo Anne Boydston, 4 (Carbondale: Southern Illinois University Press, 1969): 366. See John Dewey, *Experience and Nature* (New York: Dover Publications, 1925), *A Common Faith* (New Haven: Yale University Press, 1934), *Art as Experience* (New York: G. P. Putnam's Sons, 1934).

73. Dewey, "Introduction to Philosophy," in *Early Works* 3: 228.

74. Dewey, "The Relation of Philosophy to Theology," p. 367.

75. Dewey, "Christianity and Democracy," in *Early Works* 4: 6, 8, 9.

76. For a fuller explication of these themes, see the author's "John Dewey's Philosophy of the Common World," *Belief and Ethics*, eds. W. Widick Schroeder and Gibson Winter (Chicago: Center for the Scientific Study of Religion, 1978), pp. 21–38. An important recent study is Gibson Winter, *Liberating Creation: Foundations of Religious Social Ethics* (New York: Crossroad Publishing Company, 1981).

77. See Lewis S. Feuer, "John Dewey and the Back to the People Movement in American Thought," *Journal of the History of Ideas* 20 (October-December 1958): 545–568.

78. Elliot R. Downing, *A Naturalist in the Great Lakes Region* (Chicago: University of Chicago Press, 1922). Zonia Baber noted in the Mather hearings that she went to the Dunes for the first time as a student in 1887. See John Dewey and Evelyn Dewey, *Schools of Tomorrow* (New York: E. P. Dutton and Company, 1915).

79. John Dewey, "Evolution and Ethics," in *The Early Works* 5: 53, 38, 52.

The Dunes Movement
80. "Creed of F.O.N.L.," *Friends of Our Native Landscape Bulletin* 15 (Fall 1957): 6.

81. See R. M. Strong and Leon F. Urbain, *History of the Illinois Chapter of the Wild Flower Preservation Society*, 2 pp., Richardson Sanctuary archives, Dune Acres, Indiana.

82. See George Fuller, "An Efficient Conservation Organization," *Ecology* 19 (April 1938): 350–352.

83. The Geographic Society of Chicago, *Yearbook, 1912–1926*.

84. *Gary Post-Tribune*, June 18, 1974.

85. Walter Necker, "A Naturalist's Chicagoana—The Dune Country," *The Chicago Naturalist* 1 (1938): 63–64. For bibliographies, see *Chicago Public Library Book Bulletin*, April, 1917, p. 47; Mabel Tinkham, "Bibliography of Material on the Dunes," and "Tentative Bibliography of Lake County, Kankakee County and of the Dunes," 1918, Chicago Historical Society Library; Louis J. Bailey, "Literature of the Dunes, a Bibliography," 1922, Gary Public Library; "Indiana—Sand Dunes, a Bibliography," n.d., Indiana State Library, Indianapolis.

86. The author was present at this occasion held at Ogden Dunes Community Church, Ogden Dunes, Indiana, 1970.

87. *Dunes Summer Camp*, 1922, 4 pp., Dunes scrapbook, Chicago Historical Society Library.

88. *The School in the Dunes for Nature Study*, 1939, 4 pp., Dunes scrapbook, Chicago Historical Society Library.

CHAPTER THREE: OF TIME AND ETERNITY

A Revelation for the People
1. Stephen Mather, *Report on Sand Dunes National Park, Indiana* (Washington, D.C.: Government Printing Office, 1917), p. 25.

2. *Gary Evening Post*, June 21, 1919.

3. Harriet Martineau, *Society in America*, 2 vols. (London: Saunders and Otley, 1937) 1: 346.

4. I am indebted to James P. Wind for bringing to my attention this quotation from Harper's unpublished lecture, "The Prophetic Element in the Old Testament as Related to Christianity."

5. Jane Addams, *Twenty Years at Hull House* (New York: Macmillan Co., 1910), p. 39.

6. Mrs. Frank J. Sheehan, "Says Romance Drew Woman to Steel Town," unidentified news clipping, Dunes Scrapbook, Gary Public Library.

7. Mather, *Report*, p. 56.

8. W. H. de B. Nelson, "A Front-Rank Man in American Etching," *The International Studio* 51 (November 1913): lxxxii.

9. Earl H. Reed, *Sketches in Duneland* (New York: John Lane and Co., 1918), p. 18.

10. Ibid., p. 22.

11. *Gary Tribune*, June 4, 1931.

12. Quoted in *Businessmen for the Public Interest News-letter*, December, 1974.

13. Theodore Jessup, *Illinois State Parks* (Chicago: Chicago Literary Club, 1916), p. 14.

14. In Earl H. Reed, *Voices of the Dunes* (Chicago: Aldebrink Press, 1912), opposite Plate VIII.

15. "The Dune Trail," in *The Prairie Club Song Book* (Chicago: The Prairie Club, 1924), p. 25.

16. *Prairie Club Bulletin*, December 1920. For the scientific interest in the singing sands of the Dunes, see Frederich Shepherd, "The Story of the Dunes," *Rocks and Minerals*, June 1932, p. 45; W. D. Richardson, "Singing Sands of Lake Michigan," *Science* 50 (1919): 494; H. L. Fairchild, "Musical Sands," *Science* 51 (1920): 63; George B. Cressey, *The Indiana Sand Dunes and Shorelines of the Lake Michigan Basin* (Chicago: University of Chicago Press, 1928), pp. 19–21.

17. Phillip Kinsley, "Duneland Sings Song of Peace," *Chicago Tribune*, July 17, 1939.

18. E. Stillman Bailey, *The Sand Dunes of Indiana* (Chicago: A. C. McClurg and Co., 1917), p. 22.

19. David Sander, "Beulah Land," *Northern Indiana Dunes Review* 1 (April 1966): 7.

20. Arietta Wimer Towne, "Earl H. Reed: Artist of the Dunes," *The Club Messenger* 3 (May 1919): 9.

21. Reed, *Voices*, epigraph.

22. Reed, *Sketches*, pp. 103, 91.

23. Florence Morgan Crim, "Wonders of the Dune Country," *The Hoosier Motorist*, March 1918, p. 20. On the Dunes as the "last frontier" of Indiana, see A. H. Meyer, "Circulation and Settlement Patterns of the Calumet Region of Northwest Indiana and Northeast Illinois," *Annals of the Association of American Geographers* 44 (1954): 245–274.

24. *Indianapolis News*, June 14, 1921.

25. Anna Berg, "Solace in the Dunes," in Clarence Orvan Adams, ed., *Duneland Echoes* (Dallas: The Story Book Press, 1950).

26. Earl H. Reed, *The Dune Country* (New York: John Lane and Co., 1916), pp. 17, 23.

The Symbolism of the Center

27. For the following discussion, see Mircea Eliade, *Myth of the Eternal Return* (Princeton: Princeton University Press, 1954), *Patterns in Comparative Religion* (New York: Sheed and Ward, 1958), *The Sacred and the Profane* (New York: Harcourt Brace Jovanovich, 1959). Linda H. Graber applies Eliade's interpretation of sacred space to the American preservation movement and concludes that the movement constitutes a religion whose

sacred place is the Western wilderness. The Chicago environmentalists experienced both the wilderness and human community in the city as manifestations of the sacred. See *Wilderness as Sacred Space* (Washington, D.C.: Association of American Geographers, 1976).

28. Charles Ferguson, *The Religion of Democracy* (New York: Funk and Wagnalls Company, 1900), p. iv. Italics added.

Three Artists of the Dunes

29. Lena M. McCauley, "Earl H. Reed, Painter-Etcher," *Art and Progress* 6 (1915): 269. See also Harriet Monroe, *Catalog of an Exhibition of Original Etchings by Earl H. Reed of Chicago*, Albert Roullier's Art Galleries, Chicago, 1915, 6 pp.; Nelson, "A Front-Rank Man," pp. lxxxi–lxxxvii; David Sander, "Earl Reed: Etcher and Writer of the Dunes," *Dunes Country Magazine* 4 (Fall, 1980): 16–17; Towne, "Earl H. Reed," pp. 8–9.

30. McCauley, "Earl H. Reed," p. 271.

31. Frank V. Dudley, "The Dunes from an Artist's Point of View," *Prairie Club Bulletin*, February 1922. There is a dearth of good critical comment on Dudley's work. See, however, C. J. Bulliet, "Artists of Chicago Past and Present—Frank V. Dudley," *Chicago Daily News*, March 28, 1936; Carl Lewis, "Painter of the Dunes," *Indianapolis Star Magazine*, September 18, 1949; Maude I. G. Oliver, "Advertising with a Purpose," *The Poster*, June 1926, pp. 13–16; A. G. Richards, "Lake Michigan's Wonderful Dunes," *Fine Arts Journal* 36 (1918): 19–25; David Sander, "Frank Dudley: The Painter Who Invented the Dunes," *Dunes Country Magazine* 3 (Fall 1979): 29–30.

32. Quoted in Bulliet, "Frank V. Dudley."

33. *Chicago Tribune*, May 29, 1918.

34. J. Z. Jacobson, *Thirty-Five Saints and Emil Armin* (Chicago: L. Stein, 1929), pp. 17, 19. See C. J. Bulliet, "Artists of Chicago Past and Present—Emil Armin," *Chicago Daily News*, October 26, 1935; Ethel J. Hammer, "Attitudes Toward Art in the Nineteen Twenties in Chicago" (Ph.D. diss., University of Chicago, 1975); Maureen A. McKenna, *Emil Armin, 1883–1971* (Springfield: Illinois State Museum, 1980); David Sander, "Emil Armin: Unusual Artist of the Dunes," *Dunes Country Magazine* 3 (Spring 1980): 34–36.

35. Emil Armin Papers, Collection of Mrs. Emil Armin, Chicago, Illinois.

Where All Things Meet

36. See H. S. Pepoon, *An Annotated Flora of the Chicago Region* (Chicago: The Lakeside Press, 1927), pp. 103–136.

37. John Dean Caton, *The Last of the Illinois* (Chicago: Fergus Printing Co., 1876), p. 6.

38. Jerry S. Olson, "Indiana Sand Dune Preservation," November 8, 1951, 5 pp. mimeo., Chicago Historical Society Library.

39. *Gary Evening Post*, June 30, 1916.

40. *Gary Evening Post*, July 10, 1916, italics added. See also A. F. Knotts, "The Dunes of Northwestern Indiana," *Forty-first Annual Report of the Department of Geology and Natural Resources of the State of Indiana* (Fort Wayne: Fort Wayne Publishing Co., 1916), pp. 11–27. George Brennan describes a similar panoramic view from the top of Mount Tom, in which he

rotates north, west, south, and east, on the axis of the world, in *Wonders of the Dunes* (Indianapolis: Bobbs-Merrill Co., 1923), pp. 185-190.

41. *Gary Evening Post*, July 10, 1916.

42. Ibid., italics added.

43. Jens Jensen, "Introduction" to Brennan, *Wonders of the Dunes, and Siftings* (Chicago: Ralph Fletcher Seymour, 1956), p. 101.

44. Mather, *Report*, p. 94.

45. Edward R. Ford, "Reminiscences of Birds of the Dunes Country," *Program of Activities of the Chicago Academy of Sciences* 6 (1935): 29.

46. Brennan, *Wonders of the Dunes*, p. 183.

47. J. William Lester, "Orchids and Tumbleweeds," *Gary Post-Tribune*, January 9–February 13, 1929.

48. John O. Bowers, "Dream Cities of the Calumet," in John O. Bowers, Arthur G. Taylor, and Sam B. Woods, eds., *History of Lake County* (Gary: Calumet Press, 1929) 10: 175.

49. Mather, *Report*, p. 8. Mather was correct. The center of U.S. population in 1910 was at Indianapolis and moving slowly west.

50. Downing Mann, script for "Indiana Dunes: Playground of Mid-America," 16mm sound movie, 1958, Save the Dunes Council, Beverly Shores, Indiana.

51. "1917 Pageant of Dunes Witnessed by 40,000, Stroller Discovers," *The Valparaiso Vidette-Messenger*, 1956. The Stroller was William Ormond Wallace, who under the pen name, James Ormond Norton, likely wrote *The Man With The Funny Name*, a Dan Clevenger Detective Story set in the Dunes. See typewritten manuscript, Westchester Library, Chesterton, Indiana.

52. Sandburg to Douglas, June 27, 1958, Paul Douglas Papers, Chicago Historical Society Manuscript Collections.

53. Mather, *Report*, p. 70.

54. Ibid., p. 39. Italics added.

55. *Indianapolis Star*, December 12, 1946.

Moving Mountains

56. *Chicago Evening Post*, November 6, 1922.

57. *Gary Post*, December 4, 1933.

58. Reuben M. Strong, "Indiana's Unspoiled Dunes," *National Parks Magazine*, August, 1959, p. 7.

59. Bulliet, "Frank V. Dudley." See Reed's etching *Mt. Tom* in *Sketches in Duneland*, p. 24, and Euston's etching *Pines of Duneland from Pageant Blowout, Friends of Our Native Landscape* 2 (Autumn 1945), cover.

60. Edgar Lee Masters, "Perpetuating America's Strangest Work of Nature," *Chicago Herald*, May 27, 1917.

61. Louella Chapin, *Round About Chicago* (Chicago: Unity Publishing Company, 1907), p. 153. Italics added.

62. A. F. Knotts, "The Dunes of Northwestern Indiana," p. 25.

63. Sandburg to Douglas, June 27, 1958.

64. Quoted in Helga Sandburg, "The Walking Hills," *Chicago Tribune Magazine*, June 10, 1962.

65. Quoted in *Gary Daily Tribune*, July 6, 1914.

66. *Indianapolis News*, January 30, 1923.

67. Irwin St. John Tucker, "On the Dunes," Indiana Dunes Scrapbook, Gary Public Library.

68. E. Stillman Bailey, *The Sand Dunes of Indiana* (Chicago: A.C. Mc-Clurg & Co., 1917), pp. 98, 26–27.

69. *Indianapolis News*, July 17, 1916; *Gary Daily Tribune*, July 17, 1916.

70. G. van der Leeuw, *Religion in Essence and Manifestation*, trans. J. E. Turner (London: Allen and Unwin, 1938), p. 55. Also, Eliade: "One of the paradigmatic images of creation is an island suddenly manifesting itself in the midst of the waves." (Eliade, *Sacred and Profane*, p. 30.)

71. Frederick Webster Kirtland, "The Dunes at Gary," Adams, ed., *Duneland Echoes*.

72. James Russell Price, "The Live Sand Dunes," *The Club Messenger* 1 (June 1917): 3.

73. In his later years, Hannell turned increasingly to wood sculpture as a medium better suited to communicate his feeling for growth and movement in the Dunes landscape. Among his pieces are *Surf* and *Growth Forms*. See David Sander, "The Unique Vision of V. M. S. Hannell," *Dunes Country Magazine* 3 (Winter, 1979): 25, 27.

74. Reuben Strong, "The Indiana Dunes Project," *Friends of Our Native Landscape* 11 (Autumn 1953): 5.

75. Masters, "Perpetuating America's Strangest Work."

Creation

76. Edward W. Osann, Jr., *The Dunes Belong to the People*, Save the Dunes Council, 1957, p. 6.

77. Lester, "Orchids and Tumbleweeds."

78. Marjorie Hill Allee, *Ann's Surprising Summer* (Boston and New York: Houghton Mifflin Company, 1933), Foreword.

79. Arnold Mulder, *The Sand Doctor* (Boston: Houghton Mifflin, 1921), p. 292.

80. Laura Fermi, *Atoms in the Family* (Chicago: University of Chicago Press, 1954), p. 329.

81. Samuel A. Harper, *A Hoosier Tramp* (Chicago: The Prairie Club, 1928), p. 27.

82. The hijinks of the Cliff Dwellers' Club at their frequent Dunes parties were also decidedly sexual. Fletcher Seymour tells of one occasion in which a nude model was kept hidden in a box until the opportune moment. See Ralph Fletcher Seymour, *Some Went This Way* (Chicago: Ralph Fletcher Seymour, 1945), p. 165. The Prairie Club regularly celebrated the marriages that began as romances during pilgrimages in the Chicago environs.

83. Webb Waldron and Marion Patton Waldron, *We Explore the Great Lakes* (New York: Century Publishing Co., 1923), p. 250.

84. Ibid., pp. 249, 254.

85. Meyer Levin, *The Old Bunch* (New York: Viking Press, 1937), pp. 212, 235.

86. Thomas Rogers, *At the Shores* (New York: Simon and Schuster, 1980), pp. 14, 123, 137.

87. Van Lesley, "Diana of the Dunes," *Outdoor Indiana* (June/July 1967), p. 13. Also see James B. Lane, *City of the Century* (Bloomington: Indiana University Press, 1978), pp. 20–22.

88. Quoted in Margery Currey, "The Pageant in the Dunes," *The Prairie Club Bulletin,* May 1917.

89. Gary Nabhan, "Diana-Gone-Driftwood Dune Woman," *Great Lakes Review* 3 (Winter, 1977): 82, 89, 88. See also Jeannette Konley, "Song of Diana," *The American Bard,* January, 1958.

90. C. H. Robinson, "The Mysteries of 'Tamarack Swamp,' " *The Flower Grower,* June 1924. Robinson, former editor of the *Western Review,* was a stalwart member of the Prairie Club, and caretaker in the later years at the Beach House. The uncommon variety of wild rose he discovered in the Dunes was named by the American Rose Society in his honor "The Captain Robinson Rose." See C. H. Robinson, "The Sand Dunes of Indiana," *Nature Magazine* 26 (August, 1935): 81–84.

91. *Gary Daily Tribune,* July 17, 1916.

92. Lester, "Orchids and Tumbleweeds."

93. *Prairie Club Bulletin,* April 1921.

The Evolutionary Drama of the Dunes

94. *Hammond Times,* December 29, 1957.

95. *Chesterton Tribune,* July 9, 1914.

96. Mather, *Report,* p. 78. Italics added.

97. Thomas W. Stevens and Alden C. Noble, *The Morning Road* (Chicago: The Blue Sky Press, 1902).

98. Towne, "Earl Reed," p. 8.

99. William S. Blatchley, "A Dune Idyl," in *Boulder Reveries* (Indianapolis: The Nature Publishing Company, 1906), pp. 223–224.

100. Jeannette Vaughan Konley, *Cradled in the Dunelands* (Parkville, Missouri: Park College Press, 1956), p. 12.

101. *Gary Tribune,* June 4, 1931.

102. Charles G. Bell, *Songs for a New America* (Bloomington: Indiana University Press, 1953), p. 18.

103. Mulder, *The Sand Doctor,* p. 317. Italics added.

104. *The Survey* 37 (December 9, 1916): 263.

105. Hu Maxwell, "An Indiana Desert," *Scientific American Supplement* 80 (October 1915): 248.

106. "Why Save the Dunes?" *The Club Messenger* 1 (April 1917): 11.

107. Edwin Way Teale, *The Lost Woods* (New York: Dodd, Mead and Company, 1945), p. 310. See also *Indianapolis News,* April 26, 1946.

108. Teale, *Lost Woods,* p. 308.

109. Ibid., p. 315.

110. Ibid.

111. Pepoon, *Annotated Flora,* p. 107.

112. Ragna Eskil, "Jens Jensen," *Friends of Our Native Landscape* 9 (1951): 2.

113. Interview with Jens Jensen by Eleanor Ellis Perkins, June 14, 1940, Morton Arboretum Library archives.

114. Julian May, *Moving Hills of Sand* (New York: Hawthorn Books, Inc., 1969).

115. Brennan divides his book into two major parts: Part One, entitled "History," and Part Two, entitled "The Wonders of the Dunes." The two partners in the present stage of Dunes succession are thus given equal treat-

ment and constitute separately and together the subject matter of the work. The structure of each section *begins* with an assertion of the geographical and evolutionary centrality of the Dunes region and *concludes* with a discussion of the struggle to preserve the Dunes as a park. What lies *between* the beginning and end of each section is a comprehensive history from the earliest times to the present. Hence, Brennan's first chapter in Part One is devoted to "The Prehistoric People" of the Dunes, his next chapter to "The American Indians," and so on through the several colonial occupations to the present. In Part Two he moves from a description of the glacial epoch through the successive kinds of flora and fauna which inhabited the region, with special reference to those now extinct, and ends with a catalog of living species. The lesson is clear: written in the moving mountains of sand in microcosm is the evolutionary drama of the American continent, and its culmination is the realization of a Dunes park.

116. Carl Sandburg, *Honey and Salt* (New York: Harcourt, Brace and Co., 1963), p. 111. Critic Gay Wilson Allen found "Timesweep" to be the summation of Sandburg's socialist humanism. See Gay Wilson Allen, *Carl Sandburg* (Minneapolis: University of Minnesota Press, 1972), p. 44. A similar statement to that of Sandburg are these lines by the local Gary poet Jeannette Konley:

Behold the drama of abiding hope!
The panoramic hills of loveliness
That rise soft curved, bequeathing in their scope
A heritage that man should ever bless.
Keep forever the enchantment of this gift,
That pilgrims surfeited with worldy strife
There-in find peace; and as the shadows lift
Be one at last, with Universal Life.

(Konley, *Cradled in Dunelands*, p. 70.)

CHAPTER FOUR: THE BIRTHPLACE OF ECOLOGY

America's First Professional Ecologist

1. Interview by the author with Paul Voth, DeKalb, Illinois, March 1979. Cowles's mentors at the University of Chicago also challenged their students' prejudices about the permanence of the physical landscape by references to the "everlasting hills." Thomas Chamberlin wrote that human beings were not yet "fully emancipated from inherited impressions regarding the endurance of rocks and the immutability of the 'everlasting hills,' " and John Merle Coulter and Merle C. Coulter observed that "the 'everlasting hills' may be a phrase true enough when the comparison is with human life, but these same hills were evolved and subsequent evolution will change them." (T. C. Chamberlin, "On Lord Kelvin's Address on the Age of the Earth as an Abode Fitted for Life," in *Smithsonian Report for 1899* [Washington, D.C.: Government Printing Office, 1901], p. 223; John M. Coulter and Merle C. Coulter, *Where Evolution and Religion Meet* [New York: Macmillan Company, 1926], p. 79.)

2. The best biography of Henry C. Cowles is Sarah Gibbard Cook,

"Cowles Bog, Indiana, and Henry Chandler Cowles," Indiana Dunes National Lakeshore, Chesterton, Indiana, 1980.

3. See Donald Worster, *Nature's Economy: The Roots of Ecology* (Garden City, New York: Anchor Books, 1979), pp. 205–253. In 1898 Clements and Roscoe Pound wrote *The Phytogeography of Nebraska*, a work concerned with not only the distribution of plants, but also ecology, "the interrelations of organic elements of this floral covering." Robert P. McIntosh concludes that "Ecology in the United States was, in considerable degree, a product of the Middle West, notably . . . the University of Chicago." (Robert P. McIntosh, "Ecology Since 1900," in *Issues and Ideas in America*, ed. Benjamin J. Taylor and Thurman J. White [Norman, Oklahoma: University of Oklahoma Press, 1976], p. 353.) In addition to Cook, Worster and McIntosh, the following references were consulted for the history of ecology at Chicago: W. C. Allee, Alfred E. Emerson, Orlando Park, Thomas Park, and Karl P. Schmidt, *Principles of Animal Ecology* (Philadelphia and London: W. B. Saunder Company, 1949), pp. 13–72; Robert L. Burgess, "The Ecological Society of America," in Frank N. Egerton and R. P. McIntosh, eds., *History of American Ecology* (New York: Arno Press, 1977); Frank N. Egerton, "Ecological Studies and Observations in America before 1900," in Taylor and White, *Issues in America*; H. A. Gleason, "Twenty-Five Years of Ecology, 1910–1935," *Brooklyn Botanical Gardens Memoirs* 4: 41–49; Paul B. Sears, "Plant Ecology," in J. Evan, ed., *A Short History of Botany in the United States* (New York: Hafner, 1969), pp. 124–131; Paul B. Sears, "Some Notes on the Ecology of Ecologists," *Scientific Monthly* 83 (1956): 22–27.

4. Worster, *Nature's Economy*, p. 208.

5. Cowles studied the humanities, especially Latin and Greek, at Oberlin, edited *The Oberlin Review*, and delivered the Greek oration for his graduating class in 1893.

6. Stephen Mather, *Report on Sand Dunes National Park, Indiana* (Washington, D.C.: Government Printing Office, 1917), p. 43.

7. Gleason, "Twenty-Five Years," p. 42.

8. A. G. Tansley, "The Use and Abuse of Vegetational Concepts and Terms," *Ecology* 16 (1935): 284.

9. See H. C. Cowles, "John Merle Coulter," *The Botanical Gazette* 87 (1929): 211–217; Andrew Denny Rodgers III, *John Merle Coulter: Missionary in Science* (Princeton: Princeton University Press, 1944).

10. Charles J. Chamberlain, "Henry Chandler Cowles," speech apparently presented at Cowles's retirement, typewritten copy in possession of Dr. Paul Voth, p. 9.

11. Worster, *Nature's Economy*, p. 199. The following description of Warming's treatise is in paraphrase of Worster, pp. 198–202.

12. Ibid., p. 202.

13. Jerry S. Olson, "Rates of Succession and Soil Changes on Southern Lake Michigan Sand Dunes," *Botanical Gazette* 119 (1958): 125.

14. Rodgers, *John Merle Coulter*, p. 36.

15. Henry C. Cowles, "The Ecological Relations of the Vegetation on the Sand Dunes of Lake Michigan," *Botanical Gazette* 27 (May, 1899): 388.

16. Henry C. Cowles, "The Plant Societies of Chicago and Vicinity," *Bulletin of the Geographic Society of Chicago*, No. 2 (Chicago: The Geographic Society of Chicago), p. 75.

Plant Succession in the Dunes
17. Cowles, "The Ecological Relations of the Vegetation on the Sand Dunes of Lake Michigan," *Botanical Gazette* 27, Nos. 2, 3, 4, 5 (February, March, April, May 1899), 95–117, 167–202, 281–302, 361–391; "The Physiographic Ecology of Chicago and Vicinity; A Study of the Origin, Development, and Classification of Plant Societies," *Botanical Gazette* 31, Nos. 2, 3 (March, April 1901), 73–108, 145–182; "The Causes of Vegetative Cycles," *The Botanical Gazette* 51 (March, 1911): 161–183.

18. Cowles, "Ecological Relations," p. 95.
19. Ibid., p. 96.
20. Ibid., pp. 97, 95, 386.   22. Ibid., p. 195.
21. Ibid., p. 112.   23. Ibid., p. 302.
24. Cowles, "Physiographic Ecology of Chicago," pp. 73, 79, 81, 81.
25. Cowles, "The Causes of Vegetative Cycles," p. 179.
26. Ibid., p. 182.
27. Quoted in Worster, *Nature's Economy*, p. 211.
28. Ibid., p. 214. Clements and Pound studied Spencer's *Principles of Biology*, and as late as 1929 Clements cited Spencer as the primary support for his organismic theory.
29. Coulter, Barnes and Cowles, *Textbook of Botany for Colleges and Universities*, 2 vols. (New York, Cincinnati: American Book Company, 1910–1911), vol. 2, p. 485.
30. Sears, "Some Notes," p. 25.
31. See George D. Fuller, "Evaporation and Soil Moisture in Relation to the Succession of Plant Associations," *Botanical Gazette* 58 (1914): 193–234; "Post-Glacial Vegetation of the Lake Michigan Region," *Ecology* 16 (July 1935): 473–487.
32. Gleason, "Twenty-Five Years," p. 45.
33. See Larry Waldron, "A Conversation with Jerry Olson," *Singing Sands Almanac* 3 (November–December 1980): 2.
34. Jerry S. Olson, "Rates of Succession and Soil Changes on Southern Lake Michigan Sand Dunes," *Botanical Gazette* 119 (March 1958): 166. Olson completed his Ph.D. thesis, "Vegetation-Substrate Relationship in Lake Michigan Sand Dune Development," in 1951 under the direction of Fuller and Olmsted. His work was later summarized in four articles: see above, and "Lake Michigan Dune Development," *Journal of Geology* 66 (January–November 1958): 254–263, 345–352, 472–483.
35. Olson, "Rates of Succession," p. 167.

An Ecological Social Gospel
36. Henry Chandler Cowles, "Interactions Between Plants and Their Environment," in H. H. Newman, ed., *The Nature of the World and of Man* (Chicago: The University of Chicago Press, 1926), p. 303.
37. Sears, "Some Notes," p. 24.

38. Karl Patterson Schmidt, "Warder Clyde Allee, 1885–1955," *Biographical Memoirs of the National Academy of Sciences* 30 (1957): 16.

39. In 1909 Cowles wrote of a trip to Starved Rock: "He who returns to the city takes back something never to be lost; the strength of the cliffs, and the beauty of the trees have become a part of his being for all time." (Henry C. Cowles, *Picturesque Savanna* [Chicago: Chicago, Milwaukee and St. Paul Railway, 1909], p. 15).

40. The July, 1935 issue of *Ecology* was dedicated to Cowles. W. S. Cooper wrote: "Something more than mere respect for high scientific attainment is necessary to account for the fact that, when the plan of this special number of *Ecology* was made public, more than three hundred persons responded. With almost every contribution came a letter expressing admiration for Cowles as a scientist, as a teacher, and above all, as a man. These facts speak for themselves; formal tribute is superfluous. And yet, merely because it is a joy to do so, we make mention of a few of his many lovable traits—his unfailing good humor, his far-famed ability in telling a story, his readiness to give ungrudgingly of his time and effort in the service of students and friends, his eagerness to discover and commend whatever was meritorious in the work of a fellow scientist or admirable in the man himself." (William S. Cooper, "Henry Chandler Cowles," *Ecology* 16 [July 1935]: 283.)

41. Sears, "Some Notes," p. 25.

42. Henry C. Cowles, "A Fifteen-Year Study of Advancing Sand Dunes," *Report of the Eighty-First Meeting of the British Association for the Advancement of Science* (London: John Murray, 1912), p. 565.

43. "The International Phytogeographic Excursion in the British Isles. Impressions of the Foreign Members of the Party," *The New Phytologist* 11 (January 1912): 26.

44. See George Damon Fuller, *The International Phytogeographic Excursion in America, 1913: The Vegetation of the Chicago Region* (Chicago: July 31, 1913), 17 pp.; Henry C. Cowles, *International Phytogeographic Excursion Program,* "First Section—New York to Lincoln" (Chicago: July 24, 1913), 16 pp. The tour included Dr. H. Brockmann-Jerosch, Frau Dr. Marie Brockmann-Jerosch (Zurich), Professor Engler (Berlin), Dr. Ove Paulsen (Copenhagen), Dr. Edward Rubel (Zurich), Professor C. Schroter (Zurich), Dr. T. J. Stomps (Amsterdam), Mr. A. G. Tansley, Mrs. Tansley (Cambridge), Professor C. von Tubeuf (Munich).

45. A. G. Tansley, "International Phytogeographic Excursion in America, 1913," *The New Phytologist* 12 (November–December 1913): 324.

46. Sears, "Some Notes," p. 25.

47. H. C. Cowles, "The Economic Trend in Botany," *Science* 41 (February 12, 1915): 226.

48. Cowles was president of the Association of American Geographers in 1910, of Section G of the American Association for the Advancement of Science in 1913 (after completing a five-year term as secretary, 1907–1912), of the Ecological Society in 1917, of the Botanical Society of America in 1922, of the Chicago Academy of Sciences for some years beginning in 1923, and of the Phytological and Ecological Section of the Fifth International Botanical Congress, Cambridge, England, in 1930. His presidential address before the Association of American Geographers in 1911 was considered "of such

importance that it alone justified the forming of that organization." (Charles C. Adams and George D. Fuller, "Henry Chandler Cowles, "Physiographic Plant Ecologist," *Annals of the Association of American Geographers* 30 [1940]: 40.)

49. H. C. Cowles, "Conservation of Our Forests," *Transactions of the Illinois Academy of Science* 5 (1912): 49. Cowles was credited by his colleagues with doing as much as any other to create the Cook County forest preserve system, and he contributed greatly to the establishment of the Illinois state park system, especially Starved Rock State Park. See Adams and Fuller, "Cowles," p. 42.

50. Douglas G. Sprugal, "A 'Pedagogical Genealogy' of American Plant Ecologists," *Bulletin of the Ecological Society of America* 61 (December 1980): 197–200. Honorable Beatrice E. Willard, "What the Indiana Dunes Means to Ecology," n.d., 13-page mimeograph, Indiana Dunes National Lakeshore Science archives. "As to animal ecology, it may fairly be said to be an offspring in this country of Cowles's work on plant communities and successions." (Sears, "Plant Ecology," p. 129.) "Ecology was the prime motivating force in my becoming a biologist." (Letter of James D. Watson to J. Ronald Engel, April 16, 1982.)

51. Mather, *Report*, p. 43.

52. Ibid., p. 44. In his 1899 monograph Cowles identified the diverse physical conditions responsible for the diverse flora of the Dunes, noting that "The ecological factors thus far mentioned act together harmoniously and produce a striking composite effect upon the vegetation." (Cowles, "Ecological Relations," p. 109.)

53. Ibid., p. 45.

54. Cowles, *Phytogeographic Excursion Program*, p. 11.

55. John O. Bowers, "Salvation of Dunes Depends on Action to Prevent More Havoc," *Gary Evening Post*, April 16, 1917.

56. E. Stillman Bailey, *The Sand Dunes of Indiana* (Chicago: A. C. McClurg & Co., 1917), p. 156.

57. George A. Brennan, *The Wonders of the Dunes* (Indianapolis: Bobbs-Merrill, 1923), p. 145.

58. May Theilgaard Watts, *Reading the Landscape of America* (New York: Macmillan Publishing Co., 1957), p. 74. The island at the center of Cowles Bog stands five feet above the surrounding area from the pressure of a spring mire underneath.

59. See Jean Komaiko and Norma Schaeffer, *Doing the Dunes* (Beverly Shores, Indiana: Dunes Enterprises, 1973), p. 28.

60. Lieber to Cowles, April 1, 1929, Director's Correspondence 1919–1933, Department of Conservation, Archives Division, Indiana Commission on Public Records, Indianapolis, Indiana.

A New Earth

61. George D. Fuller, "The Plant Communities of the Dunes," *The Scientific Monthly* 38 (May, 1934): 444.

62. Ibid., p. 445.

63. See R. A. F. Penrose, Jr., "The Early Days of the Department of Geology at the University of Chicago," *Journal of Geology* 37 (May–June 1929): 293–319.

64. In 1916 Chamberlin wrote: "It is our personal view that what we conveniently regard as merely material is at the same time spiritual, that what we try to reduce to the mechanistic is at the same time volitional, but whether this be so or not, the emergence of what we call the living from the inorganic, and the emergence of what we call the psychic from the physiologic, were at once the transcendent and transcendental features of the earth's evolution." (Thomas C. Chamberlin, *The Origin of the Earth* [Chicago: University of Chicago Press, 1916], pp. 261–262.)

65. Bailey Willis, "Thomas Chrowder Chamberlin (1843–1928)," *The Smithsonian Report for 1929* (Washington, D.C.: Smithsonian Institution, 1929), p. 586. Also see Rollin Thomas Chamberlin, "Biographical Memoir of Thomas C. Chamberlin, 1843–1928," *National Academy of Sciences Biographical Memoirs* (Washington, D.C.: National Academy of Sciences, 1934), pp. 307–407; George L. Collie and Hiram D. Densmore, *Thomas C. Chamberlin and Rollin D. Salisbury, a Beloit College Partnership* (Evansville, Wisconsin: The Antes Press, 1932).

66. See William C. Alden, "Thomas Chrowder Chamberlin's Contributions to Glacial Geology," *Journal of Geology* 37 (May–June 1929): 293–319.

67. Rollin Chamberlin, "Biographical Memoir," p. 345.

68. Chamberlin, *Origin of the Earth*, p. 1.

69. Chamberlin wrote at the conclusion of *The Origin of the Earth*: "Perhaps the supreme criterion to which a hypothesis of the genesis of the earth, of the mode of its growth, and of the evolution of its inhabitants can be submitted . . . is the fitness and adequacy of its postulates for the task of maintaining, throughout all the earth's adolescent and adult stages, those delicate conditions that have made possible the long sequence of life and its wonderful ascent." (Chamberlin, *Origin of the Earth*, p. 261.) Chamberlin's ultimate concern was not for the fidelity of the earth, however, but for the fidelity of man. At the conclusion of the *Geology*, he noted that the re-peopling of the lands laid waste by the last ice incursions had taken the form of an invasion. The result has been the degradation of the land and the extinction of flora and fauna, to a degree never before seen on the face of the earth. "Man's control has not thus far been characterized by much recognition of the complicated interrelations of organisms and of the consequences of disturbing the balance in the organic kingdom, and he is reaping, and is certain to reap more abundantly, the unfortunate fruits of ignorant and careless action. For the greater part man has been guided by immediate considerations, and even these not always controlled by much intelligence, while great wantonness has attended his destruction of both plant and animal life." Yet Chamberlin thought he saw a more intelligent and sympathetic attitude emerging. (Thomas C. Chamberlin and Rollin Salisbury, *Geology*, 3 vols. [New York: Henry Holt and Co., 1904, 1906], 3: 542.)

70. Rollin Chamberlin, "Biographical Memoir," p. 393; T. C. Chamberlin, *Origin of the Earth*, p. 261.

71. Elliot R. Downing, *A Naturalist in the Great Lakes Region* (Chicago: The University of Chicago Press, 1922), pp. 88–89.

72. Mather, *Report*, pp. 32, 34, 33.

73. Rollin D. Salisbury and William C. Alden, *The Geography of Chicago and Its Environs* (Chicago: The Geographic Society of Chicago, Bulletin No. 1, 1899, revised, 1920), p. 1.

74. George Babcock Cressey, *The Indiana Sand Dunes and Shorelines of the Lake Michigan Basin* (Chicago: The Geographic Society of Chicago, Bulletin No. 8, 1928), p. 25.

75. Ibid., p. 24.

76. Mather, *Report*, p. 47.

77. *Compton's Pictured Newspaper*, May 1926. See also *Gary Post*, December 7, 1922.

78. Interview of author with Ragna Eskil, August 1, 1981.

The Beginnings of Animal Ecology

79. Salisbury and Alden, *Geography of Chicago*, p. 47.

80. Victor Shelford, "Ecological Succession. II. Pond Fishes," *Biological Bulletin* 21 (August, 1911): 128.

81. V. E. Shelford, "Preliminary Note on the Distribution of the Tiger Beetle (Cicindela) and Its Relation to Plant Succession," *Biological Bulletin* 14 (1907): 9. Shelford's Ph.D. dissertation at Chicago (1907) was entitled "Life-Histories and Larval Habits of the Tiger Beetles," and reported in *Journal of the Linnean Society of London* 30 (1908): 157–184.

82. Victor E. Shelford, "Ecological Succession. I. Stream Fishes and the Method of Physiographic Analysis. II. Pond Fishes," *Biological Bulletin* 21 (1911): 9–35, 127–151, "Ecological Succession. III. A Reconnaissance of Its Causes in Ponds with Particular Reference to Fish," *Biological Bulletin* 22 (1911): 1–38. By 1911 Shelford had mapped and catalogued the ponds and ridges of the Calumet region in detail. They consisted of a series of between seventy-five and one hundred sand ridges and ponds nearly parallel with the lakeshore. The ridges had an average width of about one hundred feet. The ponds, somewhat narrower, were on the average several miles long, and varied in depth in the course of the year from a few inches to four or five feet. With the help of George Fuller, he made a detailed inventory of the plants at the center and margin of each of the first twenty-four ponds.

83. Victor E. Shelford, *Animal Communities in Temperate America* (Chicago: University of Chicago Press, 1913), p. 33. In 1914 Shelford conceived the idea of writing a similar treatise covering all North America. This dream was realized with the publication of *The Ecology of North America* (Urbana, Illinois: University of Illinois Press, 1963).

84. Shelford, "Pond Fishes," p. 146.

85. Shelford, *Animal Communities*, p. 33.

86. In 1939 Clements and Shelford proposed that plants and animals should be included together in discussions of the super-organism created through succession. See Frederic Clements and Victor Shelford, *Bio-Ecology* (New York: Wiley, 1939).

87. Shelford, *Animal Communities*, p. 7.

88. Ibid., p. 308.

89. See Schmidt, "Warder Clyde Allee," pp. 3–40.

90. W. C. Allee, "Seasonal Succession in Old Forest Ponds," *Transactions of the Illinois Academy of Science* 4 (1911): 131.

91. W. C. Allee, "An Experimental Analysis of the Relation Between Physiological States and Rheotaxis in Isopods," *The Journal of Experimental Zoology* 13 (August 1912): 342.

92. W. C. Allee, *The Social Life of Animals* (Boston: Beacon Press, 1938, revised edition, 1951), p. 6.

93. Allee, "An Experimental Analysis," p. 282.

94. Allee, *Social Life*, p. 7.

95. See Amy Winslow, "Marjorie Hill Allee, 1890–1945," *The Horn Book Magazine*, May–June 1946. In 1923 the Allees' son was killed and during the 1930s, W. C. Allee became paralyzed from the waist down by operations for a spinal tumor. Marjorie Hill Allee was active in the League of Women Voters and the Settlement League of the university.

96. Marjorie Hill Allee, *The Great Tradition* (Boston and New York: Houghton Mifflin Company, 1937), p. 19.

97. Ibid., pp. 51, 52, 54.

98. W. C. Allee, "The Biology of Peace," *The Quaker* 1 (1920): 39–41; "The Biology of Disarmament," *The Quaker* 2 (1921): 173–174.

99. W. C. Allee, "Animal Aggregations: A Request for Information," *The Condor* 25 (1923): 129–131.

100. W. C. Allee, "Studies in Animal Aggregations: Causes and Effects of Bunching in Land Isopods," *Journal of Experimental Zoology* 45 (1926): 255–277.

101. Marjorie Hill Allee, *The Great Tradition*, p. 132.

102. W. C. Allee, "Studies in Animal Aggregations: Natural Aggregations of the Isopod, *Asellus communis*," *Ecology* 10 (January 1929): 31, 22.

103. W. C. Allee, *Animal Aggregations: A Study in General Sociology* (Chicago: The University of Chicago Press, 1931), p. 198. "A part of the difficulties we have encountered in discussing the role of different types of animal aggregations in the evolution of social groupings may be avoided if we recognize that there are many levels of social organization and that these overlap. Among the groups which we may fairly call 'social' there are: (1) those that show their social habit merely through the toleration of the close proximity of other similar individuals in the same restricted space—these may exist without any positive mutual attraction and may be called the toleration level; (2) those that form groups which react more or less definitely as units—the group integration level; (3) those which show physiological division of labor; finally (4) those that show morphologically distinct castes, each associated with some phase of the division of labor. The animals on the higher planes of social development continue to show the group attributes characteristic of the lower levels. Survival values have been demonstrated throughout this whole series and extend well below the toleration social level to the threshold of primitive life." (Ibid., p. 350.)

The Cooperative Commonwealth

104. Ibid., pp. 360, 355.

105. Ibid., p. 361.

106. Ibid., p. 362.

107. Allee et al., *Principles of Animal Ecology*, p. 54. The work is frequently referred to as AEPPS after the authors' initials.

108. See, for example, Robert Park, Ernest Burgess, and Roderick McKenzie, *The City* (Chicago: The University of Chicago Press, 1925). See also Worster, *Nature's Economy*, pp. 362–382 for the influence of the AEPPS group.

109. See Charles C. Adams, "The Relation of General Ecology to Human Ecology," *Ecology* 16 (1935): 316–335.

110. Robert Redfield, ed., *Levels of Integration in Biological and Social Systems* (Lancaster, Pa.: The Jacques Cattell Press, 1942).

111. W. C. Allee, "Human Conflicts and Cooperation: The Biological Background," in L. Bryson, L. Finkelstein, and R. M. MacIver, eds., *Approaches to National Unity. Fifth Symposium of the Conference on Science, Philosophy and Religion* (New York: Harper and Bros., 1945), p. 358.

112. W. C. Allee, "Where Angels Fear to Tread: A Contribution from General Sociology to Human Ethics," *Science* 97 (June 11, 1943): 517.

113. Ibid., p. 524.

114. Ibid., p. 520.   116. Ibid., p. 521.

115. Ibid., pp. 518, 519.   117. Ibid., p. 522.

118. See Zonia Baber, *Peace Symbols* (Chicago: Women's International League for Peace and Freedom, n.d.); T. C. Chamberlin, "World-Organization After the World War—an Omninational Confederation," *Journal of Geology* 26 (November–December 1918): 1–27.

119. Sears, "Some Notes," p. 22.

CHAPTER FIVE: HEARTH FIRES

At Home in the Universe

1. Thomas Wood Stevens, *Book of the Historical Pageant of the Dunes* (Chicago: Dunes Pageant Association, 1917), p. 15.

2. Mircea Eliade, *Sacred and Profane* (New York: Harcourt Brace Jovanovich, 1959), p. 53. Also see Joseph Rykwert, *On Adam's House in Paradise* (New York: Museum of Modern Art, 1972).

3. George Brennan, *Wonder of the Dunes* (Indianapolis: Bobbs-Merrill Co., 1923), frontispiece.

4. In American history the image of humanity "at home in the universe" is associated with the religious tradition which runs from Jonathan Edwards through Emerson to William James. William Clebsch calls this "distinctly American" religion "esthetic spirituality," and defines it as that response to the world which finds it "fundamentally hospitable to the human spirit" because of its "invitations to and gifts of harmony." (William Clebsch, *American Religious Thought* [Chicago: University of Chicago Press, 1973], pp. xvi, xvii.)

5. Earl H. Reed, *Sketches in Duneland* (New York: John Lane Company, 1918), p. 37.

6. Samuel Harper, *A Hoosier Tramp* (Chicago: The Prairie Club, 1928), p. 42.

7. Ibid., pp. 44, 45, 49.

8. In 1967 Mrs. Dudley, at the age of 96, tried with others to preserve the cabin of rough hewn logs, with its large stone fireplace and huge windows designed "to bring the dunes indoors," as a state memorial. *Chicago Tribune*, September 3, 1967.

9. Irma R. Frankenstein, *Chronicle of the Befogged Dune Bugs* (Michigan City: Tri-State Litho Printing Co., 1958).

10. Ibid.

11. Marjorie Hill Allee, *Ann's Surprising Summer* (Boston and New York: Houghton Mifflin Company, 1933), pp. 19, 21.

12. David Sander, "The Dunes, a Personal Reminiscence," *The Northern Indiana Dunes Review* 1 (April 1966): 3.

13. Arnold Mulder, *The Sand Doctor* (Boston: Houghton Mifflin Company, 1921). See Arnold Mulder, "William Morris's Socialism: An Artist's Revolt" (M.A. thesis, University of Chicago, 1910).

14. Ibid., p. 8.

15. Ibid., p. 184.

Feudal Fires

16. In the Greek myth, fire is stolen by Prometheus from Zeus and given to mankind. Afterward, Prometheus is punished for it. In the Dunes Pageant myth, the divine Creator of fire, Nanabozho, struggles to make it available to the world. For the pastoral design, see Leo Marx, *The Machine in the Garden* (New York: Oxford University Press, 1964).

17. See Mircea Eliade, *Myths, Rites, Symbols: A Mircea Eliade Reader,* Wendell Beane and William Doty, eds., 2 vols. (New York: Harper and Row, 1974) 1: 185 ff; Gerardus van der Leeuw, *Religion in Essence and Manifestation* (Gloucester, Mass.: Peter Smith, 1967), 1: 60 ff.

18. *Gary Post-Tribune*, October 27, 1919.

19. *Gary Dune Park Post*, April 16, 1917.

20. John O. Bowers, "Dream Cities of the Calumet," in John O. Bowers, Arthur G. Taylor, and Sam B. Woods, eds., *History of Lake County* (Gary: Calumet Press, 1929), 10:198.

21. Harriet Monroe, *Poets and Their Art* (New York: Macmillan Co., 1926), p. 237.

22. Louis Sullivan, *The Testament of Stone*, Maurice English, ed. (Evanston: Northwestern University Press, 1963), p. 134.

23. Donald Culross Peattie, *Journey Into America* (Boston: Houghton Mifflin Company, 1943), p. 124.

24. Interview by the author with Gladys Rizer, Chesterton, Indiana, July 19, 1981.

25. Marjorie Allee, *Ann's Surprising Summer*, pp. 32–33.

26. Mulder, *The Sand Doctor*, p. 119.

27. Carl Sandburg, *Always the Young Strangers* (New York: Harcourt, Brace, 1953), p. 379.

28. Carl Sandburg, "They Will Say," *Complete Poems* (New York: Harcourt, Brace, 1950), p. 5.

29. Carl Sandburg, "Smoke and Steel," *Complete Poems*, p. 152.

30. Earl H. Reed, *Sketches in Jacobia* (Chicago: Privately Printed, 1919), and *The Ghost in the Tower: An Episode in Jacobia* (Chicago: privately printed, 1921).

31. Reed, *Ghost in the Tower*, pp. 59, 61.

32. The version of Pokagon's life known to the early Dunes movement is found in Simon Pokagon, *Queen of the Woods* (Hartford, Michigan: C. H. Engle, Publisher, 1899). The authoritative version of the Pokagon story is Cecilia Bain Buechner, *The Pokagons* (Indianapolis: Indiana Historical Society Publications, 1933), vol. 10.

33. In the Algonquin language group of which the Potawatomi are part, "Puttawa" means to blow on a fire, and "mi" is a suffix meaning nation. There is a legend common to Potawatomi, Chippewa, and Ottawa which says the three tribes were once one. When they agreed to go separate ways, the Potawatomi were charged with keeping the council fire. Modern Potawatomi wear T-shirts that say "Fire People." See Brennan, *Wonders of the Dunes*, p. 111; John Dean Caton, *The Last of the Illinois* (Chicago: Fergus Printing Co., 1876), p. 164; Ruth Landes, *The Prairie Potawatomi* (Madison: University of Wisconsin Press, 1970), p. 17.

34. Quoted in R. A. Frederick, "Colonel Richard Lieber, Conservationist and Park Builder: The Indiana Years" (Ph.D. diss., Indiana University, 1960), p. 240.

35. Buechner, *The Pokagons*, pp. 332, 333. Pokagon's protest was especially effective because sand from the Indiana Dunes was used as fill for the 1893 Fair. A statue commemorating Pokagon was proposed for Jackson Park, and a song composed by Pokagon was adopted by Ray Public School in Hyde Park.

36. Stephen Mather, *Report on the Proposed Sand Dunes National Park, Indiana* (Washington, D.C.: Government Printing Office, 1917), p. 97.

37. Frederick, "Richard Lieber," p. 44.

38. Edwin Way Teale, *Journey Into Summer* (New York: Dodd, Mead and Co., 1960), p. 68.

39. Newsletter, Save the Dunes Council, October, 1972.

40. Julia Cooley Altrocchi, *Wolves Against the Moon* (New York: Macmillan Company, 1940). Altrocchi spent thirty summers in the Dune Country, northeast of the old Bailly trading post, beginning in 1910. She acknowledges her debt to George Brennan and Earl H. Reed, Jr., for her interest in the Bailly Homestead. See also John O. Bowers, *The Old Bailly Homestead* (Gary, Indiana: n.p., 1922).

41. Altrocchi, *Wolves Against the Moon*, p. 387. At the end of his life, Bailly platted "Baillytown" at the mouth of the Grand Calumet River in what is now Marquette Park, Gary, Indiana.

42. Robert Herrick, *The Gospel of Freedom* (New York: Macmillan and Company, 1898), p. 101. For the growth of Chicago as a completely manmade environment, see John B. Jackson, *American Space: The Centennial Years, 1865–1876* (New York: W.W. Norton and Co., 1972), p. 72 ff.

43. Brennan, *Wonders of the Dunes*, p. 128.

Jens Jensen: The Council Fire

44. The following description of the council fire is drawn from Jens Jensen, "The Camp Fire or Council Fire," in Emma Doeserich and Mary Sherburne, eds., *Outdoors with the Prairie Club* (Chicago: Paquin Publishers, 1941), pp. 352–355; Jens Jensen, "Natural Parks and Gardens," *Saturday Evening Post*, March 8, 1930; Lester Pottenger, "The Council Ring as Jensen Sees It," *Vistas*, University of Wisconsin, 1938; "Minutes," Board of Directors, Jens Jensen Centennial Meeting, June 10, 1960, Jensen Papers, Morton Arboretum Library.

45. Jensen to Mrs. T. J. Knudson, February 10, 1936, Jensen Papers, Morton Arboretum Library.

46. Jens Jensen, *Siftings* (Chicago: Ralph Fletcher Seymour, 1956), p. 111.

47. See Leonard K. Eaton, *Landscape Artist in America: The Life and Work of Jens Jensen* (Chicago: University of Chicago Press, 1974), pp. 42–45.

48. Doeserich, *Outdoors with the Prairie Club*, p. 93.

49. Interview of the author with Ragna Eskil, July, 1981, Chicago.

50. Louise B. Lemon, "The Pilgrimage to the Fallen Leaf," *Our Native Landscape* 2 (1929). Another description of a fall council fire held in the Dunes, this one devoted to a memorial service for Enos Mills, is given in the *Chicago Evening Post*, November 6, 1922.

51. Ibid., p. 7.

52. Jensen to Miss Emma Doeserich, September 14, 1928, Prairie Club archives, Chicago, Illinois.

53. Louise B. Lemon, "The Dune Shelter," *Our Native Landscape* 3 (1930).

54. See Doeserich, *Outdoors with the Prairie Club*, pp. 96–97; *Chicago Daily News*, July 6, 1914; Susan D. Windesheim, "Jens Jensen as a Planner" (M.A. thesis, Illinois Institute of Technology, Chicago, 1975).

55. Jensen, *Siftings*, p. 84.

56. Jensen to R. Alice Drought, June 16, 1932, Morton Arboretum Library archives. Jensen bought the first piece of land for the Clearing in 1919. See Mertha Fulkerson, *The Story of the Clearing* (Chicago: Coach House Press, 1972), and Jens Jensen, *The Clearing: A Way of Life* (Chicago: Ralph Fletcher Seymour, 1949).

Peattie and Teale: Nostalgia Americana

57. See Edwin Way Teale, *A Walk Through the Year* (New York: Dodd, Mead and Company, 1978), p. 90; Donald Culross Peattie, *The Road of a Naturalist* (New York: Houghton Mifflin Company, 1941), p. 9. Peattie and Teale studied the nineteenth-century naturalists and worked to make their writings available to the public. See Donald Culross Peattie, *Green Laurels, the Lives and Achievements of the Great Naturalists* (New York: Simon and Schuster, 1936), and *Singing in the Wilderness, a Salute to Audubon* (New York: G. P. Putnam's Sons, 1935). Teale edited the works of Audubon, Thoreau, Fabre, and Hudson, all with Dodd, Mead and Company. His anthology, *The Wilderness World of John Muir*, was published by Houghton Mifflin in 1955. Peattie distinguishes himself from the romantic nature writers in *The Road of a Naturalist* and *An Almanac for Moderns* (New York: G. P. Putnam's, 1935). Teale is less explicit but John Conron characterizes him as a major portrayer of twentieth-century symbiotic landscapes in *The American Landscape* (New York: Oxford University Press, 1973), pp. 477–482, 497.

58. Peattie, *Road of a Naturalist*, pp. 109–122.

59. Ibid., p. 115.

60. Donald C. Peattie, *Blown Leaves* (Chicago: University of Chicago School of Education Print Shop, 1916), p. 19.

61. Edwin Way Teale, *Dune Boy, The Early Years of a Naturalist* (New York: Dodd, Mead and Company, 1943). Frederick Breed describes a trip to the farm in the company of artist Vin Hannell in "Sand-hill Sketches," *University of Chicago Magazine* 37 (February, 1945): 10–11, 16.

62. Teale, *Dune Boy*, p. 2.

63. Ibid., p. 24.

64. Peattie, *Road of a Naturalist*, p. 122.
65. Edwin Way Teale, *The Lost Woods* (New York: Dodd, Mead and Company, 1945), pp. 3, 5.
66. Peattie, *Journey Into America*, pp. 8, 88. See also *Road of a Naturalist*, p. 62, where Peattie describes watching a Jewish schoolmate being beaten, and his reluctance to tell his parents because they believed so deeply in democracy.
67. Donald Culross Peattie, *Flora of the Indiana Dunes* (Chicago: Field Museum, 1930).
68. Edwin Way Teale, *Dune Boy*, Lone Oak Edition (New York: Dodd, Mead and Company, 1957).
69. Edwin Way Teale, *A Naturalist Buys an Old Farm* (New York: Dodd, Mead and Company, 1974).
70. Edwin Way Teale, *Autumn Across America* (New York: Dodd, Mead and Company, 1950), p. 79.
71. Quoted in William Peeples, "The Indiana Dunes and Pressure Politics," *The Atlantic Monthly*, February, 1963, p. 88.
72. Donald Culross Peattie, "A Breath of Outdoors," *Chicago Daily News*, September 14, 1937.
73. See Donald Culross Peattie, *An Almanac for Moderns* (New York: G. P. Putnam's, 1935), *A Book of Hours* (New York: G. P. Putnam's Sons, 1937), *This is Living* (New York: Dodd, Mead and Company, 1938); Edwin Way Teale, *Circle of the Seasons* (New York: Dodd, Mead and Company, 1953), *Days Without Time* (New York: Dodd, Mead and Company, 1948), *A Walk Through the Year* (New York: Dodd, Mead and Company, 1978), *The American Seasons*, 4 vols. (New York: Dodd, Mead and Company, 1976).
74. Teale, *Circle of the Seasons*, p. 160. On Teale's obsession with memory, see Edward H. Dodd, Jr., *Of Nature, Time and Teale* (New York: Dodd, Mead and Company, 1960).
75. *Chicago Daily News*, November 13, 1960.
76. Peattie, *The Road of a Naturalist*, p. 5.
77. Teale, *Circle of the Seasons*, p. 24.
78. Douglas to Teale, July 22, 1958, Paul H. Douglas Papers, Chicago Historical Society Manuscript Collections.

The Sandburgs: A House with Windows to the World
79. "Minutes," Save the Dunes Council, June 22, 1962, Beverly Shores, Indiana.
80. Helga Sandburg, *The Unicorns* (New York: Dial Press, 1965), p. 70.
81. See Helga Sandburg, "The Walking Hills," *Chicago Sunday Tribune Magazine*, June 10, 1962.
82. Ibid.
83. Helga Sandburg, *The Owl's Roost* (New York: The Dial Press, 1962).
84. Helga Sandburg, "Great Lake of My Childhood," *The Unicorns*, p. 88.
85. Carl Sandburg, "The Harbor," *The Complete Poems*, p. 5. See Richard Crowder, *Carl Sandburg* (New York: Twayne Publishers, 1964), p. 24.
86. Carl Sandburg, *The Letters of Carl Sandburg*, Herbert Mitgang, ed. (New York: Harcourt, Brace and World, 1968), p. 61.

87. For biographies of Carl Sandburg and Lillian Steichen, and critical studies of Sandburg's work pertinent to this discussion, see: Gay Wilson Allen, *Carl Sandburg* (Minneapolis: University of Minnesota Press, 1972); Roy P. Basler, "Your Friend the Poet—Carl Sandburg," *Midway* 10 (Autumn, 1969): 3–15; North Callahan, *Carl Sandburg: Lincoln of Our Literature* (New York: New York University Press, 1970); Oscar Cargill, "Carl Sandburg: Crusader and Mystic," *College English* 2 (April, 1950): 365–372; Karl Detzer, *Carl Sandburg* (New York: Harcourt, Brace and Company, 1951); Hazel Durnell, *The America of Carl Sandburg* (Washington, D.C.: The University Press, 1965); W. G. Rogers, *Carl Sandburg, Yes* (New York: Harcourt Brace Jovanovich, 1970).

88. Carl Sandburg, *Home Front Memo* (New York: Harcourt, Brace and Company, 1942), p. 154.

89. Carl Sandburg, "Letter," *Geneva Progress*, Geneva, Indiana, July 24, 1959, p. 1. Sandburg wrote a long personal letter to the one tiny newspaper in Indiana that supported Douglas's campaign for a Dunes park.

90. Quoted in Lennox Bouton Grey, "Chicago and 'The Great American Novel'" (Ph.D. dissertation, University of Chicago, 1935), p. 27.

91. Callahan, *Sandburg*, p. 129.

92. Carl Sandburg, *Abraham Lincoln: The Prairie Years*, 2 vols. (New York: Harcourt Brace and Company, 1926), 1:15.

93. Ibid., vol. 2, p. 235.

94. Carl Sandburg, *Abraham Lincoln: The War Years*, 4 vols. (New York: Harcourt, Brace and Company, 1939), vol. 4, p. 355.

95. Sandburg, "The People, Yes," *Complete Poems*, pp. 439–617.

96. Ibid., pp. 452–453.

97. Ibid., p. 443.
98. Ibid., p. 509.
99. Ibid., p. 590.
100. Ibid., p. 593.
101. Ibid., p. 617.
102. Ibid.

Paul Douglas: Where Antaeus Retouched the Earth

103. Paul H. Douglas, *In the Fullness of Time, The Memoirs of Paul H. Douglas* (New York: Harcourt Brace Jovanovich, 1971), p. 3. For the following sketch, also see Jerry M. Anderson, "Paul H. Douglas: Insurgent Senate Spokesman for Human Causes, 1949–1963," (Ph.D. diss., Michigan State University, 1964).

104. Ibid., p. 9.

105. Ibid., pp. 12, 8.
106. Ibid., p. 17.

107. Douglas completed the M.A. at Columbia in 1915, where he was influenced by John Dewey and Charles Beard. In 1923 he received the Ph.D. in economics from Columbia. In 1923 he was also appointed associate professor at the University of Chicago, and in 1925, professor, a position he held until election to the Senate in 1948.

108. Douglas developed an intense feeling for the sacred history of midwestern social democracy. One newspaper reporter recalled: "Traveling with Douglas was an experience. Routinely, he lapsed into historical monologues—about the Pullman strike in Chicago or Louis Sullivan's architecture. Driving into the town of Belvidere, Douglas once gave a rather scholarly discourse on the Latin origin of the town's name and the fact that a local Belvidere family was descended from John Stuart Mill, the nineteenth-century British po-

litical economist. With that, Douglas filled in the gaps in our knowledge of Mill. Another time, on our way to Quincy, Illinois, Douglas urged us to make sure we picked up a copy of Edgar Lee Masters' 'Spoon River Anthology.' We had to read that, he demanded." (Edward Shanahan, "The loss of a man of integrity," *In Memoriam, Paul H. Douglas*, Library of Friends Meeting of Hyde Park, Chicago.)

109. See Paul H. Douglas, *The Theory of Wages* (New York: The Macmillan Company, 1934). Douglas edited *The Worker in Modern Democratic Society* (1923) and wrote *Wages and the Family* (1925), *Real Wages in the United States* (1930), *The Movement of Money and Real Wages in the United States* (1931), *The Coming of a New Party* (1932), *Standards of Unemployment Insurance* (1933), *Controlling Depressions* (1935). In 1927 he began work on the Cobb-Douglas Production Function, his chief claim to distinction in the field of pure economics. See Paul H. Douglas, "Are There Laws of Production?" *The American Economic Review* 38 (March 1948): 2–41. Douglas was a leader in the movement to make economics an empirical science. After election to the Senate, Douglas wrote *Ethics in Government* (1952), *In Our Time* (1967), and *The Urban Environment: How It Can Be Improved* (1969).

110. See Rufus Jones, *Mysticism and Democracy in the English Commonwealth* (Cambridge, Mass.: Harvard University Press, 1932). Douglas regretted the loss of an intimate sense of all-conquering love as the foundation of life in the course of his rough-and-tumble legislative career.

111. Devere Allen, ed., *Adventuresome Americans* (New York: Farrar and Rinehart, 1932), p. 189. Although he deplored its tyranny, Douglas joined other American intellectuals of the 1920s, including Dewey, in the view that communism had brought a spiritual and moral unity to the people of Russia.

112. Douglas, *The Coming of a New Party* (New York: McGraw-Hill Book Company, 1932), pp. viii, 115, 118, 224, 223, 117. For Douglas's inclusion of his Quaker faith within James's and Dewey's pragmatic faith in voluntary association see Paul Douglas, "The Absolute, the Experimental Method, and Horace Kallen," in Sidney Ratner, ed., *Vision and Action: Essays in Honor of Horace Kallen* (New Brunswick: Rutgers University Press, 1953). Kallen, a disciple of William James and a philosopher of cultural pluralism, also argued on behalf of a democratic social religion in America. See *Secularism Is the Will of God: An Essay in the Social Philosophy of Democracy and Religion* (New York: Twayne Publishers, 1954). Douglas worked with Kallen in the cooperative and consumers' rights movements of the 1930s. Douglas was fond of quoting Marcus Aurelius: "for we have come into being for cooperation." Although he voted for Norman Thomas, he never joined the Socialist party, and never considered himself a Socialist because he could never subscribe to the doctrine that the class struggle was necessary in a constitutional democracy.

113. Douglas, *In the Fullness of Time*, p. 123.

114. A. Powell Davies, *America's Real Religion* (Washington, D.C.: All Soul's Church, 1939), pp. 18, 47. Davies also wrote *American Destiny* (1942), and *Man's Vast Future: A Definition of Democracy* (1951). See William O. Douglas, *The Mind and Faith of A. Powell Davies* (Garden City, New York: Doubleday, 1959).

115. Douglas, *In the Fullness of Time*, p. 295. In Douglas's view, Jane Addams was for her time what John Woolman was for his, and nearly every year he laid flowers on her simple Quaker grave and paused for a few minutes of prayer and meditation. For Douglas's deep attachment to Lincoln, see Paul H. Douglas, "The Significance of Gettysburg," in Allan Nevins, ed., *Lincoln and the Gettysburg Address* (Urbana, Illinois: Board of Trustees of University of Illinois, University of Illinois Press, 1964), "The European Reaction to Lincoln," in *A Portion of That Field* (Urbana: University of Illinois Press, 1967), "Abraham Lincoln," in Ralph G. Newman, ed., *Lincoln for the Ages* (New York: Doubleday, 1960). What was most important to Douglas was Lincoln's fidelity to the principle "all men are created equal," yet with "malice toward none." Congressman Paul Simon recalled that Douglas once asked him to join one of his midnight walks through Salem: "Because I had to go on to Galesburg that night, I declined, and I have always regretted it. My guess is that he would have spent a part of that walk in silence, communing with Abe, and that he might have reminisced about his own childhood." (Paul Simon, "Source, teacher, senator, friend," *Chicago Tribune Magazine*, October 14, 1973.)

116. Emily Taft Douglas, Save the Dunes Council address, unpublished manuscript in the possession of the author. Emily Douglas is an author in her own right. See *Remember the Ladies: The Story of the Great Women Who Helped Shape America* (1966), and *Margaret Sanger: Pioneer of the Future* (1969).

117. Douglas, *In the Fullness of Time*, p. 76. It may be argued that the image of Douglas's boyhood home was in part created by the midwestern religion of democracy and projected back on his Maine experience.

118. Ibid., p. 14.

119. Ibid., p. 15.

120. Ibid., p. 77.

CHAPTER SIX: STANDING ON THE LAST ACRE

A New Act in the Dunes Drama

1. See A. Powell Moore, *The Calumet Region: Indiana's Last Frontier* (Indianapolis: Indiana Historical Bureau, 1959).

2. Marjorie Hill Allee, *Ann's Surprising Summer* (Boston and New York: Houghton Mifflin Company, 1933), p. 11.

3. *Chicago Daily News*, February 15, 1930. The new city was to be named "Williams" in honor of the chairman of National Steel, just as the town of Gary was named in honor of Elbert Gary, chairman of United States Steel.

4. See Henry Z. Scheele, *Charlie Halleck: A Political Biography* (New York: Exposition Press, 1966).

5. George S. Cottman, *Indiana Dunes State Park, A History and Description* (Indianapolis: Department of Conservation, State of Indiana 1930), pp. 63, 10.

6. Milo Quaife, *Lake Michigan* (Indianapolis: Bobbs-Merrill Co., 1944), p. 310. Italics added.

7. Herbert Read, "The Dunes—The Army—The Battle," *The Izaak Walton Magazine*, February 1967, p. 10.

8. Simon Pokagon, "The Red Man's Greeting," in Cecilia Bain Buechner, *The Pokagons* (Indianapolis: Indiana Historical Society, 1933), p. 331.

9. Paul H. Douglas, *In the Fullness of Time* (New York: Harcourt Brace Jovanovich, 1971), p. 14.

10. Thomas E. Dustin, "The Battle of the Indiana Dunes," in *Citizens Make the Difference: Case Studies in Environmental Action* (Washington, D.C.: Citizens Advisory Committee on Environmental Quality, 1973), pp. 35–42.

11. Stephen Mather, *Report on the Proposed Sand Dunes National Park Indiana* (Washington, D.C.: Printing Office, 1917), p. 93.

12. "20 Reasons Why the Dunes Should Be Preserved as a National Park," unidentified news clipping, Dunes Scrapbook, Gary Public Library.

13. Earl R. North, "The Spirit of the Dunes: A Pageant," in *Book of the Spirit of the Dunes* (Michigan City, Indiana: n.p., 1916), p. 56.

14. Sigurd Olson, "Indiana Dunes Revisited," *The Izaak Walton Magazine Outdoor America*, January 1966. Italics added.

15. Quoted in R. A. Frederick, "Colonel Richard Lieber, Conservationist and Park Builder: The Indiana Years" (Ph.D. diss., Indiana University, 1960), p. 270.

16. J. Howard Euston, "Frank V. Dudley, November 14, 1868–March 5, 1957," March 10, 1957, privately printed, Library of the Art Institute of Chicago.

17. *Save the Dunes*, Spring 1917, n.p., pamphlet, Chicago Historical Society.

18. *Michigan City Evening News*, May 29, 1917.

19. Mary Kelly Graves, "The Dunes Pageant," *The Prairie Club Bulletin*, June 1917. The Prairie Club also policed its own membership. Any member caught plucking any wild plant life three times was expelled.

20. After the death of W. D. Richardson in 1936, Flora Richardson incorporated their 3.48 acres of duneland in Dune Acres as a wildlife sanctuary and not-for-profit library. See John Canright, "Richardson memorial provides nature films for 164,000," *Chesterton Tribune*, March 9, 1979.

21. Peggy Moran, "The Dunes and Dunes People," *Calumet Review* 3 (1969): 17.

22. George Brennan, *Wonders of the Dunes* (Indianapolis: Bobbs-Merrill Co., 1923), p. 323.

23. This was the conclusion of the study of the Dunes controversy, as well as sixty-seven other environmental conflicts, reached by Lynton K. Caldwell and his associates at Indiana University in 1976. See Lynton K. Caldwell, Lynton R. Hayes, and Isabel M. MacWhirter, *Citizens and the Environment: Case Studies in Popular Action* (Bloomington: Indiana University Press, 1976), pp. xi, xv, xvii, 63–65.

24. University of Chicago geographer and planning expert Harold M. Mayer stated in 1959: "There is not now, nor has there ever been, an official regional planning agency competent to carry on studies and make recommendations relative to the best use of each of the portions of the region bordering southern Lake Michigan." This statement could as well be made in 1982. (Harold M. Mayer, "Politics and Land Use: The Indiana Shoreline of Lake Michigan," *Annals of the Association of American Geographers* 54 [1964]: 519.)

25. Moran, "The Dunes and Dunes People," p. 22.

Indiana Dunes State Park

26. Biographical material on Knotts is drawn from the *Gary Post-Tribune*, June 3, 1931; Moore, *The Calumet Region;* telephone interview with Eugene Knotts, Yankeetown, Florida, January, 1982.

27. Graham Romeyn Taylor, *Satellite Cities* (New York: D. Appleton and Company, 1915), p. 180.

28. Mather, *Report*, p. 84.

29. *Gary Post*, March 19, 1919.

30. *Gary Tribune*, August 29, 1919; *Gary Post-Tribune*, February 13, 1932.

31. "Minutes," National Dunes Park Association, September 5, 1919, Gary Public Library archives.

32. Ibid., November 23, 1922. Bess Sheehan wrote to Richard Lieber that it would be a great mistake to say the federal park project failed. "What did happen, as I have analyzed it, was, that the encouragement and interest then gathering momentum in *state* officials, *state* organizations and a few Indiana men and women of vision, induced the Indiana leaders to believe that it would be *easier* and *quicker* to create a state park, than a federal, and with the rapidly encroaching civilization, time was very precious. I should therefore prefer this statement to convey the thought that the *encouragement forthcoming from Indiana people* was the determining factor in the change from the federal to the state park idea." (Sheehan to Lieber, September 5, 1929, Director's Correspondence 1919–1933, Department of Conservation, Archives Division, Indiana Commission on Public Records, Indianapolis.)

33. Indiana State Geologist Edward Barrett advocated a Dunes state park between 1910 and 1916. Jensen, Tuthill, Sheehan, and Knotts were in a correspondence with Lieber about its prospects by 1916. George Brennan claimed that he worked for the idea as early as 1887.

34. Emma Rappaport Lieber, *Richard Lieber* (private printing, 1947), p. 17.

35. Frederick, "Colonel Richard Lieber," pp. 185, 40, 17, 41.

36. Ibid., pp. 369, 355. At the end of his life, Lieber summarized his philosophy in *America's Natural Wealth* (New York: Harper & Brothers, 1942).

37. Ibid., p. 241.

38. Richard Lieber, Speech of August 17, 1926, General Office Files, Department of Conservation, Archives Division, Indiana Commission on Public Records, Indianapolis. For accounts of the history of Indiana Dunes State Park, see Frederick, "Colonel Richard Lieber," pp. 256–270; Moore, *The Calumet Region*, pp. 596–601; John O. Bowers, "The Dunes Park" in *History of the Lake and Calumet Region of Indiana*, ed. Thomas H. Cannon (Indianapolis: Historians' Association, 1927) 1:612–621; Cottman, *Indiana Dunes State Park*, pp. 34–40.

39. Frederick, "Colonel Richard Lieber," p. 257.

40. Moran, "The Dunes and Dunes People," p. 15.

41. Frederick, "Colonel Richard Lieber," p. 263.

42. *Indianapolis News*, January 30, 1923.

43. Frederick, "Colonel Richard Lieber," p. 172.

44. Later Samuel Insull also donated a strip of land %10 of a mile long and 500 feet wide between the park entrance and the South Shore railroad.

45. Frederick, "Colonel Richard Lieber," p. 275.

46. Virginia Moe, "Political Pet Dunes Newest Thing at State Park, Claim," *Gary Post,* September 18, 1930.

47. Frederick, "Colonel Richard Lieber," p. 357.

48. Ibid., p. 168. For the Dunes Nature Preserve, see William B. Barnes, "New Protection for a Famous Park," *Outdoor Indiana,* September 1971.

Save the Dunes Council

49. Frank V. Dudley, "The Dunes from an Artist's Point of View," *Prairie Club Bulletin,* February 1922.

50. In 1931, 1935, and 1944 the corps reported unfavorably on the proposal for a new harbor at Burns Ditch, citing as the principal problem the fact that it would benefit only one or two private corporations, and existing harbor facilities at Chicago, Indiana Harbor, and Michigan City were adequate. By 1949 demands on the area's harbor facilities had increased; Indiana state government officials supported development with increasing enthusiasm, and the corps was becoming more aggressive in support of public works projects.

51. Hugh Hough, "Heroine of Indiana Dunes," *Chicago Sun-Times,* December 1, 1966; U.S. Congress, Senate, Committee on Interior and Insular Affairs, *Indiana Dunes National Lakeshore: Hearings on S. 2249,* 88th Congress, 2d sess., March 5, 6, and 7, 1964, p. 123.

52. Transcript of interview by Helen Bieker with Dorothy Buell, October 17, 1968. The following biographical sketch of Dorothy Buell is derived from Bieker's interview, a personal history of Dorothy Buell prepared by her son, Robert Buell, and the following: Arthur Gorlick, "Granny Builds a Mountain," *Chicago Daily News,* November 5, 1966; Hough, "Heroine of Indiana Dunes"; Moran, "The Dunes and Dunes People"; *Chicago American,* March 4, 1962; *Chicago Tribune,* November 13, 1966; "Minutes" and "Newsletters" of the Save the Dunes Council, Beverly Shores, Indiana, 1952–1966.

53. Jerry S. Olson, "Indiana Sand Dune Preservation," November 8, 1951, 6 pp. mimeo., Chicago Historical Society.

54. Bieker transcript.

55. "Newsletter," Save the Dunes Council, June 1962.

56. *Chicago Tribune,* November 13, 1966. Among the women active in the early years were Hester Butz, Florence Broady, Laura Gent, Lois Howes, Esther Johnson, Mary Klooster, Mary Frances McAtee, Downing Mann, Arvilla Peters, Virginia Reuterskiold, Martha Mosier Reynolds, Ann Sims, Gail Snyder, Dorothy and Frances Woods.

57. See *Chicago Tribune,* October 29, 1953, *Chesterton Tribune,* October 22, 1953, *Gary Post-Tribune,* October 21, 1953.

58. Larry Waldron, "Birth of a National Park," *Singing Sands Almanac* 3 (May–June 1980): 1.

59. U.S. Congress, Senate, Committee on Interior and Insular Affairs, *Indiana Dunes National Monument: Hearings on S. 1001,* 86th Congress, 1st sess., May 13, 1959, p. 156.

60. Dorothy Buell, "Statement before the Platform Committee, Republican Party, June 20, 1960," Save the Dunes Council archives, Beverly Shores, Indiana.

334 NOTES TO PAGES 258–260

61. Dorothy Buell, "Statement before the Platform Committee, Democratic National Convention, July 2, 1960," Save the Dunes Council archives, Beverly Shores, Indiana.

62. Buell, "Statement before Republican Party."

63. See, for example, Dorothy Buell, "The Indiana Dunes," Address at Gary Public Library, October 29, 1965, Save the Dunes Council archives, Beverly Shores, Indiana.

64. Edward W. Osann, Jr., *The Dunes Belong to the People*, Save the Dunes Council, 1957, pp. 6, 4.

65. See Tippets-Abett-McCarthy-Stratton, *Preliminary Report: Feasibility of Proposed Indiana Deepwater Port*, January 28, 1956. In 1938, George A. Nelson and John W. Van Ness procured passage of bills creating the Indiana Board of Public Harbors and Terminals and appropriating a small sum of money toward acquisition of a Burns Ditch site. In the 1950s and '60s, Nelson and Van Ness, along with Halleck, were prominent advocates of the Porter County pro-port viewpoint.

66. *Chicago Daily News*, November 5, 1966.

67. See Rutherford H. Platt, *The Open Space Decision Process: Spatial Allocation of Costs and Benefits* (Chicago: University of Chicago, Department of Geography, 1972), p. 140.

68. In 1963 William Peeples, member of the *Louisville Courier-Journal's* editorial board, described a complex web of financial dealings and political relationships linking Clint W. Murchison, a Dallas multimillionaire, who controlled the Consumers Company of Chicago; the Consumers Dunes Corporation, subsidiary formed in 1954 by Consumers Company to speculate in Dunes real estate and which earned $85 for each share of $10 common stock from its sale to Bethlehem Steel; the C.T. Corporation, which acted as financial agent for Consumers Dunes Corporation, located in the Indianapolis office of Governor Craig's former law firm of White, Raub, Craig and Forrey; the Lake Shore Development Corporation, incorporated in 1956 as the land-buying agent for Bethlehem Steel; Thomas W. Moses, executive vice-president of Consumers Dunes, and president of the Indianapolis Water Company, in which the Murchison family owned over half of the stock; Frank McKinney, board chairman of the Fletcher National Bank of Indianapolis, close associate of the Murchison family, director of the New York Central Railroad (indirectly controlled by the Murchison family), and one-time national chairman of the Democratic party; the St. Lawrence Seaway Corporation, incorporated in 1959 to speculate in real estate in areas influenced by the St. Lawrence Seaway, with special reference to Burns Harbor, and headed by former Indiana Senator William Jenner; Indiana governor Harold Handley (1956–1960), who named Seaway's stock dealer, Durward E. McDonald, to the Northern Indiana Lakefront Study Committee in 1959; Indiana Democratic governor Matthew Welsh (1960–1964), protégé of Frank McKinney; and John Van Ness, who as state senator worked hard for a port in the Indiana General Assembly, and in 1959 was appointed assistant to the president of Midwest Steel (subsidiary of National Steel) and chairman of the Northern Indiana Lakefront Study Committee by Governor Handley. See William Peeples, "The Indiana Dunes and Pressure Politics," *The Atlantic Monthly*, February 1963, pp. 84–88.

69. Bieker transcript. There are conflicting accounts of Douglas's entry into the Dunes campaign. The account here is that of Mrs. Buell, which differs in some respects from that which Douglas gives in his autobiography.

70. Ibid.

71. Dorothy Buell, "Testimony," Subcommittee on Public Lands of the Committee on Interior and Insular Affairs. United States Senate, March 6, 1964. Save the Dunes Council archives, Beverly Shores, Indiana.

72. *Valparaiso Vidette-Messenger,* May 5, 1958.

The Battle for the Central Dunes

73. For the following discussion of the Dunes conflict, 1958–1976, see: Lynton K. Caldwell, Lynton R. Hayes, and Isabel M. MacWhirter, *Citizens and the Environment* (Bloomington: Indiana University Press, 1976), pp. 63–65; Paul H. Douglas, *In the Fullness of Time* (New York: Harcourt Brace Jovanovich, Inc., 1971), pp. 536–545; Paul H. Douglas Papers, 1958–1976, Indiana Dunes, Manuscript Collections, Chicago Historical Society; Thomas E. Dustin, "The Battle of the Indiana Dunes," in *Citizens Make the Difference: Case Studies of Environmental Action* (Washington, D.C.: Citizens' Advisory Committee on Environmental Quality, 1973), pp. 35–42; Gordon Englehart, "The Battle of the Dunes," July 23, 1961, "The Dunes: The Land and Its Buyers," April 22, 1962, "Holding on to an Ideal," December 9, 1962, "Indiana Dunes: Controversial Sands of Time," April 3, 1966, *Louisville Courier-Journal;* James J. Kyle, "Indiana Dunes National Lakeshore: The Battle for the Dunes," in *Congress and the Environment,* Richard A. Cooley and Geoffrey Wandesfordesmith, eds. (Seattle: University of Washington Press, 1970), pp. 16–31; Richard Lewis, "Indiana's Sand Gold," *Chicago Sun-Times,* August 17, 18, 19, 20, 1958; George Mann, "The Dunes in Danger: A Political-Industrial Scheme Threatens a Major Natural Recreation Area," *Chicago,* September 1955, pp. 28–32; Harold M. Mayer, "Politics and Land Use: The Indiana Shore line of Lake Michigan," *Annals of the Association of American Geographers* 54 (December 1964): 508–523; Peggy Moran, "The Dunes and Dune People," *Calumet Review* 3 (1969): 10–24; John B. Oakes, "Conservation: Indiana Dunes Unspoiled," *New York Times,* June 1, 1958; Edward R. Osann, "Rounding Out the Indiana Dunes," *National Parks and Conservation Magazine,* November, 1973, pp. 25–27; Rutherford H. Platt, *The Open Space Decision Process: Spatial Allocation of Costs and Benefits* (Chicago: University of Chicago, Department of Geography, 1972), pp. 138–174; Lawrence M. Preston, *The Port of Indiana: Burns Waterway Harbor* (Bloomington: Bureau of Business Research, Graduate School of Business, Indiana University, 1969); Herbert Read, "The Complete Story of the Indiana Dunes—with Port Design Problems," *The Hoosier Waltonian* (December 1959), "The Dunes—The Army—The Battle," *The Izaak Walton Outdoor America* (February 1967), pp. 10–14; Frederick Sicher, "An Indiana Dunes National Lakeshore," *National Parks Magazine* 38 (July 1964). See also the following hearings: U.S. Congress, Senate, Committee on Interior and Insular Affairs, *Indiana Dunes National Monument: Hearings on S. 1001,* 86th Congress, 1st sess., May 13, 1959; U.S. Congress, Senate, Committee on Interior and Insular Affairs, *Indiana Dunes National Lakeshore: Hearings on S. 2249,* 88th Cong., 2d sess., March 5, 6, 7, 1964; U.S. Congress, Senate, Committee on Interior and Insular Affairs, *Indiana Dunes National Lakeshore: Hearings on*

S. 360, 89th Cong., 1st sess., February 8, 1965; U.S. Congress, Senate, Committee on Interior and Insular Affairs, *Indiana Dunes National Lakeshore: Hearings on S. 820*, 93d Cong., 2d sess., September 30, 1974; U.S. Congress, House, Committee on Interior and Insular Affairs, *Indiana Dunes National Lakeshore: H.R. 51, H.R. 4412 and Related Bills, Part I*, 89th Cong., 1st sess., October 2, 1965; U.S. Congress, House, Committee on Interior and Insular Affairs, *Indiana Dunes National Lakeshore: H.R. 51, H.R. 5512, and Related Bills, Part II*, 89th Cong., 2d sess., April 4, 5, 6, 7, 26, 1966; U.S. Congress, House, Committee on Interior and Insular Affairs, *To Expand the Indiana Dunes National Lakeshore: H.R. 3571 and Related Bills*, 93rd Cong., 2d sess., June 17, 1974.

74. *The Valparaiso Vidette-Messenger*, May 5, 1958.

75. Senate Committee, *Hearings on S. 1001*, p. 195.

76. Horace M. Albright to Douglas, April 30, 1958; Mrs. Helen Price to Douglas, May 19, 1958; Warren Travoli to Douglas, June 4, 1958; Dunes files 1958, Paul Douglas Papers, Manuscript Collections, Chicago Historical Society.

77. At the urging of Edward W. Osann, Ogden Dunes in 1958 zoned all of the land owned by National Steel, the proposed harbor site, and 1,100 acres of the Bethlehem property for single family dwellings! Immediately, six suits were filed by the steel companies to enjoin the ordinance, and Porter County drew up a county zoning ordinance. See Platt, *Open Space Decision Process*, p. 160.

78. David Sander, "Beulah Land," *Northern Indiana Dunes Review* 1 (April 1966): 7.

79. Between 1958 and 1963, Douglas introduced five pieces of legislation, each of which included as its centerpiece some portion of the Central Dunes: S. 3898 (1958)—acreage 3,800; S. 1001 (1959, Hearings May and June 1959)—acreage 5,000; S. 1797 (1961)—acreage 8,000; S. 1797 amended (1961, Hearings February 1962)—acreage 9,000; S. 650 (1963)—acreage 900. All but the 1958 and 1959 bills included the 2,200-acre Indiana Dunes State Park, if donated.

80. Senate Committee, *Hearings on S. 1001*, p. 12.

81. Ibid., pp. 151-152.

82. Jerry Olson, "Report on the Scientific Importance of the Indiana Sand Dunes," July 10, 1959, 3 pp., Chicago Historical Society Library archives.

83. Quoted in Dustin, "The Battle of the Indiana Dunes," p. 36.

84. *The Portage News*, July 6, 1959.

85. *National Parks Magazine*, January, 1960, p. 2.

86. S. 1797 encompassed all undeveloped land in the Porter County Dunes region, including 2,054 acres in the Central Dunes, but deleted the National Steel and NIPSCO sites.

87. "Itinerary," July 23, 1961, Dunes files, Douglas Papers, Manuscript Collections, Chicago Historical Society; *Chicago Sun-Times*, July 24, 1961.

88. Chapman to Douglas, July 10, 1958, Dunes files, Douglas Papers, Manuscript Collections, Chicago Historical Society.

89. Save the Dunes Council mimeo., 1958.

90. The southern end of Lake Michigan was well suited for steel production. During the 1950s regional demand was ahead of production and there

was excellent transportation available for moving raw materials and finished products via railroads, the inland waterway system, the Great Lakes, and as of 1959, the St. Lawrence Seaway. But Douglas and the council did not believe that economic convenience *dictated* site selection. See Mayer, "Politics and Land-Use," p. 512. The situation changed in the 1970s. In 1982 the midwest steel industry was in serious trouble and the capacity of the Bethlehem plant was only half its originally projected size.

91. *New York Times*, May 28, 1961.

92. Read, "The Dunes—The Army—The Battle," p. 14.

93. See Preston, *The Port of Indiana*, pp. 1–3.

94. "Statement," Northern Indiana Industrial Development Association and Affiliated Organizations, 1939, n.p., Save the Dunes Council archives, Beverly Shores, Indiana.

95. *Gary Post-Tribune*, April 10, 1961.

96. *Gary Post-Tribune*, July 24, 1961.

97. *Chicago Sun-Times*, March 31, 1962.

98. Hough, "Heroine of Indiana Dunes," *Chicago Sun-Times*, December 1, 1966.

99. *Congressional Record*, February 4, 1963, p. 1589.

The Indiana Dunes National Lakeshore

100. Kyle, "Indiana Dunes National Lakeshore," p. 30.

101. *Congressional Record*, October 18, 1966. Douglas paid special tribute to "that small core group who have literally given their lives to this effort," Mrs. J. H. Buell, Thomas and Jane Dustin, Merrill Ormes, Edward W. Osann, Jr., Herbert P. Read, Fred Meyer, Mrs. Sylvia Troy, Robert Mann, Mrs. Carl Peters, Mrs. Calvin Gent, Mrs. J. C. B. Sims, Mrs. Willard Butz, Mrs. Lawrence Bieker, Florence Broady, John Nelson, Judson Harris, Mrs. Edward Howes, Mrs. K. Benninger.

102. Douglas, *In the Fullness of Time*, p. 539.

103. Ibid., p. 540.

104. *Congressional Record*, February 4, 1963.

105. Douglas, *In the Fullness of Time*, p. 542. This account of the final passage of the Dunes bill basically follows that given by Douglas in his autobiography.

106. *Congressional Record*, October 11, 1966, pp. 26100, 26104.

107. Ibid., p. 26106.

108. Ibid., p. 26110.

109. Ibid.

110. *Congressional Record*, October 12, 1966, p. 26207.

111. Douglas, *In the Fullness of Time*, p. 543.

112. Preston, *Burns Waterway Harbor*, p. v. The incident of the Goodyear blimp is described in Platt, *Open Space Decision Process*, p. 138.

113. Senator Bayh, who was unable to attend the dedication, prepared a statement that stressed the role of Stephen Mather, Paul Douglas, Dorothy Buell, and the Save the Dunes Council.

New Borders to Defend

114. "Indiana Dunes: tying up loose ends," *Audubon*, January, 1977, p. 126.

115. *Congressional Record*, September 24, 1976, p. 32311.

116. Ibid.

117. Ibid., p. 32312.

118. See Fred D. Cavinder, "Irene Herlocker and Her Prairie," *Indianapolis Star Sunday Magazine*, October 17, 1976, pp. 42, 43, 46, 47; George Neavoll, "Hoosier Prairie in peril as lakeshore bills languish," *Fort Wayne Journal-Gazette*, November 15, 1973; *Hoosier Prairie*, n.d., published by the Committee on the Hoosier Prairie.

119. The dedication was written by Glenda Daniel, Indiana Dunes National Lakeshore. The West Beach Unit of the Lakeshore was also named the Paul H. Douglas Ecological and Recreational Unit.

120. See Tanya Lee Erwin, "Indiana Dunes: Another Border to Defend," *National Parks and Conservation Magazine* 51 (October 1977): 4–8; Brenda Frantz and Robin Rich, "Two First Hand Accounts of the Bailly Fight," *Critical Mass Energy Journal* 7 (November, December 1981): 8–9, 13, 15; Herbert P. Read, "Statement Before Subcommittee on Energy and Environment," June 5, 1979, Save the Dunes Council archives, Beverly Shores, Indiana; "Chronology: Indiana Dunes National Lakeshore and the Bailly Generating Station," August 8, 1976, Science Office files, Indiana Dunes National Lakeshore.

121. *Michigan City News-Dispatch*, November 19, 1976.

122. *Fort Wayne Journal-Gazette*, May 29, 1977.

123. Frantz, "First Hand Accounts," p. 8.

124. Rich, "First Hand Accounts," p. 13.

EPILOGUE

1. The following description of the picnic on Hawk's Island is based on interviews with John Hawkinson, Herbert Read, and Lee Botts, April, 1982; and Jonathan Ela's "Hawk's Island: A Cameo Portrait," in *The Faces of the Great Lakes* (San Francisco: Sierra Club Books, 1977), pp. 90–96.

2. Gordon Englehart, "Holding onto an Ideal," *The Louisville Courier-Journal*, November 30, 1962.

3. Harlan Draeger, "Naturalist Hawkinson Fights the Giants," *Chicago Daily News*, May 23, 1970.

4. Ela, *Faces of the Great Lakes*, p. 96.

5. Draeger, "Naturalist Hawkinson."

Index

Ecology of Chicago and Vicinity: A Study of the Origins, Development and Classification of Plant Societies, The," 142, 147; on plant succession, 90, 137–38, 143–51, 169, 172, 177, 271; at University of Chicago, 56, 73–76, 78, 137–42, 159–60. See also Coulter, John M.; Cowles Bog; Ecology
Craig, George, 256, 259, 334n. 68
Creation, 99–103, 121–27. See also Creation myth; Rebirth
Creation myth, 99–100, 237–38, 298n.46; of America, 37–40, 42, 250; in Dunes literature, 24–25, 90–91, 121; of earth's origins, 159–63, 177–78. See also Creation; Rebirth; Native Americans, myth of Nanabozho
Crescendo (Armin), 106–7, 188
Cressey, George Babcock, Indiana Sand Dunes and Shore Lines of the Lake Michigan Basin, The, 165–66
Crim, Florence, 94
Croly, Herbert, Promise of American Life, The, 50
Crowd, The (Strain), 69
Cup of Sky, A (Peattie), 183
Currey, Margery, 13, 19, 21, 28, 65, 125

Dahlgreen, Charles W., 59
Daley, Richard, 265, 273
Dalstrom, Gustaf, 64
Darrow, Clarence, 54–56, 229, 247
Darwin, Charles, 179, 181
Daughters of the American Revolution, 251.
Davies, A. Powell, America's Real Religion, 229
Davis, Bradley M., 141
Davy, Randall, 64
Day, J. Edward, 276
Debs, Eugene, 55, 224, 246
Declaration of Independence, 34, 38, 40, 42, 49, 248, 250
Dell, Floyd, 64
Democracy: A Man Search (Sullivan), 194
Desert, 4, 21–22, 88–91, 94, 264, 278
Deserts on the March (Sears), 155
Des Plaines River, 152, 163–64
Despres, Leon, 261
Dewey, John, 21, 58, 71, 181, 227; Art as Experience, 76; Common Faith, A, 76; Experience and Nature, 76; as theologian of democracy, 16, 76–79, 229

Diana of the Dunes. See Gray, Alice
Dickinson, Thomas, 32, 56
Dingell, John, 271
Doeserich, Emma, Sherburne, Mary, and Wey, Anna, Outdoors with the Prairie Club, 201, 203
Douglas, Emily Taft, 78, 82, 188, 226, 229–30, 260, 266
Douglas, Paul Howard, 115, 117, 188, 211, 213, 238; Coming of a New Party, The, 227–28; Dunes campaign, 4, 6, 17, 116, 232–33, 237, 240–41, 253–54, 260–61, 263–80, 282, 284–87; In the Fullness of Time, 222–32; and Lincoln, 22, 219, 229, 231, 330n.115; life of, 13, 82, 122, 179, 182, 222–26, 229–32, 254, 277, 280–81, 284–86, 293, 328n.107; and Progressivism, 20–22, 223–27, 230, 328n.108, 329n.112; and religion of democracy, 223–24, 226–30, 272; Theory of Wages, 225. See also Indiana Dunes National Lakeshore
Douglas, William O., 229
Downing, Elliot R., 43, 78, 112, 160; Naturalist in the Great Lakes Region, A, 78, 135, 162
Doyle, Charles, 198, 281
Drama, community, 25–26, 30–32, 34, 56, 255, 299n.55, n.59, 300n.62. See also Dunes Pageant of 1917; Dunes pageants; Ritual, civic; and names of individual dramatists and plays
Dreiser, Theodore, 64
Drude, Oscar, 153
Drury, John, 64
Drury, L. H., 63
Drury, Marion, 64
Dudley, Charles G., 63
Dudley, Frank V., 17, 62–63, 68, 103–5, 116, 187–88; and Dunes movement, 4, 33, 45, 47, 81–82, 84, 203, 240, 253, 258; Paintings: Duneland, 66; Pageant, The, 17, 38; Port Chester Trail to Pageant Blowout, 17; Sun and Shadows Meet, 104, 131; View from Mount Tom, 104–5
Dudley, Maida Lewis (Mrs. Frank V.), 33, 68, 103, 187–88
Dune Acres, 229, 236, 253, 275, 280, 285
Dune Boy (Teale), 64, 208, 211
Dune Country, The (Reed), 63
Dune Creek, 113, 175, 177, 187, 253, 268, 285; in Dunes art, 47, 106; historical associations, 14–15, 110
Duneland (Dudley), 62